CONTEMPORARY'S
American Civics and Government

Matthew T. Downey

McGraw Hill | Wright Group

Author
Matthew T. Downey received his Ph.D. in American History from Princeton University. He served as Director of the Clio Project in History-Social Science Education in the Graduate School of Education at the University of California, Berkeley. He also directed the U.C. Berkeley site of the California History-Social Science Project. He has taught at the University of Colorado, the University of California at Los Angeles, and at Louisiana State University. Currently, he directs the Social Science Program and the William E. Hewitt Institute for History and Social Science Education at the University of Northern Colorado.

Senior Editor: Mitch Rosin
Executive Editor: Linda Kwil

Reviewers and Consultants
Jill DeLuccia
Social Studies Instructor
Atlanta, Georgia

Jeffrey J. Johll
K–12 District Social Studies Supervisor
Dubuque Community School District
Dubuque, Iowa

Eleanor Nangle
Social Studies Instructor
Chicago, Illinois

Brian Silva
Social Studies Instructor and Technology Coordinator
Long Beach, California

Jill Smith-Mott
Social Studies Instructor
Giddings, Texas

About the Cover
The images on the cover include (from left to right): Thurgood Marshall, Cesar Chavez, Rosa Parks, Charles Sumner, and Sandra Day O'Connor.

Photo credits are on page 490.

Wright Group

ISBN: 0-07-704444-4 (Student Softcover Edition)
ISBN: 0-07-704443-6 (Student Softcover Edition with CD)
ISBN: 0-07-704523-8 (Student Hardcover Edition)
ISBN: 0-07-704524-6 (Student Hardcover Edition with CD)

The **McGraw-Hill** Companies

Contents

The Star-Spangled Banner

O! say, can you see, by the dawn's early light,
What so proudly we hail'd at the twilight's last gleaming?
Whose broad stripes and bright stars, thro' the perilous fight,
O'er the ramparts we watched were so gallantly streaming?
And the rockets' red glare, the bombs bursting in air,
Gave proof thro' the night, that our flag was still there.
O! say, does that Star-Spangled Banner yet wave
O'er the land of the free and the home of the brave?

On the shore, dimly seen thro' the mist of the deep,
Where the foe's haughty host in dread silence reposes,
What is that which the breeze, o'er the towering steep,
As it fitfully blows, half conceals, half discloses?
Now it catches the gleam of the morning's first beam,
In full glory reflected now shines on the stream.
'Tis the Star-Spangled Banner. O long may it wave
O're the land of the free and the home of the brave.

And where is that band who so vauntingly swore,
That the havoc of war and the battle's confusion
A home and a country should leave us no more?
Their blood has wash'd out their foul footstep's pollution.
No refuge could save the hireling and slave
From the terror of flight or the gloom of the grave,
And the Star-Spangled Banner in triumph doth wave
O're the land of the free and the home of the brave.

O thus be it e'er when free men shall stand
Between their lov'd home and war's desolation,
Blest with vict'ry and peace, may the Heav'n-rescued land
Praise the pow'r that hath made and preserv'd us a nation.
Then conquer we must, when our cause it is just,
And this be our motto, "In God is our Trust.
And the Star-Spangled Banner in triumph shall wave
O'er the land of the free and the home of the brave.

To the Student

This textbook provides an overview of civics and government in the United States. It also includes sections about political and economic systems around the world. The book begins with an examination of the foundations of government in the United States. The ideas of the Founding Fathers and the decisions they made impact our lives daily.

The book next looks at the three branches of government. The legislative branch is responsible for making the laws. The executive branch is charged with enforcing the laws. The judicial branch is responsible for interpreting the laws. The three branches of government work together and also provide a system of checks and balances.

Being part of a democracy involves taking part in how government operates and exercising the rights afforded each citizen under the Constitution. However, all citizens have not always been afforded equal rights. It took more than 150 years for every citizen in the United States to achieve equality under the law. This book next examines civil liberties and civil rights. The struggle for equality included many groups of people and continues to be a topic of debate even today.

Government is an active process. Exercising your right to vote is important to the United States and to the role each of us plays in a democracy. By voting you influence how public policy is shaped. Public opinion also guides the position taken by the United States in world events. It is important to participate in government through political campaigns, voting, and being an active member of your community. There are opportunities to participate in government at the local, state, and national levels.

We live in a world of constantly changing political and economic climates. While change brings opportunities, it also causes problems. The last section of this book examines the political structures of nations around the world and the various economic systems that these countries utilize. By having an understanding of other nations and systems, you are better prepared to contribute to the world community.

Living in the United States, you have an opportunity to play an important role in your community and the government. I hope that this book helps you to better understand the importance of your role in civics and government.

Matthew T. Downey

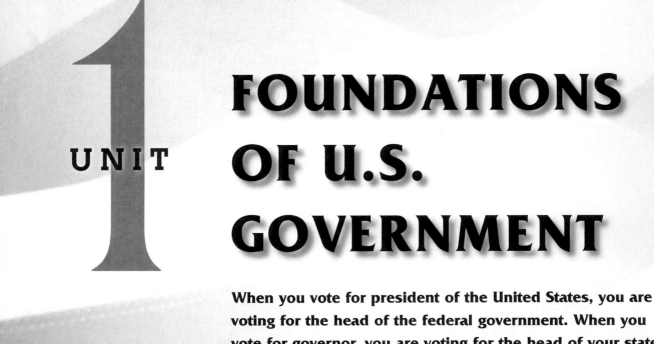

UNIT 1

FOUNDATIONS OF U.S. GOVERNMENT

When you vote for president of the United States, you are voting for the head of the federal government. When you vote for governor, you are voting for the head of your state government. When you vote for mayor, you are voting for the head of your local government.

The United States is a system of interlocking government units: federal, state, and local. How did the United States develop three sets of governments? This unit will help you answer that question. The rest of the book will answer the question "What do the three levels of government do?"

GOVERNMENT AND THE PEOPLE

Getting Focused

Skim this chapter to predict what you will be learning.

- Read the lesson titles and subheadings.
- Look at the illustrations and read the captions.
- Review the vocabulary words and terms.

What do you think this chapter is about? Do the subheadings and pictures raise any questions for you? In your notebook, write at least five questions you want answered as you read this chapter.

The New York State Capitol is located in Albany, New York. Construction of the building began in 1867 and was completed in 1899. In 1754, Albany was the site of a meeting where Benjamin Franklin proposed the Albany Plan of Union — an early attempt at unifying the 13 British Colonies.

Principles of Government

Thinking on Your Own

What does the word *government* mean to you? Make a list of what you think government does. Then think about what your life would be like if there were no government. Write a paragraph to describe how your life would be different without government.

What exactly is government? We live under local, state, and federal governments, but what are they? How does each level of government affect us? How, in turn, do we affect each level of government?

To answer these questions, we first have to ask a more basic question: What is a state—not the 50 states of the United States, but the general idea, or concept, of state? A **state** is (1) a group of people (2) living in a definite territory who have (3) a government with the power to make and enforce laws (4) without having to ask permission from a higher authority.

Government, then, is a tool of the state. **Government** is the organization by which the state maintains order, provides public services, and enforces decisions over the people living in its territory. Another word for this meaning of *state* is *nation*.

focus your reading

What is a state?

Describe the four theories about how government began.

Explain the four main purposes of government.

words to know

state

government

evolutionary theory

force theory

divine right theory

social contract theory

coercive

The U.S. Senate

Theories of How Government Began

Scholars do not know how or when the first governments came about. Some scholars have developed theories, or ideas, about the origins of government.

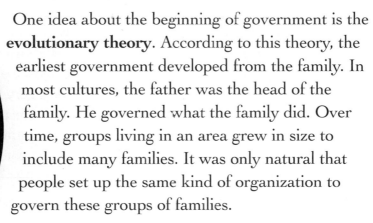

John Locke developed the social contract theory.

One idea about the beginning of government is the **evolutionary theory**. According to this theory, the earliest government developed from the family. In most cultures, the father was the head of the family. He governed what the family did. Over time, groups living in an area grew in size to include many families. It was only natural that people set up the same kind of organization to govern these groups of families.

The **force theory** explains the beginning of government differently. Scholars who support the force theory claim that the first governments were established by the use of weapons. One man or a small group of men used force to bring others in an area under their control.

According to **divine right theory**, a ruler holds power because he or she is a god or was chosen by the gods to rule. The governments of many ancient civilizations were based on this theory. The Egyptians believed that their pharaoh was like a god and was chosen by the gods to rule. Divine right theory influenced Europeans in the 1600s. The rulers of France and Russia, for example, claimed that their authority was based on God's will. This claim gave the rulers absolute power over their subjects. To disobey the ruler was to disobey God.

By the late 1600s, however, some European philosophers were questioning the divine right theory. Thomas Hobbes helped to develop the **social contract theory**. Hobbes wrote

> ### ideas to remember
>
> A state has four important characteristics
> - population, or people
> - territory, or land
> - sovereignty, or authority
> - government, or an organized way to maintain authority

that in a "state of nature," no government existed. Without government as an authority, life was "cruel, brutish, and short." According to this theory, the ruler and the people who were ruled entered into a contract. If the ruler failed to honor the rights of the people, the people could overthrow the ruler.

This idea of a social contract greatly influenced the English in 1688. Before they allowed William and Mary to take the throne, the two had to agree to the English Bill of Rights. This became the "contract" between the English monarchy and the English people. Thomas Jefferson based much of the Declaration of Independence on the social contract theory.

stop and think

With a partner, review the different theories of government. Select one of the theories. Then write a brief dialogue between a ruler and a subject that illustrates the theory. Include three sample laws that demonstrate the theory of government.

Primary Source

John Locke (1632–1704) spent much of his life thinking and writing about government and philosophy. The following excerpt explains why people develop government.

"If Man in the state of Nature be so free . . . ; if he be absolute Lord of his own Person and Possessions, equal to the greatest, and subject to no body, why will he part with his Freedom? . . . Why will [Man] . . . subject himself to the . . . Control of any other Power? . . . ['T]is obvious to answer, That tho in the state of Nature he hath such a [freedom], yet the enjoyment of it is very uncertain, and constantly exposed to the Invasion of others. For all being Kings as much as he, every Man his Equal, and . . . no strict Observers of . . . Justice, the Enjoyment of the Property he has . . . is very unsafe, very unsecure. This makes him willing to quit a Condition, which however free, is full of Fears and continual Dangers; And 'tis not without Reason, that he seeks out, and is willing to join in Society with others, . . . for the mutual Preservation of their Lives, Liberties, and . . . Property."

—John Locke, from *Two Treatises of Government*

reading for understanding

1. What does Locke mean by the term *state of Nature*?
2. How does Locke describe "others"?
3. Write a paragraph to explain Locke's reasoning about why people want government.

The Purposes of Government

As you have just read, the idea of government goes back to ancient civilizations. Governments have been around for thousands of years because they serve a purpose. In reality, they serve four main purposes.

First, government provides a way for people to live in peace. When people live together in groups, conflict often arises. Government sets up laws to handle conflict and to punish those who disobey the laws. For example, suppose a person steals money from another. The thief is arrested, tried, and sentenced to jail under the law.

Government is able to maintain law and order because its citizens have given it this power. Government has the authority to make decisions and to force its citizens to obey those decisions. This power is called **coercive**. It means that government can coerce, or force, people to obey it. The force is the fear of punishment if they do not obey. For example, many people might not willingly pay taxes. However, the fear of a fine and possible prison time forces people to pay their taxes.

Each image represents one of the purposes of government. Work with a partner to determine which purpose of government is represented by each picture.

Second, government provides public services. In general, this means that government works to ensure the general welfare, or well-being, of the people. Government takes on tasks that individuals could not afford to do on their own, such as building schools, roads, and subways. Government also promotes the health and safety of its people. Some examples are federal food and drug laws to ensure the safety of the foods we eat and the medicines we take. The federal government also sets standards for airplane safety.

National security is the third purpose of government. Typically, the national government sets foreign policy and maintains the armed forces for national defense. It also directs the nation's response to external threats, like the war on terrorism.

Fourth, government makes decisions that affect the economy and economic activities of businesses and individuals. The power to tax is one way the government regulates economic activity. Government also uses direct payments and tax credits as other ways to influence economic activity. For example, some farmers are paid to limit the number of acres they plant of certain crops, such as corn. Surplus crops can drive down the price the farmer receives and hurt the economy. Government may pass laws that give tax credits to companies that provide job retraining to workers who would otherwise lose their jobs.

> **ideas to remember**
>
> Government has four main purposes
> - to maintain social order, that is, to keep the peace
> - to provide public services
> - to provide national security
> - to make economic decisions

Putting It All Together

With a partner, make a list of three laws that match each of the four purposes of government. Then develop a list of services the government provides. The government may be national, state, or local. Share your 12 laws and your list of services with the class.

Systems and Forms of Government

Thinking on Your Own

Suppose you had to set up a government for a colony on the moon. What would you want your government to be like? Would you want it to be independent and free from interference from governments on Earth? Would you want citizens to vote for officials? Describe your ideas for a government in two or three paragraphs. Include what you have learned about the purposes of government in Lesson 1.

In Lesson 1, you learned about what government is and why people have set up governments since earliest times. This lesson discusses the systems and the forms, or types, that governments have taken over the years. There are three basic systems of government: unitary, confederation, and federal.

Knowing the system of government is different from knowing the type of government. Answering the question "Who governs?" tells you the type of government. A government may be an autocracy, an oligarchy, or a democracy.

focus your reading

What are the differences among unitary, confederation, and federal systems of government?

Compare and contrast autocracies and oligarchies.

What type of democracy is most common today?

words to know

unitary government

confederation government

federal system

autocracy

absolute monarchy

constitutional monarchy

dictator

oligarchy

democracy

direct democracy

representative democracy

The British Parliament holds all the power in the government but delegates powers to counties and local governments.

Unitary Government

Unitary government is one in which all government power is held by the national government. It uses its power to set up lesser governments, such as states and provinces. The national government gives these lesser levels of government the power to make and enforce laws. This is also called a centralized system of government. Modern European nations such as France, Italy, and Great Britain have unitary governments.

The 50 states of the United States also have unitary governments. They exercise their authority, or power, to set up local governments. These may take the form of counties, cities, towns, and villages.

Confederation Government

A **confederation government** is a loose union of independent states. The difference between a unitary government and a confederation becomes clear if you think about how the United States was formed. In 1777, the original 13 British colonies set up a national government under the Articles of Confederation. The states gave up some of their power to set up the national government. The national government did not set up the states.

Federal System of Government

Note the word *loose* in the definition of a confederation government. The union among the states was so loose under the Articles of Confederation that it was unworkable. The writers of the Constitution agreed to a federal system of government in place of the confederation government.

Congress holds only certain powers, as noted in the Constitution.

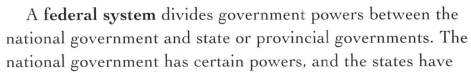

A **federal system** divides government powers between the national government and state or provincial governments. The national government has certain powers, and the states have certain powers. Besides the United States, the nations of Australia, Germany, Mexico, India, and more than 20 other nations use the federal system of government.

stop and think

Reread the description of the imaginary government that you wrote for Thinking on Your Own. Does your government fit any of these three basic systems? If your imaginary government does not match any of them, rewrite your description to fit one. Then share your description with a partner. Ask your partner to identify your system of government.

Autocracy and Oligarchy

Adolf Hitler

Autocracy and oligarchy have a characteristic in common. The people who are governed do not have a voice in their government.

In an **autocracy**, a single person holds all power. This is probably the oldest type of government. Autocrats either inherit their role or use force to get and keep it. Monarchs in Europe from the 1400s to the 1700s and the czars in Russia were autocrats, also known as **absolute monarchs**. They inherited their positions and used force to keep them. Modern autocratic monarchies are rare. The king of Saudi Arabia is a modern absolute monarch.

Today, most monarchies, such as Great Britain's, are **constitutional monarchies**. The British monarch is mainly the ceremonial head of the British government. The position has little power. Real government power is in the hands of the British Parliament. Japan, Sweden, and Spain also have constitutional monarchies. Even though the heads of these governments are monarchs, the governments are democracies. The people vote for their representative leaders.

A **dictator** is a modern autocrat. A dictator controls the government and rules with absolute power. Adolf Hitler in Germany, Joseph Stalin in the Soviet Union, and Benito Mussolini in Italy were all twentieth-century dictators. Kim Jong-Il, the leader of North Korea, was one of the few remaining dictators at the beginning of the twenty-first century.

An **oligarchy** is similar to an autocracy. The difference is that in an oligarchy, a small group of people, not just one person, rules with absolute power. Before and during World War II, Japan was run by an oligarchy of army officers and businessmen. Sometimes the group in power will hold elections. However, the only candidates up for election support the oligarchy, and voters must vote for them. This is the form of oligarchy in the People's Republic of China. The only political party is the Communist Party, and few dare to oppose it.

Democracy

Abraham Lincoln said that democracy is "government of the people, by the people, and for the people." The U.S. Constitution begins "We the people." In a **democracy**, the people rule.

There are two forms of democracy. One is direct democracy. In a **direct democracy**, individual citizens vote on issues of government in a meeting of all citizens. This was the form of democracy in ancient Athens. It is still used today in New England town meetings.

However, few places today are small enough to be governed efficiently by direct democracy. Instead, people practice **representative democracy**. They elect representatives who govern in their place. The voters give their representatives the power to make and enforce laws for the community, state, or nation.

---

ideas to remember

There are three basic types of government

* Autocracy
  * dictator
  * absolute monarchy
  * constitutional monarchy
* Oligarchy
* Democracy
  * direct
  * representative

Putting It All Together

Write a letter to the editor explaining why the United States should keep its federal system of government or change to a unitary or confederation government. What are the advantages of each? Also, take a position on whether the United States should have a more or less direct form of democracy.

Participate in Government

Volunteer for Community Service

People contribute in many ways to the society in which they live. They take part in government by voting, paying taxes, and serving on juries. They contribute to community service through nongovernmental organizations (NGOs) and as volunteers. Doing volunteer service can be important and rewarding. You can be sixteen or eighty-six and be a volunteer.

There are many ways to volunteer your time and talents. The photo on this page shows one way. You can also volunteer your time to visit the elderly. You can work on clean-ups sponsored by your community, neighborhood, school, or local businesses. Another volunteer possibility for young adults is tutoring younger children.

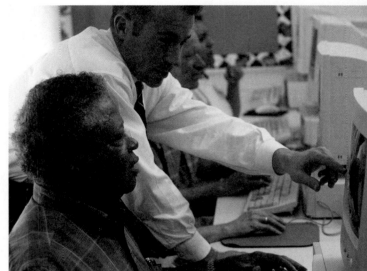

Many communities offer classes in literacy or computer skills that are taught by trained volunteers.

Sometimes young adults are elected to serve on local community boards. Often, other local boards, such as the zoning commission, are appointed positions. Towns and small cities often have a volunteer fire department that will accept young volunteers.

To find volunteer opportunities in your community, ask your school guidance counselor. Also read your local newspaper for announcements by community groups that use volunteers.

Complete the following activity.

Locate a community organization that you are interested in learning more about. Develop a list of at least five questions to ask the coordinator of volunteers for the organization. You might ask more about what the organization does and what you would be doing as a volunteer.

Skill Builder

Identifying Main Idea and Supporting Details

The **main idea** is the theme, or idea, that a piece of writing is mostly about. Your textbook can be a useful tool in helping you to identify main ideas. It is divided into chapters, which are divided into lessons, which are divided into sections. Each chapter has a main idea; so does each lesson and section.

The chapter title tells you the main idea of the chapter. The lesson title tells you the main idea of the lesson. For example, Lesson 1 in Chapter 1 explains the basic principles of government.

To find the main idea, ask yourself the following:

1. Is there a single sentence that states what the piece is about?

   If there is, then you have found the main idea. To be sure, restate the sentence in your own words. Does it still seem as if it is what the paragraph is mainly about?

2. If there is no single sentence, what does the piece seem to be about? What are the details describing or explaining?

   When you think you know, restate the main idea in your own words. This will help you to be sure you really figured out the main idea.

Complete the following activities.

1 What is the main idea of each of the following: (a) Lesson 1 in Chapter 1? (b) Lesson 2 in Chapter 1?

2 Read the section "The Purposes of Government," on pages 7–8. Identify the main idea in each paragraph. Decide whether it is stated or unstated.

Chapter

2 BEGINNINGS OF U.S. GOVERNMENT

Getting Focused

Skim this chapter to predict what you will be learning.

- Read the lesson titles and subheadings.
- Look at the illustrations and read the captions.
- Examine maps and charts.
- Review the vocabulary words and terms.

What do you already know about the British colonists' fight for independence? Make a list of at least ten facts about events that led up to the American Revolution.

Independence Hall in Philadelphia is often called the birthplace of our nation. It was in this building that the Declaration of Independence and the United States Constitution were signed. Philadelphia was the nation's capital from 1790 to 1800.

Government of the British Colonies

Thinking on Your Own

Imagine you are deciding how laws will be passed in a new government. Describe your idea of the best way to set up a legislature, or lawmaking body. Consider qualifications for lawmakers and how people will become lawmakers.

Most of the people who settled in the British colonies came from England. They brought with them the rights that they had known as British citizens. These rights evolved over many centuries and were based largely on two ideas: limited government and representative government.

Foundations of English Government

Limited government is the idea that government is not all-powerful. People have certain rights that government cannot take away. This idea was first set down in the Magna Carta in England in 1215. This document was a first step toward limiting the power of the monarch and establishing certain rights, such as trial by jury.

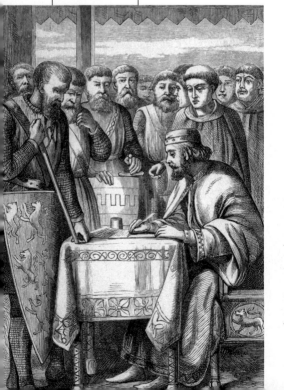

King John was forced to sign the Magna Carta in 1215.

The Petition of Right, forced on King Charles I in 1628, also limited the monarch. It prohibited the monarch from levying taxes without the agreement of Parliament, forbade the housing of soldiers in private homes, and banned the jailing of people without just cause.

focus your reading

Describe the two basic principles of government that the English brought to the colonies.

What three documents state the basic rights of the English people?

Explain how colonial constitutions and colonial legislatures relate to the two basic principles of English government.

words to know

limited government

representative government

Mayflower Compact

Fundamental Orders of Connecticut

The attempts to limit power in England did not end abuses by the government. The years between 1628 and 1688 were marked by civil war. Finally, in 1688, the leaders of Parliament overthrew King James II. They then invited his daughter Mary and her husband, William of Orange, to rule England. Before the two could be crowned, Parliament insisted they sign the Bill of Rights. Among the rights granted to the people were freedom from cruel and unusual punishment, the right to a fair and speedy trial, and freedom from excessive bail. The colonists brought these ideas about rights with them to North America.

William and Mary signed the English Bill of Rights in 1689.

The English colonists also brought with them the idea of **representative government**. The first meetings of Parliament took place in the 1200s. Parliament was, and still is, the legislative branch of English government. It is made up of an upper house, the House of Lords, and a lower house, the House of Commons. Members of the House of Lords hold office because they are part of the English nobility. Members of the House of Commons are elected by voters in their home districts. They represent the voters in Parliament. The process is similar to the way Americans vote for members of the U.S. House of Representatives.

Written Plans of Government

England did not and does not have a written constitution. The collection of laws and documents such as the Magna Carta is considered England's unwritten constitution. The early English colonists, however, developed written plans for their colonial governments.

The Pilgrims signed the Mayflower Compact in 1620.

The first such document was the **Mayflower Compact**. It was written and signed by the Pilgrims before they came ashore at Plymouth Rock in 1620. They agreed to form a government and to pass "just and equal laws" under that government.

The first formal constitution in the colonies was the **Fundamental Orders of Connecticut**, signed in 1639. Male property owners were granted the right to elect the governor and the representatives to the colonial legislature. As in Great Britain, all women, as well as any men who did not own property, were not allowed to vote. In time, each colony had a charter that set up a limited government based on rule by law. This means that government is always subject to, or under the control of, the law.

Representative Government

The colonists set up their own versions of Parliament. The first colonial legislature met in the Virginia Colony in 1619. It was called the House of Burgesses.

Each of the other 12 colonies also established legislatures. Typically, they had two houses. The upper house was usually made up of wealthy landowners who were appointed by the governor. The lower house was elected. Among the issues that the legislators dealt with were laws regulating the ownership of land, relations with native groups, and taxation.

stop and think

The basic rights of the American people are found in the Bill of Rights—the first ten amendments to the United States Constitution. Find the Bill of Rights on page 66, and compare it to the rights of English people listed in this lesson. Work with a partner to list the similarities that you find.

Putting It All Together

How were the governments of the colonies the same as and different from the government of England? With a partner, create a Venn diagram to compare and contrast the governments. Then write a paragraph explaining the similarities and differences.

Fighting for Independence

Thinking on Your Own

A compromise is the settlement of a disagreement in which each side gives up something. Parliament and King George on one side and the colonists on the other side would not compromise. Think of a disagreement you had with someone. What compromise did you or could you have proposed to settle it? Describe the compromise.

At the end of the French and Indian War in 1763, the colonists celebrated Britain's victory over France. They were proud to be citizens of the British Empire. By 1776, about one-third of the colonists were ready to declare independence from Great Britain. About one-third remained loyal to the monarchy, and the rest had no opinion. Many colonial leaders demanded independence from Britain. How did relations between the colonies and Great Britain get to this point?

focus your reading

Why did Parliament begin to place revenue taxes on the colonists?

What actions of the First Continental Congress brought the colonists closer to war with Great Britain?

What was the purpose of the Declaration of Independence?

words to know

revenue   boycott

Time Box

1754
Albany Plan of Union

1765
Stamp Act

1774
Intolerable Acts

1774
First Continental Congress

1775
Second Continental Congress

1776
Declaration of Independence

British Policies After 1763

The French and Indian War (1756–1763) in the colonies was part of a global conflict between Britain and France. The peace treaty gave Britain vast new territories in North America and India. To protect its huge empire, Britain had to keep thousands of troops stationed overseas. King George III refused to ask the people of England to pay all the costs.

They already had a large war debt to pay off. He asked Parliament to make the North American colonists help pay for their own defense.

A group of colonists dressed as Mohawk Native Americans dumped a cargo of tea in Boston Harbor.

Beginning in 1765, Parliament levied, or placed, new taxes on the colonies to raise **revenue**, or income. The first was the Stamp Act, which placed a tax on such items as newspapers, legal documents, and playing cards. Parliament had never collected a revenue tax from the colonists before. Colonists had always taxed themselves by sending representatives to their colonial assemblies. The colonists protested this as "taxation without representation," because they did not send representatives to Parliament. Parliament repealed the Stamp Act in 1766, after street protests and violence against royal tax collectors. British businesses were also suffering from the tax.

However, Parliament did not give up its right to tax the colonists. It claimed that it represented all British subjects, including the colonists. In 1773, Parliament passed the Tea Act. Among other things, it placed a tax on tea. In protest, some citizens of Boston dumped a load of imported British tea into the harbor. This is known as the Boston Tea Party. Parliament responded with the Intolerable Acts. The first of these acts closed the port of Boston until the colonists paid for the tea. The second act outlawed town meetings in Boston. The third act required the colony to pay the cost of food and housing for the British troops sent to enforce the acts. The fourth act allowed British officials accused of serious offenses while putting down riots to be sent to England for trial.

stop and think

Why would the colonists not want to send their tax money to Great Britain? Imagine you are a colonist in 1765. Write a journal entry explaining why you do not want to pay the Stamp Act. Share your writing with a partner and discuss your reasons.

Colonial Unity

The actions of King George III and Parliament created the opposite effect of what was expected to happen. Instead of forcing the colonists to obey, the Intolerable Acts pushed them toward independence. Twelve colonies sent representatives to a meeting in Philadelphia in September 1774. This meeting became known as the First Continental Congress.

The Congress rejected the Intolerable Acts and called for a **boycott** of British goods. This meant the colonists would neither sell nor buy British goods. The Congress also sent Parliament a "Declaration and Resolves" that defended the colonists' right to pass laws for themselves. The colonists claimed the right to make their own laws and to try those accused of crimes in their own courts, not in courts in England. The colonists also refused to accept Parliament's right to tax them.

Benjamin Franklin published this drawing in support of colonial unity.

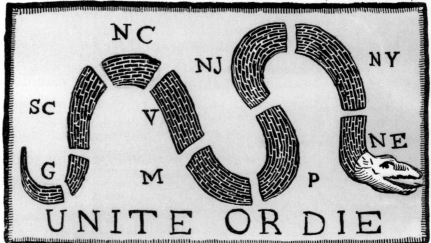

In May 1775, the Second Continental Congress met in Philadelphia. In April, colonists and British soldiers had fought the opening battles of the Revolutionary War at Lexington and Concord in the Massachusetts Bay Colony. Some members of Congress knew that declaring independence was only a matter of time. As a result, the new Congress acted to protect the colonies. It organized an army and chose George Washington as commander in chief. Congress also organized a navy and began to issue money.

Fighting between colonial and British forces continued in New England throughout 1775. Congress and King George traded petitions and proclamations. Congress's efforts at finding a peaceful solution ended with the Olive Branch Petition. It asked the king to protect the colonists from Parliament's unfair acts. The king refused to accept it and declared the colonists in rebellion.

Declaring Independence

In early 1776, support for independence from Great Britain grew rapidly. Thomas Paine's pamphlet, *Common Sense*, persuaded many colonists that the time for independence had come. He denounced King George III as a "royal brute" who could no longer be trusted to protect American rights. By spring, some colonial legislatures were telling their representatives to the Second Continental Congress to work toward independence. On June 7, Richard Henry Lee of Virginia introduced a resolution calling for independence.

Thomas Jefferson drafted the Declaration of Independence in 1776.

The representatives debated his resolution throughout June. In the meantime, Congress had named a committee to prepare a declaration of independence. The document would explain why the colonies were rejecting British rule and establishing their own national government. Thomas Jefferson was asked to write the document.

The Declaration of Independence was presented to Congress on June 28. On July 2, the Second Continental Congress passed Lee's Resolution. On July 4, the members of Congress signed the Declaration of Independence. There was no turning back. Congress then prepared to set up the new nation's government.

Putting It All Together

What steps led to the Declaration of Independence? With a partner, make a list of the actions taken by Parliament and King George III, on one side, and the colonists, on the other side, that led to the Declaration of Independence.

The Declaration of Independence

Action of Second Continental Congress, July 4, 1776

The unanimous Declaration of the thirteen United States of America

WHEN in the Course of human Events, it becomes necessary for one People to dissolve the Political Bands which have connected them with another, and to assume among the Powers of the Earth, the separate and equal Station to which the Laws of Nature and of Nature's God entitle them, a decent Respect to the Opinions of Mankind requires that they should declare the causes which **impel** them to the Separation.

WE hold these Truths to be self-evident, that all Men are created equal, that they are **endowed** by their Creator with certain **unalienable** Rights, that among these are Life, Liberty and the Pursuit of Happiness — That to secure these Rights, Governments are instituted among Men, deriving their just Powers from the Consent of the Governed, that whenever any Form of Government becomes destructive of these Ends, it is the Right of the People to alter or to abolish it, and to institute new Government, laying its Foundation on such Principles, and organizing its Powers in such Form, as to them shall seem most likely to effect their Safety and Happiness. Prudence, indeed, will dictate that Governments long established should not be changed for light and **transient** Causes; and accordingly all Experience hath shewn, that Mankind are more disposed to suffer, while Evils are sufferable, than to right themselves by abolishing the Forms to which they are accustomed. But when a long Train of Abuses and **Usurpations**, pursuing invariably the same Object, evinces a Design to reduce them under **absolute Despotism**, it is their Right, it is their Duty, to throw off such Government, and to provide new Guards for their future Security. Such has been the patient Sufferance of these Colonies; and such is now the Necessity which constrains them to alter their former Systems of Government. The History of the present King of Great Britain is a History of repeated Injuries and Usurpations, all having in direct Object the Establishment of an absolute Tyranny over these States. To prove this, let Facts be submitted to a **candid** World.

Preamble

The Preamble, or first paragraph, states that the colonists have determined that it is necessary to break away from Great Britain. However, they respect the right of others to know why they have come to this decision. The Declaration is their explanation.

impel: force

Natural Rights

This section describes the political ideas behind the colonists' desire for independence. Thomas Jefferson borrowed ideas from the French philosopher Montesquieu and the English philosopher John Locke. People create governments in order to protect their natural rights. Natural rights are rights that belong to people because they are human beings. Jefferson lists the three basic rights as "life, liberty, and the pursuit of happiness." If government leaders do not protect these rights, then the people have the right to replace the leaders. However, Jefferson notes that governments should not be replaced for unimportant reasons. People should change a government only for the most serious reasons. People have a further duty to set up a new government that will safeguard their rights.

endowed: given
unalienable: cannot be taken away
transient: passing quickly
usurpations: unjust use of power
absolute despotism: complete control of government; same as absolute monarchy

candid: fair, sincere

HE has refused his Assent to Laws, the most wholesome and necessary for the public Good.

HE has forbidden his Governors to pass Laws of immediate and pressing Importance, unless suspended in their Operation till his Assent should be obtained; and when so suspended, he has utterly neglected to attend to them.

HE has refused to pass other Laws for the Accommodation of large Districts of People, unless those People would **relinquish** the Right of Representation in the Legislature, a Right **inestimable** to them, and formidable to **Tyrants** only.

HE has called together Legislative Bodies at Places unusual, uncomfortable, and distant from the **Depository** of their public Records, for the sole Purpose of fatiguing them into Compliance with his Measures.

HE has dissolved Representative Houses repeatedly, for opposing with manly Firmness his Invasions on the Rights of the People.

HE has refused for a long Time, after such Dissolutions, to cause others to be elected; whereby the Legislative Powers, incapable of the **Annihilation**, have returned to the People at large for their exercise; the State remaining in the mean time exposed to all the Dangers of Invasion from without, and the **Convulsions** within.

HE has endeavoured to prevent the Population of these States; for that Purpose obstructing the Laws for Naturalization of Foreigners; refusing to pass others to encourage their Migrations hither, and raising the Conditions of new Appropriations of Lands.

HE has obstructed the Administration of Justice, by refusing his Assent to Laws for establishing Judiciary Powers.

HE has made Judges dependent on his Will alone, for the **Tenure** of their Offices, and the Amount and Payment of their Salaries.

HE has erected a Multitude of new Offices, and sent hither Swarms of Officers to harrass our People, and eat out their Substance.

HE has kept among us, in Times of Peace, Standing Armies, without the consent of our Legislatures.

HE has affected to render the Military independent of and superior to the Civil Power.

HE has combined with others to subject us to a **Jurisdiction** foreign to our Constitution, and unacknowledged by our Laws; giving his Assent to their Acts of pretended Legislation:

List of Charges Against King George III

Most of the Declaration lists the ways that George III had abused the rights of the colonists. Each paragraph lists an offense against the people. In truth, most members of Parliament had supported these actions. However, some members of Parliament had supported the colonists. Jefferson wanted to keep them on the colonists' side, so he made the monarch the target of the list.

relinquish: give up
inestimable: priceless
tyrant: dictator
depository: storehouse

annihilation: complete destruction

convulsions: violent disturbances

tenure: length of time in office

These are British troops stationed in the colonies after the French and Indian War.

This refers to the Quartering Act, one of the Intolerable Acts passed after the Boston Tea Party.

jurisdiction: authority, power

FOR quartering large Bodies of Armed Troops among us;

FOR protecting them, by a **mock** Trial, from Punishment for any Murders which they should commit on the Inhabitants of these States:

mock: imitation, not real

FOR cutting off our Trade with all Parts of the World:

FOR imposing Taxes on us without our Consent:

FOR depriving us, in many Cases, of the Benefits of Trial by Jury:

FOR transporting us beyond Seas to be tried for pretended Offences:

FOR abolishing the free System of English Laws in a neighbouring Province, establishing therein an **arbitrary** Government, and enlarging its Boundaries, so as to **render** it at once an Example and fit Instrument for introducing the same absolute Rules into these Colonies:

The Quebec Act allowed Canada to keep its French system of laws, which gave people fewer rights than English laws.

arbitrary: based on someone's idea rather than on laws or rules
render: make

FOR taking away our Charters, abolishing our most valuable Laws, and altering fundamentally the Forms of our Governments:

FOR suspending our own Legislatures, and declaring themselves invested with Power to legislate for us in all Cases whatsoever.

HE has **abdicated** Government here, by declaring us out of his Protection and waging War against us.

abdicated: given up

HE has plundered our Seas, ravaged our Coasts, burnt our Towns, and destroyed the Lives of our People.

HE is, at this Time, transporting large Armies of foreign Mercenaries to compleat the Works of Death, Desolation, and Tyranny, already begun with circumstances of Cruelty and **Perfidy**, scarcely paralleled in the most barbarous Ages, and totally unworthy the Head of a civilized Nation.

Not all the troops in the colonies were British soldiers. Parliament hired German mercenaries to patrol the colonies. Mercenaries are soldiers who work for foreign governments.

perfidy: disloyalty, breaking a trust

HE has constrained our fellow Citizens taken Captive on the high Seas to bear Arms against their Country, to become the Executioners of their Friends and Brethren, or to fall themselves by their Hands.

HE has excited domestic **Insurrections** amongst us, and has endeavoured to bring on the Inhabitants of our Frontiers, the merciless Indian Savages, whose known Rule of Warfare, is an undistinguished Destruction, of all Ages, Sexes and Conditions.

insurrections: rebellions

IN every stage of these Oppressions we have **Petitioned for Redress** in the most humble Terms: Our repeated Petitions have been answered only by repeated Injury. A Prince, whose Character is thus marked by every act which may define a Tyrant, is unfit to be the Ruler of a free People.

petitioned for redress: asked for a solution or remedy

NOR have we been wanting in Attentions to our British Brethren. We have warned them from Time to Time of Attempts by their Legislature to extend an unwarrantable Jurisdiction over us. We have reminded them of the Circumstances of our Emigration and Settlement here. We have appealed to their native Justice and Magnanimity, and we have **conjured** them by the Ties of our common Kindred to disavow these Usurpations, which, would inevitably interrupt our Connections and Correspondence. They too have been deaf to the Voice of Justice and of **Consanguinity**. We must, therefore, acquiesce in the Necessity, which denounces our Separation, and hold them, as we hold the rest of Mankind, Enemies in War, in Peace, Friends.

WE, therefore, the Representatives of the UNITED STATES OF AMERICA, in GENERAL CONGRESS, Assembled, appealing to the Supreme Judge of the World for the **Rectitude** of our Intentions, do, in the Name, and by Authority of the good People of these Colonies, solemnly Publish and Declare, That these United Colonies are, and of Right ought to be, FREE AND INDEPENDENT STATES; that they are absolved from all Allegiance to the British Crown, and that all political Connection between them and the State of Great-Britain, is and ought to be totally dissolved; and that as FREE AND INDEPENDENT STATES, they have full Power to levy War, conclude Peace, contract Alliances, establish Commerce, and to do all other Acts and Things which INDEPENDENT STATES may of right do. And for the support of this Declaration, with a firm Reliance on the Protection of divine Providence, we mutually pledge to each other our Lives, our Fortunes, and our sacred Honor.

conjured: asked for

consanguinity: blood relationship

Resolution of Independence and Rights

The final section declares that the colonies are "free and independent states." It then lists the rights that the new nation has. Once this document was signed by the assembled representatives of the colonies, there was no turning back.

rectitude: correctness, rightness

John Hancock	Charles Carroll	Geo. Taylor	Josiah Bartlett
Button Gwinnett	Of Carrollton	James Wilson	Wm. Whipple
Lyman Hall	George Wythe	Geo. Ross	Saml Adams
Geo Walton	Richard Henry Lee	Caesar Rodney	John Adams
Wm Hooper	Th Jefferson	Geo Read	Robt Treat Paine
Joseph Hewes	Benja Harrison	Tho M. Kean	Elbridge Gerry
John Penn	Thos Nelson Jr.	Wm Floyd	Step Hopkins
Edward Rutledge	Francis Lightfoot Lee	Phil. Livingston	William Ellery
Thos Heyward Junr.	Carter Braxton	Frans. Lewis	Roger Sherman
Thomas Lynch Junr.	Robt Morris	Lewis Morris	Samel Huntington
Arthur Middleton	Benjamin Rush	Richd. Stockton	Wm. Williams
Samuel Chase	Benja. Franklin	Jno Witherspoon	Oliver Wolcott
Wm. Paca	John Morton	Fras. Hopkinson	Matthew Thornton
Thos. Stone	Geo Clymer	John Hart	
	Jas. Smith	Abra Clark	

The Confederation Government

Thinking on Your Own

If you were going to draw up a new plan of government in 1776, how would you set up your government? How would your experience with Great Britain affect what you wanted in a government? Make a list of at least five things you would or would not want in your new government.

Once the Declaration was signed, the colonies were no longer colonies. Each became a state with the powers of a state.

States either quickly wrote new constitutions or used their colonial plans of government as their constitutions. The relationship between the states and the national government was not the same as it is today. The states were joined together in a loose union known as a confederation. The states kept most of their powers. They shared few powers with the national government.

focus your reading

Discuss why the new states set up a confederation form of government.

What did the confederation government accomplish?

Explain the weaknesses of the confederation government.

words to know

central government

ratify

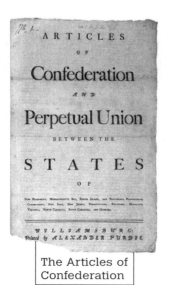

The Articles of Confederation

The Confederation Government

It soon became clear that the new states needed some form of **central government**. For example, each state could not act alone in fighting Great Britain. As a result, in 1777, the Second Continental Congress agreed on the Articles of Confederation. By 1781, all the states had **ratified**, or approved, this new plan of government. It remained the government of the new nation until it was replaced by the United States Constitution in 1789.

Great Britain had a strong central government with a great deal of power over the colonies. The new states were determined to keep another strong central government from interfering with their newly won autonomy.

The Articles of Confederation created a weak central government. It consisted of a Congress similar to the earlier Continental Congresses. It had no separate executive branch or judicial branch. Congress had the power to coin money, direct foreign affairs, make war and peace, and build a navy. It could not collect taxes, enforce laws, or regulate trade. Those important powers were left to the states. State governments sent delegates to Congress, with each state having one vote in Congress.

stop and think

Draw a diagram to illustrate how the confederation government was set up. Ask a partner to review your diagram against the text to make sure it is accurate.

Accomplishments of the Confederation Government

The confederation government had two major accomplishments. The first was that the new nation negotiated a favorable treaty with Great Britain at the end of the Revolutionary War. As a result of the U.S. victory, Great Britain recognized the independence of its former colonies. In addition, all the land from the Great Lakes and Canada south to Florida, and from the Atlantic coast west to the Mississippi River, became U.S. territory.

The second major accomplishment related to a section of the newly acquired land called the Northwest Territory. Congress passed the Land Ordinance of 1785 to set up a system for dividing, selling, and settling the lands in this area. In time, the states of Ohio, Indiana, Illinois, Michigan, Wisconsin, and part of Minnesota were made from this region.

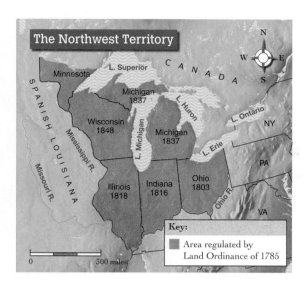

The Northwest Territory

The Northwest Ordinance, which was passed in 1787, set up government for the area. The law divided the Northwest Territory into districts. Congress appointed a governor and three judges for each district. When a district had 5,000 free adult males, it could set up a legislature and elect lawmakers. When there were 60,000 people, a district could ask for statehood. The Northwest Ordinance was important for two reasons. First, it set up the system for adding new states to the United States. Second, it established the principle that old and new states had the same rights.

Weaknesses of the Articles

The Articles of Confederation had several weaknesses that made it difficult for the government to operate. First, Congress did not have the power to pass taxes. As a result, it depended on borrowing money or asking the states for money to support it. If a state refused, there was nothing Congress could do. This was the second problem with the Articles.

Third, Congress had no power to regulate trade. As a result, trade laws varied greatly from state to state and between the states and other nations. The different trade regulations hurt the economy of the new nation.

ideas to remember

The major weaknesses of the confederation government were:

- Congress could not pass taxes.
- Congress could not force states to obey its laws.
- Congress could not regulate, or manage, trade.
- Laws needed the approval of nine of the 13 states.
- All 13 states had to agree to changes in the Articles.
- There was no executive branch.
- There was no judicial branch.

Fourth, representatives of nine of the 13 states had to approve a bill before it could become a law. However, representatives of all 13 states were rarely in Congress at the same time. Therefore, it was difficult to get laws passed.

Shays's Rebellion helped Congress realize the weaknesses of the Articles of Confederation.

Fifth, people realized over time that the Articles needed to be changed. However, the legislatures of all 13 states had to agree to changes in the Articles. No amendment was ever successful because all 13 states could never agree.

Sixth, there was no executive branch. As a result, the government could not enforce its own laws.

Seventh, there was no judicial branch. State courts heard lawsuits between the states and interpreted national laws. Interpretations could vary from court to court and state to state.

By the late 1780s, the new nation was in serious trouble. It owed millions of dollars in war loans. Economic problems were causing hardships among landowners and merchants. Small farmers suffered greatly. Many lost their land because they could not pay their debts. Something had to be done—and soon—about the confederation government.

Putting It All Together

The desire of the states to hold onto power shaped the way the Articles were written. With a partner, make a two-column table. In the left column, list the seven weaknesses of the Articles. In the right column, explain how each weakness resulted from the desire of the states not to give up power.

The Constitutional Convention

Thinking on Your Own

If you were going to revise the Articles of Confederation, what would you change? Decide based on what you know about the federal government today and what you have learned about weaknesses of the confederation government. Compare your changes with those of a partner.

By the mid-1780s, relations between Maryland and Virginia had become strained over trade issues. In 1785, George Washington asked the states to meet at Mount Vernon in Virginia to discuss the issues. The discussions went well enough that another meeting was called for the following year in Annapolis, Maryland. This time all the states were asked to attend. The purpose of the Annapolis Convention was to discuss trade issues. Only five states attended. After much discussion, the delegates called for a meeting in May 1787 to discuss ways to make the Articles of Confederation stronger.

focus your reading

What six early decisions shaped the Constitutional Convention?

Describe the compromises made by the delegates.

What were the issues in the fight over ratification of the Constitution?

words to know

exports

Anti-Federalists

Federalists

The Constitutional Convention met in 1787 with the goal of revising the Articles of Confederation.

Organizing the Constitutional Convention

Each state legislature chose delegates to attend the Constitutional Convention. The convention opened in Philadelphia on May 25, 1787. In all, 55 men were appointed to represent 12 states. Rhode Island did not send delegates because it opposed strengthening the confederation government. George Washington was selected to be president of the convention. The representatives soon realized that strengthening the Articles of Confederation was not enough— they needed to write a new constitution. Among the early decisions that shaped the convention were the following:

- Each state had only one vote.

- At least seven of the 12 states had to approve a proposal.

- The public would not be told what was happening until the convention was over.

- The Articles had to be replaced by a new plan of government.

James Madison (1751–1836)

James Madison had a great deal of political experience before the Constitutional Convention. He helped write Virginia's state constitution in 1776, and he served in the Continental Congress from 1780 to 1783 and in the Virginia legislature from 1784 to 1786. Madison had firsthand knowledge of the weaknesses of the Articles of Confederation. He went to Philadelphia prepared to write a new plan of government. He wanted a greatly strengthened central government.

Madison had a list of 15 proposals for how a new government should be organized. These suggestions formed the basis for discussions and became known as the Virginia Plan. Much of the Constitution reflects his ideas. As a result of his proposals, Madison is often called "the Father of the Constitution."

Madison's work at the convention is important for another reason. He kept the only complete record of the discussions. Because the delegates voted to keep the debates secret, his *Notes* were not published until 1840, four years after his death. It is because of his journal that we know what went on at the convention. Madison ended his public service as president of the United States from 1809–1817.

- The new government would be based on the ideas of limited government and representative government.

- The national government would be divided into three branches: executive, legislative, and judicial.

The Major Compromises

James Madison, a delegate from Virginia, arrived with a plan for a new national government. The Virginia Plan, as it was called, favored the large states, as it made a state's population the basis for representation. William Paterson of New Jersey offered a plan that favored the small states. Much of the convention was spent debating the two plans. After much debate, the convention almost broke up. It could not agree on either plan.

Finally, the Connecticut Compromise, also known as the Great Compromise, was proposed. The Connecticut Compromise was really a series of compromises that ended the deadlock. Analyze the table "Competing Plans and the Compromise Solutions" on page 34. It shows the differences between the plans and how compromise solved the problems.

stop and think

Compromise was an important part of the Constitutional Convention. With a partner, make a concept map of the four major compromises agreed to by the delegates. Draw lines and add circles to each compromise to show its most important details.

The delegates reached other important compromises. One dealt with how people would be counted to determine the number of representatives each state would have in the House of Representatives. Southern states wanted enslaved people counted. Northern states wanted only free people counted. The delegates approved the Three-Fifths Compromise to settle the disagreement. Three-fifths of the population of enslaved people would be counted in determining representation.

A third compromise also involved slavery—and trade in general. Southerners would not accept the Constitution if it banned the slave trade. They also would not accept the Constitution if it allowed the national government to tax **exports**, or goods being sold to other nations. As a result, the delegates agreed not to tax exports. However, they agreed to give the national government the power to regulate trade between states and between states and foreign nations. In return, the national government did not ban the slave trade with foreign nations until 1808.

The fourth compromise involved how the president was elected. The delegates agreed on an Electoral College. The legislature in each state would choose electors who would meet after the national election by citizens. The electors would select the president based on the number of votes each candidate received.

Competing Plans and the Compromise Solutions

Issue	Virginia Plan	New Jersey Plan	U.S. Constitution
Representation	Based on population or wealth	Equal representation for each state	Upper house (Senate) made up of two delegates from each state; Lower house (House of Representatives) based on population
Executive Branch	Single executive chosen by Congress	Executive committee chosen by Congress	Single executive (president) chosen by the Electoral College; electors selected by individual states
Legislative Branch	Two houses: Upper house elected by the people; Lower house elected by the upper house	One house: appointed by state legislatures	Two houses: Upper house (Senate) selected by state legislatures*; Lower house (House of Representatives) elected by the people
Judicial Branch	National judiciary chosen by Congress	National judiciary appointed by executive committee	National judiciary: Supreme Court and lower courts; Supreme Court justices appointed by the president and confirmed by the Senate

*The Seventeenth Amendment in 1913 changed this. Senators are now elected by the people.

The major compromises of the Constitutional Convention were

- Connecticut, or Great, Compromise that combined the Virginia Plan and the New Jersey Plan
- Three-Fifths Compromise on slavery
- compromise on commerce and the slave trade
- Electoral College compromise

Ratifying the Constitution

Nine of the 13 states had to ratify the Constitution before it could go into effect. However, its supporters knew that all 13 states had to approve it. Otherwise, the new nation would collapse.

Ratification, or approval, was not a sure thing. Opposition was centered on two issues. Some people did not want a strong central government. Others, like Thomas Jefferson, wanted a bill of rights included in the Constitution. They wanted the rights of individuals protected against government.

Anti-Federalists, those who opposed the Constitution, were especially strong in New York and Virginia.

The **Federalists** supported ratification. Several of them, including James Madison, John Jay, and Alexander Hamilton, wrote a series of essays defending the need for a strong government. The *Federalist Papers* won over the opposition in New York. A promise to include a bill of rights won over Virginians. The *Federalist Papers* and the promise of the bill of rights won over people in other states as well. By March 1789, only Rhode Island and North Carolina remained outside the new government. By May 1790, both states had ratified the Constitution.

Residents of New York City celebrate the ratification of the U.S. Constitution.

Putting It All Together

With a partner, brainstorm ideas for an ad to support ratification of the Constitution. List at least four ideas. Then choose one idea. Design an ad with text for your idea.

Participate in Government

Register to Vote

The Twenty-sixth Amendment to the Constitution set the voting age at eighteen for all federal, state, and local elections. Before 1971, the voting age in some states had been twenty-one. Setting the qualifications for voting is still the responsibility of the states. Differences among the states usually involve how long a person must live in the state or the voting district in order to be able to vote. Typically, it is 15 to 30 days before an election.

Voters may register at the office of the county, city, or town board of elections where they live. The National Voter Registration Act of 1995 made it even easier to register. The law is sometimes called the "motor-voter act" because people can now register at their state's department of motor vehicles. Voters can also register at welfare offices and at government agencies for people with disabilities. States must also accept voter registrations by mail.

When you register to vote, you will be asked for your name, address, place and date of birth, gender, Social Security number, and political party. You may register as an independent, which means that you do not indicate a political party. This may limit whether you can vote in primary elections. You will also need to provide proof that you are a U.S. citizen.

To find out how to register in your state

- Check the government pages in your telephone directory or look online for the county, city, or town board of elections.

- Call to find out what you need to register and how or where to register.

- Gather the necessary documents.

Skill Builder

Analyzing Timelines

Sequence is the order in which events happen. A timeline is a quick way to see the sequence of events. Dates and events on a timeline are arranged in chronological order. Chronological order is the same as time order. The first dates on a timeline are the earliest dates.

Being able to read a timeline is useful in understanding when certain events happened in relation to other events. For example, was the fighting at Lexington and Concord before or after approval of the Declaration of Independence? Knowing the time order of events can help you understand the causes of events. It can also tell you the effects of events. Lexington and Concord happened before the Declaration of Independence was written.

The timeline at the right uses dates and events from this chapter.

Answer the following questions.

1 When did the Annapolis Convention take place?

2 How many years passed between the Annapolis Convention and the ratification of the U.S. Constitution?

3 Which took place first: passage of the Stamp Act or passage of the Intolerable Acts?

4 For how many years were the Articles of Confederation the basis of government for the United States?

⧗ Time Box

1765
Stamp Act passed

1773
Boston Tea Party

1774
Intolerable Acts passed
First Continental Congress

1775
Battles of Lexington and Concord

1775–1781
Second Continental Congress

1776
Declaration of Independence

1777
Articles of Confederation written

1781–1789
Government under the Articles of Confederation

1785
Delegates from Virginia and Maryland met at Mount Vernon

1786
Annapolis Convention held

1786–1787
Shays's Rebellion

1787
Constitutional Convention

1788
U.S. Constitution ratified

Chapter

3

THE UNITED STATES CONSTITUTION

Getting Focused

Skim this chapter to predict what you will be learning.

- Read the lesson titles and subheadings.
- Look at the illustrations and read the captions.
- Examine the charts and diagrams.
- Review the vocabulary words and terms.

The Constitution provided a new form of government for the United States. Think about what you already know about the Constitution. Write five statements in your notebook about the kind of national government it created.

The United States Constitution was completed on September 17, 1787. The document became the "Law of the Land" when ratified on March 4, 1789.

The Basic Principles

Thinking on Your Own

A representative government is one of the basic principles of the Constitution. Based on what you already know about the U.S. government, how did the writers include this principle in the Constitution? What clues do the vocabulary terms provide about the principles of government on which the Constitution was based? Discuss these questions with a partner. Then answer them in your notebook.

The U.S. Constitution is the basic law of the United States. It describes how the national government should be set up. It also describes the relationship between the national government and the states. No law—either national or state—is higher than the Constitution.

Organization of the Constitution

The Constitution is divided into three parts. The first part is called the Preamble. It explains why the document was written.

The second part of the Constitution is made up of seven articles. These articles lay out the plan of government for the United States.

- Article I describes the legislative branch (Congress), its duties and powers, and qualifications for its members.

focus your reading

Explain how the Constitution is organized.

The Constitution is based on what six principles of government?

words to know

supremacy clause

amendments

Framers

popular sovereignty

federalism

separation of powers

checks and balances

judicial review

limited government

George Washington with a copy of the U.S. Constitution in 1787

- Article II describes the duties and powers of the executive branch and the qualifications for president and vice president. It also describes the process for electing the president and vice president.

- Article III creates the Supreme Court as head of the judicial branch.

- Article IV explains the relationship among the states and the states' relationship to the national government.

- Article V describes the process for amending, or changing, the Constitution.

- Article VI declares that the Constitution, acts of Congress, and treaties are the "supreme Law of the Land." This is known as the **supremacy clause**.

- Article VII sets out the process for ratifying, or formally approving, the Constitution.

The third part of the Constitution lists the **amendments**. The first ten are known as the Bill of Rights. These were written during the first session of Congress in 1789. They became laws when the Virginia legislature ratified them in 1791. Virginia was the ninth state to ratify them. In more than 200 years, only 17 additional amendments have been ratified.

The Foundation of the Constitution

The delegates who attended the Constitutional Convention are known as the **Framers**, or writers, of the Constitution. They based the new government on six principles. These principles are: popular sovereignty, federalism, separation of powers, checks and balances, judicial review, and limited government.

The power of the U.S. government comes from the people of the nation. **Popular sovereignty** is the term that describes this. Government is able to govern as long as it has the consent, or approval, of the governed. As Abraham Lincoln described the government, it is "government of the people, by the people, [and] for the people."

stop and think

The first three articles of the Constitution describe the branches of the national government. The men who wrote the Constitution could have described them in a single section. Why do you think they gave each branch a separate article? Discuss your ideas with a partner and write your answer in a sentence or two in your notebook.

Federalism describes the relationship between the states and the national government. In a federal system, power is divided between the states and the national government. Each has its own area of duties and responsibilities. The loose union of states under the Articles of Confederation had not worked. The members of the Constitutional Convention knew that in order to survive, the new nation had to have a central government with some power.

The delegates set up three branches of government. Each branch was given its own duties and responsibilities. This division is based on the principle of **separation of powers**.

Checks and Balances of the Federal Government

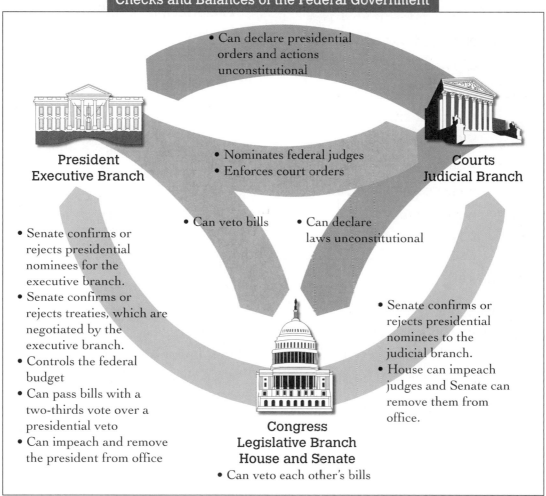

President
Executive Branch

Courts
Judicial Branch

Congress
Legislative Branch
House and Senate

- Can declare presidential orders and actions unconstitutional

- Nominates federal judges
- Enforces court orders

- Can veto bills
- Can declare laws unconstitutional

- Senate confirms or rejects presidential nominees for the executive branch.
- Senate confirms or rejects treaties, which are negotiated by the executive branch.
- Controls the federal budget
- Can pass bills with a two-thirds vote over a presidential veto
- Can impeach and remove the president from office

- Senate confirms or rejects presidential nominees to the judicial branch.
- House can impeach judges and Senate can remove them from office.

- Can veto each other's bills

The writers of the Constitution built into the central government a system of **checks and balances**. Each branch has duties that check, or restrain, the power of the other two branches. For example, the president nominates federal judges. The Senate approves or rejects the president's candidates. The diagram "Checks and Balances of the Federal Government," above, explains how the system works.

The buildings represent the three branches of the United States government. These branches provide checks and balances on each other.

ideas to remember

The Constitution is based on the following principles

- popular sovereignty
- federalism
- separation of powers
- checks and balances
- judicial review
- limited government

The principle of **judicial review** gives power to the courts. The courts can rule on the constitutionality of a law or action of local, state, or the national government. *Constitutionality* means whether a law or action violates the U.S. Constitution. The lower courts have the power of judicial review. But the U.S. Supreme Court has the final decision on what is or is not constitutional.

This power is not stated as such in the Constitution. It has developed since 1803, when Chief Justice John Marshall wrote the opinion in *Marbury* v. *Madison*. He declared unconstitutional a law that Congress had passed.

Limited government limits, or restricts, the power of government to do certain things and not others. The Bill of Rights, for example, lists those freedoms that people have and that government may not take away.

Putting It All Together

Write a definition for each of the six principles that form the basis of the Constitution. Then play "Which Principle?" with a partner. Take turns reading your definitions and asking each other to identify the principle.

The Branches of Government

Thinking on Your Own

The Framers of the Constitution wrote a plan of government they hoped would last for centuries. The government that they created had to be able to solve problems in the future. With a partner, make a list of at least five issues that the U.S. government must deal with today that the Framers could not have predicted. Write these in your notebook.

Most of the articles of the Constitution lay out the separate powers of each branch of the national government. However, the Constitution also lists powers that the branches share. For example, the executive and legislative branches must cooperate on passing the annual budget for the federal government. Declaring war and agreeing on legislation are two other areas of cooperation between the two branches.

focus your reading

Describe the expressed and enumerated powers of Congress.

What powers does the executive branch have?

What is the major duty of the judicial branch?

words to know

veto

expressed powers

enumerate

naturalization

elastic clause

jurisdiction

appeal

Congress—the Legislative Branch

Article I of the U.S. Constitution deals with Congress, the lawmaking body of the national government. Section 1 establishes Congress. Sections 2 and 3 describe the House of Representatives and the Senate.

Section 4 states how elections to the House and Senate should be held and when Congress should meet. Section 5 sets out the organization and rules of procedure for both houses. Section 6 makes the federal government responsible for paying the salaries of members of Congress.

According to Section 7, all bills related to taxation must come from the House. Section 7 also describes how a bill becomes a law and what happens if the president refuses to sign a bill. This is known as the president's **veto**. Section 7 gives Congress the power to override the president's veto by a two-thirds vote of both houses. The legislative branch is discussed in detail in Chapter 5.

The Framers of the Constitution listed specific powers for Congress. These are known as the **expressed powers** because they are stated. Section 8, Clauses 1 to 18, lists most of these powers. They are also called the enumerated powers. The word **enumerated** means "numbered."

- The first six expressed powers deal with the economy. Among these are the power to levy taxes, to regulate bankruptcies, to coin money, and to punish counterfeiters. Clause 4 also gives Congress the power to determine the **naturalization** process for people of other nations to become United States citizens. Clause 7 gives Congress the power to set up post offices.

- Clause 8 deals with copyrights and patents. Congress may pass laws to protect people's writings and inventions.

- Clause 9 gives Congress the power to set up the federal court system below the level of the U.S. Supreme Court.

- Clauses 10 through 16 give Congress powers related to defending the nation. These include the powers to set up an army and navy, and to declare war.

- Clause 17 gives Congress the power to pass laws to govern the District of Columbia.

- Clause 18 gives Congress the power to make all laws that are "necessary and proper" in order to exercise its other 17 powers. Clause 18 is also known as the **elastic clause**, because it allows Congress to stretch the use of its powers.

The "necessary and proper," or elastic, clause is one of the most important and controversial powers of Congress. The Framers were thoughtful men and realized that the nation would change over time. However, they had no way of knowing what those changes would be. But they intended the Constitution to last for centuries. The elastic clause was one solution for governing the nation in the unknowable future.

Section 9 lists powers that Congress does not have. For example, Congress may not create a system of nobles like British dukes and counts. Many of the powers denied to Congress have their basis in powers that Parliament or the monarchy had over the colonists.

Section 10 lists powers denied to the states. For example, the states may not conduct business with foreign nations or wage war on other nations. There was a reason for removing the states from areas that involved other nations or other states. It meant they were less likely to come into conflict with the federal government.

stop and think

Write a paragraph to explain how the Framers of the Constitution provided for change. Use the ideas that you wrote in Thinking on Your Own as examples in your paragraph. Share and discuss your paragraph with a partner.

The Executive Branch

Article II creates the executive branch headed by the president. This branch has the power to enforce laws. The executive branch is more than the president and vice president. Since 1789, it has evolved into 15 departments, 33 independent agencies, and 12 offices. Today more than 2.6 million employees work for the executive branch of the federal government in the United States and throughout the world.

Article II has only four sections. Section 1 states the term of office of the president and vice president, the method of election for these offices, qualifications, their salaries, and the oath of office that the president must take.

The powers of the presidency listed in the Constitution are somewhat broad and vague. Over time, presidents have used these powers to increase the duties and responsibilities of the presidency. For example, Congress determines the annual budget for the federal government. However, the discussion begins with a budget prepared by the executive branch. Congress makes the laws, but the president often suggests what those laws should be. The executive branch of the U.S. government is discussed in detail in Chapter 8.

President George W. Bush was sworn in as president for a second term on January 20, 2005.

Section 2 lists the powers of the president. The president

- is commander in chief of the nation's armed forces including state militias, now known as the National Guard.

- appoints the heads of the departments within the executive branch, ambassadors to foreign nations, federal judges, and other top officials in the executive branch. The Senate approves these appointments. This is part of the system of checks and balances.

- may pardon, set free, or reduce a prison sentence or fine of a person convicted of a federal crime.

- negotiates treaties with other nations. The Senate approves the treaties. This is part of the system of checks and balances.

Section 3 lists the duties of the president. The president

- delivers an annual State of the Union address to Congress.

- may call Congress into special session as needed.

- represents the United States with other nations.

- commissions, or approves for service, every officer in the armed forces.

- enforces all the laws that Congress passes.

Section 4 lists the reasons why the president and vice president may be impeached and removed from office. Those reasons are "treason, bribery, or other high crimes and misdemeanors." A misdemeanor is misbehavior of some kind. The Constitution leaves it to Congress to decide what a high crime or misdemeanor may be.

The Judicial Branch

The United States has two separate judicial systems. One is the judiciary of the 50 states. Each state constitution empowers its state government to set up a court system. Local communities also have courts, such as criminal court and traffic court. These courts get their power to hear cases from the state. The judicial branch of the government is discussed in detail in Chapter 11.

Article III of the U.S. Constitution creates the federal judicial branch. However, the only court mentioned by name is the

Supreme Court. The article does not say anything about the levels of federal courts that may be set up below the Supreme Court. Section 1 only states:

> The judicial Power of the United States, shall be vested [placed] in one supreme Court, and in such inferior [lower level] Courts as the Congress may from time to time ordain [create] and establish.

Section 2 describes the **jurisdiction**, or area of the law that the federal courts may hear cases about. Most cases are challenges to laws passed by Congress and cases involving the Constitution. Federal courts also hear cases related to ships and shipping on rivers, lakes, and canals within the United States.

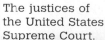

The justices of the United States Supreme Court.

The U.S. Supreme Court alone may hear cases involving officials of other nations and cases involving the states. This is called the Supreme Court's original jurisdiction. However, most cases come to the Supreme Court on **appeal** from a lower court. This happens when one party to the lawsuit requests a further hearing. This is known as the Supreme Court's appellate jurisdiction.

Section 2 also grants accused persons the right to a trial by jury. Section 3 defines the crime of treason and states the punishment for it.

Neither the executive nor the legislative branch may throw out a ruling of the Supreme Court. However, there are actions that these branches can take. One is to rewrite the law that the Court found unconstitutional. Congress and the president hope that by rewriting it, they can remove the reasons the Court found it unconstitutional. A second action is to turn the rejected law into an amendment to the Constitution. Congress then passes and sends the amendment to the states for ratification.

Putting It All Together

In your notebook, make a three-column chart with the columns labeled "Legislative," "Executive," and "Judicial." List the major powers of each branch of the national government. Share these with a partner.

The pages that follow contain the original text of the United States Constitution. Sections that are no longer enforced have been crossed out. The spelling and punctuation of the document remain in their original format. The headings are not part of the original Constitution.

The United States Constitution

We the People of the United States, in Order to form a more perfect Union, establish Justice, insure domestic Tranquility, provide for the common defence, promote the general Welfare, and secure the Blessings of Liberty to ourselves and our Posterity, do ordain and establish this Constitution for the United States of America.

Preamble

The first section of the Constitution is the Preamble. It states the purposes for which the Constitution was written. These purposes are to ensure (1) greater cooperation among the states, (2) equal justice for all, (3) peace within the nation, (4) defense against other nations, (5) the general well-being of the people, and (6) liberty now and in the future. The phrase "We the People" is based on the ideas of popular sovereignty and representative government. The phrase means that the power of the government comes from the people.

Article I   Legislative Branch

Article I.
Legislative Branch

Article I describes the legislative branch of the national government.

Section 1   Congress

All legislative Powers herein granted shall be vested in a Congress of the United States, which shall consist of a Senate and House of Representatives.

Section 1. Congress

The legislative branch is called Congress and is made up of two houses. It is the only lawmaking body for the federal government. The lower house, called the House of Representatives, is elected directly by the people in their home districts. House members represent the interests of their particular voters. As written, members of the Senate were to be elected by state legislatures and represent the overall interests of their state. The election of senators was changed by the 17th Amendment, ratified in 1912. Senators continue to represent the overall interests of their state, but they are elected directly by voters.

Section 2   House of Representatives

Clause 1: The House of Representatives shall be composed of Members chosen every second Year by the People of the several States, and the Electors in each State shall have the Qualifications requisite for Electors of the most numerous Branch of the State Legislature.

Section 2. House of Representatives

1. Election and Term of Office. *Electors* means "voters". Members of the House are elected every two years. Anyone who can vote for a candidate to a state legislature may vote for a House member. States may determine who may vote. However, Amendments 15, 19, 24, and 26 place limits on the rights of states to decide who may or may not vote.

Clause 2: No Person shall be a Representative who shall not have attained to the Age of twenty five Years, and been seven Years a Citizen of the United States, and who shall not, when elected, be an Inhabitant of that State in which he shall be chosen.

Clause 3: Representatives and direct Taxes shall be apportioned among the several States which may be included within this Union, according to their respective Numbers, ~~which shall be determined by adding to the whole Number of free Persons, including those bound to Service for a Term of Years, and excluding Indians not taxed, three-fifths of all other Persons.~~

The actual Enumeration shall be made within three Years after the first Meeting of the Congress of the United States, and within every subsequent Term of ten Years, in such Manner as they shall by Law direct.

The Number of Representatives shall not exceed one for every thirty Thousand, but each State shall have at Least one Representative; ~~and until such enumeration shall be made, the State of New Hampshire shall be entitled to chuse three, Massachusetts eight, Rhode-Island and Providence Plantations one, Connecticut five, New-York six, New Jersey four, Pennsylvania eight, Delaware one, Maryland six, Virginia ten, North Carolina five, South Carolina five, and Georgia three.~~

Clause 4: When vacancies happen in the Representation from any State, the Executive Authority thereof shall issue Writs of Election to fill such Vacancies.

Clause 5: The House of Representatives shall chuse their Speaker and other Officers; and shall have the sole Power of Impeachment.

2. Qualifications. Representatives must be at least twenty-five years old and have been a U.S. citizen for seven years. Representatives must also live in the state that they wish to represent in the House. The Constitution does not say that a House member must live in the district that he or she represents. However, custom has made this a qualification for a candidate.

3. Division of Representatives Among the States. The number of representatives that a state has is based on population. Each state must have at least one representative.

The nation counts its citizens every ten years in a census. This clause gives the government the authority to conduct a census. The first census was taken in 1790. The final sentence in Section 2, Clause 3, lists the number of representatives that each of the first 13 states had until the first census was taken.

The first House had 65 members. As the nation grew, the House added seats. In 1929, Congress limited the number of members in the House to 435. Instead of adding members to the House as the population of some states grows, states with declining populations lose representatives. In the beginning, there was one representative for about every 30,000 citizens in a state. Today, there is one member for about every 650,000 citizens in a state.

"Three-fifths of a person" refers to the Three-Fifths Compromise worked out by the Framers. Three-fifths of a state's enslaved population was counted to determine representation. The 13th Amendment replaced this clause in 1865.

Native Americans were not counted. When the Constitution was written, they were considered members of foreign nations. Since 1924, Native Americans have been U.S. citizens and included when determining representation in the House.

4. Vacancies. A member of the House may die in office or leave office for some reason before his or her term is over. Then the governor of the state calls a special election to fill the vacancy. The phrase *executive authority* refers to the governor.

5. Officers. The House has the power to choose its own officers, including the Speaker. This person calls House sessions to order and runs the business of the House. Typically, the Speaker is from the majority party in the House.

The House has the power to impeach, or bring charges against, federal officials, including the president and vice president. See Section 3, Clause 6, for the Senate's role in the impeachment process.

Section 3 Senate

Clause 1: The Senate of the United States shall be composed of two Senators from each State, chosen ~~by the Legislature thereof,~~ for six Years; and each Senator shall have one Vote.

Clause 2: Immediately after they shall be assembled in Consequence of the first Election, they shall be divided as equally as may be into three Classes. The Seats of the Senators of the first Class shall be vacated at the Expiration of the second Year, of the second Class at the Expiration of the fourth Year, and of the third Class at the Expiration of the sixth Year, so that one third may be chosen every second Year; ~~and if Vacancies happen by Resignation, or otherwise, during the Recess of the Legislature of any State, the Executive thereof may make temporary Appointments until the next Meeting of the Legislature, which shall then fill such Vacancies.~~

Clause 3: No Person shall be a Senator who shall not have attained to the Age of thirty Years, and been nine Years a Citizen of the United States, and who shall not, when elected, be an Inhabitant of that State for which he shall be chosen.

Clause 4: The Vice President of the United States shall be President of the Senate, but shall have no Vote, unless they be equally divided.

Clause 5: The Senate shall chuse their other Officers, and also a President pro tempore, in the Absence of the Vice President, or when he shall exercise the Office of President of the United States.

Clause 6: The Senate shall have the sole Power to try all Impeachments. When sitting for that Purpose, they shall be on Oath or Affirmation. When the President of the United States is tried, the Chief Justice shall preside: And no Person shall be convicted without the Concurrence of two thirds of the Members present.

Clause 7: Judgment in Cases of Impeachment shall not extend further than to removal from Office, and disqualification to hold and enjoy any Office of honor, Trust or Profit under the United States: but the Party convicted shall nevertheless be liable and subject to Indictment, Trial, Judgment and Punishment, according to Law.

Section 3. Senate

1. **Number of Members, Terms, and Voting.** Since the admission of Hawaii in 1959, the Senate has had 100 members.

2. **Staggered Elections and Vacancies.** The first part of this clause relates to the election of 1788. The division of senators into three groups staggered the terms of office of the first 26 senators. In this way, the Senate was able to set up a system in which one-third of all Senate seats are up for election every two years.

   The second part of the clause was replaced by the 17th Amendment. A state governor may fill a vacant Senate seat by calling a special election. Depending on state law, the governor may also appoint a person to fill the vacant seat.

3. **Qualifications.** A senator must be thirty years old and have been a U.S. citizen for at least nine years. A senator must also live in the state that he or she represents.

4. **President of the Senate.** The vice president presides over, or runs, the meetings of the Senate. If a vote results in a tie, the vice president votes to break the tie. Otherwise, the vice president may not vote. Presiding over the Senate is the only duty assigned to the vice president by the Constitution.

5. **Other Officers.** The Senate chooses its own officers, including a president pro tempore. *Pro tempore* means "for a time." The president pro tempore presides over Senate sessions when the vice president is absent or when he has become president. For example, when President John Kennedy was assassinated in 1963, Vice President Lyndon Johnson became president. He no longer could preside over the Senate.

6. **Impeachment.** The House impeaches a federal official, which means that it finds enough evidence of wrongdoing to bring the official to trial. The trial is held in the Senate.

   If the official being tried is the president of the United States, the Chief Justice of the Supreme Court presides over the Senate. Otherwise, the vice president presides.

   Two-thirds of the members of the Senate must vote to convict or the official is found not guilty.

7. **Penalty If Convicted.** If a person is convicted in an impeachment case, he or she is removed from office. The Senate may also bar the person from holding any other federal office. These are the only two punishments that the Senate may hand down. However, a convicted official may be tried in a regular court for any crime committed as part of the impeachment case.

Section 4 Elections and Meetings

Clause 1: The Times, Places and Manner of holding Elections for Senators and Representatives, shall be prescribed in each State by the Legislature thereof; but the Congress may at any time by Law make or alter such Regulations, ~~except as to the Places of chusing Senators.~~

Clause 2: The Congress shall assemble at least once in every Year, ~~and such Meeting shall be on the first Monday in December, unless they shall by Law appoint a different Day.~~

Section 5 Rules of Procedure

Clause 1: Each House shall be the Judge of the Elections, Returns and Qualifications of its own Members, and a Majority of each shall constitute a Quorum to do Business; but a smaller Number may adjourn from day to day, and may be authorized to compel the Attendance of absent Members, in such Manner, and under such Penalties as each House may provide.

Clause 2: Each House may determine the Rules of its Proceedings, punish its Members for disorderly Behaviour, and, with the Concurrence of two thirds, expel a Member.

Clause 3: Each House shall keep a Journal of its Proceedings, and from time to time publish the same, excepting such Parts as may in their Judgment require Secrecy; and the Yeas and Nays of the Members of either House on any question shall, at the Desire of one fifth of those Present, be entered on the Journal.

Clause 4: Neither House, during the Session of Congress, shall, without the Consent of the other, adjourn for more than three days, nor to any other Place than that in which the two Houses shall be sitting.

Section 4. Elections and Meetings

1. Elections. As written, the Constitution gives state legislatures the right to schedule elections for U.S. representatives and senators. In 1842, Congress changed part of this. It passed a law requiring that representatives be elected on the first Tuesday after the first Monday in November in even-numbered years. In 1914, Congress passed a law setting the same date for the election of senators.

2. Sessions. Congress must meet at least once every year.

Section 5. Rules of Procedure

1. Organization. As written, the Constitution gives each house the right to judge the qualifications of those elected to serve in it. However, in 1969, the Supreme Court modified this power. It ruled that Congress cannot legally exclude anyone who meets all the qualifications as stated in Article I, Section 2, Clause 2.

A quorum must be present for either house to conduct business. A quorum is half the total number plus one. In the House, a quorum is 218 of its 435 members. In the Senate, it is 51 of its 100 members.

2. Rules. The House and the Senate each have rules to guide how they conduct business. Each has methods for punishing members for unacceptable behavior. Expelling a member requires a two-thirds (287 and 66) vote of its members.

3. Record. Each house must keep a record of its daily business. The *Congressional Record* publishes a complete and official record of the daily sessions of both houses of Congress. Members' votes are included, as well as everything that is said or done during the daily session. With constant media coverage, the daily meetings of both houses are no longer secret.

4. Adjournment. Once Congress opens a session, neither house can adjourn, or stop meeting, for more than three days unless the other house agrees. For example, the House cannot decide to suspend meeting for three days without asking the Senate if it is all right. Both houses must always meet in the same place.

Section 6   Privileges and Restrictions

<u>Clause 1</u>: The Senators and Representatives shall receive a Compensation for their Services, to be ascertained by Law, and paid out of the Treasury of the United States. They shall in all Cases, except Treason, Felony and Breach of the Peace, be privileged from Arrest during their Attendance at the Session of their respective Houses, and in going to and returning from the same; and for any Speech or Debate in either House, they shall not be questioned in any other Place.

<u>Clause 2</u>: No Senator or Representative shall, during the Time for which he was elected, be appointed to any civil Office under the Authority of the United States, which shall have been created, or the Emoluments whereof shall have been encreased during such time; and no Person holding any Office under the United States, shall be a Member of either House during his Continuance in Office.

Section 7   How Bills Become Laws

<u>Clause 1</u>: All Bills for raising Revenue shall originate in the House of Representatives; but the Senate may propose or concur with Amendments as on other Bills.

Section 6. Privileges and Restrictions

1. Salary and Immunity. Members of the Confederation Congress were paid by their state legislatures. The Framers of the Constitution saw a problem with this arrangement. Members could be influenced by their state legislature because it paid them. As a result, Congress is paid by the U.S. government.

The last sentence in this clause sets up what is called "legislative immunity." *Immunity* means "exception or freedom from." Members of Congress may not be arrested on their way to or from a session of Congress or during a session. However, if they are accused of treason, felony, or breach of the peace, they may be arrested. A felony is any major crime, such as robbery. Breach of the peace is any lesser crime. Members may not be arrested for what they say in Congress.

2. Limits. *Emolument* means "salary." Members of Congress are barred from taking jobs in the executive or judicial branch if they were in Congress when the job was created. They also may not take the job if they were in Congress when the salary for the job was raised. This clause is meant to keep members of Congress from enriching themselves by their votes.

A person may not serve in Congress and the judicial or executive branch at the same time. This is one example of the Framers' efforts to reinforce the separation of powers among the branches of government.

Section 7. How Bills Become Laws

1. Revenue Bills. Revenue is income, and most government income comes from taxes. All bills that raise income must begin in the House of Representatives. This means that all tax bills begin in the House. The Senate, however, has the right to amend, or change, revenue bills that it receives from the House. The Framers gave the House the responsibility for taxation for two reasons. Originally, only its members were elected directly by the people. Second, House elections are held every two years. Therefore, members of the House are more easily accountable to the voters for their actions.

Clause 2: Every Bill which shall have passed the House of Representatives and the Senate, shall, before it become a Law, be presented to the President of the United States; If he approve he shall sign it, but if not he shall return it, with his Objections to that House in which it shall have originated, who shall enter the Objections at large on their Journal, and proceed to reconsider it. If after such Reconsideration two thirds of that House shall agree to pass the Bill, it shall be sent, together with the Objections, to the other House, by which it shall likewise be reconsidered, and if approved by two thirds of that House, it shall become a Law. But in all such Cases the Votes of both Houses shall be determined by yeas and Nays, and the Names of the Persons voting for and against the Bill shall be entered on the Journal of each House respectively.

If any Bill shall not be returned by the President within ten Days (Sundays excepted) after it shall have been presented to him, the Same shall be a Law, in like Manner as if he had signed it, unless the Congress by their Adjournment prevent its Return, in which Case it shall not be a Law.

Clause 3: Every Order, Resolution, or Vote to which the Concurrence of the Senate and House of Representatives may be necessary (except on a question of Adjournment) shall be presented to the President of the United States; and before the Same shall take Effect, shall be approved by him, or being disapproved by him, shall be repassed by two thirds of the Senate and House of Representatives, according to the Rules and Limitations prescribed in the Case of a Bill.

Section 8   Powers of Congress
Clause 1: The Congress shall have Power To lay and collect Taxes, Duties, Imposts and Excises, to pay the Debts and provide for the common Defence and general Welfare of the United States; but all Duties, Imposts and Excises shall be uniform throughout the United States;

Clause 2: To borrow Money on the credit of the United States;

Clause 3: To regulate Commerce with foreign Nations, and among the several States, and with the Indian Tribes;

2. Passing Bills and the Presidential Veto. A bill is a proposed law. A bill becomes law if both houses of Congress pass it and the president signs it. However, the president does not have to sign a bill. If the president disapproves of a bill, he has three choices. (1) He can veto the bill and send it back to Congress, explaining why he vetoed it. (2) He can allow the bill to become law. This happens if the president does not act on the bill within ten days (not counting Sundays) of receiving it from Congress. In other words, he neither signs nor vetoes the bill. (3) If the president receives the bill at the end of a session of Congress, he can use the pocket veto. To do this, the president does not act on the bill within ten days of receiving it and Congress adjourns during those ten days. As a result of adjourning, Congress cannot vote on the bill again. To pass a law over a presidential veto, two-thirds of both houses have to pass the bill.

3. Presidential Approval or Veto. Every vote that Congress takes must be sent to the president for approval or veto. The exception is a vote to adjourn. The Framers included this clause to keep Congress from passing joint resolutions. A joint resolution is an expression of opinion on an issue. A joint resolution would not need to be sent to the president for an approval or veto. The Framers wanted to prevent Congress from going around the president's authority and weakening the system of checks and balances.

Section 8. Powers of Congress
Section 8 lists 27 of the expressed powers granted in the Constitution to Congress.

1. Revenue. Congress has the power to levy and collect certain types of taxes. Duties and imposts are taxes on goods brought into the country. Excises are taxes paid on goods made and sold within the country. The purpose of raising money is to fund government operations, including the armed forces. Tax rates must be the same throughout the country.

2. Borrowing. The government, through Congress's actions, may borrow money. Generally, the money is borrowed by selling government bonds to investors. Investors receive interest on their bonds. Note that the clause does not say how much the government may borrow.

3. Commerce. This is known as the Commerce Clause. It grants Congress the power to regulate interstate and foreign trade. Over time, Congress has enlarged and extended the meaning of commerce and thus enlarged its own power. For example, Congress has passed laws regulating interstate transportation and banking based on the Commerce Clause.

Clause 4: To establish an uniform Rule of Naturalization, and uniform Laws on the subject of Bankruptcies throughout the United States;

Clause 5: To coin Money, regulate the Value thereof, and of foreign Coin, and fix the Standard of Weights and Measures;

Clause 6: To provide for the Punishment of counterfeiting the Securities and current Coin of the United States;

Clause 7: To establish Post Offices and post Roads;

Clause 8: To promote the Progress of Science and useful Arts, by securing for limited Times to Authors and Inventors the exclusive Right to their respective Writings and Discoveries;

Clause 9: To constitute Tribunals inferior to the supreme Court;

Clause 10: To define and punish Piracies and Felonies committed on the high Seas, and Offences against the Law of Nations;

Clause 11: To declare War, grant Letters of Marque and Reprisal, and make Rules concerning Captures on Land and Water;

4. **Naturalization and Bankruptcy.** Naturalization is the process by which a citizen of another nation becomes a U.S. citizen. Congress passes bankruptcy laws for the nation.

5. **Currency.** Congress has the power to issue money for the nation. It also has the power to set national standards for weights and measures. Measures include time, distance, weight, volume, and area.

6. **Counterfeiting.** Counterfeiting is the making of fake money. Congress has the responsibility for setting the punishment for counterfeiters.

7. **Postal Service.** Congress has the power to set up post offices and post roads. These are the routes over which mail is carried. Until 1970, the Post Office was one of the departments in the executive branch. In 1970, Congress created the United States Postal Service and made it a government-owned corporation. Congress can veto increases in postal rates but cannot set rates.

8. **Copyrights and Patents.** The Framers wanted to encourage the arts, science, and industry. As a result, they granted Congress the power to make laws regulating copyrights and patents. Copyrights protect the rights of writers, artists, and composers to their works for a period of time. During that time, others cannot use their works without their permission. Patents enable inventors to control how their inventions are manufactured and sold.

9. **Lower Courts.** Article III creates the U.S. Supreme Court. However, Congress has the power to set up the federal court system below the Supreme Court. *Inferior* means "lower in rank."

10. **Piracy and Other Crimes Against Nations.** Piracy is the robbing of ships on the high seas, or oceans. Congress has the power to decide what actions should be considered federal crimes committed outside the United States. Congress also has the power to decide on the punishment for these crimes.

Congress has the same power to define and set the punishment for crimes committed within the United States against another nation. Blowing up a foreign embassy in the United States is an example.

11. **Declare War.** According to the Constitution, only Congress has the power to declare war. However, presidents, as commander in chief, have sent U.S. troops into battle without a formal declaration of war. This has caused much controversy at times in the nation's history.

Letters of marque and reprisal authorize private citizens to capture and destroy enemy ships during wartime. In 1856, this practice was outlawed by international law.

Congress has the right to make rules about people and property captured in war.

Clause 12: To raise and support Armies, but no Appropriation of Money to that Use shall be for a longer Term than two Years;

Clause 13: To provide and maintain a Navy;

Clause 14: To make Rules for the Government and Regulation of the land and naval Forces;

Clause 15: To provide for calling forth the Militia to execute the Laws of the Union, suppress Insurrections and repel Invasions;

Clause 16: To provide for organizing, arming, and disciplining, the Militia, and for governing such Part of them as may be employed in the Service of the United States, reserving to the States respectively, the Appointment of the Officers, and the Authority of training the Militia according to the discipline prescribed by Congress;

Clause 17: To exercise exclusive Legislation in all Cases whatsoever, over such District (not exceeding ten Miles square) as may, by Cession of particular States, and the Acceptance of Congress, become the Seat of the Government of the United States, and to exercise like Authority over all Places purchased by the Consent of the Legislature of the State in which the Same shall be, for the Erection of Forts, Magazines, Arsenals, dock-Yards, and other needful Buildings;--And

Clause 18: To make all Laws which shall be necessary and proper for carrying into Execution the foregoing Powers, and all other Powers vested by this Constitution in the Government of the United States, or in any Department or Officer thereof.

12. Army. Congress has the power to set up an army. However, bills to finance the army may not request money for more than two years at a time. The purpose of this clause is to keep the control of the army in the hands of the civilian Congress.

13. Navy. Congress also has the power to set up and finance a navy.

14. Rules for the Armed Forces. Congress has the power to make rules for the army and navy. These rules were collected into the Uniform Code of Military Justice in 1950.

15. Militia. State militias were first organized in 1792. They became the National Guard in 1916. Guard members take an oath of loyalty to their state and to the federal government. Federal laws authorize the use of Guard members for three reasons. The Guard may be asked to uphold the laws of the nation, to put down rebellions, and to fight off invasions. For example, in 1957, the Arkansas National Guard protected African-American students who were integrating Little Rock Central High School in Arkansas. In 2001, Guard members provided security at airports and train stations after the events of September 11, 2001.

16. National Guard. The states are responsible for appointing National Guard officers and training the Guard. However, Congress provides the funding to equip the Guard. Congress also has the power to make rules for the Guard when members are called into federal service.

17. Nation's Capital. Virginia and Maryland donated land for the nation's capital, Washington, D.C. This was one of the compromises to win ratification of the Constitution. Virginia's land was never used and was returned in 1846.

Congress has the power to make laws for the District of Columbia. Among the laws are ones setting up a city government for the District and allowing residents to vote in presidential elections (23rd Amendment).

18. Elastic Clause. This is also known as the "necessary and proper" clause. Congress is granted the power to make whatever laws are needed to carry out its other powers. Congress has used this clause to enlarge and extend its authority. This clause is the basis for the implied powers of Congress.

Section 9   Powers Denied to the Federal Government

<u>Clause 1</u>: ~~The Migration or Importation of such Persons as any of the States now existing shall think proper to admit, shall not be prohibited by the Congress prior to the Year one thousand eight hundred and eight, but a Tax or duty may be imposed on such Importation, not exceeding ten dollars for each Person.~~

<u>Clause 2</u>: The Privilege of the Writ of Habeas Corpus shall not be suspended, unless when in Cases of Rebellion or Invasion the public Safety may require it.

<u>Clause 3</u>: No Bill of Attainder or ex post facto Law shall be passed.

<u>Clause 4</u>: No Capitation, or other direct, Tax shall be laid, unless in Proportion to the Census or Enumeration herein before directed to be taken.

<u>Clause 5</u>: No Tax or Duty shall be laid on Articles exported from any State.

<u>Clause 6</u>: No Preference shall be given by any Regulation of Commerce or Revenue to the Ports of one State over those of another: nor shall Vessels bound to, or from, one State, be obliged to enter, clear, or pay Duties in another.

<u>Clause 7</u>: No Money shall be drawn from the Treasury, but in Consequence of Appropriations made by Law; and a regular Statement and Account of the Receipts and Expenditures of all public Money shall be published from time to time.

<u>Clause 8</u>: No Title of Nobility shall be granted by the United States: And no Person holding any Office of Profit or Trust under them, shall, without the Consent of the Congress, accept of any present, Emolument, Office, or Title, of any kind whatever, from any King, Prince, or foreign State.

Section 9. Powers Denied to the Federal Government

1. Slave Trade. This is the Commerce Compromise reached by the Framers. In return for Southern support, the Framers agreed not to ban the foreign slave trade for 20 years. In 1808, Congress outlawed the importing, or bringing into the United States, of enslaved persons. However, the trade in slaves within the United States was allowed to continue.

2. Habeas Corpus. The writ, or order, of habeas corpus is one of the basic rights of English citizens. *Habeas corpus* is Latin, meaning "you have the body." A judge issues a writ of habeas corpus to a law official. The writ directs the official to bring a prisoner to a court hearing in order to find out if the person is being held legally. The writ may be suspended only during a rebellion or an invasion.

3. Bill of Attainder. A bill of attainder punishes a person without a trial. *Ex post facto* means "something done after the fact." An ex post facto law makes an action a crime after the action has been done. Congress may pass neither type of law.

4. Taxes. A capitation tax is a "head" tax, a tax on each person. Direct taxes are ones paid by taxpayers directly to the government. Income tax is a direct tax. The federal tax on gasoline is an indirect tax. Motorists pay it to the gasoline company, which then pays it to the government. The 16th Amendment changed part of this clause. The amendment allows Congress to levy an income tax directly on taxpayers.

5. Tax on Exports. Congress may not tax goods that are exported, or sent out of the country. This was part of the Commerce Compromise reached by the Framers. Congress may tax imports, or goods brought into the country.

6. Single System of Treatment. All ports (and states) must be treated the same. Congress may not pass laws that favor one port (or state) over another. Goods shipped by water from one state to another may not be taxed.

7. Appropriations Law. An appropriation is money set aside for a particular use. Congress must pass a law to authorize the spending of any federal money. The government must regularly publish a record of all the money it receives and spends.

8. Nobility. Congress may not set up a system of nobles such as princes and duchesses. No public official may accept a present, salary, job, or title of nobility from another government. The purpose was to keep other governments from trying to bribe, or buy the support of, U.S. officials.

Section 10 Powers Denied to the States

Clause 1: No State shall enter into any Treaty, Alliance, or Confederation; grant Letters of Marque and Reprisal; coin Money; emit Bills of Credit; make any Thing but gold and silver Coin a Tender in Payment of Debts; pass any Bill of Attainder, ex post facto Law, or Law impairing the Obligation of Contracts, or grant any Title of Nobility.

Clause 2: No State shall, without the Consent of the Congress, lay any Imposts or Duties on Imports or Exports, except what may be absolutely necessary for executing it's inspection Laws: and the net Produce of all Duties and Imposts, laid by any State on Imports or Exports, shall be for the Use of the Treasury of the United States; and all such Laws shall be subject to the Revision and Controul of the Congress.

Clause 3: No State shall, without the Consent of Congress, lay any Duty of Tonnage, keep Troops, or Ships of War in time of Peace, enter into any Agreement or Compact with another State, or with a foreign Power, or engage in War, unless actually invaded, or in such imminent Danger as will not admit of delay.

Section 10. Powers Denied to the States

1. Limits on Power. This clause lists nine powers that the states do not have. The first part of the clause forbids states from conducting relations with other nations. The purpose of most of this clause is to prevent conflicts between the national government and state governments. Both levels of government could not conduct foreign policy with other nations, for example, or have two sets of money.

State governments may not grant letters of marque and reprisal. This power was reserved for the national government. See Article I, Section 8, Clause 11.

States may not issue their own money or use anything but national currency. They may not issue bills of credit, or notes promising to pay debts.

Like the national government, state governments may not pass bills of attainder and ex post facto laws. Article I, Section 9, Clause 3, prohibits Congress from passing these kinds of laws.

State governments may not interfere with contracts between individuals.

State governments also may not give anyone a title such as duke or princess.

2. Taxes on Exports and Imports. Imposts are taxes on imports, goods brought into a country. Only Congress may levy taxes on imports. However, states may charge a small fee for inspecting goods.

Neither the national government nor the states may tax exports. The ban on the national government is stated in Article I, Section 9, Clause 5.

3. Taxes, Armed Forces, War. A duty of tonnage is a tax on ships based on how much cargo they can carry. States may not levy this kind of tax.

States may not keep an army or navy. However, Congress recognizes their right to set up militias. The National Guard is the modern form of the state militia.

States may enter into compacts, or written agreements, with other states if Congress agrees. However, based on this clause, Congress does not permit states to enter into agreements with foreign nations.

A state may not go to war on its own unless it is attacked or it is about to be attacked and cannot wait for Congress to act. This clause expressly denies certain powers to the states that the Constitution grants to the national government.

Article II   Executive Branch

Section 1   President and Vice-President

<u>Clause 1:</u> The executive Power shall be vested in a President of the United States of America. He shall hold his Office during the Term of four Years, and, together with the Vice President, chosen for the same Term, be elected, as follows

<u>Clause 2:</u> Each State shall appoint, in such Manner as the Legislature thereof may direct, a Number of Electors, equal to the whole Number of Senators and Representatives to which the State may be entitled in the Congress: but no Senator or Representative, or Person holding an Office of Trust or Profit under the United States, shall be appointed an Elector.

<u>Clause 3:</u> ~~The Electors shall meet in their respective States, and vote by Ballot for two Persons, of whom one at least shall not be an Inhabitant of the same State with themselves. And they shall make a List of all the Persons voted for, and of the Number of Votes for each; which List they shall sign and certify, and transmit sealed to the Seat of the Government of the United States, directed to the President of the Senate. The President of the Senate shall, in the Presence of the Senate and House of Representatives, open all the Certificates, and the Votes shall then be counted. The Person having the greatest Number of Votes shall be the President, if such Number be a Majority of the whole Number of Electors appointed; and if there be more than one who have such Majority, and have an equal Number of Votes, then the House of Representatives shall immediately chuse by Ballot one of them for President; and if no Person have a Majority, then from the five highest on the List the said House shall in like Manner chuse the President. But in chusing the President, the Votes shall be taken by States, the Representation from each State having one Vote; A quorum for this Purpose shall consist of a Member or Members from two thirds of the States, and a Majority of all the States shall be necessary to a Choice. In every Case, after the Choice of the President, the Person having the greatest Number of Votes of the Electors shall be the Vice President. But if there should remain two or more who have equal Votes, the Senate shall chuse from them by Ballot the Vice President.~~

<u>Clause 4:</u> The Congress may determine the Time of chusing the Electors, and the Day on which they shall give their Votes; which Day shall be the same throughout the United States.

<u>Clause 5:</u> No Person except a natural born Citizen, or a Citizen of the United States, at the time of the Adoption of this Constitution, shall be eligible to the Office of President; neither shall any Person be eligible to that Office who shall not have attained to the Age of thirty five Years, and been fourteen Years a Resident within the United States.

Article II.
Executive Branch

Section 1. President and Vice President

1. Term of Office. The "executive power" gives the president the power to enforce the laws passed by Congress and to run the executive branch of government. The president and vice president are elected for four-year terms. See also the 22nd Amendment, which sets limits on how long a person may serve as president.

2. Election Process. The Framers set up an Electoral College to elect the president and vice president. Candidates are not elected directly by the voters. Instead, voters elect each state's electors, who meet in December to cast their ballots for president and vice president. The number of electors for each state is based on the state's combined number of senators and members of the House. Political parties nominate the electors. State law determines the election process for electors. No U.S. senator, representative, or official may be an elector.

3. Former Method of Electing the President and Vice President. This clause was replaced by the 12th Amendment in 1804. The amendment was approved and ratified as a result of the election of 1800. Before the 12th Amendment, ballots did not indicate which person was a candidate for president and which was a candidate for vice president. In the election of 1800, the top two candidates received the same number of votes. The election had to be decided in the House of Representatives.

4. Date of Election. Congress has set the date for presidential elections as the first Tuesday after the first Monday in November. Electors vote on the Monday after the second Wednesday in December.

5. Qualifications. To be president, a person must have been born a citizen of the United States and have lived in the United States for at least 14 years. The person must also be at least thirty-five years old. The 22nd Amendment also sets limits on how long a person may serve as president.

Clause 6: ~~In Case of the Removal of the President from Office, or of his Death, Resignation, or Inability to discharge the Powers and Duties of the said Office, the Same shall devolve on the Vice-President,~~ and the Congress may by Law provide for the Case of Removal, Death, Resignation or Inability, both of the President and Vice President, declaring what Officer shall then act as President, and such Officer shall act accordingly, until the Disability be removed, or a President shall be elected.

Clause 7: The President shall, at stated Times, receive for his Services, a Compensation, which shall neither be encreased nor diminished during the Period for which he shall have been elected, and he shall not receive within that Period any other Emolument from the United States, or any of them.

Clause 8: Before he enter on the Execution of his Office, he shall take the following Oath or Affirmation:—"I do solemnly swear (or affirm) that I will faithfully execute the Office of President of the United States, and will to the best of my Ability, preserve, protect and defend the Constitution of the United States."

Section 2   Powers of the President

Clause 1: The President shall be Commander in Chief of the Army and Navy of the United States, and of the Militia of the several States, when called into the actual Service of the United States; he may require the Opinion, in writing, of the principal Officer in each of the executive Departments, upon any Subject relating to the Duties of their respective Offices, and he shall have Power to grant Reprieves and Pardons for Offences against the United States, except in Cases of Impeachment.

Clause 2: He shall have Power, by and with the Advice and Consent of the Senate, to make Treaties, provided two thirds of the Senators present concur; and he shall nominate, and by and with the Advice and Consent of the Senate, shall appoint Ambassadors, other public Ministers and Consuls, Judges of the supreme Court, and all other Officers of the United States, whose Appointments are not herein otherwise provided for, and which shall be established by Law: but the Congress may by Law vest the Appointment of such inferior Officers, as they think proper, in the President alone, in the Courts of Law, or in the Heads of Departments.

Clause 3: The President shall have Power to fill up all Vacancies that may happen during the Recess of the Senate, by granting Commissions which shall expire at the End of their next Session.

6. Vacancies. If the president is removed, dies, resigns, or is unable to carry out his duties, the vice president becomes president. The 25th Amendment states the process for deciding whether the president is unable to fulfill his duties. The process for filling the vice presidency, if it becomes vacant, is also described by this amendment.

7. Salary. Since 1999, the president receives $400,000 in salary and $50,000 as a taxable expense account. In addition, the president receives $100,000, which is nontaxable, for travel and entertainment.

Salary and benefits may not change while a president is in office. A president may not receive other income from the national government or state while in office.

8. Oath of Office. The president takes this oath when being sworn into office. Typically, the Chief Justice of the U.S. Supreme Court administers the oath. However, any judicial official may administer it.

Section 2. Powers of the President

1. Military, the Cabinet, and Pardons. The Framers made the president the head of the armed forces. This ensures that the military is under civilian control.

This clause is also the basis for the cabinet. The cabinet is made up of the heads of the executive departments and advises the president.

The president may grant reprieves and pardons for federal crimes only. The exception is impeachment. A reprieve is the postponement of punishment and a pardon is forgiveness of punishment.

2. Treaties and Appointments. The president has the responsibility for deciding on and conducting foreign policy. Negotiating treaties is one part of this responsibility. However, as a check on presidential power, two-thirds of the Senate must ratify any treaties. Over time, presidents have used executive agreements as a way to avoid Senate debate and possible vetoes of treaties.

The president also has the power to appoint ambassadors to other nations and to the United Nations, justices to the Supreme Court, and other officials of the executive branch. Again, the Senate must approve each appointment. Only the highest-level officials are appointed in this manner. Most government workers receive their jobs through the civil service system. This is covered by the last part of the clause.

3. Vacancies in Federal Offices. The president may fill any vacancy that occurs when the Senate is in recess. The appointment is called a "recess appointment" and is temporary.

Section 3   Duties of the President

He shall from time to time give to the Congress Information of the State of the Union, and recommend to their Consideration such Measures as he shall judge necessary and expedient; he may, on extraordinary Occasions, convene both Houses, or either of them, and in Case of Disagreement between them, with Respect to the Time of Adjournment, he may adjourn them to such Time as he shall think proper; he shall receive Ambassadors and other public Ministers; he shall take Care that the Laws be faithfully executed, and shall Commission all the Officers of the United States.

Section 4   Impeachment

The President, Vice President and all civil Officers of the United States, shall be removed from Office on Impeachment for, and Conviction of, Treason, Bribery, or other high Crimes and Misdemeanors.

Section 3. Duties of the President

The president must deliver to both the House and the Senate information about how the nation is doing. This information is to be accompanied by suggestions about possible laws. The president's annual State of the Union address fulfills this section. The president addresses a joint session of Congress each year at the beginning of the first session of Congress. The speech is given in the evening and is televised so the public can see it. Within a few weeks, the executive branch also delivers the president's annual budget request to Congress. In addition, the president may send special messages to Congress on matters that he considers important.

This section gives the president the power to call special sessions of one or both houses of Congress. The president may also adjourn Congress if the two houses cannot agree on a date.

In his role as maker of foreign policy, the president receives ambassadors from other nations.

The president also sees that the nation's laws are enforced.

The president also approves the promotion of all officers in the armed forces.

Section 4. Impeachment

This section lists the reasons for which the president and vice president may be impeached and removed from office. The causes are treason, bribery, and "other high crimes and misdemeanors." The Framers left it to Congress to decide what makes actions high crimes and misdemeanors. Article I, Section 2, Clause 5, and Section 3, Clauses 6 and 7, set out the process for impeachment.

Article III Judicial Branch

Section 1 Federal Courts

The judicial Power of the United States, shall be vested in one supreme Court, and in such inferior Courts as the Congress may from time to time ordain and establish. The Judges, both of the supreme and inferior Courts, shall hold their Offices during good Behaviour, and shall, at stated Times, receive for their Services, a Compensation, which shall not be diminished during their Continuance in Office.

Section 2 Extent of Judicial Powers

<u>Clause 1</u>: The judicial Power shall extend to all Cases, in Law and Equity, arising under this Constitution, the Laws of the United States, and Treaties made, or which shall be made, under their Authority;—to all Cases affecting Ambassadors, other public Ministers and Consuls;—to all Cases of admiralty and maritime Jurisdiction;—to Controversies to which the United States shall be a Party;—to Controversies between two or more States;—between a State and Citizens of another State; —between Citizens of different States, —between Citizens of the same State claiming Lands under Grants of different States, and between a State, or the Citizens thereof, and foreign States, Citizens or Subjects.

<u>Clause 2</u>: In all Cases affecting Ambassadors, other public Ministers and Consuls, and those in which a State shall be Party, the supreme Court shall have original Jurisdiction. In all the other Cases before mentioned, the supreme Court shall have appellate Jurisdiction, both as to Law and Fact, with such Exceptions, and under such Regulations as the Congress shall make.

Article III.
Judicial Branch

Section 1. Federal Courts

This section sets up the federal court system and empowers it to hear cases. The only court that is mentioned by name is the Supreme Court. However, this section states that Congress may set up lower federal courts as needed. Congress has used this power to establish federal district courts and, above them, federal courts of appeal.

Federal judges may keep their positions "during good behavior." For the most part, this means until they die or retire.

The salary of judges may not be decreased while they serve.

Section 2. Extent of Judicial Powers

1. General Jurisdiction. Jurisdiction is an area of the law where a court has authority to act. This section lists the areas of the law where the federal courts have jurisdiction, or authority. For the most part, federal courts deal with cases involving the Constitution, laws passed by Congress, and treaties.

Lawsuits involving ambassadors, public officials, and consuls—those who also deal with foreign nations—are heard in federal courts.

Federal courts hear cases involving ships and shipping on the oceans, and within the nation on rivers, lakes, and canals.

Any lawsuit against the United States is heard in federal court.

Lawsuits brought by a state or states against another state, lawsuits between citizens of different states, and lawsuits between citizens of the same state who claim land in different states come within the jurisdiction of federal courts.

The 11th Amendment changed the court system in which citizens of foreign nations could bring lawsuits against a state. The amendment sent these lawsuits to state courts.

2. The Supreme Court Jurisdiction. Original jurisdiction gives a court the right to hear a case in the first place. Appellate jurisdiction means the court may hear the case only if it is appealed from a lower court. An appeal is a request to rehear the case.

The Supreme Court has original jurisdiction in all cases involving ambassadors, public officials, and consuls, as well as any case in which a state is involved.

The Supreme Court has appellate jurisdiction in all other cases. Most cases come to the Supreme Court on appeal from federal appeals courts and state supreme courts.

<u>Clause 3</u>: The Trial of all Crimes, except in Cases of Impeachment, shall be by Jury; and such Trial shall be held in the State where the said Crimes shall have been committed; but when not committed within any State, the Trial shall be at such Place or Places as the Congress may by Law have directed.

Section 3   Treason

<u>Clause 1</u>: Treason against the United States, shall consist only in levying War against them, or in adhering to their Enemies, giving them Aid and Comfort. No Person shall be convicted of Treason unless on the Testimony of two Witnesses to the same overt Act, or on Confession in open Court.

<u>Clause 2</u>: The Congress shall have Power to declare the Punishment of Treason, but no Attainder of Treason shall work Corruption of Blood, or Forfeiture except during the Life of the Person attainted.

Article IV   The States

Section 1   Recognition of Each Other's Acts

Full Faith and Credit shall be given in each State to the public Acts, Records, and judicial Proceedings of every other State. And the Congress may by general Laws prescribe the Manner in which such Acts, Records and Proceedings shall be proved, and the Effect thereof.

Section 2   Citizens' Rights in Other States

<u>Clause 1</u>: The Citizens of each State shall be entitled to all Privileges and Immunities of Citizens in the several States.

3. Jury Trials. Those who are accused of a federal crime have the right to a trial by jury in a federal court. The trial must take place in a federal court in the state where the crime was committed. The exception is anyone who is impeached. That person's trial is held in the Senate.

Various amendments further spell out the rights of the accused in court. The 5th and 7th Amendments deal with the federal courts. The 14th Amendment provides guarantees for accused persons in state courts. The 6th Amendment applies to both.

Section 3. Treason

1. Definition. Treason is defined as making war against the United States or supporting the nation's enemies. Two people must witness the act of treason and testify against the accused. The only other way a person can be convicted is to confess. The Framers defined treason carefully for a reason. They wanted to prevent government officials from charging opponents of the government with treason.

2. Punishment. Deciding on the punishment for treason is the duty of Congress. Sentencing guidelines list a prison term of from five years to life in prison. A person may also be fined $10,000. According to this section, the children of a person convicted of treason may not be punished. Also, the property of a convicted person may not be taken from his or her children.

Article IV. The States

Section 1. Recognition of One Another's Acts

This section is known by the name "full faith and credit." It requires that each state recognizes the laws, public records, and court rulings of every other state. This section is limited to civil actions and laws. States cannot enforce one another's criminal laws.

Section 2. Mutual Duties of States

1. Privileges and Immunities. Privileges and immunities are rights and freedoms. States may not discriminate against residents of other states. However, they may consider some reasonable differences between their residents and nonresidents. For example, they may charge nonresidents higher fees for fishing licenses. States may also require new residents to live in the state for a period of time before being able to vote.

Clause 2: A Person charged in any State with Treason, Felony, or other Crime, who shall flee from Justice, and be found in another State, shall on Demand of the executive Authority of the State from which he fled, be delivered up, to be removed to the State having Jurisdiction of the Crime.

Clause 3: ~~No Person held to Service or Labour in one State, under the Laws thereof, escaping into another, shall, in Consequence of any Law or Regulation therein, be discharged from such Service or Labour, but shall be delivered up on Claim of the Party to whom such Service or Labour may be due.~~

Section 3   New States and Territories

Clause 1: New States may be admitted by the Congress into this Union; but no new State shall be formed or erected within the Jurisdiction of any other State; nor any State be formed by the Junction of two or more States, or Parts of States, without the Consent of the Legislatures of the States concerned as well as of the Congress.

Clause 2: The Congress shall have Power to dispose of and make all needful Rules and Regulations respecting the Territory or other Property belonging to the United States; and nothing in this Constitution shall be so construed as to Prejudice any Claims of the United States, or of any particular State.

Section 4   Guarantees to the States

The United States shall guarantee to every State in this Union a Republican Form of Government, and shall protect each of them against Invasion; and on Application of the Legislature, or of the Executive (when the Legislature cannot be convened) against domestic Violence.

2. **Extradition.** Extradition is the returning of a person wanted for a crime to the state where he or she is wanted. The purpose is to prevent people from escaping justice by fleeing from state to state.

3. **Fugitive-Slave Clause.** Enslaved persons could not escape into free states and become free. This clause was in force from 1788 until the end of the Civil War. In 1865, the 13th Amendment was ratified and slavery was abolished.

Section 3. New States and Territories

1. **New States.** The power to admit new states to the Union is given to Congress. New states may not be created from land belonging to another state unless the state legislature and Congress agree. Maine was created in this way. It had been part of Massachusetts. The exception is West Virginia, which was created from Virginia. It occurred during the Civil War, and Virginia was considered in rebellion against the United States.

2. **Territories and Property.** This clause empowers Congress to manage territories, lands, and other property that belong to the federal government. Although the United States has acquired territory over the years, there is nothing in the Constitution that says that it can.

Section 4. Guarantees to the States

This section lists the three obligations of the national government to the states. The national government must guarantee representative government to each state. The national government must also protect states from attacks and from riots and civil disorder. If a state's legislature or governor requests help, the federal government may send federal troops to restore law and order. However, over time, presidents have sent federal troops to uphold the law and the Constitution without a request.

Article V   Amending the Constitution

The Congress, whenever two thirds of both Houses shall deem it necessary, shall propose Amendments to this Constitution, or, on the Application of the Legislatures of two thirds of the several States, shall call a Convention for proposing Amendments, which, in either Case, shall be valid to all Intents and Purposes, as Part of this Constitution, when ratified by the Legislatures of three fourths of the several States, or by Conventions in three fourths thereof, as the one or the other Mode of Ratification may be proposed by the Congress; ~~Provided that no Amendment which may be made prior to the Year One thousand eight hundred and eight shall in any Manner affect the first and fourth Clauses in the Ninth Section of the first Article; and~~ that no State, without its Consent, shall be deprived of its equal Suffrage in the Senate.

Article VI   National Supremacy

<u>Clause 1</u>: All Debts contracted and Engagements entered into, before the Adoption of this Constitution, shall be as valid against the United States under this Constitution, as under the Confederation.

<u>Clause 2</u>: This Constitution, and the Laws of the United States which shall be made in Pursuance thereof; and all Treaties made, or which shall be made, under the Authority of the United States, shall be the supreme Law of the Land; and the Judges in every State shall be bound thereby, any Thing in the Constitution or Laws of any State to the Contrary notwithstanding.

<u>Clause 3</u>: The Senators and Representatives before mentioned, and the Members of the several State Legislatures, and all executive and judicial Officers, both of the United States and of the several States, shall be bound by Oath or Affirmation, to support this Constitution; but no religious Test shall ever be required as a Qualification to any Office or public Trust under the United States.

Article V. Amending the Constitution

The Framers wanted the Constitution to be flexible and adaptable to changing times. However, they did not want to make it too easy to amend the Constitution. The result is a two-step process: first, proposing an amendment and, second, ratifying an amendment.

Amendments may be proposed by a two-thirds vote of both houses of Congress.

Amendments may also be proposed by a national constitutional convention called by Congress. However, two-thirds of the state legislatures must request a constitutional convention. So far, no constitutional convention has been held to propose an amendment.

Amendments may be ratified by three-fourths of the state legislatures or by three-fourths of special conventions called by the states to consider the amendment. Congress decides which method to use. Only the 21st Amendment has been ratified by special state conventions.

The part that is no longer in force deals with an amendment to outlaw the international slave trade. The slave trade with other nations was banned in 1808.

Article VI. National Supremacy

1. Public Debts and Treaties. The Framers promised to repay all debts that were run up during the Revolution and under the confederation government.

2. The Supreme Law. This clause is known as the Supremacy Clause. It declares that the Constitution, federal laws, and treaties are the supreme law of the new nation. They are superior, or more important, than any state or local government law. State and local governments may not pass laws that conflict with federal law. The decision in *McCulloch v. Maryland* was based on this clause. The 14th Amendment reinforced the supremacy of national law over state law.

3. Oaths of Office. Members of national and state executive, legislative, and judicial branches must take an oath to support the Constitution. This clause reaffirms the Supremacy Clause.

No religious qualifications can be required to determine a person's fitness for office. The 1st Amendment reinforces and enlarges on the separation of church and state.

Article VII Ratification

The Ratification of the Conventions of nine States, shall be sufficient for the Establishment of this Constitution between the States so ratifying the Same. Done in Convention by the Unanimous Consent of the States present the Seventeenth Day of September in the Year of our Lord one thousand seven hundred and Eighty seven and of the Independence of the United States of America the Twelfth In witness whereof We have hereunto subscribed our Names,

George Washington, President and Deputy from Virginia

Delaware
George Read
Gunning Bedford, Junior
John Dickinson
Richard Bassett
Jacob Broom

Maryland
James McHenry
Daniel of St. Thomas
  Jenifer
Daniel Carroll

Virginia
John Blair
James Madison, Junior

North Carolina
William Blount
Richard Dobbs Spaight
Hugh Williamson

South Carolina
John Rutledge
Charles Cotesworth
  Pinckney
Charles Pinckney
Pierce Butler

Georgia
William Few
Abraham Baldwin

New Hampshire
John Langdon
Nicholas Gilman

Massachusetts
Nathaniel Gorham
Rufus King

Connecticut
William Samuel
  Johnson
Roger Sherman

New York
Alexander Hamilton

New Jersey
William Livingston
David Brearley
William Paterson
Jonathan Dayton

Pennsylvania
Benjamin Franklin
Thomas Mifflin
Robert Morris
George Clymer
Thomas FitzSimons
Jared Ingersoll
James Wilson
Gouverneur Morris
Attest: William
  Jackson, Secretary

The pages that follow contain the original text of the amendments to the United States Constitution. Sections that are no longer enforced have been crossed out. The spelling and punctuation of the document remain in their original format. The headings are not part of the original amendments.

Amendments to the Constitution

Amendment 1   (1791) Religious and Political Freedom

Congress shall make no law respecting an establishment of religion, or prohibiting the free exercise thereof; or abridging the freedom of speech, or of the press; or the right of the people peaceably to assemble, and to petition the Government for a redress of grievances.

Amendment 2   (1791) Right to Bear Arms

A well regulated Militia, being necessary to the security of a free State, the right of the people to keep and bear Arms, shall not be infringed.

Amendment 3   (1791) Quartering of Soldiers

No Soldier shall, in time of peace be quartered in any house, without the consent of the Owner, nor in time of war, but in a manner to be prescribed by law.

Amendments to the Constitution

The first ten amendments are known as the Bill of Rights. Supporters of the Constitution agreed to propose these amendments in order to win ratification of the Constitution. When first adopted, the Bill of Rights applied only to actions of the national government. However, the Supreme Court has enlarged these guarantees. Many of these same rights safeguard citizens against mistreatment by the states.

Amendment 1. Religious and Political Freedom (1791)

The 1st Amendment safeguards civil liberties. Civil liberties are those protections that citizens have against abuse, or mistreatment, by the government. The 1st Amendment, however, does not mean that these freedoms are unlimited. People may use these rights as long as they do not interfere with the rights of others.

The 1st Amendment protects the right of people to practice their religion. It also sets up separation between church and state.

Freedoms of speech and press guarantee people the right to speak, publish, and express their opinions.

The right to assemble means that people may gather together in a public meeting. It also protects their right to join political parties, public interest groups, and other organizations.

The right to petition guarantees the right to ask the government to correct injustices. In other words, it guarantees the right of the people to influence public policy.

Amendment 2. Right to Bear Arms (1791)

States may set up militias for their protection. Over time, the state militias have developed into the National Guard. This amendment guarantees the right of people to have weapons. However, the national and state governments may regulate the possession, or ownership, of guns.

Amendment 3. Quartering of Soldiers (1791)

Quartering means "housing." This amendment was passed to safeguard people's privacy. During the colonial period, the British government housed troops in private homes. This amendment forbids that action.

Amendment 4   (1791) Search and Seizure

The right of the people to be secure in their persons, houses, papers, and effects, against unreasonable searches and seizures, shall not be violated, and no Warrants shall issue, but upon probable cause, supported by Oath or affirmation, and particularly describing the place to be searched, and the persons or things to be seized.

Amendment 5   (1791) Life, Liberty, and Property

No person shall be held to answer for a capital, or otherwise infamous crime, unless on a presentment or indictment of a Grand Jury, except in cases arising in the land or naval forces, or in the Militia, when in actual service in time of War or public danger; nor shall any person be subject for the same offence to be twice put in jeopardy of life or limb; nor shall be compelled in any criminal case to be a witness against himself, nor be deprived of life, liberty, or property, without due process of law; nor shall private property be taken for public use, without just compensation.

Amendment 6   (1791) Rights of the Accused

In all criminal prosecutions, the accused shall enjoy the right to a speedy and public trial, by an impartial jury of the State and district wherein the crime shall have been committed, which district shall have been previously ascertained by law, and to be informed of the nature and cause of the accusation; to be confronted with the witnesses against him; to have compulsory process for obtaining witnesses in his favor, and to have the Assistance of Counsel for his defence.

Amendment 4. Search and Seizure (1791)

Besides taking property, *seizure* refers to arresting a person. In order to conduct a search, police must have a search warrant, or order, from a judge. The judge gives the order only if the police can show "probable cause." The police must give reasons why they think someone has done something illegal or has goods that are illegal or stolen.

The Supreme Court has enlarged the protections of this amendment. Court rulings have developed the Exclusionary Principle. Goods seized without a search warrant may not be used as evidence in a trial. This amendment is now applied to state as well as federal courts.

Amendment 5. Rights of the Accused (1791)

A presentment, or indictment, is a formal charge of wrongdoing. A federal grand jury must determine if there is enough evidence to bring an accused person to trial. Only then can a person be brought to trial for a federal crime.

The exception is members of the armed forces and the militia, or National Guard. They are tried under military law.

A person may not be tried twice in federal court for the same crime. This is known as double jeopardy. However, if a trial ends without a verdict, a person may be tried again.

A person cannot be forced to testify against himself or herself.

The government may take private property for public use. This is called the Right of Eminent Domain. However, the government must pay the owner for the loss of the property.

The Due Process of Law Clause is very important and the basis of many rights of the accused. Due process means that the government may not act in an unfair or unreasonable way. The 14th Amendment extends due process to people's dealings with the states.

Amendment 6. Right to a Speedy and Fair Trial by Jury (1791)

An accused person has the right to a (1) speedy trial (2) in public (3) before a jury. Holding a person for a long time before trial is punishing someone without the benefit of a trial. Holding the trial in public is one way to ensure that it is fair.

The trial must be held where the crime was committed. This ensures that witnesses will be available.

The accused must be told what he or she is charged with.

The accused must also be allowed to question witnesses against him or her.

The accused must be allowed to have his or her own witnesses testify.

The accused must be allowed a lawyer. In 1963, the Supreme Court ruled that a lawyer must be provided for a defendant who is too poor to hire one.

Amendment 7 (1791) Right to Trial by Jury

In Suits at common law, where the value in controversy shall exceed twenty dollars, the right of trial by jury shall be preserved, and no fact tried by a jury, shall be otherwise re-examined in any Court of the United States, than according to the rules of the common law.

Amendment 8 (1791) Bail and Punishment

Excessive bail shall not be required, nor excessive fines imposed, nor cruel and unusual punishments inflicted.

Amendment 9 (1791) All Other Rights

The enumeration in the Constitution, of certain rights, shall not be construed to deny or disparage others retained by the people.

Amendment 10 (1791) Rights of States and the People

The powers not delegated to the United States by the Constitution, nor prohibited by it to the States, are reserved to the States respectively, or to the people.

Amendment 7. Civil Lawsuits (1791)

This amendment applies only to civil lawsuits in federal court. A civil lawsuit is between two private parties or between the government and a private party. *Party* means "a person or group of persons, or a business or group of businesses." Civil lawsuits often involve money or property. There is no crime involved.

If the money involved is more than $20, the 7th Amendment guarantees a jury trial. In practice, federal courts hear civil suits only if much larger amounts of money are involved. Also, the parties to the lawsuit may agree to have the case heard just by a judge.

Common law is not a law passed by legislatures. It is law that has developed from court decisions and custom. It has the force of laws passed by legislatures.

Amendment 8. Bail and Punishment (1791)

Bail is money that a person must give the court as a guarantee that he or she will appear for trial. In place of being sentenced to prison or in addition to a prison sentence, a convicted person may have to pay a fine. Neither bail nor fines can be out of proportion to the crime. A serious crime requires a higher bail and/or fine.

"Cruel and unusual punishment" safeguards convicted persons from unreasonable punishment, such as whipping.

Amendment 9. Powers Reserved to the People (1791)

Amendment 9 declares that the people have more civil rights than those listed in the Constitution and its amendments.

Amendment 10. Powers Reserved to the States (1791)

The Constitution lists certain powers that belong to the national government. Certain other powers are denied the people and the states. The 10th Amendment declares that all other powers belong to the people or to the states. The purpose of this amendment is to safeguard the rights of the people and the states. The fear was that the national government would become too powerful.

Amendment 11   (1795) Suits Against a State

The Judicial power of the United States shall not be construed to extend to any suit in law or equity, commenced or prosecuted against one of the United States by Citizens of another State, or by Citizens or Subjects of any Foreign State.

Amendment 12   (1804) Election of President

The Electors shall meet in their respective states, and vote by ballot for President and Vice-President, one of whom, at least, shall not be an inhabitant of the same state with themselves; they shall name in their ballots the person voted for as President, and in distinct ballots the person voted for as Vice-President, and they shall make distinct lists of all persons voted for as President, and of all persons voted for as Vice-President, and of the number of votes for each, which lists they shall sign and certify, and transmit sealed to the seat of the government of the United States, directed to the President of the Senate;

The President of the Senate shall, in the presence of the Senate and House of Representatives, open all the certificates and the votes shall then be counted;

The person having the greatest number of votes for President, shall be the President, if such number be a majority of the whole number of Electors appointed; and if no person have such majority, then from the persons having the highest numbers not exceeding three on the list of those voted for as President, the House of Representatives shall choose immediately, by ballot, the President. But in choosing the President, the votes shall be taken by states, the representation from each state having one vote; a quorum for this purpose shall consist of a member or members from two-thirds of the states, and a majority of all the states shall be necessary to a choice.

~~And if the House of Representatives shall not choose a President whenever the right of choice shall devolve upon them, before the fourth day of March next following, then the Vice-President shall act as President, as in the case of the death or other constitutional disability of the President.~~

The person having the greatest number of votes as Vice-President, shall be the Vice-President, if such number be a majority of the whole number of Electors appointed, and if no person have a majority, then from the two highest numbers on the list, the Senate shall choose the Vice-President; a quorum for the purpose shall consist of two-thirds of the whole number of Senators, and a majority of the whole number shall be necessary to a choice. But no person constitutionally ineligible to the office of President shall be eligible to that of Vice-President of the United States.

Amendment 11. Lawsuits Against the States (1795)

The 11th Amendment repeals part of Article III, Section 2, Clause 1. A resident of a state or of a foreign nation must bring a lawsuit against a state in state court. Such lawsuits may not be heard in federal court.

The Supreme Court has enlarged the meaning of this amendment. It has ruled that a foreign nation may not sue a state in federal court. Also, a resident of a state may not sue that state in federal court.

Amendment 12. Election of the President and Vice President (1804)

This amendment changes Article II, Section 1, Clause 3. It was added because of the election of 1800. Until the ratification of the 12th Amendment, ballots were not marked "president" and "vice president." In the election of 1800, two candidates tied for president. The House of Representatives had to decide the election. The 12th Amendment states that separate ballots are to be cast for president and vice president.

Electors may not vote for two candidates from their home state for president and vice president.

The amendment sets up a process if no single candidate for president receives a majority of Electoral College votes. All but the top three vote-getting candidates are eliminated, and House members vote for president among these three.

The Senate chooses the vice president if no candidate receives a majority in the Electoral College. The Senate chooses from the two highest vote-getting candidates.

The deleted section was changed by the 20th Amendment.

The vice president must have the same qualifications as the president. This enlarges on Article II, Section 1, Clause 5.

Amendment 13 (1865) Abolition of Slavery

<u>Section 1</u> Neither slavery nor involuntary servitude, except as a punishment for crime whereof the party shall have been duly convicted, shall exist within the United States, or any place subject to their jurisdiction.

<u>Section 2</u> Congress shall have power to enforce this article by appropriate legislation.

Amendment 14 (1868) Civil Rights in the States

<u>Section 1</u> All persons born or naturalized in the United States, and subject to the jurisdiction thereof, are citizens of the United States and of the State wherein they reside. No State shall make or enforce any law which shall abridge the privileges or immunities of citizens of the United States; nor shall any State deprive any person of life, liberty, or property, without due process of law; nor deny to any person within its jurisdiction the equal protection of the laws.

<u>Section 2</u> Representatives shall be apportioned among the several States according to their respective numbers, counting the whole number of persons in each State, excluding Indians not taxed. But when the right to vote at any election for the choice of electors for President and Vice President of the United States, Representatives in Congress, the Executive and Judicial officers of a State, or the members of the Legislature thereof, is denied to any of the male inhabitants of such State, being twenty-one years of age, *(See Note 15)* and citizens of the United States, or in any way abridged, except for participation in rebellion, or other crime, the basis of representation therein shall be reduced in the proportion which the number of such male citizens shall bear to the whole number of male citizens twenty-one years of age in such State.

<u>Section 3</u> No person shall be a Senator or Representative in Congress, or elector of President and Vice President, or hold any office, civil or military, under the United States, or under any State, who, having previously taken an oath, as a member of Congress, or as an officer of the United States, or as a member of any State legislature, or as an executive or judicial officer of any State, to support the Constitution of the United States, shall have engaged in insurrection or rebellion against the same, or given aid or comfort to the enemies thereof. But Congress may by a vote of two-thirds of each House, remove such disability.

Amendment 13. Abolition of Slavery (1865)

This amendment ended slavery in the United States and in territory under U.S. control. In addition to enslavement of African Americans, it ended the enslavement of persons to repay debts.

Section 2. Enforcement. Congress may make all laws that are needed to ensure that the amendment is carried out.

Amendment 14. Rights of Citizens (1868)

Section 1. Definition of Citizenship. This amendment grants U.S. citizenship to everyone born within the United States and to all naturalized persons. As a result, all former enslaved African Americans became citizens.

States are forbidden to pass any laws that would interfere with the "privileges or immunities" of citizens.

States may not take "life, liberty, or property" from someone without "due process of law." The 12th Amendment extends the Due Process Clause of the 5th Amendment to dealings between states and individuals.

All citizens are entitled to equal protection under the law. The Supreme Court used the Equal Protection Principle to overturn segregation in *Brown* v. *Board of Education*.

Section 2. Representation in Congress. The Three-Fifths Clause, Article I, Section 2, Clause 3, counted enslaved African Americans as three-fifths of the population in deciding the number of representatives for each states in the House of Representatives. Section 2 of the 14th Amendment did away with this clause. Native Americans were not considered citizens and were not counted.

There was a penalty if a state refused to allow African Americans to vote. The number of representatives that the state had in the House would be reduced. This section was never enforced. African Americans' voting rights were guaranteed by the 24th Amendment and other civil rights laws.

Section 3. Punishment for Rebellion. The section is aimed at officials and military officers who joined the confederacy. Anyone who once swore to uphold the Constitution and then rebelled against the United States may not hold a job in federal or state government. Congress is empowered by a vote of two-thirds of both houses to remove this ban. By the end of the 1870s, almost all former Confederate officials had been allowed to hold public office again.

Section 4 The validity of the public debt of the United States, authorized by law, including debts incurred for payment of pensions and bounties for services in suppressing insurrection or rebellion, shall not be questioned. But neither the United States nor any State shall assume or pay any debt or obligation incurred in aid of insurrection or rebellion against the United States, or any claim for the loss or emancipation of any slave; but all such debts, obligations and claims shall be held illegal and void.

Section 5 The Congress shall have power to enforce, by appropriate legislation, the provisions of this article.

Amendment 15   (1870) Black Suffrage

Section 1 The right of citizens of the United States to vote shall not be denied or abridged by the United States or by any State on account of race, color, or previous condition of servitude.

Section 2 The Congress shall have power to enforce this article by appropriate legislation.

Amendment 16   (1913) Income Tax

The Congress shall have power to lay and collect taxes on incomes, from whatever source derived, without apportionment among the several States, and without regard to any census or enumeration.

Amendment 17   (1913) Direct Election of Senators

Section 1 The Senate of the United States shall be composed of two Senators from each State, elected by the people thereof, for six years; and each Senator shall have one vote. The electors in each State shall have the qualifications requisite for electors of the most numerous branch of the State legislatures.

Section 2 When vacancies happen in the representation of any State in the Senate, the executive authority of such State shall issue writs of election to fill such vacancies: Provided, That the legislature of any State may empower the executive thereof to make temporary appointments until the people fill the vacancies by election as the legislature may direct.

Section 3 This amendment shall not be so construed as to affect the election or term of any Senator chosen before it becomes valid as part of the Constitution.

Section 4. Public Debt. Both the Union and the Confederacy piled up huge debts in the Civil War. This section states that the Union debt was valid, or legal. However, the Confederate debt was declared invalid, or illegal. It would not be repaid.

In addition, former slaveholders were not to be paid for the loss of their enslaved persons.

Section 5. Enforcement. Congress may make all laws that are needed to ensure that this amendment is carried out.

Amendment 15. The Right to Vote (1870)

Section 1. African-American Voting Rights. This amendment bars the states from discriminating against anyone "on account of race, color, or previous conditions of servitude." *Servitude* refers to slavery.

Section 2. Enforcement. Congress may make all laws that are needed to ensure that the amendment is carried out.

Amendment 16. Income Tax (1913)

Congress is given the power to levy a tax on income. This is a direct tax and changes Article I, Section 9, Clause 4, which bars Congress from collecting direct taxes.

Amendment 17. Direct Election of Senators (1913)

Section 1. Election Process. Section 1 changes the process for the election of senators described in Article I, Section 3, Clause 1. Voters in each state now vote for senators. This is known as direct election of senators. Before this amendment, state legislators elected U.S. senators.

Senators still serve for six years and still have one vote each in the Senate.

Electors mean "voters." Anyone who is eligible to vote for state legislators is eligible to vote for U.S. senators.

Section 2. Vacancies. Section 2 changes the process for filling a Senate vacancy described in Article I, Section 3, Clause 1. The governor must call a special election to fill the opening. If the state legislature authorizes it, the governor may appoint someone as senator until the election is held.

Section 3. Timing. The amendment must be ratified before it can go into effect. Until then, no election or temporary appointment of a senator will be affected.

Amendment 18   (1919) National Prohibition

~~Section 1 After one year from the ratification of this article the manufacture, sale, or transportation of intoxicating liquors within, the importation thereof into, or the exportation thereof from the United States and all territory subject to the jurisdiction thereof for beverage purposes is hereby prohibited.~~

~~Section 2 The Congress and the several States shall have concurrent power to enforce this article by appropriate legislation.~~

~~Section 3 This article shall be inoperative unless it shall have been ratified as an amendment to the Constitution by the legislatures of the several States, as provided in the Constitution, within seven years from the date of the submission hereof to the States by the Congress.~~

Amendment 19   (1920) Women's Suffrage

The right of citizens of the United States to vote shall not be denied or abridged by the United States or by any State on account of sex.

Congress shall have power to enforce this article by appropriate legislation.

Amendment 20   (1933) "Lame-Duck" Amendment

Section 1 The terms of the President and Vice President shall end at noon on the 20th day of January, and the terms of Senators and Representatives at noon on the 3d day of January, of the years in which such terms would have ended if this article had not been ratified; and the terms of their successors shall then begin.

Section 2 The Congress shall assemble at least once in every year, and such meeting shall begin at noon on the 3d day of January, unless they shall by law appoint a different day.

Section 3 If, at the time fixed for the beginning of the term of the President, the President elect shall have died, the Vice President elect shall become President. If a President shall not have been chosen before the time fixed for the beginning of his term, or if the President elect shall have failed to qualify, then the Vice President elect shall act as President until a President shall have qualified; and the Congress may by law provide for the case wherein neither a President elect nor a Vice President elect shall have qualified, declaring who shall then act as President, or the manner in which one who is to act shall be selected, and such person shall act accordingly until a President or Vice President shall have qualified.

Amendment 18. National Prohibition (1919)

The 18th Amendment outlaws the making, selling, or transporting of alcoholic beverages in the United States. Over time, many Americans openly disobeyed the law. The 21st Amendment repealed Prohibition in 1933.

Amendment 19. Women's Suffrage (1920)

Women may not be denied the right to vote in federal and state elections. This is extended to local elections.

Congress may make all laws that are needed to ensure that the amendment is carried out.

Amendment 20. "Lame-Duck" Amendment and Succession (1933)

A lame duck is someone who is defeated or not eligible for reelection but serves out his or her term.

Section 1. New Starting Dates for Terms of Office. The Framers set the inauguration of the president and vice president for March 4. This was four months after the election. In the late 1700s, it could take months for the presidential and vice presidential candidates to make their way to the capital and prepare to take office. However, by the 1930s, travel was much easier and there was no need for so much time. As a result, inauguration day was changed to January 20. This shortened the time that a defeated or retiring president remained in office.

Section 2. Meeting Time for Congress. Every two years, Congress had a lame-duck session. At least some senators and members of the House were retiring or were defeated. Like the president and vice president, they served until March. The 20th Amendment moved the opening of the new Congress to January 3 of the year after the election.

Section 3. Succession of the President and Vice President. Article II and the 12th Amendment also deal with presidential selection. A president-elect is a person who has been elected president by the Electoral College but who has not yet been inaugurated.

If the president-elect dies before taking office, the vice president-elect becomes president.

If there is no president-elect, the vice president-elect may become president temporarily.

Congress is empowered to choose a temporary president if no one qualifies as either president or vice president.

The purpose of the section is to try to cover all possibilities in which no president or vice president is elected or able to serve.

Section 4 The Congress may by law provide for the case of the death of any of the persons from whom the House of Representatives may choose a President whenever the right of choice shall have devolved upon them, and for the case of the death of any of the persons from whom the Senate may choose a Vice President whenever the right of choice shall have devolved upon them.

Section 5 Sections 1 and 2 shall take effect on the 15th day of October following the ratification of this article.

Section 6 This article shall be inoperative unless it shall have been ratified as an amendment to the Constitution by the legislatures of three-fourths of the several States within seven years from the date of its submission.

Amendment 21   (1933) Repeal of Prohibition

Section 1 The eighteenth article of amendment to the Constitution of the United States is hereby repealed.

Section 2 The transportation or importation into any State, Territory, or possession of the United States for delivery or use therein of intoxicating liquors, in violation of the laws thereof, is hereby prohibited.

Section 3 This article shall be inoperative unless it shall have been ratified as an amendment to the Constitution by conventions in the several States, as provided in the Constitution, within seven years from the date of the submission hereof to the States by the Congress.

Amendment 22   (1951) Presidential Term of Office

Section 1 No person shall be elected to the office of the President more than twice, and no person who has held the office of President, or acted as President, for more than two years of a term to which some other person was elected President shall be elected to the office of the President more than once. But this article shall not apply to any person holding the office of President when this article was proposed by the Congress, and shall not prevent any person who may be holding the office of President, or acting as President, during the term within which this article becomes operative from holding the office of President or acting as President during the remainder of such term.

Section 4. Filling a Presidential Vacancy. This section deals with several "if's." The Electoral College votes for the president and vice-president. If one presidential candidate does not get a majority of electoral votes, then the election is sent to the House of Representatives. If a presidential candidate dies before the House chooses a president, the House has to figure out what to do. It has to pass a law to solve the problem. If no vice-presidential candidate wins a majority in the Electoral College, then the Senate has to choose the vice president. If a vice-presidential candidate dies while the Senate is deciding on the vice president, the Senate must decide what to do.

Section 5. Using the New Starting Dates. This section states when the new starting dates in Sections 1 and 2 will go into effect. The president elected in November 1936 was the first president to take office on January 20. The members of Congress elected in 1934 were the first group to take their seats on January 3.

Section 6. Time Limit on Ratification. Three-fourths of the state legislatures must ratify the 20th Amendment within seven years from March 2, 1932. This was the date that Congress proposed the amendment. The states took less than a year to ratify the amendment.

Amendment 21. Repeal of Prohibition (1933)

Section 1. Ending Prohibition. *Repeal* means "to cancel or end." The 21st Amendment repealed the 18th Amendment and ended Prohibition.

Section 2. Limit. States and territories could continue to ban the shipping of alcoholic beverages across their borders. Any state or territory that wished to make it a crime would have to pass its own laws against the transportation of alcoholic beverages.

Section 3. Time Limit on Ratification. This amendment also contains a clause putting a seven-year time limit on ratification. Congress proposed the amendment in February 1933, and special state conventions ratified it by the end of December 1933.

Amendment 22. Presidential Term of Office Limits (1951)

Section 1. Term Limits. This amendment limits presidents to two elected terms in office.

A vice president can become president if the president dies in office or resigns. If the vice president serves more than two years of the previous president's term, he or she may be elected only once. If the vice president serves less than two years, then the vice president may be elected for two terms (eight years) of his or her own.

This section states that the amendment does not cover anyone who is president when the amendment is proposed or until the amendment goes into effect.

Section 2 This article shall be inoperative unless it shall have been ratified as an amendment to the Constitution by the legislatures of three-fourths of the several states within seven years from the date of its submission to the states by the Congress.

Amendment 23   (1961) Voting in the District of Columbia
Section 1 The District constituting the seat of government of the United States shall appoint in such manner as the Congress may direct:

A number of electors of President and Vice President equal to the whole number of Senators and Representatives in Congress to which the District would be entitled if it were a state, but in no event more than the least populous state; they shall be in addition to those appointed by the states, but they shall be considered, for the purposes of the election of President and Vice President, to be electors appointed by a state; and they shall meet in the District and perform such duties as provided by the twelfth article of amendment.

Section 2 The Congress shall have power to enforce this article by appropriate legislation.

Amendment 24   (1964) Abolition of Poll Taxes
Section 1 The right of citizens of the United States to vote in any primary or other election for President or Vice President, for electors for President or Vice President, or for Senator or Representative in Congress, shall not be denied or abridged by the United States or any state by reason of failure to pay any poll tax or other tax.

Section 2 The Congress shall have power to enforce this article by appropriate legislation.

Amendment 25   (1967) Presidential Disability and Succession
Section 1 In case of the removal of the President from office or of his death or resignation, the Vice President shall become President.

Section 2 Whenever there is a vacancy in the office of the Vice President, the President shall nominate a Vice President who shall take office upon confirmation by a majority vote of both Houses of Congress.

Section 3 Whenever the President transmits to the President pro tempore of the Senate and the Speaker of the House of Representatives his written declaration that he is unable to discharge the powers and duties of his office, and until he transmits to them a written declaration to the contrary, such powers and duties shall be discharged by the Vice President as Acting President.

Section 2. Time Limit on Ratification. Congress set a seven-year time limit on ratification. Congress proposed the amendment in March 1947, and it was not ratified until 1951.

Amendment 23. Voting in the District of Columbia (1961)
Section 1. Voting Rights. Residents of the District of Columbia could not vote in presidential elections until this amendment was passed. The District now has three electors. This is equal to the number of senators and representatives it would have if it were a state. However, the District is not represented in Congress, although Congress supervises its government.

Section 2. Enforcement. Congress may make all laws that are needed to ensure that the amendment is carried out.

Amendment 24. Abolition of Poll Taxes (1964)
Section 1. Some southern states used the poll tax to discriminate against African Americans. In order to vote, people had to pay this tax. The 24th Amendment banned the payment of any tax in order to vote in a primary or regular election for federal offices. A federal office includes president, vice president, and members of Congress. In 1966, the Supreme Court extended the ruling to include state elections.

Section 2. Enforcement. Congress may make all laws that are needed to ensure that the amendment is carried out.

Amendment 25. Presidential Disability and Succession (1967)
Section 1. Filling a Presidential Vacancy. This section spells out what happens if the president dies, resigns, or is removed from office. The vice president becomes president. This section makes clear what Article II, Section 1, Clause 6, implies.

Section 2. Filling a Vice-Presidential Vacancy. If a vice president dies, resigns, or is removed from office, the president selects a replacement. The nominee must be approved by a majority of members of both the Senate and the House.

Section 3. Replacing the President with His Agreement. From time to time, a president may be unable to carry out his duties. Usually, the reason is a health problem. The president must notify the president pro tempore of the Senate and the Speaker of the House of the problem in writing. The vice president then becomes acting president. When the president is able to resume his duties, he again notifies the president pro tempore of the Senate and the Speaker of the House in writing. The vice president then gives up his duties as acting president.

Section 4 Whenever the Vice President and a majority of either the principal officers of the executive departments or of such other body as Congress may by law provide, transmit to the President pro tempore of the Senate and the Speaker of the House of Representatives their written declaration that the President is unable to discharge the powers and duties of his office, the Vice President shall immediately assume the powers and duties of the office as Acting President.

Thereafter, when the President transmits to the President pro tempore of the Senate and the Speaker of the House of Representatives his written declaration that no inability exists, he shall resume the powers and duties of his office unless the Vice President and a majority of either the principal officers of the executive department or of such other body as Congress may by law provide, transmit within four days to the President pro tempore of the Senate and the Speaker of the House of Representatives their written declaration that the President is unable to discharge the powers and duties of his office. Thereupon Congress shall decide the issue, assembling within forty-eight hours for that purpose if not in session. If the Congress, within twenty-one days after receipt of the latter written declaration, or, if Congress is not in session, within twenty-one days after Congress is required to assemble, determines by two-thirds vote of both Houses that the President is unable to discharge the powers and duties of his office, the Vice President shall continue to discharge the same as Acting President; otherwise, the President shall resume the powers and duties of his office.

Amendment 26   (1971) Eighteen-Year-Old Vote

Section 1 The right of citizens of the United States, who are 18 years of age or older, to vote, shall not be denied or abridged by the United States or any state on account of age.

Section 2 The Congress shall have the power to enforce this article by appropriate legislation.

Amendment 27   (1992) Congressional Salaries

No law varying the compensation for the services of the Senators and Representatives shall take effect until an election of Representatives shall have intervened.

Section 4. Replacing the President Without His Agreement. A president's health problem may be so severe that he is unable to send a message to Congress. That happened when President Ronald Reagan was shot in 1981. Section 4 gives the job of notifying the president pro tempore and the Speaker to others. The vice president and either a majority of the heads of the executive departments or a majority of Congress must send a written message stating that the president is unable to carry out his duties.

When the president sends a written message that he is no longer disabled, he once again assumes his duties. However, the vice president and a majority of department heads or members of Congress may disagree. They then have four days to notify the president pro tempore and the Speaker. Congress then must decide by a two-thirds vote of both houses if the president is capable. If not, the vice president continues as acting president.

Amendment 26. Eighteen-Year-Old Vote (1971)

Section 1. Voting Age. Because of this amendment, eighteen-year-olds have the right to vote in all federal, state, and local elections. Before this amendment, twenty-one had been the minimum voting age.

Section 2. Enforcement. Congress may make all laws that are needed to ensure that the amendment is carried out.

Amendment 27. Congressional Salaries (1992)

This amendment changed Article I, Section 6, Clause 1. When the members of Congress approve a raise for themselves, the raise may not go into effect until after the next election for Congress. The purpose is to keep members from enriching themselves at the taxpayers' expense.

Amending the Constitution

Thinking on Your Own

Does your school have a set of rules or policies for students? Would you like to see any of the rules amended by having the present rules changed? List at least four rules that you would like to amend. Write the rules as they are now. Then rewrite them your way. Share these with a partner.

The Framers understood the need to make the Constitution adaptable. As a result, they built into the document a way to amend, or change, the Constitution. This is the formal amendment process. However, informal ways of changing the Constitution have also developed since 1789.

focus your reading

Describe the formal process for adding amendments to the U.S. Constitution.

What are the informal ways to change the Constitution?

words to know

executive agreements

judicial restraint

Formal Methods for Amending the Constitution

The chart on page 78 lists the 27 amendments to the Constitution. The first 10 are called the Bill of Rights. As you remember, supporters of the Constitution agreed to add them in order to win ratification of the Constitution. The other 17 amendments were added as the nation and the role of government changed over time.

Adding an amendment to the Constitution requires two steps: (1) proposing an amendment and (2) ratifying the proposed amendment.

There are two ways to propose an amendment. First, the amendment may be introduced into the House of Representatives and the Senate. Two-thirds of the members of both the House (287) and the Senate (67) must approve the proposed amendment. Under the second method, two-thirds of

the 50 states (34) petition, or request, Congress to call a constitutional convention. The convention proposes, discusses, and approves the amendment. The constitutional convention method of proposing an amendment has never been used.

Once an amendment is approved, there are two ways it may be ratified. According to the first way, three-fourths (38) of the state legislatures of all 50 states must ratify it. For the second method, Congress asks the states to call special constitutional conventions to ratify the proposed amendment. If that method is used, then three-fourths (38) of all 50 state constitutional conventions must ratify it.

Congress determines which method of ratification to use. Since 1789, special constitutional conventions have been called only once to ratify an amendment. The Twenty-first Amendment was ratified in this way in 1933. The other 26 amendments were proposed by Congress and ratified by state legislatures.

Informal Changes to the Constitution

The Constitution leaves the day-to-day operation of the government to the people who run it. When the Constitution was first written, there were a few million people living in 13 states. Today, the nation has grown to more than 280 million people and 50 states. Yet the Constitution still works as the plan of government for the nation.

One reason is that the Framers left many details to be filled in later. As you have just read, amendments are one way that the Constitution changes with the times. There are also informal ways. Informal changes do not revise the wording of the Constitution. Instead, they develop as Congress, presidents, and the courts go about the daily business of running the government.

The first source of informal change is legislation. Congress passes laws that explain and enlarge on the powers given to Congress in Article I. For example, the Framers gave Congress the power to levy taxes. However, the questions of what kinds of taxes, on whom, and how much, were left to Congress to answer.

Amendments to the Constitution

Amendment	Year	Subject
First	1791	Guarantees freedom of religion, speech, assembly, press, and petition
Second	1791	Protects the right of states to have militias and the right of citizens to carry guns
Third	1791	Limits how and when soldiers may be housed in private homes
Fourth	1791	Protects against "unreasonable searches and seizures"
Fifth	1791	Guarantees the right to a speedy and fair trial by a jury
Sixth	1791	Guarantees the right of "due process" under the law
Seventh	1791	Guarantees the right to a jury trial
Eighth	1791	Protects against high bail and "cruel and unusual punishment"
Ninth	1791	States that people's rights are not limited to those listed in amendments 1 through 8
Tenth	1791	States that powers not granted to the federal government and not forbidden to the states belong to the states and the people
Eleventh	1795	Forbids certain kinds of lawsuits against the states
Twelfth	1804	Changes how the Electoral College votes for president and vice president
Thirteenth	1865	Abolishes slavery
Fourteenth	1868	Defines citizenship and states the rights of citizens to due process and equal protection of the laws
Fifteenth	1870	Guarantees the right to vote regardless of race, color, or previous enslavement
Sixteenth	1913	Grants Congress the power to tax incomes
Seventeenth	1913	Provides for the election of senators by the people
Eighteenth	1919	Sets up Prohibition, which forbids the sale and manufacture of alcohol
Nineteenth	1920	Grants women the right to vote
Twentieth	1933	Changes the beginning dates for presidential and congressional terms of office
Twenty-first	1933	Repeals, or ends, Prohibition
Twenty-second	1951	Places a limit on the number of terms a president may serve
Twenty-third	1961	Grants citizens in the District of Columbia the right to vote in presidential elections
Twenty-fourth	1964	Prohibits the poll tax, a tax that voters had to pay in order to vote
Twenty-fifth	1967	Sets policies for presidential succession, filling a vice presidential vacancy, and presidential illness
Twenty-sixth	1971	Lowers the voting age to eighteen
Twenty-seventh	1992	Places limits on raises for members of Congress

The second source of informal change is practice, or how things are done. For example, the Constitution gives the House the power to impeach a federal official. However, the Framers did not define "high crimes and misdemeanors" in Article II, Section 4. They left it to members of the House of Representatives to decide.

Presidential actions are a third source of informal change. Beginning with Theodore Roosevelt (1901–1909) and Woodrow Wilson (1913–1921), presidents in the twentieth century began asserting their power with Congress. The Framers gave Congress the power to make laws. However, since Theodore Roosevelt, presidents have been more assertive. They regularly send proposed legislation to Congress and threaten to veto bills that they do not want passed.

Another example of presidential action is the power to declare war. The Framers gave Congress this power but made the president the commander in chief of the armed forces. This is part of the system of checks and balances. However, presidents have sent United States troops into battle many times without asking Congress for a declaration of war. Modern presidents also get around Congress's power to approve treaties. They make **executive agreements**. These are informal documents with other nations, rather than treaties. The Senate must approve treaties, but the Constitution does not mention executive agreements.

The fourth method of informal change is court decisions. The principle of judicial review developed from Supreme Court decisions. By hearing cases and handing down decisions, the federal judiciary interprets the Constitution and laws passed by Congress. Some critics of the judiciary claim that it reads into the Constitution things that the Framers never meant. These

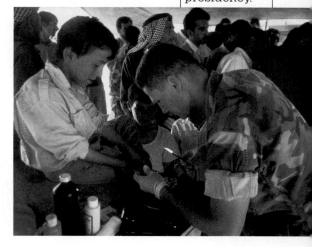

Using the military for humanitarian missions is one of the powers of the presidency.

critics believe in **judicial restraint**. However, others believe that the Court should be involved in how the government makes and enforces laws. These people support judicial activism.

Customs and usage also result in informal change. For example, the Constitution says nothing about political parties. However, political parties began to take shape as early as George Washington's first term. Since the early 1800s, elections have been based on party differences. Congress is organized according to party membership.

Putting It All Together

With a partner, create a table to list the formal and informal ways that the Constitution changes over time. Your table should have three columns and a title. In the first column, list the methods for change. In the second column, explain the method. In the third column, list an example.

Civics Today

National Constitution Center

One of the most important government documents ever written is the U.S. Constitution. But how do you honor a document? How do you make a document come to life? Visit the National Constitution Center in Philadelphia. If you cannot visit in person, then visit online. Millions of people have taken a virtual tour of the center since it opened in September 2003. One million people visit the actual building every year. The goal of the center is to increase "public understanding of, and appreciation for, the Constitution, its history, and its contemporary relevance."

The National Constitution Center is just two blocks from Independence Hall, where the Constitution was written. One exhibit has life-sized statues of each delegate to the Constitutional Convention. You can walk among the delegates and look eye to eye with Benjamin Franklin and James Madison.

Visit the interactive center and learn about the Constitution's effect on Americans' rights. Type in a description for yourself, such as an enslaved person in 1860, or a woman in 1880 who wants to vote. Then learn if the Constitution granted you any rights. If not, continue with your search to find out when you did gain your rights.

Participate in Government

Work for a Candidate

Political campaigns are a good way to become involved in politics. Candidates, especially in local elections, need volunteers. You do not have to be old enough to vote in order to volunteer.

Volunteers do all kinds of jobs to get the message about their candidate out to voters. Volunteers stuff envelopes with campaign literature. They also canvass neighborhoods for votes. They go door-to-door, handing out campaign information and talking about their candidate. On election day, volunteers may drive voters to the polls or call voters to remind them to vote.

To Find Out More About Volunteering:

• Decide which candidate you support in the election.

• Check the phone book or the Internet for the phone number of the political party of this candidate. Call the party to find the local campaign office for the candidate.

• Look at an ad for the candidate or at campaign literature you receive.

• Call for information or visit the campaign office to sign up as a volunteer.

Skill Builder

Reading a Diagram

A diagram presents information by using pictures and symbols. For example, in Lesson 3, you read about the steps in proposing and ratifying an amendment to the Constitution. Instead of using text, the author might have used a diagram like the one below. A diagram is especially useful in presenting information that includes steps or a sequence. It can make it easier to remember information.

Proposing and Ratifying an Amendment to the Constitution

STEP 1: Amendment Proposed by:	STEP 2: Amendment Ratified by:	
A two-thirds vote of both houses of Congress	Three-fourths of the 50 state legislatures	
or	**or**	**New Amendment**
A constitutional convention called by Congress on petition of two-thirds of the 50 states	Three-fourths of the special constitutional conventions called by the 50 states	

→ Used for all amendments except the Twenty-first

→ Used only for the Twenty-first Amendment (repeal of Prohibition)

→ Never used

To read a diagram:

1. Read the title first to find out what the diagram is about.

2. Read the legend to identify symbols and colors.

3. Read all the labels and check them against symbols or pictures to understand the diagram.

4. Locate any arrows or numbers to identify the sequence or movement within the information shown.

5. Summarize for yourself what the diagram shows.

Answer the following questions about the diagram on this page.

1 What method of ratification has never been used?

2 Adding an amendment requires how many steps?

3 What method of proposing an amendment has been used most often?

4 How many of the 50 states must ratify an amendment for it to become law?

Chapter

4 THE FEDERAL SYSTEM

Getting Focused

Skim this chapter to predict what you will be learning.

- Read the lesson titles and subheadings.
- Look at the illustrations and read the captions.
- Examine the chart and diagram.
- Review the vocabulary words and terms.

Federalism requires cooperation between the national government and the states. Think of a time when you and another person or group cooperated to get something done. Write a paragraph in your notebook describing what you had to do and how everyone cooperated to get it done.

Federal funds are used for many projects, including the construction of the nation's highway system.

Division of Powers

Thinking on Your Own

This lesson focuses on powers of the national and state governments. Title a page in your notebook "Powers of Government" and create a two-column chart. In the left-hand column, include the powers listed in the Words to Know box. In the right-hand column, add the definition of each kind of power as you read about it. Be sure to leave space between each power to provide room for a full-sentence definition.

As you read in earlier chapters, the Constitution is based on six principles. One of those principles is federalism. In a federal system, power is divided between the states and the national government. This is known as the **division of powers**. Both the national government and the state governments have their own duties and responsibilities. These are described in the Constitution. However, these duties and responsibilities have shifted and changed over the years as the nation has grown and changed.

Powers of the National Government

The Constitution delegates, or gives, the national government three types of powers. Together, these are known as the **delegated powers**. They are expressed powers, implied powers, and inherent powers.

Expressed powers are expressed, or stated directly, in the Constitution. Articles I, II, and III contain most of these powers. For example, Article I, Section 8, Clauses 1 to 18, lists 27 powers delegated to Congress. Among them are the power to tax and to set up an army and navy.

focus your reading

Explain the differences among expressed, implied, and inherent powers of the national government.

How is power distributed to the states?

What guarantees and obligations exist between the national and state governments?

Describe the role of the U.S. Supreme Court in the division of powers.

words to know

division of powers

delegated powers

expressed powers

implied powers

inherent powers

denied powers

reserved powers

concurrent powers

Implied powers are those not stated directly in the Constitution. However, they can be reasonably assumed, or suggested, by the expressed powers. Clause 18 of Article I, Section 8, is the basis for the implied powers. This is the "necessary and proper" clause. It gives Congress the power to make laws that are needed for the government to function. The implied powers enable the government to meet the needs of changing times. For example, the modern Congress funds a national railroad system, regulates the nuclear power industry, and sets laws about environmental pollution. All these are based on Congress's implied powers. None of these topics would have been known in 1787.

Congress has the power to set up an army and navy.

Inherent powers are not directly stated in the Constitution. They belong to the national government. To act as the government of a nation, the government must have and use certain powers. For example, the national government must have the power to regulate immigration. It must also deal with other nations.

The Constitution also denies certain powers to the national government. **Denied powers** include the right to tax exports. Exports are goods sent out of the country for sale. Powers expressly denied Congress, for example, are stated in Article I, Section 9. The first ten amendments to the Constitution also deny the national government certain powers. For example, the national government may not limit freedom of speech or of religion.

In addition, any power that is not an expressed, implied, or inherent power is denied the national government. For example, the national government cannot set up a national system of public schools. There is nothing in the Constitution that gives the national government that right. The Tenth Amendment gives powers to the states that are not given to the federal government.

Powers of the States

Like the national government, the 50 states have certain powers that belong to them alone. These are called **reserved powers**. There are also certain powers denied to the states. The states and the national government exercise some of the same powers. These are known as **concurrent powers**.

The powers reserved, or set aside, for the states are not listed in the Constitution. The Tenth Amendment, however, provides guidance on state powers. It declares that those powers belong to the states that are neither given to the national government nor forbidden to the states. For example, only states may set up local governments such as counties and cities. Only states may create public school systems and license teachers.

stop and think

Your school probably has a student government. With a partner, think of an expressed, implied, and inherent power that your student government probably has. Also, think of a denied power. In your notebook, write a sentence describing each power. For example, the constitution for the student government denies it the power to develop cafeteria menus.

People in the News

Candy Lightner and MADD

The National Minimum Purchase Act was announced in 1983.

What do you do if you want all 50 states to pass a particular law? If you are Candy Lightner, you lobby, or push your case, in Congress. Lightner's thirteen-year-old daughter was killed by a drunk teenage driver. In 1980, Lightner founded Mothers Against Drunk Driving (MADD) to educate the public about the problem of underage drinking. MADD set up chapters in all 50 states. They campaigned to get laws passed to raise the minimum drinking age to twenty-one. Of the 50 states, 31 allowed people under age twenty-one to drink alcohol in 1980.

Lightner and MADD decided that there was a quicker way than approaching every state legislature. They wanted Congress to pass the law setting the minimum drinking age at twenty-one. There was one problem. Congress did not have the power to pass a minimum drinking age law. That power rested with the states.

Lightner and her supporters in Congress, as well as Secretary of Transportation Elizabeth Dole, found a way. They used the federal power to fund highways as a tool. Under their National Minimum Purchase Act, if a state did not raise its minimum legal drinking age to twenty-one by 1988, the federal government would withhold ten percent of the state's federal highway funds. The bill passed and was signed into law in 1984.

Division of National and State Powers

NATIONAL GOVERNMENT	**NATIONAL and STATE GOVERNMENTS**	**STATE GOVERNMENTS**
(Expressed, Implied, and Inherent Powers)	*(Concurrent Powers)*	*(Reserved Powers)*
• Regulate foreign and interstate commerce	• Levy taxes	• Regulate intrastate commerce
• Coin money	• Borrow money	• Establish local government systems
• Provide an army and navy	• Spend for general welfare	• Administer elections
• Declare war	• Establish courts	• Protect the public's health, welfare, and morals
• Establish federal courts below the Supreme Courts	• Enact and enforce laws	
• Conduct foreign relations		
• Exercise powers implied from the expressed powers		

Article I, Section 10, lists powers expressly denied to the states. For example, states may not negotiate treaties with foreign nations. States also may not grant titles of nobility. The Bill of Rights and the Thirteenth, Fourteenth, Fifteenth, Nineteenth, Twenty-fourth, and Twenty-sixth Amendments place the same limits on the states as they do on the national government. For example, the states may not allow slavery or keep women from voting in elections.

Concurrent powers are those that the national and state governments both have. For example, both levels of government have the power to levy taxes. The national government and state governments also have the power to create their own court systems.

President Eisenhower signed the proclamation making Hawaii a state on August 21, 1959. Admitting a state is the responsibility of Congress; however, the president has the power of veto. Once admitted, all states are treated equally.

Guarantees and Obligations

Article IV, Sections 3 and 4, lists the responsibilities of the national government toward the states. First, the national government must guarantee each state "a republican form of government." This means making sure that each state has a representative government. Congress enforced this guarantee after the Civil War. It refused to seat senators and House members from Southern states that had not ratified the Thirteenth, Fourteenth, and Fifteenth Amendments. These amendments ended slavery and recognized the rights of African Americans.

Second, the national government guarantees to protect the states from invasion and from domestic disorder, such as riots or rebellion. If a foreign nation invades one state, it is considered an attack on the nation itself.

The states have the primary duty of enforcing laws and keeping order within their borders. However, there are times when state forces are overwhelmed by violence, and the governor asks for help. There is also the issue of upholding federal law when state or local officials will not. For example, in 1957, President Dwight Eisenhower sent federal troops to enforce integration at Little Rock Central High School. This was the result of the governor trying to prevent the desegregation of schools.

> **ideas to remember**
>
> The national government
> - has certain delegated powers, which are expressed, implied, or inherent.
> - is denied certain powers.
> - shares concurrent powers with the states.

Federal troops were called in to enforce desegregation at Little Rock Central High School in 1957.

LITTLE ROCK CENTRA

The national government also guarantees the territorial integrity of the states. *Territorial integrity* means the legal existence and physical boundaries of the states. A new state may not be made from an existing state unless the legislature of the existing state agrees.

In turn, the states have certain obligations toward the national government. The states are responsible for national elections. These are the elections for president and vice president, senators, and members of the House of Representatives. The states run the elections and pay for them.

The Role of the Federal Courts

The Framers realized the possibility of conflicts between the national government and the states. As a result, the Framers included Article VI, Clause 2, known as the Supremacy Clause. It states that the Constitution, all laws made by the United States, and United States treaties are the "supreme Law of the Land." In other words, state constitutions and state laws must agree with the U.S. Constitution and national laws.

The Supreme Court often acts as umpire in disputes between states and the federal government.

When conflicts arise, lawsuits are brought in the federal court system. Federal courts determine whether the state action or law is constitutional or not. This is known as the power of judicial review. As you have read, this power developed from court decisions. The first time it was applied to conflicts between states and the national government was in *McCulloch* v. *Maryland*. In that 1819 ruling, the Supreme Court denied states the right to tax a national bank established by Congress.

Putting It All Together

Review the list of powers and their definitions that you have been keeping in your notebook. Quiz a partner to see if she or he knows the definitions. Then ask your partner to quiz you.

State-to-State Relations

Thinking on Your Own

The United States is one of only 11 nations in the world that has a federal system. The others have unitary governments. That is, they have one national authority but no state or provincial governments. Federal systems face special problems. They have to keep each state from going its separate way. What would happen if your state refused to enforce a neighboring state's laws, loan contracts, or jail sentences? Write a paragraph to describe life without state governments.

The unwillingness of the states to give up power was a major reason why the Articles of Confederation had been so weak. The Framers of the Constitution were determined not to have this happen again. They strengthened the powers of the national government. They also laid out rules for how the states are to deal with one another. Article IV, Sections 1 and 2, states the mutual duties of the states.

Full Faith and Credit Clause

Article IV, Section 1, is known as the Full Faith and Credit Clause. It requires that every state recognize or accept, the "public Acts, Records, and judicial Proceedings of every other State." For example, every state must accept the legality of the birth certificates of every other state.

Public acts are laws passed by state legislatures that relate to civil matters, not criminal ones. The Full Faith and Credit Clause refers to civil actions and laws only. One state's criminal laws cannot be enforced by another state.

---

focus your reading

What is the effect of the Full Faith and Credit Clause?

Discuss how the Privileges and Immunities Clause protects citizens of different states.

What is the purpose of the Extradition Clause?

Explain how states resolve conflicts among themselves.

words to know

privileges

immunities

extradition

interstate compacts

Records are documents such as mortgages, deeds, leases, and wills. For example, a will signed in one state will be valid in all 50 states.

Judicial proceedings under Article IV refer to court decisions in civil lawsuits only. A civil court ruling in one state must be recognized and enforced in the other 49 states. For example, a person cannot move from New Jersey to California to avoid paying damages in a lawsuit he or she lost. The person who won the case could bring a suit in California. The courts there would have to enforce the New Jersey decision.

All authority within a state comes from the state government. States create local governments, including counties, cities, towns, villages, and boroughs. Each local unit of government gets its authority to act from the state. Like the states, local governments may not pass laws that conflict with the Constitution.

Privileges and Immunities

Article IV, Section 2, Clause 1, states that "the Citizens of each State shall be entitled to all Privileges and Immunities" of citizens of every other state. Because of this clause, a state may not discriminate against residents of other states. **Privileges** and **immunities** refer to freedoms, or rights.

There is no complete list of privileges and immunities. However, over time, the courts have recognized certain rights. For example, people may travel freely from one state to another. People may freely change residence from state to state. People are also free to buy, sell, and own property in any state or enter into contracts to do business in any state.

However, the courts have recognized the right of states to make "reasonable distinctions" between their own residents and residents of other states. For example, states may charge out-of-state students more to attend state-funded universities. States may also require that voters live in the state for a period of time before being allowed to vote. States may also have residency requirements before a person may become a public official in the state.

States have the right to set different tuition rates. Students may be charged more money to attend a state university if they are not from that state.

stop and think

Imagine that a neighboring state has just passed a set of laws refusing to let citizens of your state buy property, attend schools, and collect debts there. In your notebook, write a letter to the governor of that state explaining why these laws are unconstitutional.

Extradition

Article IV, Section 2, Clause 2, deals with extradition. When a person is wanted for a crime, or is convicted and flees before he or she can be jailed, the person is known as a fugitive. **Extradition** means the returning of a fugitive to the state where he or she is wanted. The purpose of the clause is to make sure that criminals and suspected criminals do not escape justice by fleeing from state to state. The governor of the state where the fugitive is found is responsible for having the person sent back.

Governors have usually responded to requests for a fugitive by turning the person over. However, sometimes a governor has refused. Finally, Congress made the issue a federal matter. Crossing state borders to avoid prosecution for a felony became a federal crime. In 1987, the Supreme Court declared that federal courts are empowered to order governors to turn over fugitives.

ideas to remember

The Constitution lists three ways that the states must cooperate with one another

- give "full faith and credit" to the laws, court decisions, and records of other states
- extend the "immunities and privileges" of their citizens to citizens of all states
- extradite fugitives

Interstate Compacts

What if states disagree about an issue? How can they settle the disagreement? Article I, Section 10, Clause 3, declares that states may enter into compacts, or agreements, with one another. However, Congress must agree to the terms of these **interstate compacts**. Once a compact is signed, state governments may not change their minds. The U.S. Supreme Court enforces compacts.

The National Governors Association is a bipartisan group that helps governors in developing state policies and in lobbying the national government for policies that aid the states.

Compacts are rare. Congress has agreed to and states have signed about 200 interstate compacts. Early ones dealt mainly with disagreements over state borders. Modern ones often deal with regional issues such as air and water pollution, use of water resources, and prevention of forest fires.

When states cannot agree on a solution, they may bring lawsuits against one another. More than 220 such lawsuits have been filed since the beginning of the nation. The U.S. Supreme Court hears these cases. It is the only court authorized to hear lawsuits filed by states against states.

Putting It All Together

With a partner, create a concept map about interstate relations. Draw a large circle and label it "Interstate Relations." Then add smaller circles connected by lines to the large circle. Label these with the three ways that the states must cooperate. Add the two ways states have of settling conflicts among themselves.

Federalism: The Ongoing Process

Thinking on Your Own

One way the federal government relates to states is by providing money for special programs. Federal money might pay for more police officers or new highways. Make a list in your notebook of problems in your community that more federal money could help solve.

Federalism is defined as the division of powers between the national government and the states. What powers are involved? How are they divided? As you have learned, the Constitution lists many of the powers that are divided, shared, or denied the national government and the states.

However, the nation has changed and grown since the document was written. Laws, court decisions, and practice have added duties and responsibilities to both the national

The Framers could not have planned for federal aid to fund school lunches. Public education did not exist in 1787.

and state governments. With these changes, the relationship between the national government and the states has shifted. In other words, federalism continues to develop over time. It is not the same as it was in 1787.

focus your reading

What is the difference between states' rights and nationalist positions?

What powers has the national government used to expand its reach?

How has federal aid to the states expanded the power of the national government?

How does the political process affect federalism?

words to know

states' rights position

nationalist position

war power

commerce power

power to tax

guidelines

public policy

Balance Between the States and the National Government

One area of disagreement over the years has been the balance of power between the states and the national government. What is the right balance?

The **states' rights position** is that the state and local governments should deal with social, economic, and other problems. The **nationalist position** is that the national government is better suited to act for all the people in dealing with these problems. The chart below shows the arguments that each side uses to support its viewpoint.

Balance of Power

States' Rights Viewpoint	Nationalist Viewpoint
1. The national government was created by the states, which gave it only limited powers.	1. The people created the states and the national government.
2. The national government only acts for, or in place of, the states.	2. The national government is not subordinate to the states.
3. States are closer to the people and better understand what the people want and need.	3. The national government represents all the people, not just the people of one state.
4. States' rightists base their view on the Tenth Amendment. Part of the Bill of Rights, it states that powers not delegated to the national government are reserved to the state or the people.	4. Nationalists base their view on the "necessary and proper clause" (Article I, Section 8, Clause 18). It states that the government of the United States will make all laws "necessary and proper for carrying out the foregoing Powers and all other Powers" placed in that government. Powers reserved to the states or the people do not limit how the national government may act or what it should do.
5. States' rights advocates usually insist on a narrow, or strict, interpretation of the Constitution.	5. Nationalists usually favor a broad, or loose, interpretation of the Constitution.

The issue of states' rights was a major cause of the Civil War. Southern states believed the states should regulate slavery. Today, many states' rightists think states should control all school spending. Nationalists believe the U.S. government should control federal grants to schools for education.

A good example of the nationalist argument is Franklin Roosevelt's New Deal. The New Deal was created to provide employment during the Depression. These programs greatly expanded the role of the national government. The Supreme Court's first rulings found them unconstitutional. Later, they upheld them.

In the late 1990s, the Supreme Court appeared to be moving toward the states again. In cases involving gun control laws and the Americans with Disabilities Act, the Court ruled that Congress was overreaching its powers.

The New Deal allowed construction of power plants under the direction of the Tennessee Valley Authority.

stop and think

Make a list in your notebook of the reasons why you think the national government should or should not be allowed to expand its powers. Add to this list as you continue reading this lesson.

Expansion of the National Government

When the Framers met in Philadelphia in 1789, the new United States was a nation of farms. In the late 1800s, the nation shifted from farming to industry as its major business. The modern United States is moving from selling manufactured goods to selling services and information. The national government has expanded its powers to meet the changes in society as well as in the economy. Much of this expansion is based on three constitutional powers.

• **War power**: The Constitution gives the national government the power to wage war. Modern war is more than protecting the nation from attack. A great amount of time and energy of the executive and legislative branches is taken up with foreign affairs and the resources of the nation.

Waging war may involve building coalitions, or partnerships, with other nations. It may mean going to war to fulfill our obligations to foreign partners. The impact of war on the economy has to be considered. What effect will spending billions of dollars on defense have on programs at home, such as worker training and health care? Decisions about defense impact all parts of the economy and society.

- **Commerce power:** Congress has the power to regulate commerce. Over time, Congress has broadened this power to include more than buying and selling goods across state borders and with other nations. Commerce has come to mean almost everything involved in the making, selling, buying, and transporting of goods.

Congress used this expanded power as the basis for its civil rights legislation in the 1960s. It banned racial discrimination in interstate travel, based on the commerce clause. Various Supreme Court rulings have confirmed Congress's expanded definition of its commerce power.

U.S. troops served in Kosovo as part of a NATO force during the 1990s.

ideas to remember

The national government has expanded its reach based on three constitutional powers:

- war power
- commerce power
- power to tax

- **Power to tax:** The major purpose of taxes is to raise revenue, or money, for the government. About half of the national government's revenue comes from personal and corporate income taxes. No state can match this amount of revenue. It gives the national government huge resources to spend on national, state, and local programs.

Federal Aid to States

Another way that the national government has expanded its power is through grants to states. The federal government collects taxes in order to fund programs. Some of the money for programs such as Social Security and unemployment payments goes directly to citizens. Some pays for services for older Americans such as Medicare. Other funds go directly to the state and local governments.

These federal grants enable the national government to expand into areas that are not delegated to it by the Constitution. For example, the national government offers grants to fund low-income housing. Once a state or local government accepts grant money, it must obey federal **guidelines**, or rules, for using the money. Federal money means federal control. For this reason, not everyone likes the idea of grants from the national government.

The Influence of Federalism

Federalism has a far-reaching influence on the political life of the nation. For example, it affects how and by whom public policy is made. **Public policy** is the goals that a government sets for itself in order to solve problems.

The national government sets public policy for the nation as a whole. However, state and local governments also set public policy. At times, their solutions have been adopted by the national government or by other state and local governments. For example, Florida's Government-in-the-Sunshine Law became a model for other states. The law prohibits public officials from closing their meetings to the public.

Federalism also affects political parties and political participation. A strong political party system is one result. Because there are many government units, one party may lose control of the presidency and Congress, but remain strong in state and local politics. This happened to the Democratic Party after the Civil War and to the Republican Party during the Great Depression.

Because the United States has a federal system, citizens benefit from having thousands of governments—state and local—trying out public policy solutions. Citizens also have many opportunities to become active in politics. A person might become involved to protect local parkland or to oppose a new highway. As a person becomes more involved in politics and government, he or she has a greater chance of influencing public policy.

The U.S. Conference of Mayors meets annually in June. It is the official organization of the nation's 1,183 U.S. cities with populations of 30,000 or more.

Putting It All Together

Is federalism a good thing for the nation or not? Discuss the question with a partner. When you reach a conclusion, write a sentence stating your conclusion. Use the sentence as the introduction to a paragraph answering the question. Use at least five examples from the lesson to support your answer.

Participate in Government

Become an Informed Voter

The right to vote comes with a responsibility. That responsibility is to be an informed voter. There are many ways that voters can learn about candidates and issues.

Candidates and political parties pay for and distribute all kinds of campaign information. They

- hand out brochures.

- pay for ads on television, cable, and radio.

- put up Web sites.

- sponsor campaign rallies and meet-the-candidate question-and-answer sessions.

- appear on cable and television talk shows. and talk radio programs.

- host town hall meetings.

- participate in political debates.

Read campaign literature carefully. Do not expect it to be objective. It will present the best view of the candidate and the worst view of the opponents.

A better way to find out about candidates and issues is to read news stories and interviews with candidates. Even when listening to candidates, pay attention to the accuracy of what they say. Does their record agree with what they say? Are they exaggerating their own record or their opponents' records? Do not believe everything you hear, see, or read. Investigate, analyze, and make informed voting decisions.

Find Out More:

Check the phone book to see if your community has a local branch of the League of Women Voters. This is a nonpartisan group that monitors elections. Contact your local branch for information about the candidates running in upcoming elections.

Skill Builder

Participating in Discussions

Does this ever happen to you? You are having a discussion with someone and the other person cuts you off in the middle of a sentence. Do you ever do this to others? Being a courteous listener and speaker are important skills. You want your ideas to be heard. You have to let others have their say. The following tips will help you be a good participant in a discussion.

1. Be willing to listen to other people's ideas. This means not cutting them off when they are speaking.

2. Be willing to share your ideas and opinions. Do not just say someone else is wrong. Explain your reasons.

3. Be clear when you explain your ideas. If someone does not understand, restate your idea in a different way.

4. Restate what the other person said to be sure you understand.

5. Respect what others have to say. Everyone has the right to an opinion. Do not laugh at someone else's ideas.

6. Do not make disagreements personal. You can disagree with someone's ideas without disagreeing with the person.

7. Speak calmly.

8. Most important, if you are having a discussion in class, be sure you are prepared. Read your assignment.

Complete the following activities.

1 Choose the two tips from this list that you think would be the most helpful in your discussions with friends, teachers, or parents. Then write a paragraph explaining how the tips you chose might help your conversation or listening skills.

2 Discuss the following question with a partner: How does federalism affect relations between the states? Use the tips for discussion as a guide.

UNIT 2

THE LEGISLATIVE BRANCH

- The National Legislature
- Congress
- The House of Representatives
- The Senate

What do these terms mean? Who are our national legislators? What do they do? How are they chosen? In writing the Constitution, the Framers gave Congress a great deal of power. How do members of Congress use this power? How do their actions affect our daily lives? This unit will help you answer these questions.

Chapter 5

CONGRESS

Getting Focused

Skim this chapter to predict what you will be learning.

- Read the lesson titles and subheadings.
- Look at the illustrations and read the captions.
- Examine the maps and table.
- Review the vocabulary words and terms.

What do you already know about Congress? Draw a table with three columns in your notebook. Label the first column "What I Know." Label the second column "What I Want to Learn." Label the third column "What I Learned."

Fill in column one before you examine this chapter. Then think about what the photographs and other illustrations show and what the subheadings say. In column two, write some questions you would like to answer as you read the chapter. After you study the chapter, complete column three.

On January 4, 2005, newly elected members of the 109th Congress took an oath of office in the House of Representatives.

The National Legislature

Thinking on Your Own

Suppose you wanted to run for election to the House of Representatives. What issue would you campaign on? Think of an important issue that faces the nation today. Make up a slogan to advertise your viewpoint on the issue.

Congress is the lawmaking body of the national government. It is a **bicameral legislature**, which means that it has two houses. The upper house is the Senate. The lower house is the House of Representatives. The **Senate** is the smaller body, with 100 members. Membership in the **House of Representatives** was set at 435 in 1929. Until then, members were added as new states were admitted to the Union and the population grew.

Congress meets for **terms**, or periods of time. Each term is two years and is divided into two one-year sessions. A term begins on January 3 of odd-numbered years.

Usually Congress meets from January until November or December. There are **recesses**, or breaks, for holidays and vacations. Members of both houses must vote to **adjourn**, or take a break. If either house wants to adjourn for more than three days, the other house must approve. Article I and the Twentieth Amendment set out how Congress organizes itself.

focus your reading

What are the differences and similarities between representatives and senators?

What is the purpose of reapportionment?

Why is redistricting a political issue?

words to know

bicameral legislature

Senate

House of Representatives

term

recess

adjourn

constituents

incumbent

reapportionment

redistricting

gerrymandering

New members of the Senate were sworn in on January 4, 2005.

Members of Congress and Their Jobs

Who are the members of Congress? The average member of Congress is a white male in his fifties. However, this average does not reflect the growing gender and ethnic diversity in Congress. In a recent congressional term, there were 63 women in the House of Representatives and 14 in the Senate. The same congressional term had 39 African Americans, 23 Latinos, 5 Asian Americans, and 3 Native Americans.

The major duties of members of Congress are to (1) pass laws, (2) represent what they think is best for their constituents, (3) oversee the workings of the federal government, and (4) help their constituents solve problems with the federal government. **Constituents** are the people back home in the member's state or district. The table on page 105 shows some of the differences and the many similarities between the two houses of Congress.

Reelecting Incumbents

Once a person is elected to office, it is easier for him or her to be reelected. In other words, anyone who challenges an incumbent has a difficult time being elected. An **incumbent** is a person who already holds the office. For example, about 90 percent of all incumbents in Congress were reelected between 1945 and 1990. Sometimes an incumbent does not even face a challenger. Opponents feel they have little chance to defeat an incumbent.

There are four major reasons why incumbents are difficult to beat. First, raising campaign funds is easier for incumbents. People know them and what they have done in office. Being better known than challengers is the second reason. Third, the district may have been set up so that the majority of voters belong to the incumbent's political party. Party members tend to vote for their party's candidates. Fourth, incumbents do favors and solve problems for their constituents. This develops loyalty among voters.

Incumbent Congresswoman Loretta Sanchez (D-California) wins reelection, while her sister Linda Sanchez (left) also wins a seat in the House.

Differences and Similarities Between the House of Representatives and the Senate

Categories	House of Representatives	Senate
Qualifications	• Be twenty-five years of age • Be a citizen for at least seven years • Live in the state from which he or she is elected	• Be thirty years of age • Be a citizen for at least 14 years • Live in the state from which he or she is elected
Term of Office	• Two years	• Six years
Salary	• Representatives: $158,000 • Speaker: $193,600 • Majority and minority leaders: $172,900	• Senators: $158,000 • President pro tempore: $193,600 • Majority and minority leaders: $172,900
Privileges and Benefits	• Tax deduction because they keep homes in their districts and in Washington, D.C. • Free postage for all official business • Free printing of speeches, newsletters • Pension plan • Low-cost health and life insurance	• Tax deduction because they keep homes in their states and in Washington, D.C. • Free postage for all official business • Free printing of speeches, newsletters • Pension plan • Low-cost health and life insurance
Some Duties of Members	• Serve on committees • Help constituents in dealing with the federal government	• Serve on committees • Help constituents in dealing with the federal government
Some Duties of Each House	• Propose revenue, or tax, laws • Elect president in the event of a tie	• Confirm or reject presidential nominees • Confirm or reject treaties with other nations

Reapportionment

The Framers were divided about how to choose members of Congress. They worked out the Great Compromise to solve the problem. It provided for electing members of the House of Representatives based on population. However, population can change over time. Some states gain people, whereas other states lose people.

Until 1929, Congress just added representatives as territories became states. However, the Reapportionment Act of 1929 set the number of members of the House at 435. The law set up a process for **reapportionment**. Seats are reassigned after each ten-year census based on gains or losses in a state's population. The map on page 106 shows the gains and losses after the 2000 census.

stop and think

How are the House of Representatives and the Senate alike and different? Use information from the table on page 105 to create a Venn diagram in your notebook. Share your diagram with a partner. Discuss whether you have included all of the important facts.

Redistricting

When states gain or lose seats in the House of Representatives, they must redraw their districts. This is called **redistricting**. State legislatures draw new congressional districts. For example, after the 2000 census, California gained one representative for a total of 53 members in the House. The state legislature redrew its districts to add one more. Connecticut had the opposite problem. It had to collapse its six districts into five.

The political party in power in a state often tries to set up districts so that its members will win elections.

ideas to remember

Incumbents generally win reelection because

- it is easier for them to raise campaign funds.
- they are better known than challengers.
- their districts were drawn to favor their party.
- they help their constituents solve problems.

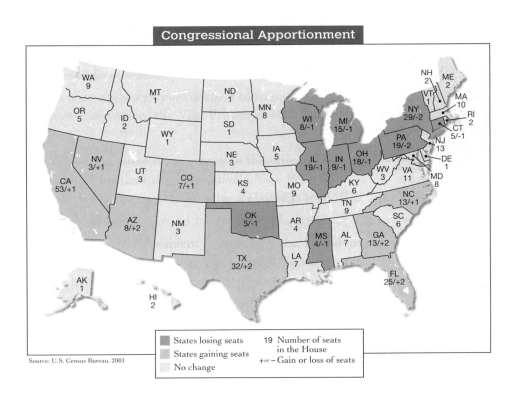

Congressional Apportionment

Source: U.S. Census Bureau, 2001

States losing seats
States gaining seats
No change

19 Number of seats in the House
+ or − Gain or loss of seats

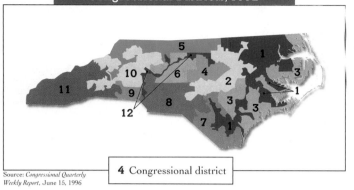

Redistricting Example: North Carolina Congressional Districts, 1992

Source: *Congressional Quarterly Weekly Report*, June 15, 1996

4 Congressional district

As a result, the shape of congressional districts is sometimes very strange. Creating a district to favor one party over another is called **gerrymandering**.

There are two ways to gerrymander districts. One way is to push as many voters from the minority party as possible into a few districts. Then voters from the party in power become the majority in most of the districts. The second way is to divide the minority party's voters into many districts. The result is the same. The party in power is able to elect more of its candidates to office.

Over the years, redistricting has resulted in several important Supreme Court decisions. Read the landmark cases on page 107 to learn about these decisions.

Remember, according to Article I, no matter how few people a state has, it must have at least one representative.

Landmark Supreme Court Cases: Redistricting

- *Wesberry v. Sanders* (Georgia, 1964): The difference in the number of voters in Georgia's new districts violated the Constitution. The Court ruled that the Framers intended that votes have equal value. This is the principle of "one person, one vote." As a result, congressional districts in all states now have about the same number of voters, 650,000.

- *Shaw v. Reno* (North Carolina, 1993): Race cannot be used as the major factor in redistricting. The purpose of creating districts with a majority of African Americans was to elect more African Americans to office. The Supreme Court ruled that these districts violated the Fourteenth Amendment rights of white voters. This ruling also applied to states that drew new districts with a majority of Latino voters.

This 1812 political cartoon shows how political districts were redrawn to the advantage of Governor Eldridge Gerry.

Putting It All Together

Imagine that you are a member of Congress who wants to be reelected for another term. With a partner, discuss the things you can do to improve your chances of reelection. Write a paragraph in your notebook explaining what you have decided upon.

The House of Representatives

Thinking on Your Own

There are 435 members of the House of Representatives. Imagine that you are one of 60 new members who are called "freshmen members." How would you go about meeting other freshmen and learning how the House is run? List four things you could do to learn about your fellow members and about the House.

The United States has a two-party system. Most people think of themselves as either Democrats or Republicans and vote that way. As a result, both the House and the Senate are organized along political party lines. The **majority party** is the party that has the most members in the Senate or the House during a term. A term lasts for two years.

The majority party in the House during a term may be different from or the same as the majority party in the Senate. For example, from 2001 to 2003, the Republicans were the majority party in the House, whereas the Democrats were the majority party in the Senate. The party with fewer seats is called the **minority party**.

focus your reading

Describe the leadership roles in the House of Representatives.

What are the duties of the House Rules Committee?

words to know

majority party

minority party

caucus

majority leader

majority whip

minority leader

minority whip

committees

The elephant is the symbol of the Republican Party, and the donkey is the symbol of the Democratic Party.

Leadership in the House of Representatives

The majority political party manages the business of each house. The Speaker of the House belongs to the majority party. The Speaker is the most important and powerful member of the House. He or she is chosen by a **caucus**, or closed meeting, of the majority party. The full House, however, must vote to approve the choice.

The jobs of the Speaker of the House include keeping order in the House as presiding officer; leading the majority party in the House; appointing members to certain committees; scheduling bills for votes in the House; and sending bills to the proper committees. The Speaker is also next in line to become president after the vice president.

The **majority leader** is the second-most powerful member of the House. First, he or she helps the Speaker and other party leaders plan the party's legislative agenda, or program. Together, they decide what bills the House will work on during the session. Second, the majority leader guides the party's agenda through the House. He or she pushes committees to complete their work on bills and then schedules bills for votes. Third, the majority leader is the main spokesperson for his or her party in the House.

The majority leader has assistants, known as the **majority whip** and deputy majority whips. The job of the whips is to see that party members vote as the leadership wants them to. First, whips talk to party members before votes to see how they plan to vote. Second, whips try to convince members to vote with the party leaders. Third, whips make sure that party members are present when it is time to vote. Fourth, whips report to party leaders what party members think about issues.

stop and think

With a partner, create a table to list the duties of the majority leader and whips and the minority leader and whips. Be sure to give your table a title.

The minority party in the House also has a **minority leader**, **minority whip**, and deputy minority whips. Their duties are similar to the majority party's leader and whips. In addition, the minority leader determines how his or her party will react to the majority party's programs. He or she takes the lead in criticizing the majority party's programs. The minority leader delivers this criticism through news conferences, interviews, and press releases.

House minority leader Nancy Pelosi (D-California) in 2005

The floor leaders and whips are political jobs. They are not official positions in the House.

The Business of the House of Representatives

The chief business of the House of Representatives is to pass laws for the nation. Most of the work of the House is done in

A bill is dropped in the hopper in the House chamber.

committees. These are small groups of representatives who work out the details of bills. All laws begin as bills. The chairperson of each committee belongs to the majority party. The majority of the members on a committee will always be from the majority party. Committees review and discuss the bills. Chapter 7 describes in detail how a proposed bill moves through Congress.

Each year, between 10 and 20 percent of bills—a few hundred bills—are "reported out of committee." This means that a committee votes to send the bill to the full House for a vote. First, however, the bill goes to the powerful Rules Committee. The Rules Committee is called the "traffic cop" of the House. It must issue an order called a "rule" before a bill can be sent to the House. The Rules Committee decides how quickly or slowly a bill will be voted on. Its members may also decide to keep a bill from reaching the House floor at all.

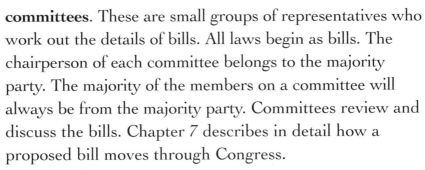

The House requires a quorum of 218 members before a vote can be taken.

The Rules Committee sometimes limits how long the House can debate a bill. It may also limit the number of amendments that can be added to a bill. When a bill is finally sent to the House, it is placed on the calendar for debate and a vote. You will learn more about how a bill becomes a law in Chapter 7.

Putting It All Together

With a partner, create a concept map to illustrate the business of the House of Representatives. Make "Business of the House" the label for your central circle. Then draw lines out from the circle to connect smaller circles that list supporting details.

The Senate

Thinking on Your Own

Over the years, the House has developed a system for managing its members. Would you use the same system to organize the Senate, which is a much smaller group? Why or why not? Explain your reasons in a paragraph in your notebook.

The organization of the Senate is similar to that of the House of Representatives. The members are organized along party lines, and most work is done in committees. However, the Senate is less formal than the House. The rules about how the Senate works are more flexible. This is done on purpose. The goal is to allow senators time to discuss a bill, think about the issues, and discuss the bill again—and again. The debate on a bill may run for weeks before a vote is ever taken on it. During that time, any senator who wants to express his or her views on the issues may do so.

> ### focus your reading
>
> What are the leadership roles in the Senate?
>
> How is a bill scheduled for a vote in the Senate?
>
> Explain the purpose of a filibuster.
>
> ### words to know
>
> president pro tempore
>
> filibuster   cloture

Leadership in the Senate

According to Article II of the Constitution, the vice president is the presiding officer of the Senate. The vice president may not vote except to break a tie. Generally, the vice president has other duties and rarely chairs the daily sessions.

In place of the vice president, the **president pro tempore** chairs daily sessions. The title means "president for a time" and is usually shortened to president pro tem. Generally, the president pro tem is the senior member of the majority party. The whole Senate elects the president pro tem. Like the Speaker of the House, the president pro tem manages the daily sessions and keeps order. The position, however, lacks the power of the Speaker of the House.

Senator Ted Stevens (R-Alaska), president pro tem of the Senate, in 2005

Senate majority leader Bill Frist (R-Tennessee) (left) and Senator Mitch McConnell (R-Kentucky) in 2003

Like the House of Representatives, the Senate has majority and minority leaders. It also has majority and minority whips and assistant majority and minority whips. They are elected by their party. All these positions are political.

Like the majority leader in the House, the Senate majority leader, with other party leaders, sets the agenda for the Senate. The majority leader guides bills through the Senate. The minority leader develops his or her party's position on bills. The minority leader then makes sure that party members support their party's views. Both the majority and minority leaders are the main spokespeople for their party in the Senate.

The whips work with the leaders to see that members are present for votes. Like the House whips, they find out before a vote how their party's senators plan to vote. They try to persuade their party's members to vote with the party leaders. The whips also let party leaders know what members are thinking about the issues.

stop and think

With a partner, create a Venn diagram to compare and contrast the organization of the House of Representatives with that of the Senate. Then write a paragraph to explain how the organization of the two houses is similar and how it is different.

The Business of the Senate

Like the House of Representatives, the major job of the Senate is to pass laws. However, the Senate also votes on nominees for federal judgeships and some high-level government positions. The Senate also confirms or rejects treaties.

Any member of the Senate may introduce a bill. However, there is no Speaker to decide which committee to send it to. There is no Rules Committee to decide when or if a bill will be voted on. Instead, the majority leader has the power to decide what happens to the bill.

The system of reviewing and discussing bills in the Senate is similar to the system in the House. Committees review bills, call witnesses, and discuss the issues. A bill may or may not be reported out of committee. If a bill is sent to the Senate for a vote, it is put on the calendar. The majority leader consults with the minority leader to decide when to schedule a debate and a vote. However, the majority leader has the final say. He or she may delay the debate and a vote until he or she has enough votes to pass the bill. The majority leader can also kill a bill by never bringing it to a vote.

Senators prepare to vote on the Homeland Security bill in 2002.

The Senate does not set time limits for discussing bills. Usually, however, the majority and minority leaders agree ahead of time when the debate will end. At that point, the Senate calls unanimously for a vote. However, if even one senator disagrees, the vote cannot be taken. Debate goes on. The Senate prides itself on being open to unlimited debate. The purpose is to make sure that all sides of an issue are heard.

Congress's Informal Networks—the Caucus

You learned that each political party holds a caucus to set up its organization for the session. However, there is another kind of caucus in Congress. This caucus is a group of members of Congress who share an interest or characteristic.

Three of the best-known caucuses are the Congressional Black Caucus, the Congressional Hispanic Caucus, and the Congressional Women's Caucus. Each caucus includes members of both the House of Representatives and the Senate.

The Congressional Black Caucus (CBC) was founded in 1970 to be "the voice of the voiceless." Its members work for universal health care for all Americans, equal educational opportunities for all children, and strong enforcement of civil rights.

The Congressional Hispanic Caucus (CHC) was formed in 1976. Members support laws that will aid Hispanic Americans, including greater educational and economic opportunities.

The Congressional Women's Caucus first met in 1977. The Women's Caucus focuses on issues important to women and families.

People in the News

The Filibuster

Suppose a group of senators does not want a bill to pass or a presidential nominee to be approved. Suppose they also know that there are not enough votes to kill the bill or the nomination. They may use a **filibuster** to talk until the sponsor of the bill or nomination agrees to modify or withdraw the bill. Senators talk and talk for hours, days, and even weeks in an effort to wear down the opposition. The filibustering senators hope to force the opposition to give up on the bill or to change the parts they object to.

In May 2005, cots were set up in Senate offices to accommodate staff during an all-night debate over the use of the filibuster.

The Senate can end filibusters. Three-fifths of the senators, or 60 members, must vote for cloture. **Cloture** limits the time for debate. Once cloture has been approved, the Senate may spend only 30 more hours discussing the bill. Then the Senate must vote on the bill. It is not easy to reach cloture, however. Senators fear that their opponents could turn around one day and use cloture against them.

Filibusters used to close down all business in the Senate. However, the Senate changed its rules. It now conducts regular business for a period of time each day during a filibuster.

Putting It All Together

How does a bill go from introduction to a vote in the Senate? Create a flowchart to answer this question. Share your flowchart with a partner. Ask your partner to check to make sure you included all of the most important supporting details.

Participate in Government

Ask Your Senators or Representative

You might contact a member of your congressional delegation when

- you want to tell your senators what you think about an upcoming bill.

- your family is going to visit Washington, D.C., and would like to tour the White House.

- you think you might like to go into government service and would like an internship to find out.

- your school district wants to fund an after-school program, and the superintendent needs information on possible funding.

These are just some of the items that senators and representatives can help their constituents with.

Each member of Congress has his or her own home page within either the House or the Senate's main Web site. The home pages list what are known as Constituent Services. These are services that members of Congress offer their constituents. Members of Congress also help with problems related to veterans' benefits, visa issues, and similar federal programs.

To Contact Your Senators or Representative:

- Check your local phone book for the address and phone number of the office nearest you.

- Find your senators and representative by visiting the House and the Senate's Web sites.

- Send him or her an e-mail. Click on the "contact" link button on the home page of your senators and representatives.

Skill Builder

Read a Congressional District Map

A state's congressional district map shows its election districts for the U.S. House of Representatives. Each district represents one member of the House. The state legislature draws the boundaries for the districts. Each district has to have 650,000 people.

However, some districts cover much larger areas of land than others. Districts that are smaller in size mean that they are more densely, or heavily, populated. Small-sized districts have more large cities than districts with more land area. Because of the "one-person, one vote" principle, every district has the same number of people.

To read a congressional district map or any map:

- Read the title of the map first. What is the map about?

- Read the map key. What do the symbols stand for?

- Examine the map. Look at the placement of symbols carefully.

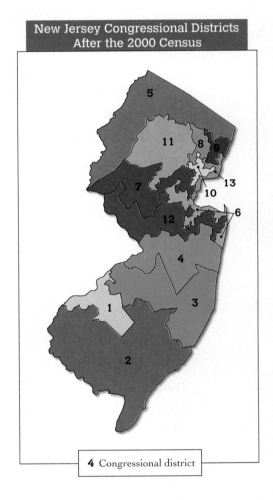

New Jersey Congressional Districts After the 2000 Census

4 Congressional district

Use the map above to answer the following questions:

1 Which district has the smallest area?

2 Which district has the largest area?

3 Which part of the state probably has more cities—north, south, or central?

Chapter 6 POWERS OF CONGRESS

Getting Focused

Skim this chapter to predict what you will be learning.

- Read the lesson titles and subheadings.
- Look at the illustrations and read the captions.
- Examine the tables.
- Review the vocabulary words and terms.

The federal government makes laws that affect many areas of daily life. Think of at least four activities that are regulated by federal law. For example, airport security is under the authority of the federal government.

The Transportation Security Administration (TSA) was created in response to the terrorist attacks of September 11, 2001. It is part of the Aviation and Transportation Security Act signed into law by President George W. Bush on November 19, 2001. The TSA became part of the Department of Homeland Security in March 2003.

Constitutional Powers

Thinking on Your Own

In your notebook, write three facts that you already know about the powers of Congress. As you read the lesson, add at least two new facts.

Congress receives its powers to act from the Constitution. Article I sets up Congress and lists its duties and responsibilities. The major job of Congress is to pass legislation. However, it also has nonlegislative duties and responsibilities.

Conflict Over Congress's Power

Since 1789, Congress has enlarged its powers and, therefore, the powers of the national government. Americans have argued ever since about how powerful the national government should become. The argument centers on the interpretation of the Constitution.

Strict constructionists believe the Constitution should be interpreted narrowly. The result would be a government with limited powers. The national government could use the expressed powers as much as it wanted, because the Constitution lists those powers. However, the government could use

focus your reading

What is the difference in viewpoint between strict constructionists and loose constructionists?

What are some legislative powers of Congress?

Describe nonlegislative powers of Congress.

words to know

strict constructionist

loose constructionist

tax-and-spend

appropriations bill

commerce

copyright

patent

Congress has the power to impose taxes on many items, including gasoline.

implied powers only when they were absolutely necessary to fulfill expressed powers.

Loose constructionists interpret the Constitution more broadly. They claim the Constitution is a living document that gives the government whatever powers it needs to grow and change with the changing nation. Generally, loose constructionists have had more influence in Congress, in the presidency, and on the Supreme Court. They have succeeded in expanding the powers of the national government.

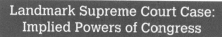

Landmark Supreme Court Case: Implied Powers of Congress

McCulloch v. *Maryland* (1819): Congress set up a national bank in 1816. Strict constructionists did not believe the Constitution gave Congress this power. The Court ruled that Congress had an implied power to set up the bank. The implied power was based on the "necessary and proper" clause. The national bank aided Congress in fulfilling its duties to tax, borrow money, create money, and regulate commerce, or business.

McCulloch v. *Maryland* was also important because the Court ruled that federal law took priority over state law.

Legislative Powers

The legislative powers of Congress can be grouped into four categories. They are money powers, commerce powers, military and foreign policy powers, and other powers stated in Article I, Section 8, Clauses 1–17. These are known as the enumerated powers.

Row two of the table on page 120 lists the expressed powers of Congress. Implied powers often come from the expressed powers. Row three lists some of the implied powers that Congress has found in the expressed powers. Remember that the "necessary and proper" clause, Clause 18, justifies the principle of implied powers.

Congress has the power to authorize the creation of money.

Powers of Congress

Type of Power	Money Power	Commerce Power	Military and National Defense Power	Other Legislative Powers
Expressed Powers	• To tax (Clause 1) • To borrow money (Clause 2) • To regulate bankruptcies (Clause 4) • To print and coin money (Clause 5) • To punish counterfeiters (Clause 6)	• To regulate business between states and business with other nations (Clause 3)	• To punish crimes at sea (Clause 10) • To declare war (Clause 11) • To set up, fund, and regulate the armed forces (Clauses 12, 13, and 14) • To provide for, regulate, and call into service a militia (the National Guard) (Clauses 15 and 16)	• To establish laws for naturalization (Clause 4) • To set up post offices (Clause 7) • To grant copyrights and patents (Clause 8) • To set up a system of federal courts beneath the Supreme Court (Clause 9) • To govern Washington, D.C. (Clause 17) • To make all laws necessary and proper for carrying out the other powers (Clause 18)
Some Implied Powers	• To punish those who do not pay their taxes • To use tax revenue to support programs such as education and public housing	• To outlaw discrimination in movie theaters, restaurants, hotels, and similar places • To set a minimum wage • To protect those with disabilities	• To draft Americans into the armed forces	• To limit and regulate immigration

The money powers give Congress the power to tax and appropriate, or authorize the spending of, the income from taxes. Because of its **tax-and-spend** powers, Congress has a great deal of control over the nation's policies. Congress must approve all funding for every program that the federal government sets up.

All bills that raise money for the government begin in the House. The Framers set up this system on purpose. Representatives are elected every two years. As a result, the Framers thought they would be more careful to follow the wishes of voters.

Heart of Atlanta Motel v. United States (1964): Congress passed the Civil Rights Act of 1964 to ban discrimination in restaurants, hotels, motels, and jobs. The owner of the Heart of Atlanta Motel sued to have the law declared unconstitutional. The owner claimed that it was a local business. However, the motel advertised on interstate highways and attracted travelers from out of state. The Supreme Court ruled that the motel was part of interstate commerce. The Civil Rights Act was declared constitutional.

In order to pay for programs, Congress passes **appropriations bills**. Requests to fund programs usually come from the president. Each year, the president sends a budget proposal to Congress. Both houses review the proposed budget. Committees hold hearings to determine how much they think the executive departments need.

Commerce is the buying and selling of goods and services. The Constitution gives Congress the power to regulate commerce between states and with other nations. However, over the years, Congress has enlarged the meaning of commerce. Today, *commerce* means "any business that crosses state lines." For example, Congress regulates banking, television and cable, clean air, and working conditions.

Congress and the president share military and national defense powers. The president is commander in chief of the armed forces. However, he must ask Congress to declare war. Congress has declared war five times in U.S. history. Yet, U.S. troops have fought in more than 200 undeclared wars. In 1973, Congress attempted to get back its power to declare war. It passed the War Powers Act. A president must notify Congress within 48 hours if he sends U.S. troops into battle. Congress must approve the use of troops in a war zone for more than 60 days.

The Constitution gives Congress six other legislative powers. Clause 18 is the all-important "necessary and proper" clause. The other five expressed powers deal with particular topics. **Copyrights** protect the rights to their works of writers, artists, and composers for a period of time. **Patents** enable inventors to control how their inventions are manufactured and sold. Congress was given the power to set up all federal courts under the Supreme Court in Clause 9. Clause 7 allows Congress to set up the post offices, Clause 4 to set laws for citizenship, and Clause 17 to govern Washington, D.C.

> **stop and think**
>
> What are implied powers? Write a paragraph to explain implied powers. Be sure to include at least two examples. Ask a partner to check your paragraph to see if it is clear and complete. Revise it based on your partner's suggestions.

President Andrew Johnson was tried and acquitted by the U.S. Senate in 1868.

Nonlegislative Powers

The House and the Senate have certain nonlegislative powers. These are powers that are not related to the passing of laws. In most cases, the House and the Senate have separate duties in fulfilling these powers. The table on page 123 lists the powers and then explains the duties of each house.

The House has only had to choose a president twice. In 1800, they chose Thomas Jefferson, and in 1824, they chose John Quincy Adams.

In 1973, Congress confirmed Gerald Ford as vice president. He succeeded Spiro Agnew, who had resigned. Then, in 1974, Congress confirmed Nelson Rockefeller as vice president. He replaced Ford, who had become president when Richard Nixon resigned the presidency.

Since 1789, the House has impeached 17 federal judges, and the Senate has convicted seven. Congress has also impeached and tried two presidents, Andrew Johnson in 1868 and Bill Clinton in 1998. Both were acquitted.

In 2005, the Senate held confirmation hearings for the appointment of Alberto Gonzales as Attorney General.

Confirmation power over presidential appointees belongs to the Senate alone. The Secretary of State and the Attorney General of the United States are examples of the heads of executive departments who are appointed. The Senate's confirmation duties also include approving justices to the U.S. Supreme Court, some diplomats, and some top-level military positions.

The executive branch has the responsibility to make treaties. The Senate alone has the power to ratify, or approve, treaties. This is part of the system of checks and balances.

Putting It All Together

Make a T-chart in your notebook. On one side, list four expressed powers of Congress that affect you. On the other, list four implied powers that affect you. Discuss your selections with a partner, and make any changes to which you both agree.

Nonlegislative Powers of Congress

Power	Source of Power	House of Representatives	Senate
Power to appoint the president and vice president	• Twelfth Amendment • Twentieth Amendment, Sections 3 and 4 • Twenty-fifth Amendment, Section 2	**Twelfth Amendment** • A joint session of Congress counts the Electoral College votes. • If no presidential candidate has a majority, House selects from top three candidates. **Twentieth Amendment** • House and Senate together pass legislation to deal with the death of a presidential or vice presidential candidate if the person died before taking office. **Twenty-fifth Amendment** • A majority vote of House and Senate must approve a nominee to replace a vice president who died or resigned.	**Twelfth Amendment** • A joint session of Congress counts the Electoral College votes. • If no vice presidential candidate has a majority, Senate selects from top two candidates. **Twentieth Amendment** • House and Senate together pass legislation to deal with the death of a presidential or vice presidential candidate if the person died before taking office. **Twenty-fifth Amendment** • A majority vote of House and Senate must approve a nominee to replace a vice president who died or resigned.
Power to remove a federal official from office, including federal judges	• Article II, Section 2, Clause 5: the House • Article I, Section 3, Clause 6: the Senate	The House impeaches a federal official. This means the House finds enough evidence of wrongdoing to turn the official over to the Senate for trial.	The Senate tries the impeached official. If found guilty, the person is removed from office.
Power to confirm federal nominees	• Article II, Section 2, Clause 2	No responsibilities	Senate must confirm presidential nominees for the • heads of executive departments and their highest level of assistants. • heads of regulatory agencies. • federal judges. • major diplomatic positions. • major military positions.
Power to ratify treaties	• Article II, Section 2, Clause 2	No responsibilities	• Senate must approve any treaty with another nation by a two-thirds vote.
Power to propose amendments to the Constitution	• Article V	• This power is shared with the Senate. • The House must propose an amendment by a two-thirds vote.	• This power is shared with the House. • The Senate must propose an amendment by a two-thirds vote.

The Work of Committees

Thinking on Your Own

Have you ever been on a sports team or served on a committee or group that made decisions? What was the hardest part of working as a team? What was the most enjoyable part? If you have never been part of a team or committee, think about a time when you had to work with someone else to get something done. Answer each question with two or three sentences in your notebook.

As you just read, the Constitution gives Congress expressed powers and implied powers. Congress also has inherent powers. **Inherent powers** are not directly stated in the Constitution. These powers belong to the government because it is the government. The government must have and use certain powers in order to carry out its duties.

Two of these inherent powers belong to Congress. One is the power to investigate issues and topics that are viewed as important. The other is the power to oversee how laws are carried out. This is known as **legislative oversight**.

Congress usually works through committees and subcommittees when it uses its investigative and oversight powers. Most of Congress's work is done through committees. By serving on committees in both the House of Representatives and in the Senate, members of Congress become experts in specific topics.

focus your reading

Describe the committee system in Congress.

How does Congress use its investigative power?

What is Congress's legislative oversight?

words to know

inherent power

legislative oversight

standing committee

subcommittee

seniority system

select committee

joint committee

conference committee

subpoena

perjury

immunity

contempt

federal bureaucracy

power of the purse

The Committee System

Both the Senate and the House have their own committees. The Senate has 18 permanent committees, or **standing committees**. The House has 19 standing committees.

Each committee is divided into several subcommittees. **Subcommittees** are small working groups of members of the standing committees. Each subcommittee deals with a piece of the larger committee's work. For example, the House Committee on Veterans' Affairs has four subcommittees. Its Subcommittee on Disability Assistance and Memorial Affairs handles all issues related to salaries and pensions of the armed forces. The Senate has about 70 subcommittees, and the House has about 80. These numbers change as the responsibilities of committees change.

Senator Diane Feinstein (D-California), shown here at the 2004 Democratic National Convention, serves on the Senate Judiciary Committee.

The members of committees are chosen by the party leaders in the House and the Senate. Senators and representatives request committees based on how they can best serve their constituents. For example, a representative from New Jersey might ask to be assigned to the Homeland Security Committee. This would be useful because New Jersey is home to Newark Airport, an airport that serves the New York metropolitan area.

The majority of members on committees are from the majority party in the House and the Senate. For the 109th Congress (2005–2007), for example, the Republican Party won more seats in Congress than the Democrats. As a result, the majority on every committee was made up of Republicans.

Each committee has a chairperson. The chair of every committee for the 109th congress was also a Republican. The chair is usually the person from the majority party who has been on the committee the longest. This is known as the **seniority system**.

> **ideas to remember**
>
> The committee system in Congress is made up of
> - standing committees.
> - subcommittees.
> - select committees.
> - joint committees.
> - conference committees.

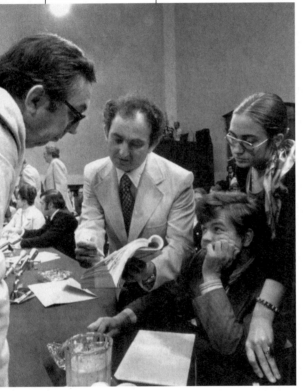

Hillary Rodham (Clinton) served on the Watergate Committee in 1974, officially known as the Select Committee on Presidential Campaign Activities.

Each senator sits on three or four standing committees and several subcommittees. Representatives generally sit on one or two committees and several subcommittees. Much of the senators and representatives' time is spent on committee work. That is why the House and the Senate do not hold sessions on Monday or before noon on other days.

There are three other types of committees in Congress. **Select committees**, also known as special committees, are temporary. They are set up to study one topic or issue and report on it to the House or the Senate. Both the House and the Senate have their own select committees. The Senate committee that investigated the Watergate break-in and the involvement of President Richard Nixon in the cover-up was a select committee.

Joint committees are made up of members of both houses. Joint committees may be permanent or temporary. Most joint committees are permanent, however. For example, the Joint Committee on Printing oversees the printing of all government publications.

Conference committees are temporary and made up of members of both houses. Their job is to work out differences in House and Senate versions of a bill. As you will learn, a bill must pass both houses before it goes to the president. The two versions must be exactly the same. The members of conference committees come from the House and the Senate committees that proposed the bills. However, the majority party in each house has more members on a conference committee.

stop and think

Read the committees listed in the table on page 127. If you were a member of Congress, on which three committees would you want to serve? Discuss your choices with a partner. Write three reasons for each of your choices.

Permanent Committees of the House and the Senate

House Standing Committees	Senate Standing Committees	Joint Committees
Agriculture	Agriculture, Nutrition, and Forestry	Economic
Appropriations	Appropriations	Printing
Armed Services Budget	Armed Services	Taxation
Education and the Workplace	Banking, Housing, and Urban Affairs	
Energy and Commerce	Budget	
Financial Services	Commerce, Science, and Transportation	
Government Reform	Energy and Natural Resources	
Homeland Security	Environment and Public Works	
House Administration	Finance	
International Relations	Foreign Relations	
Judiciary	Health, Education, Labor, and Pensions	
Resources	Homeland Security and Governmental Affairs	
Rules	Indian Affairs	
Science	Judiciary	
Small Business	Rules and Administration	
Standards of Official Conduct	Small Business and Entrepreneurship	
Transportation and Infrastructure	Veterans' Affairs	
Veterans' Affairs		
Ways and Means		

House Select, or Special, Committees	Senate Select, or Special, Committees
Permanent Select Committee on Intelligence	Select Committee on Ethics
	Special Committee on Aging
	Select Committee on Intelligence

Power to Investigate

Standing committees, subcommittees, and select committees conduct investigations. Investigations take the form of hearings, in which witnesses testify. Congressional committees have the power to **subpoena** witnesses. Witnesses are served with a legal order to appear before the committee. Witnesses do not always testify under oath. If a witness is caught lying under oath, however, he or she can be charged with **perjury**. As in a regular court of law, a witness before a committee can be prosecuted for perjury.

Executives from Enron Corporation testified before the Senate in the early 2000s about corruption and the eventual financial failure of the corporation.

Sometimes a committee will grant a witness **immunity**. The person will not be charged with any crime that he or she testifies about committing. A committee grants immunity for one reason. The witness has information about others involved in the crime and the committee wants that information. If a person refuses to testify, he or she can be charged with **contempt**. This is a crime.

Congressional investigations have several purposes. First, investigations may be conducted to determine whether a law is needed. Second, a committee may hold hearings to gather information to help it write a better bill. Third, some investigations look into possible wrongdoing by members of Congress or others. Fourth, hearings may be held to educate the public on issues of importance.

Major General Antonio Taguba testified before the Senate Armed Services Committee in 2004.

GEN. TAGUBA

Power of Legislative Oversight

Legislative oversight, or review, is an important part of the system of checks and balances. Congress makes the laws, and the executive branch carries them out. Through legislative oversight, Congress checks on what the departments of the executive branch are doing and how they are doing it.

Congress exercises its legislative oversight through its committees. However, committees do not have the time or staff to review the daily workings of the huge departments that make up the federal bureaucracy. The **federal bureaucracy** includes everyone who works for the government, including nonelected employees. Departments are run smoothly and efficiently for the most part. What the public hears about are the cases where problems arise. This is when Congress's oversight power is important.

Congress has several ways to use this power. Committees can and do require departments to send yearly reports about their activities. Congress has a support agency called the General Accounting Office (GAO). Committees can request that the GAO investigate how departments are using their budgets.

Luis V. Gutierrez (D-Illinois) is a member of the House Committee on Veterans' Affairs.

Committees hold hearings each year on the budget requests of each department. Committee members often lecture members of the executive departments on how they should do their jobs and what their departments should or should not be doing. Committees hold what is called the **power of the purse**. They use it by adding money for certain programs, cutting spending on others, or ending funding for some programs completely. In these ways, committees can pressure the executive branch to do what their committee members want.

Putting It All Together

For the Stop and Think activity, you selected the committees you would want to serve on if elected to Congress. Research what one of those committees might investigate. Select an issue or problem that you might investigate as a member of the committee. In your notebook, list three people or kinds of people whom you would ask your committee to subpoena as witnesses. Write three questions you would like to ask them.

Congressional Power and Presidential Power

Thinking on Your Own

Think of a time when you worked with a group to complete a project or to play a sport. What kinds of conflicts came up? How did the group settle those conflicts? Write a paragraph in your notebook to describe a conflict and how it was settled.

The president comes to Congress once a year—to give the annual State of the Union address. However, the president's influence is felt in Congress every day. This has not always been the case.

Some presidents have taken a more active role in shaping national policy than others. Andrew Jackson used his veto power to keep Congress in check. Both Theodore Roosevelt and Franklin D. Roosevelt pushed legislation they wanted through Congress. Active presidents often have conflicts with Congress. This is especially true when the two branches are controlled by different political parties.

focus your reading
Explain why conflicts develop between Congress and the president.
How has Congress tried to limit presidential power?

words to know
staff members
impoundment

President George W. Bush delivered the State of the Union address on February 2, 2005.

Conflict Between Congress and the President

Party politics can be a major reason for conflict between Congress and the president. When the president and the majority of both houses belong to the same political party, there are few conflicts.

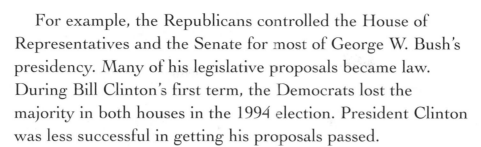

For example, the Republicans controlled the House of Representatives and the Senate for most of George W. Bush's presidency. Many of his legislative proposals became law. During Bill Clinton's first term, the Democrats lost the majority in both houses in the 1994 election. President Clinton was less successful in getting his proposals passed.

Second, the rules and organization of Congress can also cause conflicts. The filibuster, for example, means that the opposite party can talk until a bill fails in the Senate. Even members of the president's own party may not support his proposals. For example, southern Democrats used the filibuster to try to stop President Lyndon Johnson's civil rights legislation in the 1960s.

President Ronald Reagan met with congressional leaders of both parties in the Oval Office in February 1981.

As you just read, both houses are organized into committees to work on legislation. Committees review and rework the president's proposals. The resulting bill may be greatly changed from what the president wanted. Committees may also delay a bill from one session to another or kill it by not bringing it out of committee.

Third, the president represents the nation as a whole. Members of Congress represent their districts or states. Different parts of the country may have different concerns about issues. For example, western landowners want to develop their lands, but environmentalists want to save western forests. The president sends a proposal to Congress to set aside thousands of acres as national forests in western states. Senators and representatives from those states put the interests of their constituents first. They fight the proposed law. This occurred during Clinton's presidency. In the end, President Clinton issued an executive order to set aside the land. An executive order is a rule issued by the president that has the force of law. When President George W. Bush came into office, the executive order was overruled.

A fourth reason for conflict between Congress and the presidency is the system of checks and balances. The Framers meant it as a way to balance the power of the branches of government. However, the system sets Congress against the president if he vetoes or threatens to veto a bill. The threat of a veto forces members of Congress to try to change the bill enough so that the president will sign it. If the president actually vetoes a bill, then supporters must try to get enough votes to override, or overturn, the veto. Since President George Washington, presidents have used their veto power 2,552 times. Congress has overridden only 107 of these vetoes.

Social Security was a source of tension between the president and Congress in 2005.

stop and think

With a partner, make a T-chart to show the five reasons why conflicts develop between Congress and the presidency. Label the left column "Reasons for Conflicts." Label the second column "Examples."

Fifth, presidents and members of Congress have different political timetables. A president has four years, or perhaps eight, to see his proposals become laws. Members of Congress may be reelected as many times as they are willing to run. Members of Congress may believe that their constituents are not yet ready for certain policies. As a result, they may not be willing to support the president. This is true even when the president is from their own party. This appeared to be the case when President George W. Bush proposed a major change to Social Security. After Republicans listened to constituents' concerns, they were not willing to make the changes that the president wanted.

Acting to Limit Presidential Power

By the 1970s, Congress began to take back some of the power it had lost. First, it added people to help committees and subcommittees. **Staff members** do much of the work gathering and reviewing information and writing reports for committee members.

As you read in Lesson 1, Congress passed the War Powers Act in 1973. It requires the president to tell Congress if troops are sent into a battle area. President Richard Nixon vetoed the bill. Congress overrode the veto. In 2002, Congress gave up some of its recently gained power. It passed a resolution to give President George W. Bush the power to take any steps "necessary and appropriate" in the face of threats by Saddam Hussein in Iraq. The result was the invasion of Iraq in 2003.

In 1990, the Senate Committee on the Judiciary conducted hearings about the War Powers Act.

A third limit on presidential power was passage of the National Emergencies Act in 1976. Congress has voted to give presidents emergency powers in times of war and other troubles. These emergency powers include the power to declare martial law and take over the transportation system. In 1943, Congress voted to declare a state of national emergency because of World War II. After the war, the state of emergency was never lifted. Later presidents used it to deal with problems without asking Congress for the power to do so. Congress ended the nation's state of emergency in 1978. The National Emergencies Act requires presidents to tell Congress if they are going to declare a national emergency. The state of emergency may last for one year. Congress may end it at any time by passing a law.

A fourth area where Congress has tried to limit presidential power is the budget. Two efforts, the legislative veto and the line-item veto, were declared unconstitutional. The Budget

Impoundment and Control Act of 1974 was more successful. **Impoundment** is the refusal of the president to spend money that Congress has set aside for a program. This was one way that a president could force the government to do or not do what he wanted. The Budget Impoundment Act ended this practice. Presidents must spend the money for programs unless Congress agrees that the money will not be spent.

The 1974 act also set up standing Budget Committees for both the Senate and the House. It also created the Congressional Budget Office (CBO). The staff of the CBO reviews the annual budget requests of the executive branch and provides Congress with economic data and analyses.

Putting It All Together

Write a two-line newspaper headline about three of the tensions between Congress and the presidency. Then write a two-line headline about each of the ways Congress has tried to limit the president's power. Work with a partner to decide which ideas to write about. Then write the headlines together.

Civics Today

Library of Congress

What houses 29 million books and other print materials, 2.7 million recordings, 12 million photographs, 4.8 million maps, and 58 million manuscripts—on 530 miles of bookshelves in three buildings? The Library of Congress!

The Library of Congress was set up in 1800 as a place for members of Congress to do research. Today, the Library is a rich resource for anyone with a computer. Many of the Library's materials, including recordings, are available online.

The Library has so many books, maps, sheet music, photographs, and recordings (records, tapes, CDs, and DVDs) because the Library also handles copyrights. Anyone who wishes copyright protection for his or her work applies to the Library's division of copyrights. Two copies of each work to be copyrighted are sent to the Library with an application form.

The first Library of Congress was housed in the Capitol. It was burned when the British set fire to Washington, D.C., during the War of 1812. President Thomas Jefferson offered to sell his own collection of books to the government to replace it. Congress agreed and paid him $23,950. His 6,487 books were shipped to the Capitol in 1815. Over time, the Library outgrew its space. The current building opened in 1897. As the collections grew, two more buildings were added.

Participate in Government

Contact a Government Agency

Do you need to find the nearest state motor vehicle office? Are you looking for the phone number of the state's office of student loans? Do you have a question about the local services available for an elderly relative?

Two sources of information will help you find addresses and phone numbers for local, state, and federal government departments and agencies. One source is the telephone book and the other is the Internet.

To Contact a Government Agency:

- Use your phone book. Phone books have a section called "The Blue Pages of Government Listings." The pages are edged in blue so you can find them easily. These Blue Pages are divided into listings for local, state, and federal government departments and agencies. You will find phone numbers and addresses. Some agencies have toll-free 800 numbers. The listings in each section are in alphabetical order.

- Use the Internet. Every state and some local communities have their own Web sites. The Web sites are set up so that you can link to pages for state, county, or local departments, agencies, and services. You can find addresses and phone numbers as well as the names of people to contact. Many times, you can e-mail a message to the person you are looking for and ask your question that way.

Skill Builder

Summarizing and Paraphrasing

A **summary** is a brief retelling of something longer. It may be something that you have read, heard, or seen. For example, when you retell the story of a movie, you are giving a summary of the movie. You are briefly describing the main idea and giving only the most important details.

Be sure to leave out minor details, descriptions, and examples. They can confuse your audience and get in the way of their understanding of the basic information you want to tell. Minor details, descriptions, and examples also add length to your summary. Remember, a summary should be brief.

In writing reports, you often need to **paraphrase** what you have read. When you paraphrase, be careful not to write word for word what you have read. Use your own words and keep the important details as well as the main idea. A paraphrase may be about the same length as the original.

To write a summary, remember to

- state the main idea

- use only the most important details

- make the summary short

To paraphrase, remember to

- state the main idea

- include all important details

- make it as long as needed

Complete the following activities:

1 Reread the section under the subheading "The Committee System," on pages 125–126. Find the main idea of each paragraph.

2 Paraphrase the section "Power to Investigate," on page 127.

3 Write a summary of the section "Conflict Between Congress and the President," pages 130–132.

Chapter

7 CONGRESS AT WORK

Getting Focused

Skim this chapter to predict what you will be learning.

- Read the lesson titles and subheadings.
- Look at the illustrations and read the captions.
- Examine the diagram.
- Review the vocabulary words and terms.

You have learned that the main job of Congress is to pass laws. You have also learned that most of the work of Congress is done in committees. This chapter is titled "Congress at Work." Make a list of at least three things that you think Congress does.

When you have finished studying the chapter, review your list. Check how accurate your predictions were. Write an essay of three or four paragraphs to explain what the chapter was about.

Vol. 150   WASHINGTON, MONDAY, OCTOBER 11, 2004   No. 13

Congressional Record

The *Congressional Record* is the official record of the proceedings and debates of the United States Congress. It is published daily when Congress is in session.

United States
of America

How a Bill Becomes a Law

Thinking on Your Own

You want Congress to pass a law that will provide summer jobs for teenagers. You e-mail your representative in Congress to urge him or her to introduce such a bill. Which of the vocabulary words would help you explain what you hope to accomplish?

Each year, members of Congress propose thousands of bills. However, less than ten percent actually become laws. The 108th Congress (1999–2001), for example, introduced more than 8,000 bills. Only 504 became laws.

There are several reasons why so few proposals become laws. First, the process for passing bills is very long. As you can see from the diagram on page 140, many steps are involved. A bill can be delayed or killed several times during the process.

Second, a bill's sponsors may delay a bill on purpose. **Sponsors** are the senators or representatives who introduce a bill. They delay it because they know there are not enough votes to pass it.

Third, a bill may be killed because powerful members of Congress, the president, or special interest groups oppose it. Interest groups may also oppose a bill or work on members of Congress to kill it.

focus your reading

Summarize the different types of bills and resolutions.

What is the first step in getting a bill through Congress?

Explain what happens once a bill is reported out of committee.

What is the final step in how a bill becomes a law?

words to know

sponsor
public bill
private bill
rider
simple resolution
joint resolution
concurrent resolution
interest group
bipartisan
pigeonhole
quorum
compromise bill
pocket veto
override

Bills and Resolutions

Congress considers two kinds of bills. One is the **public bill**. It deals with an issue of general interest that applies to the entire nation. An example is the Clean Air Act of 1990. A **private bill** deals with an issue of interest only to certain people and places. An example is a bill to allow an immigrant to enter the United States without waiting until his or her turn comes up on the list of applicants for visas. Both kinds of bills become laws when both houses pass them and the president signs them.

According to Article I, Section 7, Clause 1, all revenue bills must begin in the House of Representatives. All other kinds of bills may begin in either the House or the Senate. The House Ways and Means Committee deals with most tax legislation. However, the Senate also has a role in setting tax policy. Article I, Section 7, Clause 1, goes on to state that the Senate may propose amendments to tax bills. The Senate Committee on Finance works on tax policy.

After being printed, proposed legislation and the federal budget are distributed to members of Congress.

As it passes through Congress, a bill may have a series of riders added to it. A **rider** is an amendment to a bill that does not have anything to do with the subject of the bill. For example, a rider was added to a budget bill in 2001 to allow drilling for oil in the Arctic National Wildlife Refuge in Alaska.

Congress also considers several types of resolutions. A **simple resolution** is a decision that concerns only the Senate or the House. A new rule about how bills are introduced in the Senate would be a simple resolution. It is not a law and the president does not sign it.

Joint resolutions and concurrent resolutions are passed by both houses of Congress. **Joint resolutions** deal with some special cases. The two houses passed a joint resolution after the terrorist attacks of September 11, 2001. It gave the president the power to use whatever force necessary to pursue those responsible for the disaster. The president must sign a joint resolution for it to become a law. A **concurrent resolution** is not signed by the president and is not a law. Setting the date for Congress's adjournment for vacation requires a concurrent resolution.

How a Bill Becomes Law

Action	House	Senate
Introduction of a Bill	1. A representative introduces a bill. 2. The bill is given a House number and title. 3. The bill is sent to a House committee.	1. A senator introduces a bill. 2. The bill is given a Senate number and title. 3. The bill is sent to a Senate committee.
Committee Action	1. The committee may pigeonhole the bill, kill it, or send it to a subcommittee. 2. The subcommittee holds hearings on the bill. 3. The subcommittee marks up the bill. 4. If the subcommittee votes to approve the marked-up bill, it is sent back to the standing committee. 5. The standing committee reviews the marked-up bill. 6. The standing committee may pigeonhole the bill, kill it, or report it out to the House for debate.	1. The committee may pigeonhole the bill, kill it, or send it to a subcommittee. 2. The subcommittee holds hearings on the bill. 3. The subcommittee marks up the bill. 4. If the subcommittee votes to approve the marked-up bill, it is sent back to the standing committee. 5. The standing committee reviews the marked-up bill. 6. The standing committee may pigeonhole the bill, kill it, or report it out to the Senate for debate.
Floor Action	1. The Rules Committee decides on a time limit for debate and whether amendments may be added. 2. The House debates the bill and votes. Amendments may be added. 3. The bill passes and is sent to the Senate for approval; **OR** If the House version is different from the Senate version, it is sent to a conference committee.	1. The Senate debates the bill and votes. There is no time limit on debate in the Senate. Amendments may be added. 2. The bill passes and is sent to the House for approval; **OR** If the Senate version is different from the House version, it is sent to a conference committee.

Conference Committee

Members of both the House and the Senate meet to work out differences between the two bills. A compromise bill is sent back to both houses to vote on.

Floor Action	The House votes and passes the bill.	The Senate votes and passes the bill.

Presidential Action

The president takes one of four actions:

1. Signs the bill. 2. Keeps the bill for ten days without taking any action.	3. Vetoes the bill and sends it back to Congress. 4. Uses a pocket veto. This happens if Congress adjourns during the ten days the president has the bill.	The bill becomes a law.	**Congressional Action** Congress attempts to override the veto by a two-thirds majority vote in both houses. If both houses vote to override the veto, the bill becomes a law. If one house does not have a two-thirds majority, the bill is killed, or stopped.

The First Steps

Ideas for bills can come from anyone. In Chapter 4, you read how Candy Lightner wanted the legal drinking age raised through federal action. Often, a bill comes from the president. However, bills are also written by members of Congress and by interest groups. **Interest groups** are made up of people who share common ideas and come together to influence government policy.

Even if a bill comes from the president, only a senator or representative may introduce it in Congress. Often, several members of the House or the Senate will co-sponsor a bill. At times, members of both parties will sponsor a bill. This **bipartisan**, or two-party, effort shows that the bill has support from members of both parties.

After a bill is introduced, it receives its first reading. This involves the clerk of the House or the Senate numbering the bill and giving it a title. The bill is printed in the daily *Congressional Record* and the daily *Journal* of the house in which it was introduced.

Representative Charles Rangel (D-New York), at center, discusses Social Security privatization in 2005.

Next, the bill is sent to the standing committee that has responsibility for the topic of the bill. For example, a Senate bill asking for more pollution controls on cars would be sent to the Senate Commerce, Science, and Transportation Committee. Once a bill goes to the committee chair, any of the following may occur. (1) The bill can be **pigeonholed**. The committee does not act on the bill, so it does not progress. This is what happens to most bills that are introduced in Congress. (2) The committee can vote to kill the bill. (3) The committee chair can send the bill to a subcommittee to deal with. (4) The committee or subcommittee can act on the bill.

If a subcommittee decides to consider a bill, the next step is to hold hearings. As you learned in Chapter 6, committees and subcommittees can call witnesses to testify. These witnesses have some special knowledge of or interest in the bill. They may be government officials or outside experts. Witnesses may also be private citizens, businesspeople, or members of public interest groups.

Once the hearings are over, the subcommittee meets to "mark up" the bill. The members go through the bill and make changes to it. A majority of members must agree to every change.

Once the changes are made, the subcommittee has several choices. It may pigeonhole the bill or vote to kill it outright. Members may also vote to send the revised bill back to the standing committee. The standing committee can also kill the bill or report the bill out of committee. If the bill is reported, it is sent to the House or the Senate for debate.

Floor Action

In the House of Representatives, the Rules Committee sets a time limit for floor debate. The committee also decides whether amendments may be added to the bill during debate. The Senate does not ban amendments or have time limits.

The clerk of the House or the Senate reads the bill for the second time. Amendments may be proposed after each section is read. A majority of members must approve an amendment before it can be added. Amendments are proposed for several reasons. Sometimes members believe that the changes are truly important and needed. At other times, opponents of a bill add amendments as a way to kill the bill.

Once the bill is read and all the amendments have been added, the bill is read again. After this third reading, a vote is taken. A **quorum**, or majority, of senators or representatives is needed for a vote to take place. If a quorum is not present, no vote can be taken. To pass a bill, a majority of the members present must vote to approve it.

The House uses voice votes, standing votes, and electronic voting. In a voice vote, members call out either "aye" or "no." In a standing vote, members stand to show whether they are for or against a bill. In 1973, the House introduced electronic voting. Members push buttons at their seats to vote yes or no. Each member's vote appears on a large panel behind the Speaker.

The Senate also uses voice and standing votes. It uses a roll-call vote instead of electronic voting. Each senator calls out his or her vote.

Final Steps

Usually, House and Senate bills on the same topic are different. Their subcommittees may have included different issues. When the bills reach floor debate, senators and representatives may have raised new concerns. One house may have added amendments that the other house did not. To become a law, House and Senate versions of a bill must be exactly the same.

A public hearing of the Joint Congressional Intelligence Committee in 2002

Once the two versions of a bill have passed their houses, the bills go to a conference committee. The committee is made up of members from both houses and both parties. The committee works out the differences between the two bills. The **compromise bill** is then sent back to the two houses for a vote.

If the compromise bill is passed in both houses, it is sent to the president. The president may sign the bill and it becomes a law. The president may also choose not to take action. If the president holds the bill for ten days, it becomes a law. There is one exception. If Congress adjourns during those ten days, then the bill is vetoed. This is called a **pocket veto**. The president may also veto a bill outright. Then he sends the bill back to Congress with an explanation of why he vetoed it.

Congress may choose to rework the bill and try to pass a new version. However, Congress may also try to **override** the president's veto. To do this, both houses must repass the bill with a two-thirds majority vote. If either house fails to get a two-thirds majority vote, the bill dies.

President George W. Bush signed the Garrett Lee Smith Memorial Act on October 21, 2004.

Putting It All Together

Write a one-paragraph summary explaining how a bill becomes a law. Refer to the information in this lesson, and use as many vocabulary words as you can.

Working for the Folks Back Home

Thinking on Your Own

Your congressional representative has just visited your U.S. government class. Her parting words were "If I can be of help in any way, please contact my office." List at least three ways that she might be able to help you or your school.

The "folks back home" are a Congress member's constituents. Everyone in a representative's district or a senator's state is a constituent. There are two main ways that members of Congress aid their constituents. One is to help them solve problems with federal agencies. The second is to bring money and jobs to their state or district.

focus your reading

Explain how members of Congress help individual constituents.

How do members of Congress help their districts and states?

Describe how constituents influence members of Congress.

words to know

casework

pork-barrel legislation

logrolling

Handling Casework

Citizens often turn to their senator or representative to help them with problems such as:

Representative Rush Holt (D-New Jersey) at work in the Capitol and at home at a rally

- A veteran was denied medical benefits and cannot find out why.

- A student was turned down for a Pell Grant, the federal student loan program. The loan agency rejects her complaint that it used incorrect information.

- A U.S. citizen asks for help in getting his German-born wife back into the United States. She went to Germany for a visit. The U.S. immigration service says her visa has expired. She cannot return to the United States.

Every member of Congress hires staff members to handle **casework**. A caseworker's job is to help constituents solve problems with federal agencies. On his Web site in 2005, Senator Richard Lugar (R-Indiana) lists 11 categories of "common needs and concerns with which my constituent services team" can help Indiana residents. Other representatives and senators offer similar help.

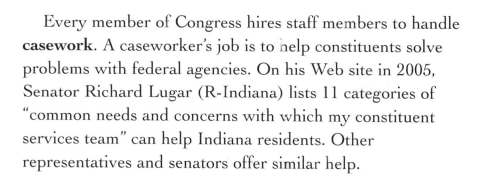

Casework Services from Senator Richard Lugar's Office

Military and Veterans' Issues

- Enlistments and discharges
- Veterans' benefits
- Awards and medals

Labor

- Pensions and benefits
- Unemployment insurance
- Workers' compensation

Education

- Student loans, grants, and scholarships
- Vocational rehabilitation
- Job training programs

Social Security

- Retirement benefits
- Disability applications
- Medicare

Over the years, casework has become an important part of the work of members of Congress. First, helping constituents can help senators and representatives win reelection. Casework shows that a congressional member is interested in the needs and concerns of constituents. People talk about their problems and the help they get to solve them. At election time, this kind of free word-of-mouth advertising is priceless.

Second, casework helps members of Congress with legislative oversight. By listening to constituents' problems, members of Congress get an idea of how certain federal agencies and departments are working. They can tell how well the executive branch is carrying out programs.

Senator Barack Obama (D-Illinois) greets constituents after being elected in 2004

stop and think

Look at the list you wrote before you began this lesson. Pick one of the items and write a letter to your congressional representative asking for help in solving one of the problems.

Third, casework truly provides a service for constituents. The federal government is a huge bureaucracy run by rules and systems. It can be overwhelming for a person to try to deal with. The caseworker can cut through all of this to the heart of the problem to get an answer.

Bringing Home Jobs and Money

Members of Congress also serve their constituents by bringing jobs and federal funds to their state or district. There are three ways that members of Congress do this.

The first is through public works projects. Many of these projects are very much needed. For example, a rapidly growing region needs a rail system to ease traffic jams. There is general agreement among members of Congress that this is a good use of federal money.

However, a number of projects every year are known as **pork-barrel legislation**. For example, a senator sponsors a bill to spend $50 million to build a road to a town with 200 people. The only value is to the senator's constituents. It will make travel easier into and out of the town. The project will also bring jobs to the area.

Over time, a number of members of Congress have criticized pork-barrel legislation. However, the practice is difficult to stop.

Metrolink, the mass transit system in Los Angeles, is an example of a federally funded public works project.

What is one senator's "pork" is another senator's aid to constituents. As a result, little is done to stop passage of pork-barrel legislation. In fact, senators or representatives at times promise to support one another's pork-barrel bills. This is known as **logrolling**.

The second way a member of Congress brings home money and jobs is through federal contracts and grants. The federal government spends billions of dollars every year. Much of it goes out in contracts and grants. For example, the federal government awarded billions of dollars in contracts to fight the war in Iraq. The money bought supplies such as uniforms, weapons, and food as well as services such as security for U.S. officials in Iraq.

Federal grants are awards of money given for many different kinds of activities. A grant might be $100,000 to improve the downtown area of a small city. A grant might also be millions of dollars to a major university for research. Federal grants and contracts bring money and jobs into an area.

This leads to the third way that federal lawmakers aid their states and districts. Once they get federal contracts or grants, members of Congress work hard to keep them. For example, the closing of military bases is often contested by local cities and towns. In recent years, the Defense Department closed bases across the nation. A base closing can badly hurt the economy of a district and state. Senators and representatives worked with state and local officials and others to argue against closing their base.

Humvees are fortified with armor at a Fairfield, Ohio, facility.

Putting It All Together

Imagine that you want a summer job with one of your state's U.S. senators. Imagine that he or she has an office in your community. Write a letter explaining why you want the job and why the senator should hire you. Use information from this lesson to support your request. Share your letter with a partner. Ask your partner to help you make your letter more convincing.

Helping Constituants Across Maine — Senator Susan M. Collins (R-Maine)

The following was written by Senator Susan M. Collins, a Republican senator from Maine. The column appeared in a local Maine newspaper.

"What do you do when the Social Security Administration insists . . . that you're dead? . . .

"It's as simple as the old phrase: you write (or phone, or fax, or e-mail) your representatives in Congress. And in each case, Maine citizens were helped by the dedicated staff in one of the six offices I maintain in the various parts of our state. . . . I'm very proud of the personal assistance my staff have given to Mainers in need. It can be frustrating for people to try to navigate the often muddy waters of federal regulations. . . .

"[M]y state office staff . . . acts as an important liaison between federal agencies and the people of our state. They understand the cares and concerns of the local areas in which they work because that's where they come from, and they have the expertise to investigate and resolve problems. . . .

"[Y]ou are always welcome just to walk into any of my state offices where my staff will be glad to greet you. . . . It may seem strange to think of asking one arm of the government to help clear up a problem with another, but it's important to remember why we're here—to serve the people of Maine."

—Senator Susan M. Collins, *Magic City Morning Star*, January 9, 2004

reading for understanding

1. What reason does Senator Collins give to explain why people ask her office for help?
2. Why are the staff in Senator Collins's offices so good at helping Mainers?
3. According to Senator Collins, what is her and her staff's purpose?

Participate in Government

Contribute to a Political Campaign

Running political campaigns is very expensive. Presidential campaigns cost more than $200 million. A state governor's race may cost as much as $40 million. Even a mayor's race in a big city can cost millions. Where does the money to fund campaigns come from?

Federal campaign finance laws regulate large contributions, as you will learn in Chapter 16. However, much of the money to fund campaigns comes in small amounts. Ordinary citizens who want to support causes and candidates give what they can.

The Democratic National Committee and the Republican National Committee regularly mail out fund-raising letters. They go to registered party members and anyone who has given in the past. The two national committees also have Web sites where contributions are accepted by credit card.

State and local candidates and political parties may also have their own Web sites. They, too, mail out fund-raising letters and hold fund-raisers.

A fund-raiser may be a $25,000-a-plate dinner at a fancy restaurant for a Senate candidate. In this case, the speaker would be an important national political figure, such as the president. A fund-raiser for a city council member may be a $25 coffee-and-bagels get-together at a supporter's home.

To Find Out More About Contributing to a Political Campaign:

- Check the candidate's or party's Web site to see if it accepts contributions online.

- Call the county office of the political party you want to support.

- Call the campaign office of the state or local candidate you want to support.

Skill Builder

Understand the Difference Between Percents and Actual Numbers

Understanding percents is important in analyzing information. Percents do not represent actual numbers. For this reason they can sometimes be misleading. People might make decisions based on a very small number, but think it is larger because it is a percent.

For instance, suppose a newspaper reports that 75 percent of people surveyed believe that veteran's should receive more benefits. Seventy five percent represents a significant number of people who share this belief. However, you need to know the actual number to make better sense of this percent. If only four people were surveyed, then three people represent the 75 percent. But, if 10,000 people were surveyed, then 7,500 represent the 75 percent. These numbers might have an impact on how you would vote or feel about increasing benefits.

Newspapers often report information as percentages rather than actual numbers. This information often comes from polls or surveys. By reading closely you can find out how many people were surveyed.

WASHINGTON, JULY 7—A national study shows that the number of births to immigrants in Broward County almost doubled between 1990 and 2002. In that time, births to immigrant mothers went from 22.7 percent to 43.2 percent.

Births went from 22.7 percent to 43.2 percent. What does this information mean? What is the number of children who were born to immigrant mothers in 2002? You cannot answer this question because the news story only gives you a percentage. To answer the question, you need to know the **actual number**. The actual number is the number represented by the percentage.

Sometimes the actual number is given along with the percentage. Sometimes, however, you have to do some work with the information. Suppose the article went on to say that the total number of births in Broward County was 22,134 children. Then you could find the actual number of children born to immigrant mothers. You would multiply the total number of children by the percentage born to immigrant mothers.

22,134 × 0.432 = 9,562 children born to immigrant mothers

Why is it important to know an actual number instead of just a percentage? The actual number could be anything from 1 to 1 million. A person who is against immigration could read the article and be alarmed. On the other hand, percentage does not give a supporter of immigration any facts to help his or her arguments. Actual numbers help people form opinions based on facts.

Read the following news article and answer the questions.

WASHINGTON, JULY 28—The Transportation Security Administration unfolded a new plan for airport screening. Kennedy International Airport will lose nearly ten percent of its 1,844 screeners, or 184. Newark Airport will go from 1,319 to 1,281 screeners, or about three percent fewer people.

1 How many screeners will Kennedy International Airport lose?

2 How do you know this number?

3 What percentage of Kennedy's screeners is this?

4 How many screeners will Newark Airport lose?

5 How did you find this number?

6 Why is the information in this article easier to understand than the information than in the first article?

UNIT 3

THE EXECUTIVE BRANCH

When you think of the executive branch, you may think only of the president—and maybe the cabinet. In reality, more than 2.7 million people are employed in the executive branch. That does not count the 1.4 million men and women on active duty in the armed forces.

How did the federal government get to be so big? Over the years, the federal government has developed thousands of programs. What do all those federal employees do? They work for you.

Chapter 8

THE PRESIDENCY

Getting Focused

Skim this chapter to predict what you will be learning.

- Read the lesson titles and subheadings.
- Look at the illustrations and read the captions.
- Examine the tables.
- Review the vocabulary words and terms.

What do you already know about the job of president?
Think about what you have read or heard about what the
current president is doing. Think, too, about what you
have learned already about the powers of the president.
Make a list of at least five things you already know about
the job of president.

When you finish studying this chapter, add to your list.
Write at least five new things that you learned about the
presidency.

In 2005, there
were four living
former presidents:
Jimmy Carter,
George H. W. Bush,
Bill Clinton, and
Gerald Ford.

The President and Vice President

Thinking on Your Own

What qualities do you want in your president? Write a list in your notebook of personal or political characteristics that you expect in a president. Then use your list as the basis for an essay. Title your essay "What I Want in My President."

Like the legislative and judicial branches, the executive branch has grown and changed. In some ways, the modern presidency is similar to the presidency of George Washington. The constitutional duties are the same. However, the size of the federal government is much larger. The nation's importance in the world is vastly greater. When George Washington was president, the nation was just trying to survive. Today, the United States is the most powerful nation in the world.

Geraldine Ferraro was the first female candidate for executive office. She ran as Walter Mondale's running mate in 1984.

focus your reading

What are the official and unofficial qualifications for the presidency?

What is the job of the vice president?

What happens if the president resigns or dies in office?

words to know

liberal

conservative

moderate

balance the ticket

The Presidency

The presidency includes many roles. The president is the chief official of the executive branch, the head of the nation, and the commander in chief of the armed forces. He or she represents the nation to the rest of the world. You will learn about duties of the presidency in Chapter 9.

The table on page 155 lists the basic qualifications, term, salary, and other privileges of the president. Any vice-presidential candidate must meet the same qualifications.

The official qualifications tell only part of the story. Anyone running for president must also meet some unofficial qualifications. First, the person probably will have had some experience in government. Being either

a U.S. senator or a state governor has been the usual road to the presidency. Holding past elective office shows that the person can be elected. He or she can win votes. It also means that the person has built up a network of political allies who will offer support.

Second, a candidate must have a large "campaign chest." This means that the person must be able to raise millions of dollars to run for the presidency.

Third, a candidate must hold views that attract the majority of voters. Moderates tend to be elected over very liberal or very conservative candidates. A **liberal** believes that the federal government should expand its role by actively promoting programs such as health care and equal opportunity. A **conservative** believes that the federal government should limit its role in social and economic programs. A **moderate's** views are somewhere in between.

stop and think

With a partner, create a table with two columns. Label the columns "Qualifications" and "Why Important." Label the rows "Formal Qualifications" and "Informal Qualifications." Fill in the qualifications for president. Then discuss with a partner why each of the qualifications is important. In the second column, write a sentence to explain your reasons.

Qualifications, Term, and Salary of President

Categories	President
Qualifications	• Be a native-born citizen of the United States • Be at least thirty-five years old • Have lived in the United States for at least 14 years
Term of Office	• Possible two terms of four years each • A vice president who steps into the presidency and serves two years or less of the president's term may be elected for two full terms of four years each. (Twenty-second Amendment)
Salary and Benefits	• $400,000 in salary • $100,000 travel allowance • $50,000 expense allowance • Free health care • Living rent-free in the White House • Retirement pension
Privileges	• Use of *Air Force One* (the presidential airplane) • Use of Camp David (the presidential retreat) • Use of other aircraft, including helicopters, and land vehicles

The vice president lives at the Naval Observatory in Washington, D.C.

The Job of Vice President

People often wonder what the vice president does. The answer depends on the president. The Constitution lists only two duties for the vice president. According to Article I, Section 3, Clause 4, the vice president presides over the Senate and votes only when needed to break a tie. The Twenty-fifth Amendment also defines another role for the vice president, described on page 157.

Until the presidency of Dwight Eisenhower in the 1950s, vice presidents had few responsibilities. Their role was to **balance the ticket** at election time. Suppose a presidential candidate was from a Northeastern industrial state. A running mate from a Midwestern farm state may have been selected.

Since the 1950s, however, vice presidents have been given more duties. For example, Vice President Al Gore was given the job by President Bill Clinton of reducing the number of federal employees. President George W. Bush asked Vice President Dick Cheney to put together a new energy policy. Both vice presidents served as trusted advisers to their presidents.

Presidential Succession

Since 1789, 42 men have served as president. Nine were vice presidents who became president on the death or resignation of a president. Article II, Section 1, Clause 6, creates a process for having the vice president take over the duties of president. The clause does not provide a way for a disabled president to step aside or be removed, or for a president who has been removed for illness to return to office after recovery. To cover all possible events, Congress proposed the Twenty-fifth Amendment. It was ratified in 1967.

First, the amendment clears up the language of Article II. The amendment clearly states what happens if the president dies, resigns, or is removed from office. The vice president becomes president.

Second, the amendment also states what happens if a vice president dies, resigns, or is removed from office. The president selects a replacement. A majority of both the Senate and the House of Representatives must approve the person.

Representative Gerald Ford was sworn in as vice president in December 1973, after the resignation of Spiro Agnew.

In 1973, President Richard Nixon had to replace his vice president, Spiro Agnew, who had resigned because of criminal charges. Nixon nominated Gerald Ford, and Congress approved him. In 1974, President Ford had to replace himself. He had become president when President Nixon resigned because of the Watergate scandal. President Ford nominated Nelson Rockefeller, and Congress approved him. This was the only time in U.S. history that neither the president nor vice president was elected to office.

Third, the Twenty-fifth Amendment deals with replacing a president who is unable to carry out presidential duties. The president must notify the president pro tempore of the Senate and the Speaker of the House in writing. The vice president then becomes acting president. When the president is again able to carry out the duties of the office, notification must be sent to the president pro tem and the Speaker in writing. The vice president then gives up the duties as acting president.

Vice President George H. W. Bush temporarily assumed the responsibilities of president after the failed assassination attempt on President Ronald Reagan in 1981.

The amendment also states what happens if the president is unable to notify Congress. The vice president and either a majority of the heads of the executive departments or a majority of Congress must notify Congress in writing. The president once again takes up the duties of the office when a written message is sent indicating that the disability is no longer an issue.

If both the president and vice president are unable to carry out their duties, then the Succession Act of 1947 applies. The Speaker of the House is next in line to become president. If the Speaker is unable, the president pro tem of the Senate takes over. The table on page 159 lists the further order of presidential succession.

Putting It All Together

Imagine that a public figure whom you admire has just been nominated to run for president. In your notebook, write him or her an e-mail that lists the qualifications of the person he or she should look for in a vice-presidential running mate. Explain why each qualification is important.

The Cabinet as Advisors

Thinking on Your Own

Suppose you have just been elected president. One of your first jobs is to name people to run the executive departments. What qualifications would you want in your department heads? Discuss this question with a partner. Together, come up with two or three qualifications and list them in your notebook.

Voters elect a president to lead the nation and manage the federal government. However, he or she does not do these jobs alone. Once a candidate is elected, people are appointed to run the executive departments. The Constitution has only one mention of the relationship between the president and the heads of executive departments. Article II, Section 2, Clause 1, states that the president

focus your reading
Who makes up the president's cabinet?
What qualifications do heads of executive departments need to have?
What are the roles of the cabinet?

words to know
cabinet   inner cabinet

> . . . may require the opinion, in writing, of the principal officer in each of the executive departments, upon any subject relating to the duties of the respective offices . . .

However, the heads of executive departments play an active role in government decision-making.

Frances Perkins, the first female member of a president's cabinet, served as secretary of labor from 1933–1945.

The Cabinet

Since George Washington, every president has had a **cabinet**. These people advise the president and help set policy for the nation. In Washington's time, the heads of the executive departments made up his cabinet. In modern times, the president's cabinet also includes the vice president and several other top officials. These other officials are part of the Executive Office of the President, which you will read about in Lesson 3.

Being named to head an executive department is a great honor. However, not everyone accepts. These jobs are very stressful and not very high-paying. If a person accepts, he or she must be confirmed by the Senate.

The person must appear before the Senate committee that deals with the department the person will run. Usually, the hearing is friendly, and the committee sends the nominee's name to the full Senate for approval. However, sometimes a person's past actions may raise issues among committee members. Questioning may become heated. However, in the end, committees usually send the person's name to the full Senate.

Selecting the Heads of Departments

The president weighs a number of factors in deciding whom to appoint to lead executive departments. First, the person should have experience with the work of the department. For example, the head of the agriculture department should have firsthand knowledge of the issues involved in modern farming. Second, the person should have experience managing large organizations. The executive departments have thousands of workers and budgets in the billions of dollars. For this reason, presidents often choose successful business executives.

Cabinet-Level Officials

Heads of Executive Departments

Secretary of State
Secretary of the Treasury
Secretary of Defense
Attorney General (Justice Department)
Secretary of the Interior
Secretary of Agriculture
Secretary of Commerce
Secretary of Labor
Secretary of Health and Human Services
Secretary of Transportation
Secretary of Energy
Secretary of Housing and Urban Development
Secretary of Education
Secretary of Veterans Affairs
Secretary of Homeland Security

Other Cabinet Members

Vice President

White House Chief of Staff
Director, Office of Management and Budget
Director, Environmental Protection Agency
United States Trade Representative
Director, Office of National Drug
    Control Policy

The order shown here is the order of succession named in the Twenty-fifth Amendment.

Robert Weaver (left), the first African-American member of a president's cabinet, served as secretary of housing and urban development in the administration of President Lyndon Johnson. Madeline K. Albright (second from left), the first woman to serve as secretary of state, was appointed by President Bill Clinton. Elaine Chao (second from right), secretary of labor during the George W. Bush administration, is the first Asian American to serve in a president's cabinet. President Ronald Reagan appointed Lauro F. Cavazos (right) as secretary of education, the first Hispanic to serve in a president's cabinet.

Third, the president has to consider interest groups. Interest groups often play important roles in electing candidates to office. They expect their candidates, once elected, to be responsive to their interests. Suppose the airline industry has helped to elect the president. They then expect the president to appoint someone to the Department of Commerce who will help the airlines.

Fourth, the president also tries to balance the members of the cabinet. He tries to select people from different parts of the country and from urban and rural backgrounds. Geographic balance helps ensure that the concerns of all regions are heard.

Gender and ethnic balance are also important. Since the 1960s, presidents have become more aware of balancing ethnic backgrounds and gender.

The Role of the Cabinet

Cabinet members who are heads of executive departments have two duties. One is to run the departments they head. The other is to act as adviser to the president. However, presidents have not always called on their cabinets for advice.

Very strong presidents have tended to tell their cabinets what to do. Abraham Lincoln and Lyndon Johnson, for example, set national policy and expected their cabinets to carry it out.

Later presidents have used the experience of their cabinets to help shape policy. Both George H. W. Bush and Bill Clinton consulted their cabinets regularly. These two presidents would put ideas on the table and ask for cabinet members' opinions.

Review the paragraph that you wrote in Thinking on Your Own. How do your ideas match what actual presidents look for in department heads? Discuss the similarities and differences with a partner. Revise your paragraph to include at least two qualifications that an actual president considers. If your ideas match, then revise your paragraph to add another qualification from the president's list.

Even when presidents rarely consult their full cabinets, they do listen to certain cabinet members. These are generally the heads of the four main departments: Defense, State, Treasury, and Justice. They make up what is called the **inner cabinet**. These department heads meet regularly one-on-one with the president. The secretaries of other departments tend to meet with the president only in large cabinet meetings. Some presidents call full cabinet meetings weekly, and some rarely call them at all.

A president wants a department head who will be loyal. Once they take office, however, department heads may find this difficult. Members of their own departments, members of Congress, and special interest groups compete for their loyalty. All three groups have their own ideas about what the secretary should do. Their ideas may not be the same as the president's. This can set up tension between the secretary and the president.

The White House staff and members of the Executive Office of the President may also become close advisers to presidents. They usually are intensely loyal to the chief executives they serve. The president may find them more trustworthy than a cabinet member who is trying to advance his or her own interests. Most presidents place a high value on loyalty and trust.

Putting It All Together

Work with a partner. Draw a small circle inside a larger circle. Then draw a bigger circle around these two. Label the smallest circle "President." In the middle circle, write the names of the executive departments that make up the president's inner cabinet. Also in the middle circle, include the offices in the cabinet that are not heads of executive departments. In the outer circle, write the names of the other executive departments.

The Executive Office and the White House Staff

Thinking on Your Own

What personal qualities do you think an adviser to the president should have? Discuss this question with a partner and list at least three personal qualities in your notebook.

The main constitutional job of the president is to oversee the executive branch. Today, this is an enormous task. The executive branch has over 2.7 million civilian employees in 15 departments and other agencies and commissions. Two offices have evolved to help the president with this job. They are the **Executive Office of the President** (EOP) and the **White House Office**.

In general, the people who work in the EOP and the White House Office have three main goals. First, they offer

The West Wing houses the offices of the executive branch.

advice and information to help the president make decisions. They usually have special expertise in the areas they work in. For example, the people in the Office of Management and Budget (OMB) have financial and budgeting experience.

Second, members of the EOP and White House Office help carry out the president's ideas. For example, offices such as that of the U.S. Trade Representative may write bills for Congress to consider. An office such as the Environmental Protection Agency may actually carry out laws. EOP and White House staff members also push members of Congress to act on the president's proposals.

Third, the EOP and White House Office help the president to manage the executive branch. The president's advisers and staff members keep in touch with the executive departments, agencies, and commissions. They pass information back and forth. In this way, the president knows what is going on and the executive branch knows what the president expects.

Presidential Libraries

Every president since Herbert Hoover has built a library to house his presidential papers. Actually, the 12 presidential libraries and the Nixon Presidential Materials Project maintain much more than documents. Each building is both a museum and a library.

The interior of President Herbert Hoover's Presidential Library (top) and President Bill Clinton's Presidential Library (bottom)

Together, they store 400 million pages in print or electronic form. There are also close to 10 million photographs; 15 million feet of movie film; nearly 100,000 hours of material on discs, audiotapes, and videotapes; and about 500,000 objects. Among the objects are presidential family photos as well as gifts given to presidents by leaders of other nations.

The documents of each administration, however, are the most valuable part of each library. They provide historians with firsthand accounts of the thinking behind policy decisions.

Each library is built with private contributions. Each library must also set up a fund to help maintain the library. The rest of the money comes from the federal government.

Some Offices Within the Executive Office of the President

Office	Responsibility
Council of Economic Advisers	• Helps the president decide on economic policy for the nation • Is the president's major source of information on the health of the economy • Predicts future economic growth • Suggests solutions to economic problems such as high unemployment • Helps write the annual *Economic Report of the President*
Council on Environmental Quality	• Advises the president on environmental issues • Works with the Environmental Protection Agency and the Interior, Energy, and Agriculture Departments to ensure that environmental policies are carried out
Domestic Policy Council	• Aids the president in developing and carrying out long-range policies in all areas that are not concerned with foreign affairs; for example, an energy policy for the nation
National Economic Council	• Helps carry out long-range economic policies
National Security Council	• Advises the president on foreign policy issues that affect the nation's security • Chaired by the president • Includes the vice president and Secretaries of State and Defense, as well as other advisers • Managed by the National Security Adviser
Office of Administration	• Handles the day-to-day needs of the other EOP groups such as clerical help and library services
Office of Faith-Based and Community Initiatives	• Oversees efforts to expand the work of religious and other private groups working to fight drug abuse, illiteracy, and similar problems of society
Office of Management and Budget	• Reviews budgets submitted by each executive department and other agencies and commissions • Recommends to the president changes in the budgets of executive departments, agencies, and commissions • Uses information from all departments, agencies, and commissions and prepares the federal budget that the president sends to Congress each year • Reviews how the funds in the approved budget are used during the year • Reviews all bills proposed by executive departments before they are sent to Congress to ensure they agree with the president's policies
Office of National AIDS Policy	• Develops and advises on the nation's policy and programs for the prevention and potential cure of HIV-AIDS
Office of National Drug Control Policy	• Develops long-range policies on the control of illegal drugs
Office of Science and Technology Policy	• Advises the president on scientific, engineering, and technology issues
Office of the United States Trade Representative	• Negotiates trade agreements with other nations
President's Critical Infrastructure Protection Board	• Advises the president on security issues related to cyberspace
President's Foreign Intelligence Advisory Board	• Advises the president on how effective the intelligence, or spy, agencies are in collecting information to keep the nation secure from enemies

Executive Office of the President

Congress created the Executive Office of the President (EOP) in 1939 to provide the president the staff needed to oversee the executive branch. It has grown over time, as every president adds offices, councils, and boards. A president changes the EOP to meet changes in the nation and to provide information necessary to perform the duties of president. For example, before the late 1980s there was no reason to have an Office on National AIDS Policy. AIDS was not an issue.

As the nation has grown, its problems have become more complex. Presidents must make decisions about how to deal with these very complex issues. As a result, the president must be able to ask the advice of people who have experience with these issues. For example, the growth of the World Wide Web resulted in the creation of the President's Critical Infrastructure Protection Board. This board deals with dangers to the nation's security from cyberspace.

stop and think

For which group within the EOP would you like to work? Why? List at least four reasons why you want to work for that group. Share your list with a partner. Ask your partner how you could make your ideas clearer.

Offices within the EOP coordinate federal efforts to address issues. For example, the nation's anti-drug program is managed by 50 agencies. The Office of National Drug Control Policy was created to oversee the activities of these agencies. The office is supposed to make sure that there are no overlaps among the agencies' programs.

Three of the most important agencies in the EOP are the Council of Economic Advisers, the National Security Council, and the Office of Management and Budget (OMB). The OMB is the largest group within the EOP.

With each new president, offices, councils, boards, and agencies within the EOP may change. Even during a president's term, he or she may add or do away with a group within the EOP.

The White House Office

The White House Office is part of the Executive Office of the President. It includes the president's key staff and personal advisers. They have a great deal of influence in shaping policies for the nation. They decide who sees the president. They also decide which of the thousands of reports that come from the executive departments to send to the president.

The Oval Office is the official office of the president of the United States.

The president appoints the main members of the White House Office. Unlike the heads of departments and some EOP members, none of the White House staff need to be confirmed by the Senate. Many of the top White House staff have worked with the president for years in previous jobs or as friends and unpaid advisers.

Among the most important positions are the chief of staff, White House counsel, and the press secretary. The chief of staff manages the White House Office. The White House counsel provides legal advice to the president on policy. The press secretary handles daily, and sometimes hourly, **briefings** to the reporters who follow the actions of the president.

Putting It All Together

With a partner, write a summary of this lesson. Be sure to include only the most important ideas. Do not include your own opinions.

Participate in Government

Be a Poll Watcher

A poll watcher is called a poll checker in some states. *Poll* is another word for ballot, or vote. Poll watchers monitor, or check, what goes on at the polling place. They are volunteers working for a political party. Their job is to make sure that anyone from their party who is registered to vote is allowed to vote. They also make sure that no one votes more than once.

Poll watchers sit near the check-in table with election workers. A voter comes to the table to sign in. An election worker calls out the voter's name. The poll checkers read down their lists. If the voter is a Republican, the Republican poll watcher checks off his or her name. If the voter is a Democrat, the Democratic poll watcher checks it off.

Suppose there is a problem. A voter is newly registered. By accident, his or her name is not yet in the registration book. The poll watcher watches to make sure that the voter is allowed to cast a provisional ballot.

Poll watchers may not wear any political buttons or signs. They may not talk about a candidate while on duty. However, they may carry signs and ask voters to vote for their candidate outside the polling place.

- Check the phone book for the number of your local or county political party committee. Call and ask what the qualifications are to be a poll watcher.

- Visit your local candidates' offices.

Skill Builder

Outline Information

An outline is an organized listing of information. Only the most important information about a topic is presented. The form for an outline is always a combination of Roman and Arabic numerals and capital and small letters.

I. Roman numerals for main ideas
    A. Capital letters for important details
        1. Arabic numerals for supporting details
           a. Small letters for less important details

Use Roman numerals for the biggest ideas—the main ideas. Use capital letters, Arabic numerals, and small letters as the information gets more detailed. If the information is not too detailed, you might need only capital letters or capital letters and Arabic numerals.

Outlines are useful for studying and for writing. Outlining a lesson or chapter helps to focus on just the important information to study. Outlining before writing an assignment helps to organize main ideas and supporting details.

A partial outline for Lesson 1 looks like this:

I. The Presidency
    A. Qualifications
        1. Native-born
        2. At least thirty-five years old
    B. Campaign chest
II. The Job of Vice President

Complete these activities.

1 Outline Lesson 2 to help you study the information.

2 Write an essay of at least three paragraphs to describe how cabinet members are chosen and what cabinet members do. Before you write, plan your writing by creating an outline. Use one Roman numeral for each paragraph. Add information with capital letters and Arabic numerals to help you fill out each paragraph.

Chapter

9

THE POWERS OF THE PRESIDENCY

Getting Focused

Skim this chapter to predict what you will be learning.

- Read the lesson titles and subheadings.
- Look at the illustrations and read the captions.
- Examine the table.
- Review the vocabulary words and terms.

As you learned from skimming this chapter, the president has many responsibilities. In your notebook, list the five duties of a president that you consider to be the most important.

President George W. Bush with Secretary of State Condoleezza Rice, in the oval office.

Executive Powers

Thinking on Your Own

Name two or three U.S. presidents who are remembered as powerful chief executives. What did they do to expand the powers of the presidency? List as many facts as you can in your notebook about each president.

The Framers could not have imagined the many issues that a modern president deals with, such as terrorism, the Internet, and relations with more than 190 other nations. However, the Framers were very wise. Their idea for the presidency allows for growth and change as the nation grows and changes.

Constitutional Source of Power

Article II of the U.S. Constitution creates the executive branch and the office of president. The first job of the president is to run the executive department. This is part of the oath of office that the president takes at his inauguration.

President Nixon's 1972 visit to China represents the foreign policy powers of the presidency.

He promises to "faithfully execute the office of president." **Execute** in this context means to carry out, or perform, the duties of president.

Section 2 of Article II lists the powers of the president. Power comes with duties, and Section 3 lists the president's duties. The president's powers and duties can be grouped as executive, military, diplomatic, legislative, and judicial. That is, the president appoints department heads, ambassadors, and federal judges; is commander in chief; and issues pardons. The president's powers and duties are discussed in Chapter 3.

The checks and balances written into the Constitution limit the president's powers. For example, his power to appoint federal judges and department heads is checked by the Senate. The Senate has the power to approve or reject his appointments. Presidents can ignore the Senate by making **recess appointments** when that body is not in session. These appointments last only until the end of Congress's next session. The Senate still has the last word.

Informal Sources of Power

Despite the limited powers granted by the Constitution, presidents have found ways to increase the powers of the office. They have expanded its inherent, or informal, powers. As a result, the presidency is more powerful today than it was in the days of George Washington.

One reason for this increase in power is the way presidents do their job. Strong presidents exercise firm control over the federal government. In exercising control, they expand what the presidency can do. For example, Thomas Jefferson agreed to buy the Louisiana Territory from France. The Constitution does not state that the president—or the nation—has the power to add territory.

However, Jefferson and his advisers found an inherent power in the Constitution. Inherent power is power that the president has because he is the president. Using inherent power, Jefferson bought the Louisiana Territory. Once Jefferson set the pattern, later presidents acquired more territory. They added the rest of the continental United States and also Alaska, Hawaii, Puerto Rico, Guam, and other territories.

Presidents have also gained power during times of national crises. In 1861, the federal government was not prepared for the Civil War. President Abraham Lincoln took it upon himself to expand the army and navy. He later asked Congress to approve his actions by passing the necessary laws. Franklin D. Roosevelt strengthened the presidency by taking bold action during the Great Depression.

> **stop and think**
>
> Create a concept map to show the sources of the president's powers. Draw a large circle in the center and label it "Sources of Power." Then add smaller circles as needed. Work with a partner. When you have finished your concept map, write a statement to explain the sources of the president's powers.

President Ronald Reagan and Vice President George H. W. Bush.

His White House staff wrote many of the bills that Congress passed to put people back to work.

The mandate of the people is the third, and probably the greatest, source of presidential power. A **mandate** is strong support from the people. In 1980, Ronald Reagan won 489 electoral votes, representing 44 states and 50 percent of the vote. He claimed a mandate from the people to put his ideas into practice.

Presidents use a variety of ways to get their ideas across to the public. They use televised speeches and interviews. They also give interviews to newspaper and magazine reporters. Presidents also send out the heads of executive departments to talk about presidential policies. The goal of all these actions is to keep up public support for the president's policies.

Limits on Presidential Powers

Congress, the federal courts, the federal bureaucracy, and public opinion all limit a president's power. The Senate has the power of "advice and consent" over presidential nominees. In fact, few nominees are ever rejected. It is a courtesy to allow the president to choose his own cabinet members. However, nominees for federal judgeships are sometimes rejected. This includes nominees for the Supreme Court.

As you read in Chapter 7, Congress may override a presidential veto and has the power of the purse. Congress decides on the federal budget each year. It may or may not fund programs at the amount that the president asks. Congress also has impeachment power over the president.

Federal courts have the power to rule on the constitutionality of presidential actions. The Landmark Case on page 173 describes an example.

Public opinion can give the president a mandate to act, but it can also turn against a president. If people do not like a president's policies, it shows up in opinion polls. If presidents lose public support, getting Congress to pass their proposals can be difficult.

Landmark Supreme Court Case: Presidential Authority

Youngstown Sheet and Tube Company v. *Sawyer* (1952): During the Korean War, steelworkers were threatening to strike. President Harry Truman believed a steel strike would harm the war effort. The president took over most of the nation's steel mills and had the military run them. He said the inherent powers of the presidency allowed him to act. The Supreme Court ruled against him.

Public opinion played a large role during the Vietnam war and influenced President Johnson's decision not to seek reelection.

Putting It All Together

Outline this lesson. Review outlining on page 168 if necessary. Share your outline with a partner. Ask your partner to check it for completeness. If you missed important information, revise your outline.

Roles and Duties of the President

Thinking on Your Own

Read the Ideas to Remember in this lesson. It lists the roles of the president. Create a table in your notebook with two columns. In the left column, write the seven roles of the president. As you study this lesson, fill in the right column. Write at least one fact about each role of the president, and name a president who was a model for that role.

Article II, Sections 1 and 2, of the U.S. Constitution describe the powers and duties of the president. He or she has five roles, or responsibilities, based on these powers and duties. They are: head of state, chief executive, chief legislator, chief diplomat, and commander in chief.

Anyone who has ever watched a presidential nominating convention knows that the president has a sixth role. He is the leader of his political party. Also, since Franklin Roosevelt, the president has been the chief economic planner for the nation. These two roles are not part of the president's constitutional powers and duties. They developed over time.

focus your reading

What are the official constitutional duties of the president?

What are the unofficial duties of the president?

words to know

ceremonial duties

diplomat

executive order

partisan

President George W. Bush and former Presidents Bush and Clinton attend the funeral of Pope John Paul II in 2005.

Constitutional Roles

Head of state: The president as the head of state represents the United States to the world and to the nation and performs certain **ceremonial duties**.

For example, on Veterans Day, the president lays a wreath at the tomb of the Unknown Soldier in Arlington National Cemetery. Welcoming leaders from other nations to the White House is another ceremonial duty.

Chief executive: The president is also the chief executive of the United States. It is the president's job to see that the government carries out the laws that Congress passes. The president must also see that decisions of the federal courts are put into effect.

Chief legislator: The president is also the chief legislator. In this role, the president proposes the annual budget and other legislation to Congress. The executive departments and the EOP actually write proposed laws. These are then sent to Congress, as described in Chapter 7.

Chief diplomat: A **diplomat** is a person who represents the nation in dealings with governments of other nations.

The Constitution gives the president the power to make treaties, or formal agreements, with other nations. However, the Senate has the power to approve or reject them. The president also has the power to make executive agreements. These are agreements between the president and the heads of other nations. However, the Senate does not have to approve them. This is one way that presidents get around a Senate that does not agree with their foreign policies.

The president as chief diplomat also has the power to recognize other nations. To recognize means to accept the legal existence of another nation. For example, Communists defeated the non-Communist government of China in 1949. They set up a new government and declared it the People's Republic of China (PRC). However, it was not until 1972 that President Nixon recognized the PRC as China's government.

Commander in chief: The president is commander in chief of the armed forces. This role allows the president to use the military to support foreign policy goals. For example, President George W. Bush believed that Saddam Hussein had a program to build weapons of mass destruction (WMD) in Iraq. To rid Iraq of the WMD and Hussein, he took the United States into war.

As chief legislator, President Johnson met with congressional officials (top). In his role as chief diplomat, President Clinton welcomed South African President Nelson Mandela to the White House (middle). President George W. Bush greeted the troops as commander in chief.

The president decides when and if the nation should go to war. The president also approves or rejects requests from the armed forces for funding. However, Congress also has a role. It alone has the power to declare war. Congress also must approve all funding requests. However, as you read in Chapter 6, presidents have involved the nation in undeclared wars many times. As a result, Congress passed the War Powers Act in 1973.

Presidential Influence

	Influence in the Role of Chief Executive
Executive Orders	• **Executive orders** are regulations about how laws are to be carried out. For example, President Lyndon Johnson used an executive order to set up affirmative action. The order spelled out how the federal government is to award contracts for federal building projects. An executive order has the "force of law." This means it must be obeyed the same way a law must be obeyed.
Appointment of Officials	• Presidents appoint executive department heads and another 2,200 top-level officials. A president chooses men and women who agree with his policies and will work to carry them out. • Presidents also appoint federal judges, including Supreme Court justices. This is an area where a president's views can greatly affect government policy. Modern Republican presidents tend to appoint judges with more conservative views. Some of the justices on the Supreme Court are strict constructionists, which you read about in Chapter 6. Democratic presidents tend to appoint judges with more liberal views.
Removal of Officials	• Executive department heads, top-level officials, and members of the EOP and the White House Office serve "at the pleasure of the president." This means that if they oppose the president, they may find themselves out of a job. President George W. Bush fired his first secretary of the treasury for opposing his tax cuts.
	Influence in the Role of Chief Legislator
Granting Political Favors	• Presidents use political favors to gain congressional support for their policies. For example, the president might agree to campaign for a senator in return for his or her vote on a program.
Veto Power	• Presidents can always use the veto against a bill they do not want to become law. However, the threat of a veto can work as well. Congress will delay a bill or revise it rather than have it vetoed. Overriding a president's veto is difficult.

stop and think

Which constitutional role of the president do you think is the most important? Review the table that you created. Review what you have read up to this point. Select four roles and list one reason why each role is important. Discuss your ideas with a partner.

Presidents have another kind of power besides the powers given to them by the Constitution. They have the power of influence. They can use favors and try to persuade, pressure, and encourage Congress and others to do what they want. The table on page 176 lists the kinds of influence that presidents have.

Unofficial Roles

The five roles that you just read about are based on the Constitution. Over time, the presidency has expanded to include two more roles.

The role of economic planner became important during Franklin Roosevelt's terms in office. The nation was deep in the Depression. President Roosevelt took control of economic planning to pull the nation out of the Depression. The president sends a report on the state of the economy to Congress each year. In addition, the president sends the annual federal budget to Congress.

The president is also the head of his political party while he is in office. As party leader, he appears at fund-raisers for the party and for candidates. He also campaigns for his party's candidates for public office.

A president has to walk a fine line between partisan politics and public policy. **Partisan** means "following a certain party." Presidents are supposed to represent all Americans, not just those who belong to their political party.

ideas to remember

Official, constitutional duties and roles of the president

- head of state
- chief executive
- chief legislator
- chief diplomat
- commander in chief

Unofficial duties and roles of the president

- economic planner
- political party leader

Putting It All Together

Play "What Role Am I?" with a partner. Write a definition of each of the president's seven roles. End each definition with the question "What role am I?" Take turns with your partner asking and answering questions. Use the information from your table to write questions.

Presidential Leadership

Thinking on Your Own

What does the word *leadership* mean to you? Think of someone you know who is a leader. What qualities, or characteristics, do you think make a good leader? List at least three qualities of a good leader in your notebook. Add to your list as you read the lesson.

What makes a good president? Political scientists have debated this question for years. **Political scientists** study the principles and organization of government. They take opinion polls to find out what Americans think of their presidents. They also examine the records of past presidents to learn the effects of their actions. They have found that successful presidents share a number of qualities. Not all presidents have every quality. However, successful presidents have several of them.

focus your reading

What are the six qualities of presidential leadership?

Why is isolation a problem for presidents?

words to know

political scientists

landslide

political courage

The Qualities of Presidential Leadership

Successful presidents understand the hopes and fears of the American public. This understanding helps presidents gain public support. With public support, a president is better able to convince Congress to pass his or her proposals.

A good example is the 1932 election. President Herbert Hoover was a strong believer in limited action by the federal government. However, the American public wanted help in dealing with the Depression. Because of his ideas about limited government, Hoover could not address their needs. Franklin D. Roosevelt was more flexible. He promised that

the federal government would take forceful action to end the Depression. As a result, voters elected him president over President Hoover. Because he won in a landslide, Roosevelt was able to push his policies through Congress. A **landslide** is a victory with a huge number of votes.

The ability to communicate policies to the public is another important leadership quality. President Ronald Reagan, a former movie actor, was known as the "Great Communicator." He was very good at explaining his policies to the public and gaining support. President Reagan was in his seventies and a Republican. However, two-thirds of Americans in their twenties and early thirties believed the Republican Party had more new ideas and energy than the Democratic Party did.

Third, presidents need a sense of timing. They need to know whether or not the time is right to act. This may mean introducing a new program or changing an existing one. One of President Bill Clinton's greatest accomplishments was reforming the welfare system. He sensed that the rising costs of the program made the public ready to accept change.

reading for understanding

1. What is the subject of the president's speech?
2. What is the question that the president is trying to answer?
3. What is his answer?

A president needs leadership skills in difficult times. One of the most difficult is wartime. For example, the United States and its allies invaded Iraq in 2003. By mid-2005, many Americans wondered if the war was worth the monetary cost and the cost in lives. President George W. Bush went on television on June 28, 2005, to boost the nation's spirits. The following is part of that speech.

"Our mission in Iraq is clear. . . . We are helping Iraqis build a free nation that is an ally in the war on terror. We are advancing freedom in the broader Middle East. We are removing a source of violence and instability and laying the foundation of peace for our children and our grandchildren.

"The work in Iraq is difficult and it is dangerous. Like most Americans, I see the images of violence and bloodshed. Every picture is horrifying— and the suffering is real. Amid all this violence, I know Americans ask the question: Is the sacrifice worth it? It is worth it, and it is vital to the future security of our country."

—George W. Bush, *Address to the Nation*, June 28, 2005

Fourth, presidents should be flexible in their thinking. They need to be willing to listen to and accept new ideas. One way they do this is by encouraging their advisers to voice differing opinions in discussions. Both Presidents George H. W. Bush and Bill Clinton welcomed debate among their advisers.

Fifth, a president should be willing to compromise. Compromise is an important part of the interaction between opposing views. Democrats and Republicans have many differences. However, they also have many common interests. A successful president works with the opposite party and with those within his own party who disagree with him. President Bill Clinton compromised with the Republican-controlled Congress to get a series of proposals passed in 1996. In compromising, he angered some of his own party members. His supporters said that the president showed political courage, another leadership quality.

Political courage is the courage to do what a person thinks is right even though the person's own party and voters disagree. Sometimes a president is proven right and sometimes not. For example, in 1968, much of the nation turned against the Vietnam War. However, President Lyndon Johnson continued to send troops to Vietnam. He had to pull out of the presidential election because of lack of support from his own party and from the American public.

President Clinton is often credited as having political courage.

The Isolation of Presidents

The president has many advisers in the cabinet, the EOP, and the White House Office. These people work for the president. Within this larger circle, there is often a small group of advisers. This inner circle is perhaps ten or fewer people. The president sees them on a daily basis. Usually, many of them have been with the president for a long time. They may have worked for him in other jobs. They may also have helped him win election to the presidency. He trusts them completely.

President Richard Nixon in 1969

This small inner circle of advisers represents a potential danger. Sometimes staff members limit others' access, or contact, with the president on purpose. They may do this to enlarge their own influence on the president. They may also do it because they truly believe the president is already too busy. If the president hears only from the same people, he or she can become isolated. The president may hear only praise for the various policies that are in place and never hear conflicting points of view.

Different presidents have reacted to presidential isolation in different ways. President Richard Nixon did not want people around him who disagreed with him. As the Watergate scandal unfolded, he closed himself off more and more from outside opinions. President George H. W. Bush, on the other hand, enlarged his circle of trusted advisers. He included many members of his cabinet in it. He did not rely on just an inner circle.

Putting It All Together

Review the list of leadership qualities that you wrote in Thinking on Your Own. In your notebook, list three qualities that you would add after having read this lesson. Identify at least one quality that would help prevent a president from becoming isolated. Then exchange your list with a partner and decide if your partner could make his or her list clearer. Suggest how your partner could revise the topics on the list.

Participate in Government

Become a Candidate

Do you want to have a say in school board decisions? Are you interested in improving public services such as garbage collection in your community? Do you think your county should spend more on road repair? Do you want your state legislature to repeal the state income tax?

Steve Allen, nineteen, was elected to the Riverside Town Council in Riverside, AL, in 2004.

These are some of the reasons that prompt people to run for public office. Being elected to public office gives a person a direct say in government. Age is not always a problem. High school students have been elected to school boards and to town councils. State legislators are sometimes in their twenties.

Age, length of residency, and other requirements vary from state to state. The process for becoming a candidate also varies. This is true for local as well as statewide elections. Usually, a person who wants to run for office must

- obtain an official petition from the state or local elections board.
- gather the required number of signatures from registered voters.
- file the petition with the elections board by the deadline.

Running for office costs money. Candidates need to pay for newspaper, television, cable, and radio ads. They also need to pay for printing brochures and mailing them to voters. A major expense is telephones. Volunteers use them to call voters to talk about the candidate and ask for support. No candidate can be successful without excited volunteers.

Skill Builder

Analyze Primary and Secondary Sources

A primary source describes an event or idea firsthand. It may be a speech, letter, memo, report, autobiography, photograph, painting, cartoon, poem, or song. The creator may have been part of the event or an eyewitness to it. A primary source may also be a person's explanation of his or her ideas. President Bush's speech on page 179 is a primary source.

A secondary source is not an eyewitness account. The creator pulls together information from others to create the work. Government reports are secondary sources. Newspaper articles may also be secondary sources if they summarize information.

The following is an excerpt from a newspaper article that was published before the president's speech:

WASHINGTON (AP)—President George W. Bush is using the first anniversary of Iraq's sovereignty to try to ease Americans' doubts about the mission. . . .

In a prime-time address from Fort Bragg, N.C., home of the Army's elite 82nd Airborne Division, Bush was to argue that there is no need to change course in Iraq despite the upsetting images produced by daily insurgent attacks. . . .

Secretary of State Condoleezza Rice said today that Bush will stress the need for patience. . . .

Tapping into Americans' emotions over terrorists' attacks, White House Press Secretary Scott McClellan said Bush will talk about insurgents killing innocent people and how stopping the violence "will be a major blow to the ambitions of the terrorists."

—*Columbia Daily Tribune*, June 28, 2005

Answer the following questions.

1 What is the news article about?

2 Does it reprint the president's speech or summarize it?

3 What information does the news article give that the speech does not?

Chapter

10 THE FEDERAL BUREAUCRACY

Getting Focused

Skim this chapter to predict what you will be learning.

- Read the lesson titles and subheadings.
- Look at the illustrations and read the captions.
- Examine the tables.
- Review the vocabulary words and terms.

What do you already know about the federal agencies and commissions listed below? Write a sentence to explain what each of the following does. Answer as many as you can.

- Internal Revenue Service
- Federal Bureau of Investigation
- Secret Service
- Amtrak
- Food and Drug Administration
- Coast Guard
- United States Postal Service

The United States Coast Guard, along with dozens of other agencies, represents part of the vast federal bureaucracy.

Departments, Agencies, and Commissions

Thinking on Your Own

Turn each subheading in this lesson into a question in your notebook before you read. After you read the lesson, answer each question that you wrote.

The first Congress created three executive departments—foreign affairs, war, and treasury—and the position of attorney general. Today, there are 15 executive departments to deal with the issues facing the nation in the twenty-first century. The executive branch also has independent agencies, corporations, boards, and commissions. In 1801, the federal government had 2,120 civilian employees. Today, 2.7 million civilian employees work for the federal government.

focus your reading

What areas of government do executive departments manage?

Explain the role that independent agencies play in the federal government.

What is the purpose of regulatory commissions?

words to know

independent agency

government corporation

independent regulatory commission

deregulation

The Executive Departments

In Chapter 8, you read that the heads of the executive departments make up the president's cabinet. Their main role, however, is to manage the departments of the executive branch. The table on pages 186–187 describes the main responsibilities of each department.

Each department is further divided into agencies. These are smaller groups that have particular duties within the larger executive department. For example, the National Park Service (NPS) is part of the Department of the Interior. The NPS takes care of all national parks, national seashore areas, national battlefields, and national monuments.

The Executive Departments

Executive Department	Main Responsibilities and Important Agencies
State, 1789 **(originally Foreign Affairs)**	• Advises the president on foreign affairs • Protects the rights of U.S. citizens traveling in other nations • Represents the United States at the United Nations and in other global organizations • Maintains embassies and other agencies in foreign countries
Treasury, 1789	• Prints paper money and makes coins • Collects taxes through the Internal Revenue Service • Borrows money for the federal government • Regulates the production and sale of alcohol, tobacco, and firearms
Defense, 1789 (originally War)	• Maintains the armed forces to protect the nation
Interior, 1849	• Protects and manages public lands such as national parks and national historic sites • Oversees the use of natural resources • Provides aid to Native Americans living on reservations
Justice, 1870 **(attorney general became head** **of the department)**	• Advises the president on legal issues • Investigates and prosecutes anyone accused of a federal crime • Enforces federal laws such as civil rights laws • Operates federal prisons
Agriculture, 1889	• Develops and administers soil and water conservation programs • Provides financial aid to farmers and ranchers through loans and subsidies, or interest-free payments • Manages the national forests • Oversees food stamp and school lunch programs
Commerce, 1903	• Takes the national census, which means it counts the nation's population every ten years • Issues patents for inventions and registers copyrights for creative works such as books • Sets standards, or values, for weights and measurements; for example, a pound is always 16 ounces • Encourages the nation's economic growth by supporting business and technological development
Labor, 1913	• Enforces federal laws on working conditions, the minimum wage, and pension benefits • Manages unemployment insurance and worker compensation programs • Develops and runs job-training programs • Encourages cooperation between business and labor

Executive Department	Main Responsibilities and Important Agencies
Housing and Urban Development, 1965	• Enforces federal fair-housing laws • Works to preserve and renew cities and neighborhoods • Manages home mortgage, rent subsidy, and public housing programs
Transportation, 1966	• Regulates the nation's transportation systems • Regulates oil and gas pipelines
Energy, 1977	• Develops the nation's energy policy • Conducts research on and develops new energy technologies such as solar, or sun, power • Encourages energy conservation • Conducts research on nuclear weapons
Health and Human Services, 1979	• Manages Medicare and Medicaid • Funds medical research • Approves new drugs for sale • Runs disease prevention and control programs through the Center for Disease Control • Enforces pure food and drug laws
Education, 1979	• Enforces federal education laws such as Individuals with Disabilities Education Act (IDEA) and No Child Left Behind (NCLB) • Oversees federal funding programs for public and private schools • Oversees federal loan programs for students
Veterans Affairs, 1989	• Operates veterans' hospitals • Manages educational training, pension, and medical benefits programs for veterans • Operates military cemeteries
Homeland Security, 2002	• Oversees the security of the nation's borders, transportation systems, oil and gas pipelines, electric power sources, and similar resources • Enforces immigration laws • Manages emergency preparedness and the response to emergencies • Protects the president, vice president, and other top-level officials through the Secret Service

In 2002, Congress created the Department of Homeland Security to deal with terrorism. Many of the executive departments had to give up some of their agencies. These were agencies that dealt with the nation's borders, transportation security, and response to emergencies.

The National Park Service monitors the Golden Gate Bridge during a heightened security alert.

Independent Agencies

As you just read, each executive department is made up of agencies. In addition, the executive branch has close to 150 **independent agencies**. These are not part of any executive department. Some, like the Social Security Administration, are as large as, or larger than, executive departments.

stop and think

Reread the table on executive departments on pages 186–187. Make a list of the departments that affect your life in some way. Next to each department, write a sentence to explain how it affects your life. Share your list with a partner and compare your experiences.

Some Government Corporations

Government Corporation	Area of Business
Corporation for Public Broadcasting	• Oversees public-supported radio and television stations • Provides some funding for developing programs
Federal Deposit Insurance Corporation (FDIC)	• Insures bank accounts up to a certain limit. If a bank fails, its depositors will get their money up to that limit.
Federal Election Commission (FEC)	• Enforces federal laws dealing with campaign funding
National Railroad Passenger Corporation (Amtrak)	• Operates the nation's passenger railroad service
Pension Guaranty Corporation	• Protects employees pension plans when companies go bankrupt
Tennessee Valley Authority (TVA)	• Operates electric power plants in eight southeastern states
United States Postal Service (USPS)	• Runs the nation's mail service

Congress creates independent agencies for two main reasons. First, some agencies do not match the work of any executive department. For example, the General Services Administration (GSA) is responsible for all federal buildings. It is the federal government's housekeeper. The GSA oversees the construction of all federal buildings and their upkeep after they are built. No executive department has similar duties.

Second, Congress sets up some independent agencies that need to be free from political pressure. The Government Accountability Office (GAO), for example, investigates how executive departments and other agencies use government resources. It needs to be free from interference to do its job.

The federal government also runs more than 50 **government corporations**. These, too, are considered independent agencies. Congress sets up these corporations to be run as businesses. Executives and a board of directors head them. Any profits go back into the business. The federal government covers losses. As you can see by the table on page 188, government corporations run many kinds of businesses.

U.S. Consumer Product Safety Commission Chairman Hal Stratton shows a product that was recalled due to safety concerns.

ideas to remember

The federal bureaucracy is made up of

- executive departments
- independent agencies
- government corporations
- regulatory commissions

It is important to remember that independent agencies and government corporations are not independent of the government. They are part of the executive branch. Although established by Congress, they report to the president. The president appoints their chief executives, boards, and often other top officials.

Independent Regulatory Commissions

Independent regulatory commissions make rules that govern how industries and businesses operate. There are ten independent regulatory commissions. The table on page 190 lists them.

Independent Regulatory Commissions

Independent Regulatory Commission	Major Duties
Consumer Product Safety Commission (CPSC)	• Creates and enforces safety standards for products • Oversees recalls of unsafe products
Commodity Futures Trading Commission (CFTC)	• Regulates the commodities markets, which buy and sell goods, such as farm products, and metals, like aluminum
Federal Communications Commission (FCC)	• Regulates television, cable, radio, and satellite businesses
Federal Energy Regulatory Commission (FERC)	• Sets rates for and regulates the oil, natural gas, and electricity industries
Federal Maritime Commission (FMC)	• Regulates the shipping industry
Federal Reserve System (the Fed)	• Oversees the banking system • Regulates the money supply
Federal Trade Commission (FTC)	• Enforces laws against unfair business activities
National Labor Relations Board (NLRB)	• Enforces labor-management laws
Nuclear Regulatory Commission (NRC)	• Regulates all uses of nuclear materials by civilians
Securities and Exchange Commission (SEC)	• Regulates investment companies, stock and bond brokers, and stock and bond exchanges • Enforces laws against dishonest investment activities

Independent regulatory commissions are different from independent agencies and government corporations in several ways. Independent regulatory commissions do not report to the president. They are independent of both the executive and legislative branches. Congress set them up in this way so political pressure would not affect their decisions.

A board of commissioners directs each independent regulatory commission. A commission has from 5 to 11 members. They serve from 4 to 14 years, depending on the commission. This means that many members will serve longer than the president who appointed them. No more than half the members, plus one, may belong to any single political party. The Senate must approve all nominees. Presidents cannot fire commissioners once they are appointed.

Independent regulatory commissions have both legislative and judicial powers. Commissions make rules for the industries they oversee. For example, the FCC decides how many television and cable stations a company may own in an area of the country. When commissions investigate supposed wrongdoing in an industry, they use their judicial powers. In the early 2000s, the SEC investigated fraud by various corporations. When the SEC found wrongdoing, it fined the corporations heavily.

For years, critics charged that business was too heavily regulated. Since the 1970s, Congress and both Democratic and Republican presidents have worked to lessen regulations. Regulations in the airline, trucking, and railroad industries were greatly reduced. This is known as **deregulation**.

Putting It All Together

Create a three-column chart. Write "Executive Departments," "Independent Agencies," and "Regulatory Commissions" at the top of the columns. In each column, explain in one or two sentences how that type of government agency is different from the other two.

The Civil Service System

Thinking on Your Own

Review the information about departments, agencies, and commissions in Lesson 1. Choose one that you might like to work for. List three reasons for your choice in your notebook. How would you apply for this job? Write a paragraph, using the vocabulary words, stating your choice and explaining your reasons.

Who works in the federal bureaucracy? Who gets these jobs? What are the qualifications for working for the federal government? How are people hired for these jobs?

The Beginning of the Civil Service System

The **civil service system** is the process the federal government uses to hire, employ, and promote workers. Federal government workers are called **civil servants**. To be hired, a person must have the required education and skills. He or she may also have to pass a competitive exam.

From the beginning of the nation, presidents appointed supporters to government jobs. It was a way to thank them. Government jobs were called **patronage**. Appointing supporters to public offices became known as the **spoils system**. After he took office, President Andrew Jackson, for example, fired about 1,000 federal employees. Their jobs went to his supporters. Many politicians, not just

focus your reading

Explain why Congress created the civil service system.

Describe how ordinary people get jobs in the federal government today.

Why are political appointees given jobs in the federal government?

Why are government workers not allowed to participate in political activities?

words to know

civil service system

civil servant

patronage

spoils system

political appointee

career civil servant

"Keep her head straight for Civil Service reform" is the original caption of this cartoon of President Grover Cleveland at the helm of a ship in stormy weather.

presidents, gave government jobs to supporters. Big-city politicians and state leaders created their own spoils systems.

As early as the 1850s, people were calling for reform of government employment. However, little was done until 1883. In that year, Congress passed the Pendleton Act. It created the present civil service system. Congress acted after President James A. Garfield was killed in 1881. A man who had been turned down for a government job shot him.

About 2,200 jobs in the executive department are not part of the civil service system. The president names people to these jobs. Those who get them are called **political appointees**. Congress must approve some of the appointees. These include the heads of executive departments and ambassadors.

U.S. Ambassador to Great Britain Robert H. Tuttle, a political appointee, signs a guest book in London after the terror attacks in July 2005.

These high-level jobs go to political supporters of the president. They may not have experience with the issues in the particular group they run. They hold their jobs only as long as the president is in office. Because of this, career civil servants run the departments, agencies, and commissions on a day-to-day basis. They also create much of the policy that each department, agency, and commission carries out. A **career civil servant** is a not a political appointee. It is a person who expects to work for the government for many years.

The Modern Civil Service

The Office of Personnel Management (OPM) handles employment for the federal government. The OPM is an independent agency in the executive branch. The president appoints the director. The Senate must approve the person.

Scientists at the National Institutes of Health (left) are part of the civil service system. U.S. Ambassador to Pakistan John K. Bauman (right) is a political appointee.

The OPM is the main recruiter for federal employees. Job openings are advertised on bulletin boards in post offices and in newspapers. They are also posted on the OPM's Web site. The OPM gives the civil service exams for clerical and secretarial jobs. It also keeps lists of the people who pass. The top three candidates are sent to an agency when a job opens for which they qualify. The OPM also recruits professionals such as lawyers, doctors, accountants, and social workers.

stop and think

How did the civil service system change the way employees were hired and fired for government jobs? Discuss this question with a partner. Make notes. Then, write a paragraph to answer the question. Share your paragraphs.

One reason for creation of the civil service system was to protect workers' jobs. Government employees, however, can be fired. A manager who wants to fire an employee must have serious reasons. He or she must go through a number of hearings to prove that the person should be let go.

Political Activities

In the past, many people feared that political parties would take advantage of government workers. The party in power might try to force workers to campaign for it or to contribute money to it. Workers who refused might be fired or overlooked for promotions. To make sure this did not happen, Congress passed the Hatch Act in 1939. The Hatch Act allowed federal government workers to vote. However, they could not take part in any other political activities. In more recent times, federal employees claimed the act violated their right to free speech.

The U.S. Office of Special Counsel is responsible for enforcing the Hatch Act and the Federal Employees Political Activities Act.

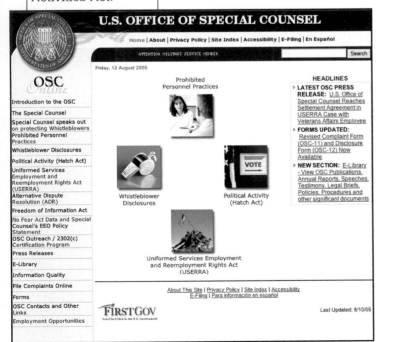

In 1993, Congress passed the Federal Employees Political Activities Act. A federal employee now has many more political rights. For example, federal employees may register new voters. They may make contributions to political parties and candidates and take part in political campaigns. However, there are still limits on federal employees' actions. They may not run for political office. They may not do any political party work while on the job or on government property. This includes wearing a campaign button or displaying campaign literature. Federal employees may not collect political contributions from those they manage or from the general public. Some states have adopted similar rules for their government employees.

Putting It All Together

The way people get jobs with the federal government has changed over time. So have the limits on political activities in which federal employees can participate. In your notebook, list five or six ways that these changes have impacted federal employees. Share your list with a partner. Revise your list if necessary.

reading for understanding

1. What kinds of tests should the civil service system give to people applying for jobs?

2. According to the law, how are jobs to be filled?

The Pendleton Act (1883)

The Pendleton Act was passed in 1883 to create a fair way to hire, promote, and fire federal employees. The following is an excerpt from the law:

"... [R]ules shall provide ... as follows:

"First, for open, competitive examinations for testing the fitness of applicants for the public service ... Such examinations shall be practical ... and ... shall relate to those matters which will fairly test the ... capacity and fitness of the persons examined to discharge the duties ...

"Second, that all offices, places, and employments ... shall be filled ... from among those graded highest as the results of competitive examinations."

—from U.S. Information Service, based on U.S. Statutes at large 22 (1883): 403

Primary Source

The Many Jobs of the Bureaucracy

Thinking on Your Own

The federal bureaucracy grew from 2,120 people in 1801 to about 2.7 million in 2001. Why do you think this happened? List at least two reasons. To help you, think about how the U.S. has changed during the past 200 years.

The federal government has 2.7 million civilian employees. What do they do? How do they interact with ordinary citizens? What is their relationship with the legislative and judicial branches? Only about 300,000 federal employees work in the Washington, D.C., area. Some represent the United States in other nations. Most, however, live and work in cities and towns throughout the United States. Your postal carrier is a federal employee. The person who helps a retiree fill out forms at the local office of the Social Security Administration is also a federal employee.

focus your reading

Describe the different duties of the federal bureaucracy.

Why is the bureaucracy able to make decisions about policy?

Who influences bureaucratic decisions?

words to know

bureaucrat

client group

intelligence gathering

lobbyist

iron triangle

The Work of the Bureaucracy

Federal employees are called **bureaucrats**. Their main job is to carry out the laws of the United States. In reality, the job of the bureaucracy is much more than that. Bureaucrats not only carry out the nation's policy, they make national policy.

Writing regulations is one way that the bureaucracy influences national policy. Congress writes and passes laws. But they do not state the details—the who, what, where, when, and how a law will be enforced.

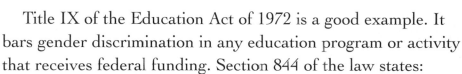

Title IX of the Education Act of 1972 is a good example. It bars gender discrimination in any education program or activity that receives federal funding. Section 844 of the law states:

> The Secretary . . . shall prepare and publish . . . proposed regulations implementing the provisions of Title IX relating to prohibition of sex discrimination in Federally assisted educational programs which shall include . . . intercollegiate athletic activities.

Congress gives the executive department the duty to write the rules and regulations describing the law. The bureaucrats in the Department of Health, Education, and Welfare (now the Department of Education) had to figure out what the Title IX law meant and how to carry it out.

Bureaucrats also influence laws while they are being written. As you read in Chapter 7, congressional committees hold hearings on proposed laws. They call expert witnesses to testify. Often, these witnesses are from the federal government's own bureaucracy. They have information that the lawmakers need in order to make reasonable decisions. Lawmakers also know that they will need the cooperation of bureaucrats in a particular department, agency, or commission to carry out the law.

Often, bureaucrats actually write a proposed law and pass it to Congress to review and debate. This is one way that bills are introduced into Congress. Medicare, for example, began as a proposal from the old Department of Health, Education, and Welfare, and from labor unions and hospitals.

Independent agencies like the Social Security Administration and the regulatory commissions have judicial powers. They settle arguments and claims in their area of authority. In settling disagreements, they interpret what rules and regulations mean. These decisions determine national policy. For example, the SSA makes decisions about who may or may not receive disability benefits. These decisions are interpretations of its regulations. They give others guidance

President Johnson signs Medicare into law in 1965, as former President Truman looks on.

on whether or not they will qualify for the same benefits. Once laws are passed, bureaucrats also provide information and advice. One of the most important duties of the federal bureaucracy is to gather data about the nation: its people, resources, and economy. Bureaucrats share this data with members of Congress and the political appointees in top positions in each department, agency, and commission. This information helps officials make decisions about whether current policy is or is not achieving its goals.

The Growing Influence of Bureaucrats

In the early 1800s, and even through the beginning of the 1900s, bureaucrats did not have so much influence. What changed?

The first reason for the change is the growth of the nation. In 1801, the United States extended west only to the Mississippi River. Today, the nation has 50 states, a number of territories, and more than 280 million people.

President Clinton posed in front of the White House with thousands of government documents as he launched an initiative to reduce the number of reports required annually.

Second, technology has become more complex and widespread. When Franklin Roosevelt was president, television was just beginning. Since the 1980s, cable television, computers, cell phones, and the Internet have been developed. Each new technological development has raised issues. Congress has created agencies to deal with these issues or given responsibility for them to existing agencies.

Third, economic problems have also increased the size of the federal bureaucracy.

Fourth, Congress has created executive departments and other agencies to deal with the needs of certain groups. Executive departments, agencies, and commissions have their own sets of **client groups**.

Fifth, international crises have added to the bureaucracy. After World War II, the nation was involved in the Cold War with the Soviet Union. To ensure that the nation's military was strong, Congress added workers and responsibilities to the Department of Defense. Aid was increased to other nations to ensure they became U.S. allies.

The terrorist attacks in 2001 focused attention on the nation's security preparedness. How well was the nation able to deal with terrorism? President George W. Bush asked Congress to create the Department of Homeland Security. Twenty-two existing agencies were placed within the department. In 2005, the Office of the Director of National Intelligence was set up to oversee **intelligence gathering**. New counterterrorism agencies were added in the Justice Department as well.

Influence on Bureaucrats

Others influence the decisions that bureaucrats make. For example, Congress uses its powers to influence the bureaucracy. It can pass laws that overrule, or change, regulations that a department, agency, or commission has written. Congress can also cut or threaten to cut funding for a program.

> ### ideas to remember
>
> The federal bureaucracy has grown in importance for the following reasons:
> - the growth of the nation
> - the growth of technology
> - economic problems
> - the pressure of client groups
> - years of international problems

However, client groups are the biggest influence on bureaucratic decisions. Each department has its own set of client groups. For example, labor unions are a major client group for the Labor Department. Client groups often hire lobbyists to represent them in Washington, D.C. A **lobbyist's** job is to attempt to influence members of Congress as they prepare and vote on bills. Client groups, congressional committees, and a federal department, agency, or commission may form an **iron triangle**. The three groups depend on one another and work closely to develop policies and programs. Each side of the triangle has something that the other two need.

The Defense Department is a good example. When the budgets are passed, the department needs the support of the congressional committees on defense. Members see that the department's budget requests are filled. Members of the congressional committees need information from the department to help them write laws.

The department also needs the goods that the defense contractors make. These goods include weapons systems, military ships and planes, and similar equipment. The contractors need the billions of dollars that the department gives out each year. In return, the defense contractors support the department's budget requests.

stop and think

Review the list of reasons you wrote for Thinking on Your Own. How does your list match the reasons described in the lesson for the growth of the bureaucracy? Share your list with a partner. Discuss the similarities and differences between your lists and the text.

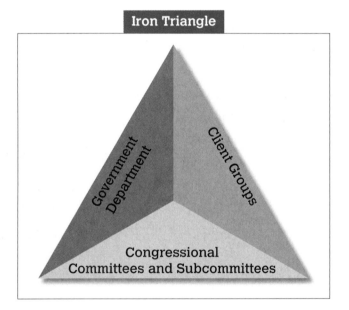

Iron Triangle

Government Department

Client Groups

Congressional Committees and Subcommittees

When they write bills, the congressional committees on defense need the experience of the defense contractors. In return, defense contractors provide political support for committee members. They make campaign contributions and work for their reelection. In return, the congressional committees write legislation that favors the client group.

Putting It All Together

Imagine that you have been asked to debate the following proposition: "Resolved, that bureaucrats have too much influence over the federal government." Using information from this lesson, make an outline in your notebook of the reasons you would use to support or oppose this proposition. Review or revise the list after discussing your reasons with a partner.

Participate in Government

A Career in Government

Are you interested in a job in the federal government? You do not have to move to Washington, D.C., to work for the government. You can stay in your home community or you can move to Antarctica. The government runs a research base in Antarctica staffed with government scientists.

The Office of Personnel Management is the official recruiter of workers for the federal government. Visit its Web site to find out the kinds of jobs that federal employees do. The home page also has links to information on salaries, wages, and benefits. On the link to student jobs, you can search for information on different kinds of jobs and create your resumé.

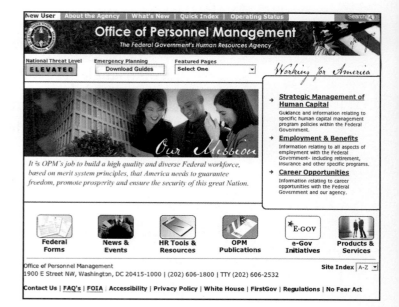

You can also find out about scholarship opportunities. In addition to student jobs, summer jobs and internships are available for qualified students. Some departments have co-op and mentoring programs. In a co-op, or cooperative job, students get to work on real-world projects that use what they are learning in school. The goal of all these student programs is to attract future full-time employees to government work.

To learn more about job opportunities in the federal government:

• Click on the OPM Web site.

• Use the buttons to find out more.

• Download information and talk to your guidance counselor.

Skill Builder

Distinguish Fact from Opinion

A fact is a statement
- of specific information.
- that can be proven true or false.

An opinion
- is what a person thinks or feels.
- cannot be proven true or false.

Client groups, congressional committees, and executive departments form iron triangles.

This sentence states a fact. It gives specific information that could be proven true or false through additional research.

Iron triangles are bad for the taxpayer.

This sentence states the author's personal belief about iron triangles. The author provides no evidence to support the statement.

Look for signal words and phrases to help you decide if a statement is a fact or an opinion. Opinion statements often use

- words such as *none, no one, every, always, never, perhaps, probably, maybe, excellent, greatest, best, worst, bad, good,* or *poor.*

- phrases such as *I think, I believe, in my opinion, in my judgment,* or *as far as I am concerned.*

Decide whether each of the following is a statement of fact or of opinion. Explain how you decided.

1 Article I of the Constitution creates the legislative branch.

2 I think Franklin Roosevelt was the greatest president.

3 The civil service system was a much-needed reform.

4 The executive branch has 15 departments, and their heads are part of the president's cabinet.

5 The growth of technology is probably the greatest cause of the increase in the bureaucracy.

UNIT 4

THE JUDICIAL BRANCH

Article III of the U.S. Constitution created the Supreme Court. The Framers left it to Congress to decide what inferior, or lower, courts were needed. Over the years, Congress has filled in the federal court system. Today, there are 113 courts that hear cases concerning the Constitution, federal laws, federal officials, the states, and foreign governments.

The U.S. Supreme Court has only nine justices. The Court hears cases for only part of the year. It accepts only a few of the many cases sent to it for review. However, the decisions of the U.S. Supreme Court greatly affect national policy. That is why a decision by the Court, or an appointment of a justice, creates so much national interest.

Chapter

11 THE FEDERAL COURT SYSTEM

Getting Focused

Skim this chapter to predict what you will be learning.

- Read the lesson titles and subheadings.
- Look at the illustrations and read the captions.
- Examine the map, tables, and diagram.
- Review the vocabulary words and terms.

What do you know about what goes on in a courtroom? Think about television shows or movies that take place in courtrooms. Write down five things in your notebook that you have learned about courtrooms from watching these shows or movies.

The John Joseph Moakley United States Courthouse in Boston, MA, was completed in 1998. It serves as headquarters for the United States Court of Appeals for the First Circuit and the United States District Court for the District of Massachusetts. The building has two courtrooms for the Court of Appeals and 25 courtrooms for the District Court. It also has 40 judges' chambers, a Circuit law library, the office of a United States congressman, and offices for the United States attorney.

Organization of the Federal Courts

Thinking on Your Own

Look through the lesson. Read the subheadings, diagram, map, and table. What questions about the information come to mind? Write at least three questions in your notebook that you would like answered by the end of the lesson.

Article III of the Constitution mentions only setting up a Supreme Court. Congress has created the lower levels of federal courts as needed. For example, the latest lower court was set up in 1988 to deal with veterans' claims.

It is important to remember that the federal courts deal with cases involving the Constitution, federal laws, and certain other issues. Each state has its own system of courts and laws. State and local courts cannot hear cases involving federal laws or the Constitution.

focus your reading

Explain the organization of the federal court system.

What kinds of cases do federal courts hear?

How are federal judges appointed?

words to know

constitutional court
legislative court
civil case
tariff

The Lower Federal Courts

The diagram on page 206 shows the levels of courts and the types of courts in the federal court system. The courts shown in blue on the diagram are known as **constitutional courts**. Congress set up these 108 courts under the authority of Article III of the Constitution. These courts hear both criminal and civil cases related to federal laws.

The other six federal courts are special courts, also known as **legislative courts**. Congress created these courts to hear particular kinds of cases. The cases are related to Congress's power to govern under Article I. For example, Congress has the power to tax. It set up the Tax Court to hear cases involving federal tax law.

Federal District Judge Sonia Sotomayer of New York issued a ruling that ended the Major League Baseball strike during the 1995–1996 season.

The courts shown in green on the diagram are not part of the federal system. However, appeals of decisions in these courts are sent to federal courts. Appeals of decisions in regulatory commissions such as the Federal Communications Commission are also appealed in federal court.

Constitutional Courts

The constitutional courts are the (1) federal district courts, (2) federal courts of appeals, (3) U.S. Court of Appeals for the Federal Circuit, and (4) U.S. Court of International Trade. The map on page 207 shows that the United States is divided into 94 districts and 12 circuits. Each state has at least one district court. Circuits cross state boundaries. The courts of appeals are divided into circuits.

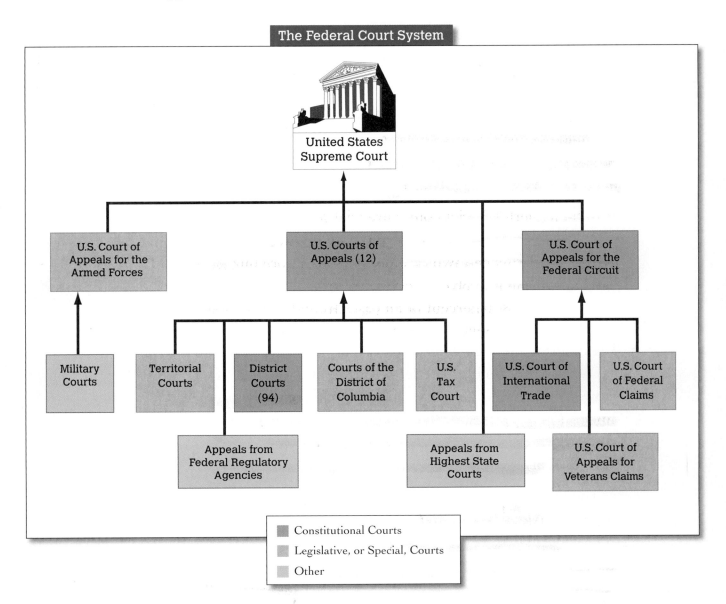

The Federal Court System

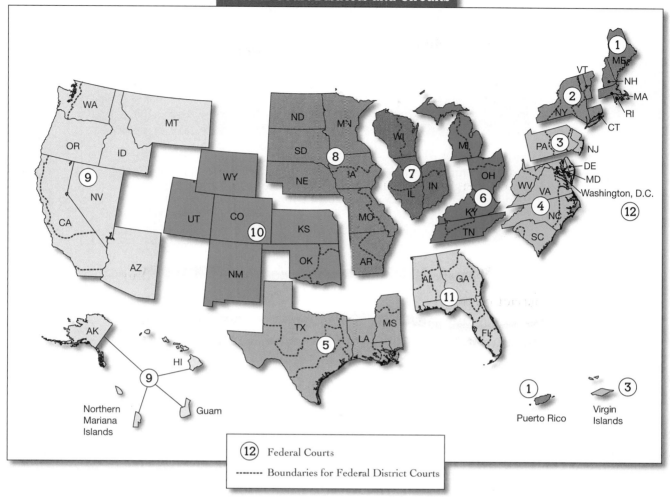

Federal Court Districts and Circuits

12 Federal Courts

------- Boundaries for Federal District Courts

The 94 federal district courts are trial courts. They hear both civil and criminal cases. A **civil case** involves a disagreement between two or more persons or organizations. There is no crime involved. Federal district courts hear 80 percent of all cases brought to federal courts in a year. This totals hundreds of thousands of lawsuits.

The 12 courts of appeals hear appeals of decisions by the federal district courts. Most cases end in the district courts. However, about 55,000 cases a year are appealed to the next level, the courts of appeals. These courts do not have trials. Judges rule based on arguments and documents that are presented by lawyers.

stop and think

Create a table in your notebook of the types of federal courts to help you organize the information in the first two subheadings. Work with a partner to make sure that you include all the important information.

Thurgood Marshall, appointed to the Supreme Court by President Lyndon Johnson in 1967, was the first African American on the Court. President Ronald Reagan appointed Sandra Day O'Connor, the first female justice on the Court, in 1981. Louis Brandeis, the first Jewish member of the Court, was appointed by President Woodrow Wilson in 1916.

The Court of Appeals for the Federal Circuit hears appeals for only certain types of civil cases. It takes appeals from the Court of International Trade, the U.S. Court of Federal Claims, and the U.S. Court of Appeals for Veterans Claims;

Federal Court System and Judges

Court	Number of Courts	Number of Judges	Term of Appointment
Supreme Court	1	9	Life
District Courts	94	642	Life
Court of Appeals	12	179	Life
Court of Appeals for the Federal Circuit	1	12	Life
Trade Court	1	9	Life
Court of Appeals for the Armed Forces	1	5	15 years
Tax Court	1	19	15 years
Court of Federal Claims	1	16	15 years
Court of Appeals for Veterans Claims	1	7	15 years

appeals involving patents and copyrights that were heard in a federal district court; and decisions made in some executive departments. Unlike the other federal appeals courts, the Court of Appeals for the Federal Circuit may take a case from any area of the country. Few cases ever go to the Supreme Court from this court. Like the 12 courts of appeals, there are no trials in the Court of Appeals for the Federal Circuit.

The Court of International Trade hears cases related to tariffs and other trade issues. A **tariff** is a tax on imports, or goods coming into the country for sale. The court sits in New York, but travels to other cities with major ports.

Legislative, or Special, Courts

Congress created the legislative courts to deal with particular issues. These issues are related to the power of Congress to carry out its legislative powers. Look at the diagram on page 206 to see where appeals from each court are heard.

The Government Printing Office

Need a copy of a Supreme Court decision? Want to read what your representative or senator said in Congress today? Looking for a committee's report on homeland security? The Government Printing Office (GPO) can provide each of these documents. The GPO prints the daily *Congressional Record* and the *Federal Register*. It also prints everything from Supreme Court decisions and executive department reports to consumer information and national park guides.

The mission of the GPO is "Keeping Americans Informed." Its Web site says that the GPO "is the federal government's primary centralized resource for gathering, cataloging, producing, providing, and preserving published information in all its forms." This means the GPO prints hard copies of government documents and also produces them in digital formats. The GPO's Web site provides 275,000 documents free to anyone with an Internet connection. Printed products such as booklets and full-length books are provided for the cost of printing.

For example, in 2004, the GPO provided the complete copy of *The 9-11 Commission Report* online at no cost.

The Tax court hears trials related to tax disputes between taxpayers and the IRS or the Treasury Department. It is a national court.

Territorial courts were created by Congress in Guam, the Virgin Islands, and the Northern Mariana Islands. These are territories governed by the United States. Each court system hears criminal and civil trials.

The Court of Appeals for Veterans Claims hears appeals of rulings by the Board of Veterans' Appeals in the Department of Veterans Affairs. Individuals appeal if they believe the board has denied them their lawful veterans' benefits.

The Court of Federal Claims is a national court. It hears cases asking for damages from the federal government. *Damages* refer to the payment of money for loss or injury.

The Court of Appeals for the Armed Forces hears appeals of verdicts in military court cases. Military courts are not part of the federal court system.

Appointing Federal Judges and Supreme Court Justices

Federal judges are appointed by the president and approved by the Senate. Most federal judges serve "during good behavior." Generally, this means they serve until they choose to retire or resign. Judges in the special courts serve 15-year terms. The reason for the long terms is judicial independence. Judges do not have to worry about their jobs. As a result, political pressure to rule one way or the other has little effect on them.

In choosing candidates for federal judgeships, presidents tend to look for two things. Usually, they choose people from their own party and people who share their views on issues likely to come before the court.

This is especially true of appointments to the Supreme Court. As you will read in Chapter 12, the Supreme Court's rulings can have a great impact on national policy.

Putting It All Together

Using the table of the Federal Court System and Judges on page 208, write a one-paragraph summary of the federal court system.

Judicial Jurisdiction and Power

Thinking on Your Own

Suppose a friend of yours disagrees with a brother or sister or another friend over the ownership of a CD. They have asked you to settle the disagreement. Describe in a paragraph in your notebook what you could do to help your friend.

The job of the federal court system is the same as that of state and local courts. Courts apply the law to cases that come before them. For federal courts, the cases may be civil, criminal, or constitutional. Federal courts get their power to hear cases and hand down decisions from the Constitution.

focus your reading

Explain the types of jurisdiction held by federal courts.

How did the power of judicial review develop?

words to know

jurisdiction

original jurisdiction

appellate jurisdiction

Jurisdiction of Federal Courts

Federal courts cannot hear just any type of law case. Federal courts have the authority to hear only certain types of cases. This authority is called a court's **jurisdiction**. Article III, Section 2, Clause 1, of the Constitution lists the types of cases that federal courts can hear. They are classified by the topic of the case and by the parties involved. The table on page 212 gives the jurisdiction of federal courts.

How does jurisdiction work in reality? For many years, the states of New Jersey and New York argued over ownership of Ellis Island in New York Harbor. The case was finally decided in the federal courts. Ellis Island was given to the state of New Jersey. Suppose a citizen of California sues a citizen of Nevada for damages from a car accident. The case is heard in federal district court. If the Nevada resident loses, the person may appeal to the U.S. Court of Appeals.

Trials are heard in federal district courts.

Federal Court Jurisdiction

Cases by Topic	Cases by Parties Involved
• U.S. Constitution	• Representatives of foreign governments, such as ambassadors
• Federal laws, including federal bankruptcy laws	• Governments of two or more of the 50 states
• Treaties	• Federal government or one of its officials or departments
• Admiralty law (laws relating to activities on the oceans, and on U.S. rivers, lakes, and canals)	• A state or one of its citizens and a foreign country or one of its citizens
• Maritime law (laws relating to shipping activities)	• Citizens of different states
	• A state and a citizen of a different state
	• Citizens of the same state who claim land under grants from different states

The 94 federal district courts have only **original jurisdiction** in cases. They are the first, or original, court to hear a case. The federal courts of appeal have only **appellate jurisdiction**. They hear only appeals.

The Supreme Court has both original and appellate jurisdiction. However, the Court's original jurisdiction is limited. The case must involve a representative of a foreign government or be a certain type of case involving a state. The total number of such cases usually amounts to fewer than five a year.

The U.S. Supreme Court's main work is hearing appeals from lower federal courts of appeals. The Supreme Court also hears cases appealed from state supreme courts. However, the case must be related to the Constitution or to federal law. The U.S. Supreme Court is able to rule only on the federal issue in the case. For example, the Supreme Court will not decide if a convicted murderer is innocent or guilty. The Court can only decide whether the person received a fair trial.

Power of Judicial Review

Of the three branches of government, the Framers had the least to say about the judicial branch. Article III, Section 1, Clause 1, states simply that the "judicial power of the United States, shall be vested [held] in one Supreme Court, and in such inferior Courts as the Congress may . . . establish." What exactly does this mean?

Congress began to spell out the power of the federal judiciary by passing the Judiciary Act of 1789. This act created the first of the lower federal courts. It also gave the Supreme Court the power to review state constitutions and state laws. If they disagreed with the U.S. Constitution, the Court had the power to declare them unconstitutional.

John Marshall added to the power of the federal judiciary. He served as Chief Justice of the Supreme Court from 1801 to 1835. In Marbury v. Madison, the Court declared a part of a federal law unconstitutional. In doing this, the Court took for itself the power to review acts of Congress. This is known as the power of judicial review. Since then, neither Congress nor any president has ever argued that the Supreme Court does not have this power.

Chief Justice John Marshall

Landmark Supreme Court Case: Judicial Review

Marbury v. Madison (1803): Democrat Thomas Jefferson had won the election of 1800. John Adams was the outgoing president and a Federalist. He wanted to appoint as many Federalists as possible to office. He appointed 42 judges in the District of Columbia. By the time Adams left office, several men had not received their appointment papers. The new secretary of state, James Madison, refused to deliver them. William Marbury sued Madison for his papers. The Supreme Court heard the case because it involved an official of the federal government. The Court decided that the Constitution did not grant the power to rule on this case. It ruled that part of the Judiciary Act of 1789 was unconstitutional.

Putting It All Together

Review what you wrote in Thinking on Your Own. Suppose your friend did not like the way you settled the disagreement. How could your friend appeal your decision? Who might serve as an appellate court in this case?

Participate in Government

Serve on a Jury

Jury duty is one of the few responsibilities that citizens have. To serve on a jury, you must

- be a U.S. citizen
- be at least eighteen years of age
- understand English
- never have been convicted of a serious crime

Serving on a jury is one of the civic responsibilities of citizenship.

People are chosen for jury duty at random. Names are drawn from lists of registered voters or those holding driver's licenses. When you are called to jury duty, you receive a jury summons in the mail. It will tell you when and where to report. Ignoring a jury summons is a serious offense. If you do not report, you can be charged with a crime.

At the courthouse, you will not be assigned to a jury right away. Potential jurors go into a jury pool. First, you will be asked to fill out some forms. Then you will be given a number and sent to a room with other possible jurors. You may be asked to answer a list of questions.

When your number is called, you will be taken to a courtroom. The case could be either criminal or civil. Lawyers for both sides will ask you questions. The judge may also question you. They want to see what or who you know that could affect your decision as a juror. For example, the case involves a hit-and-run. The person charged with the crime was found drunk nearby. A possible juror has been the victim of a drunk driver. The juror would probably be excused from hearing that case.

If you are not called to serve on a jury the first day, you usually do not have to come to the jury room again. You may only have to call in each day to see if your number has been called. Whether you serve or not, you are doing your duty and supporting the rule of law.

Skill Builder

Draw Conclusions

A conclusion is the result of thinking. In order to reach a conclusion, you have to gather and analyze, or think about, information. Then you have to decide what it means.

You draw conclusions every day without noticing what you are doing. You consider buying one of three shirts. You look at the prices and the colors. You think about what you can wear with each shirt. Then you put all these ideas together to find out which shirt best meets your needs. Perhaps you want to buy a computer. You analyze the features on four computers and compare them to your needs. Then you reach a conclusion about which computer is best for you.

Juries are asked to draw conclusions when they decide verdicts in trials. They base their conclusions on the evidence and the law. Appellate judges also draw conclusions based on the evidence and the law.

To Draw a Conclusion:

- Gather information about the topic.

- List any other facts you already know about the topic.

- Put all your information together.

- Analyze the information and decide what it means.

Answer the following questions by drawing conclusions.

1 Where would a case involving federal drug charges first be heard? Explain how you reached your conclusion.

2 Where would a lawsuit brought by a Native-American nation against the federal government first be heard? Explain how you reached your conclusion.

Chapter 12

THE SUPREME COURT AT WORK

Getting Focused

Skim this chapter to predict what you will be learning.

- Read the lesson titles and subheadings.
- Look at the illustrations and read the captions.
- Examine the diagram.
- Review the vocabulary words and terms.

After skimming the chapter, write at least five things in your notebook that you already know about the U.S. Supreme Court.

The first session of the U.S. Supreme Court was convened on February 1, 1790. However, it took almost 145 years for the Supreme Court to find a permanent location. The U.S. Supreme Court Building was constructed between 1932 and 1935. When the cornerstone of the building was put in place on October 13, 1932, Chief Justice Charles Evans Hughes stated, "The Republic endures and this is the symbol of its faith."

How the Court Process Works

Thinking on Your Own

Everyone is entitled to his or her opinion. Every year, the U.S. Supreme Court issues dozens of opinions. Write a paragraph in your notebook about why a Court opinion would outweigh yours.

The Supreme Court's term begins in October. The nine justices hear cases from the first week in October until early May. The term is named for the year in which it begins. For example, the term that begins in October 2007 is the 2007 term.

During the term, justices hear oral arguments for two weeks each month. **Oral arguments** are the presentations that lawyers make before the justices. Remember that the Supreme Court acts as a court of appeals. These courts decide whether to uphold or reverse a lower court's decision or send the case back for a retrial.

The Court hears arguments from Monday through Wednesday and sometimes on Thursdays. The justices meet among themselves on most Wednesday afternoons and Friday mornings. In these **conferences**, the justices discuss the cases before them for rulings. They also discuss which new cases to take.

focus your reading

Why do cases reach the Supreme Court?

Explain the process the Supreme Court uses for hearing and deciding on cases.

words to know

oral arguments

conference

law clerk

rule of four

cert

affirmative action

brief

precedent

amicus curiae brief

swing vote

opinion

William Rehnquist was sworn in as Chief Justice of the U.S. Supreme Court on September 26, 1986.

In 2000, the Supreme Court heard arguments regarding the presidential election between Al Gore and George W. Bush. Theodore Olson, an attorney for George W. Bush, spoke to reporters on the steps of the Supreme Court Building after making his argument to the Court.

During the rest of the time, the justices read, work on decisions, and meet with their law clerks. Clerking for a Supreme Court justice is an important job. The **law clerks** do most of the legal research for each justice. They are young men and women who graduated near the top of their classes from the nation's best law schools. Justices value their ideas. Law clerks can help shape a justice's opinion about a case.

Getting on the Court's Calendar

How do cases get to the Supreme Court? As you read in Chapter 11, a few cases come under the original jurisdiction of the Court.

Most cases arrive at the Court by writ of certiorari. The writ is called cert for short. The cert is issued as the result of a petition, or legal request, by a party—person or group—involved in a case. The petition asks the Court to review the case. Four justices must agree to take the case. This is known as the **rule of four**. Decisions are made during the justices' weekly conferences. If at least four justices vote "yes," the Court issues the writ of certiorari. The **cert** directs the lower court to send up the records of the case. The case is then scheduled for a hearing. If the Court refuses to take a case, the decision of the lower court is final.

About 8,000 requests for review are sent to the Supreme Court each year. Fewer than 100 are heard in open court and receive full written opinions.

Why do justices take some cases and not others? Typically, the justices take a case for only two reasons: it must raise either an important constitutional or legal question. For example, in the 2003 term, the Court dealt with two cases on affirmative action in education. **Affirmative action** is a government policy related to women and minority groups. Its

The issue of affirmative action received national attention when the Supreme Court heard a case involving the University of Michigan.

"Do you ever have one of those days when <u>nothing</u> seems constitutional?"

stop and think

Make an outline in your notebook of the most important information that you read in this lesson so far. Compare your outline with that of a partner. Add to it as you continue reading.

goal is to make up for past discrimination against these groups. The 2003 cases involved admissions policies at the University of Michigan law school and undergraduate school. The cases raised the issue of whether affirmative action was itself discriminatory.

The Decision-making Process

The first step once a cert is issued is scheduling the case on the Court's calendar. The attorneys take the next step. Each side submits a **brief.** This document describes the legal arguments in favor of the lawyer's side. It also includes facts and legal precedents. A **precedent** is an example from a similar case that has already been decided. Typically, the Supreme Court uses precedents as a guide in deciding cases. The justices usually rule in the same way in similar cases.

Sometimes people who are not directly involved in a case file briefs, too. These are called **amicus curiae briefs.** The phrase means "friend of the court." Their purpose is to provide additional information to support one side or the other in the case. Government departments, agencies, and commissions, as well as individuals and lobbying groups, submit amicus curiae briefs. For example, both pro-gun and anti-gun lobbyists would submit briefs in a gun control case.

Law clerks, such as those who work with Justice Clarence Thomas, play a key role at the Supreme Court.

The next step is oral arguments. Each lawyer is given 30 minutes to present the case for his or her side. The lawyer summarizes the brief and highlights the major legal points. During the presentations, justices often question the lawyers. They may challenge the lawyer's argument or ask questions that help to draw out the lawyer's points. At the end of the half hour, the lawyer's time is up—even if the lawyer is mid-sentence.

The next step is the justices' conferences on Wednesdays and Fridays. The room is empty except for the nine justices—and 20 or more carts. These contain petitions for writ of certiorari, as well as briefs and paperwork related to the cases the justices are

Justice David H. Souter

hearing. The Chief Justice runs the conferences. Any petitions for cert are discussed and decided. Then the justices discuss the cases they have heard in the past two weeks. The Chief Justice begins by summarizing the case. He or she also explains what he or she thinks about it. Each justice in turn expresses his or her opinion. The Chief Justice then takes a vote.

The vote may be unanimous—meaning that all the justices agree—or there may be majority and minority views. At least five justices must agree on one point of view to make a majority. About one-third of the votes are unanimous. When the vote is tied, four to four, the fifth and deciding vote is called the **swing vote.**

Once the vote is taken, the justices have to turn their decision into a written opinion. The **opinion** is a document stating the legal reasoning behind the decision. If the decision is unanimous, then the opinion is a unanimous opinion. If the vote is split, one of the justices on the majority side will write the majority opinion. Sometimes a justice will agree with the final decision but arrive at the conclusion differently. Then the justice may write a concurring opinion. Often, a justice who disagrees will write a dissenting opinion.

After the conference, the justices and their law clerks go to work to write the opinions. The opinions are sent around for the other justices to review. This step in the process can go on for months. At some point during the term, however, the decision is announced and the opinion, or decision, is published.

Decision-making at the Supreme Court

Case is scheduled.

Lawyers file briefs.
The Court requests amicus curiae briefs.
Amicus curiae briefs are filed.

The Court hears oral arguments.

Case is discussed during a conference.
Vote is taken.
The opinion is assigned.

Justices and their law clerks work on majority, concurrent, and dissenting opinions.
Opinions are sent to the other justices to review.

The opinions are finalized.

The decision is announced.
The opinions are published.

Putting It All Together

Write a summary of this lesson. Use the outline you made in the Stop and Think activity for information. If necessary, review the Skill Builder on page 136.

Influences on the Supreme Court

Thinking on Your Own

Do other people ever influence what you do? Think of something that you did or bought because someone else told you it was a good idea. Write two sentences in your notebook that describe the situation.

Supreme Court justices do not decide cases in isolation. The nine men and women on the Court are the products of their backgrounds and education. The interaction among justices also influences decisions. Public opinion plays a role as well. Remember, too, that the Court is one branch among three. As a result, the system of checks and balances also impacts the Court. However, the Constitution and federal law are the basic guides to decision-making for the justices.

The seal of the United States Supreme Court

focus your reading

Describe the role of the Constitution and laws in the decisions of the Supreme Court.

Why does a justice's views and interaction with other justices affect his or her decisions?

Explain how public opinion may affect Supreme Court decisions.

List how the executive and legislative branches influence the Supreme Court.

words to know

view

court packing

nominee

The Basic Guides

Why are there dissenting opinions in Supreme Court cases? How can three justices agree on the reasoning behind a decision and a fourth justice disagree on the reasoning? Yet that fourth justice agrees with the end result of the

V. BRYAN UNITED STATES COURTHOUSE

The scales of justice appear in front of the Albert V. Bryan United States Courthouse in Alexandria, VA.

"Call it 'legislating from the bench,' if you will, but on this occasion I should like to repeal the First Amendment."

others' thinking. A fifth justice may disagree with both sets of ideas but agree with the end result. The other three justices disagree with the reasoning and the vote. Is the law not the law?

The principles of the Constitution remain the same. However, the Framers described general principles in the Constitution. They left it to later people to apply these principles. For example, the Constitution gave Congress the power to regulate commerce. It did not spell out the meaning of that term. Differences in how justices interpret such powers can result in different Supreme Court opinions.

The Justices

The **views**, or philosophies, of the justices and their relationships with one another also influence decisions. As you read in Chapter 4, there are two very different views of the Constitution. One view is strict constructionist and the other is loose constructionist. Strict constructionists are considered conservatives, and loose constructionists are considered liberals. Those in between are considered moderates. Since the 1970s, Republican presidents have tended to name more conservative justices. President Bill Clinton, a Democrat, appointed justices in the 1990s who were more moderate.

Differences in views influence how justices look at and interpret the Constitution and the law. Conservative justices stay as close as possible to what they think the Framers meant. Liberal justices tend to be more flexible about what the Constitution permits. For example, in the 2003 term, the majority of justices upheld affirmative action in two education cases. The two justices who are the most conservative disagreed strongly with this opinion.

Chief Justice William Rehnquist confers with Justices O'Connor and Ginsburg.

Replacing a justice can become a huge political issue. This occurred twice in 2005 when President George W. Bush had to replace Justice Sandra Day O'Connor, who retired, and Chief Justice William Rehnquist, who passed away.

stop and think

Make a heading in your notebook entitled "Why Justices Disagree." List the reasons you have already read about. Add to the list as you continue reading.

Conservative Republicans wanted conservative replacements. Democrats and moderate Republicans wanted more moderate justices. John Roberts was confirmed as Chief Justice, to replace Rehnquist in September 2005.

The Chief Justice can also influence the Court's decisions. He or she makes up the list of what will be discussed in each weekly conference. He or she summarizes each case and presents his or her viewpoint before the other justices speak. The Chief Justice can also keep conflicts among justices from getting out of hand. This results in a better working relationship among justices.

United States Society

The justices are members of U.S. society. They read and hear the same news every day as other Americans. Their values and beliefs are shaped by living and working in this country. As a result, their viewpoints reflect the values and beliefs of other Americans.

reading for understanding

1. What did Justice Marshall force his fellow justices to consider?
2. How does this excerpt show how justices influence one another?

The Influence of One Justice on Another

Thurgood Marshall was the first African American named to the U.S. Supreme Court. He had been a justice for 14 years before Sandra Day O'Connor joined the Court in 1981. The following is from an article she wrote when Justice Marshall retired in 1992.

Primary Source

"Although all of us come to the Court with our own personal histories and experiences, Justice Marshall brought a special perspective. His was the eye of a lawyer who saw the deepest wounds . . . in the social fabric and used law to help heal them. . . . His was the mouth of a man who knew the anguish of the silenced and gave them a voice.

"At oral arguments and conference meetings, in opinions and dissents, Justice Marshall imparted not only his legal acumen but also his life experiences, constantly pushing and prodding us to respond not only to the persuasiveness of legal arguments but also to the power of moral truth."

—Justice Sandra Day O'Connor, "A Tribute to Justice Thurgood Marshall"
(44 Stan L. Rev. 1217), *Stanford Law Review*, June 1992

In deciding which cases to take, justices tend to weigh public opinion. What do most Americans think about the issue? How strongly do they hold those views? Is the nation ready to take a step beyond those views? Justices look at the same questions when making their rulings.

A good example is the University of Michigan admissions cases in 2003, discussed in Lesson 1. Justice Sandra Day O'Connor wrote the majority opinion. She stated that in 25 years, affirmative action policies might no longer be necessary. However, there is evidence to show the need for them now.

The Executive and Legislative Branches

As you remember, the Framers set up a system of checks and balances among the three branches of government. The purpose was to make sure that no branch had too much power. As a result, the other two branches also influence the Court's decisions.

This 1937 political cartoon addresses the issue of court packing by President Roosevelt.

The most important way that presidents affect the Court is by the power of appointment. The president fills openings on the Court. As you read on page 210, presidents usually appoint judges who share their philosophies. However, presidents inherit Courts that were named by earlier presidents. These justices may not share the new president's views. Even a justice whom a president appoints may be a surprise. A justice may also turn out not to hold exactly the same views as the president who named him or her.

President Franklin Roosevelt was faced with such a Court. The justices declared unconstitutional a number of Roosevelt's New Deal programs. In 1937, he tried to add six members to the Court. He wanted more justices who would support the New Deal. Republicans accused Roosevelt of trying to fill the Court with justices who would support his beliefs. In Congress, conservative Democrats joined with Republicans to defeat the measure. They thought **court packing** would upset the system of checks and balances created by the Constitution.

Congress has several tools if it does not like a ruling by the Court. It can enact a law to limit the impact of the ruling. For example, in 2004, Congress passed a law against what it called partial-birth abortion. The law was meant to limit the Court's 6-3 decision in *Roe* v. *Wade*. This case established a woman's right to seek an abortion.

Congress can also use constitutional amendments to get around a Court ruling. This is not done often. However, the Sixteenth Amendment came about as the result of a Court ruling. In 1895, the Court declared unconstitutional a federal income tax law. Congress then proposed and approved the Sixteenth Amendment, which created a federal income tax. The amendment was ratified by the states.

The president appoints the justices, but the Senate must approve them. The Senate Judiciary Committee questions nominees very carefully. Committee members want to know what the nominees' judicial philosophies are. They review how nominees have decided certain issues in the past. The most heated constitutional issues in the late twentieth and early twenty-first centuries tend to deal with social policies. These include affirmative action, abortion, and gay marriage.

The Senate can and has refused to approve nominees. **Nominees** are people who have been selected to fill a vacant position. It can also threaten to reject nominees with certain views on issues. As a result of its consent power, the Senate can greatly influence how the Court will rule on certain cases in the future.

ideas to remember
Five factors help shape Supreme Court decisions: • the Constitution and federal law • the justices' own backgrounds and views • the interaction among justices • U.S. society • the executive and legislative branches

Putting It All Together

Create a concept map that shows the influences on Supreme Court decisions. Draw a large circle and label it "Influences on the Supreme Court." Then draw smaller circles for each influence. Connect each smaller circle with a line to the large circle. Label each smaller circle. Share your concept map with a partner.

The Supreme Court and National Policy

Thinking on Your Own

Have you ever made a decision and then changed your mind? What happened to make you change your mind? Write a paragraph in your notebook to describe your decision, and then explain why you changed it.

As you just read, the Supreme Court hears cases and hands down decisions. However, the Court does more than just decide individual cases. By the cases it chooses and the opinions it delivers, the Court sets government policy. It sets policy just as much as the executive and legislative branches do. This is why appointing a justice to the Supreme Court is so important.

focus your reading

In what ways does the Supreme Court affect national policy?

Name some limits on the power of the Supreme Court.

words to know

struck down

reverse

civil liberties

Judicial Review and Interpreting the Law

The Supreme Court has three tools to shape national policy. The first is its power of judicial review. The Court declared this power in *Marbury* v. *Madison*. In the 200 years since, the Court has **struck down**—declared unconstitutional—about 150 federal laws and over 1,000 state and local laws.

Judicial review affects public policy in two ways. First, once a law is struck down, legislators tend not to pass similar laws. Second, a Court decision can greatly affect how the nation deals with an issue. For example, the decision in *Miranda* v. *Arizona* changed the way law officers are allowed to question suspects. They must inform them of their rights. These include the right to remain silent and the right to have an attorney, or lawyer, present during questioning.

Miranda v. *Arizona* ensured the rights of people under arrest.

The way that justices interpret the laws also affects national policy. Congress writes federal laws in general terms. The House and the Senate leave it to the bureaucracy to add the details. Not everyone agrees on those details. That is one reason that cases go to the Supreme Court. The Court acts as an umpire. In its opinions, the Court spells out how it interprets, or explains the meaning of, the law. This interpretation becomes what people must obey.

For example, in 1990, Congress passed the Americans with Disabilities Act. The law required employers and public places such as office buildings to make "reasonable accommodations" for people with disabilities. Entrances with ramps and automatic doors are two outcomes of the law. Another goal was to end employment discrimination against people with disabilities.

What disabilities does the law cover? Some people believed it covered those with HIV. Not all employers agreed. A lawsuit, *Bragdon v. Abbott*, was filed. The case reached the Supreme Court, and it agreed to hear the appeal. In 1998, the Court ruled that the law included people who were HIV-positive. As a result of this ruling, people with HIV and AIDS are protected against discrimination in the workplace.

> **ideas to remember**
>
> The Supreme Court shapes national policies
>
> - by its use of judicial review
> - by the way it interprets laws
> - by overturning earlier decisions

Landmark Supreme Court Case: Separate but Equal

Plessy v. Ferguson **(1896):** By the 1890s, African Americans and whites were separated by law in the South. For example, African Americans were barred from eating in the same restaurants as whites. They could not use the same drinking fountains. African Americans were forced to sit in their own sections in theaters, railroad trains, and other public places.

Homer Plessy, an African American, tested a Louisiana segregation law. The law required separate but equal accommodations, or facilities, for African Americans and whites. Plessy sat down in a whites-only railroad car and refused to leave. He was arrested. A court convicted him of breaking the state law. Plessy appealed.

The Supreme Court upheld Plessy's conviction. The justices said the state law was constitutional. It did not violate the equal protection clause of the Fourteenth Amendment. The clause (Section 1) guarantees that all citizens will be treated alike under the law. The justices ruled that the law was constitutional because it said that the separate accommodations had to be equal. This principle of "separate but equal" lasted for more than 50 years. It was used both by the courts and legislators to continue segregating society.

Linda Brown
in 1964

Brown v. Board of Education of Topeka (1954): By the 1950s, racial ideas in the United States outside the South were changing. A growing number of Americans began to question segregation. How could the United States fight World War II to defend democracy in Europe and Asia while denying rights to African Americans at home? In reality, facilities for African Americans were not equal. Segregated schools did deprive African-American children of equal opportunities. That was well established in a legal brief presented to the Supreme Court in the case of *Brown v. Board of Education of Topeka* (1954). The brief was prepared by the National Association for the Advancement of Colored People (NAACP). Thurgood Marshall, the lawyer who argued the case, later became the first African American to be appointed to the Supreme Court.

In 1954, the Supreme Court used *Brown v. Board of Education of Topeka* to overturn *Plessy*. The case involved Linda Brown, who could not attend the school closest to her. It was an all-white school. Instead, she had to go to an all-black school across town. The justices reversed the precedent, or ruling, in *Plessy*. They declared that separate was not equal and that segregation violated the equal protection clause of the Fourteenth Amendment. States were ordered to end segregation. Different times, along with different justices, resulted in a different decision.

Reversing Past Decisions

Very rarely, the Court **reverses**, or overturns, a previous court decision. This is another way the Court influences national policy. For example, at one point in time, a Court decision represents the justices' thinking on an issue. However, those justices retire over a period of years. New justices are appointed. They may have different philosophies than the justices who decided the original case. A shift in public opinion may also have taken place during these years. When a similar case comes before the new justices, they decide it differently.

This proves the truth of what you learned in Lesson 2. In many ways, Supreme Court justices represent the same attitudes as the general public. Over time, the nation's attitudes about certain issues change. The Supreme Court's views change along with them. Two important civil rights cases stand out as an example of a change in judicial viewpoints.

As you read in Lesson 1, the rulings of the Supreme Court set precedents. However, there are decisions such as the one in *Plessy* that later justices no longer believe are correct.

stop and think

Write the following heading in your notebook: *"Brown v. Board of Education."* Under it, list three "lessons" that we can learn from this case about the United States Supreme Court. Review what you have read and keep this assignment in mind as you continue reading.

Limits on the Supreme Court

The majority of Supreme Court cases involve **civil liberties**. These are a person's protection against abuse by the government. For example, in 1963, Clarence Gideon petitioned the Court because he said he did not get a fair trial. He was too poor to hire a lawyer to represent him. In *Gideon* v. *Wainwright*, the Court declared that courts must appoint an attorney for anyone too poor to hire one.

The Supreme Court also takes cases related to economic issues. These may involve environmental protection regulations or anti-trust laws. Other cases involve suits against federal officials or between the national government and the states.

In deciding which cases to take, the Court looks at what is involved. First, the case must make a difference in some way. *Gideon* v. *Wainwright*, expanded the civil liberties of the poor. Second, there must be real harm involved. Without a lawyer, Clarence Gideon was sent to jail. Third, the case must apply to a large number of people. Gideon was not the only poor person to go through a trial without a lawyer.

THE CASE

OF

THE CHEROKEE NATION

against

THF STATE OF GEORGIA:

ARGUED AND DETERMINED AT

THE SUPREME COURT OF THE UNITED STATES,

JANUARY TERM 1831.

WITH

AN APPENDIX,

Containing the Opinion of Chancellor Kent on the Case ; the Treaties between the United States and the Cherokee Indians ; the Act of Congress of 1802, entitled 'An Act to regulate intercourse with the Indian tribes, &c.'; and the Laws of Georgia relative to the country occupied by the Cherokee Indians, within the boundary of that State.

BY RICHARD PETERS,
COUNSELLOR AT LAW.

Philadelphia:
JOHN GRIGG, 9 NORTH FOURTH STREET.
1831.

The Supreme Court sided with the Cherokee Nation in a land dispute during the 1830s.

ideas to remember

Limits on the Supreme Court include

- the issues it chooses to consider
- the types of cases it chooses to hear
- lack of control over when cases are sent to it
- no power of enforcement

A fourth limit on the Court's influence is its lack of enforcement power. The Framers gave the executive branch the power to carry out laws and to enforce the Court's rulings. In the 1832 case *Worcester* v. *Georgia*, the Court ruled that the state of Georgia had no authority in Cherokee land. President Andrew Jackson said, "John Marshall has made his decision. Now let him enforce it." In other words, Jackson ignored the Court and the Cherokee were forced to move to Indian Territory.

Putting It All Together

Write three paragraphs summarizing the following topics: 1) The Supreme Court works slowly and carefully. 2) Court decisions are influenced by society. 3) The Supreme Court has an impact on American life.

Participate in Government

File a Civil Rights Complaint

Unfortunately, discrimination on the basis of race, gender, religion, ethnic background, and disability still occurs. People face discrimination in education, credit, employment, housing, law enforcement, voting, and public services. Public services include restaurants, movies, hotels, and public transportation.

Everyone has the right to file a civil rights complaint when discrimination occurs.

If a person believes that he or she has been discriminated against, that person can take action. A civil rights complaint can be filed. The U.S. Commission on Civil Rights offers a booklet entitled *Getting Uncle Sam to Enforce Your Civil Rights.* It is available online from the commission. The commission does not investigate complaints but can help you find the right agency to contact.

Usually, complaints need to be filed within 180 days of the alleged discrimination. The commission sets out the following guidelines for filing a complaint. The complaint must

- be typed or printed neatly, dated, and signed.

- include your name, address, and telephone number.

- state the name and address of the person or place of business that discriminated against you.

- explain the act or acts of discrimination. The date, place of the action, and the basis for the discrimination need to be identified and explained. For example, was it because of your skin color?

- include the names, addresses, and telephone numbers of any witnesses or others who have information about your complaint.

When your complaint is investigated, you may also need to offer proof. This can be receipts, contracts, or any other records that support your complaint.

Skill Builder

Understand Cause and Effect

A cause is what makes something happen. An effect is the result or the outcome of the cause. For example:

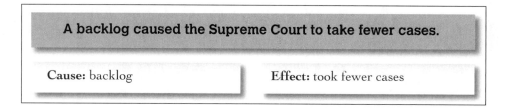

A backlog caused the Supreme Court to take fewer cases.

Cause: backlog | **Effect:** took fewer cases

Identifying the cause and the effect in this sentence is easy. The verb *caused* signals the relationship between the backlog and the Court's taking fewer cases. A flowchart is one way to determine cause-and-effect relationships.

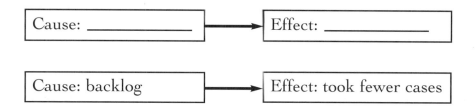

Cause: ____________ → Effect: ____________

Cause: backlog → Effect: took fewer cases

Sometimes the effect of one event is the cause of another. Then your flowchart would look like this:

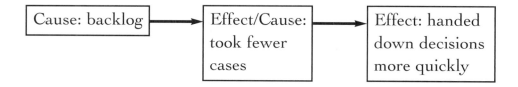

Cause: backlog → Effect/Cause: took fewer cases → Effect: handed down decisions more quickly

Use the information from Chapter 12 to complete these activities.

1. Create a cause-and-effect flowchart to describe why the Sixteenth Amendment was passed, page 225.

2. Create a cause-and-effect flowchart to describe how the Court ruled in *Plessy* and *Brown*, pages 227 and 228.

3. Use a cause-and-effect flowchart to write a summary of the influences on the Supreme Court.

5
UNIT

CIVIL LIBERTIES AND CIVIL RIGHTS

Civil liberties and civil rights are often taken for granted by Americans. However, it took almost 200 years before these were guaranteed by law to all Americans. In the photograph at the right, A. Philip Randolph, march director (right); Roy Wilkins, Executive Secretary of the National Association for the Advancement of Colored People (second from right); and the Rev. Martin Luther King, Jr., (seventh from right) led the March on Washington on August 28, 1963. On that day, thousands of people walked along Constitution Avenue in Washington, D.C.

Do you want to start a petition to ask the mayor and council to fix up the local basketball court? Do you want to organize a march to city hall to present the petition? In some nations, you would be arrested and sent to jail for these actions. In the United States, these actions are expressions of a person's civil liberties. The U.S. Constitution guarantees civil liberties. It also guarantees civil rights.

This unit will explain the differences between civil liberties and civil rights. You will also learn how these liberties and rights have been expanded over time.

Chapter

13 CIVIL LIBERTIES: CONSTITUTIONAL FREEDOMS

Getting Focused

Skim this chapter to predict what you will be learning.

- Read the lesson titles and subheadings.
- Look at the illustrations and read the captions.
- Examine the table.
- Review the vocabulary words and terms.

What rights does the Bill of Rights guarantee? List as many rights as you can remember. Check your list against the Constitution. Add to or revise your list as needed.

Freedom of religion is one of the liberties guaranteed by the U.S. Constitution. Judaism, Islam, Catholicism, and Protestantism are four of the main religions in the United States.

Constitutional Rights

Thinking on Your Own

What do you know about the Fourteenth and Ninth Amendments? Create a four-column chart in your notebook. Label the first column "What I Know About the Fourteenth Amendment." Label the third column "What I Know About the Ninth Amendment." Fill in those two columns with what you already know. Label the second and fourth columns "What I Learned." Fill in those columns after you study the lesson.

Civil liberties are the freedoms guaranteed by the U.S. Constitution. The Bill of Rights, the first ten amendments to the Constitution, lists many of these civil liberties. Among them are freedom of speech, religion, and assembly.

Civil rights are the rights of everyone to equal protection under the law. No one can be discriminated against on the basis of race, religion, gender, or ethnic origin. The Fifth and Fourteenth Amendments protect us from discrimination by the government or by any other group or individual.

Some states would not ratify the Constitution until 1788 when the Bill of Rights was added. However, it took almost 200 years for the nation to recognize the civil rights of women, African Americans, and other groups.

The right to vote is a civil liberty.

---

focus your reading

What civil liberties are guaranteed by the Bill of Rights?

How does the principle of incorporation affect civil liberties?

Explain why the Ninth Amendment is important.

words to know

civil liberties

civil rights

alien

incorporation

The Bill of Rights

The first ten amendments to the Constitution make up the Bill of Rights. Review the table on page 78, which lists what each amendment guarantees. Both citizens and aliens are guaranteed these rights.

Aliens are non–U.S. citizens in the United States. In a number of cases, the Supreme Court has ruled that they have the same basic rights as citizens. The Bill of Rights applies to them as well as to citizens. They also have the same guarantees of due process that you will read about in Lesson 5. However, aliens may not vote or serve on juries.

Incorporation of Rights

The first members of Congress who proposed the Bill of Rights meant for these amendments to apply only to the national government. Remember that they had just won their independence from Great Britain. They did not fear the power of their own state governments. The British government had tried to limit people's rights, and members of Congress feared the national government might do the same. In 1868, the Fourteenth Amendment was added to the Constitution. It states that citizens are citizens of both the United States and their state. No state may pass any laws that violate the rights of citizens of the United States. In addition, no state may "deprive any person of life, liberty, or property without due process of law." Beginning in 1925, the Supreme Court interpreted the Fourteenth Amendment to include people's dealings with both state and local governments. This is known as **incorporation**.

The U.S. Constitution guarantees the right to an attorney in a criminal trial.

The Court began by expanding the rights guaranteed under the First Amendment. Since the 1960s, the Court has expanded the "due process" guarantee to include other amendments in the Bill of Rights. For example, the decision in *Malloy* v. *Hogan* extended the protection of the Fifth Amendment into state courts. A defendant in state court has the right to remain silent and not incriminate himself or herself. This is the same right that someone tried in federal court has. By the end of the twentieth century, almost all the guarantees of the Bill of Rights had been incorporated. Why is incorporation important? State constitutions also guarantee civil liberties. However, states have not always used those guarantees to protect their people. Almost 100 years of discrimination against African Americans is an unfortunate example of state government abuse. Expansion of the guarantees of the U.S. Constitution offers protection to all people in all states.

stop and think

In your notebook, explain how the Fourteenth Amendment and the Court's rulings on incorporation have helped protect your civil liberties. Work with a partner to explain how the Ninth Amendment adds to that protection.

Ninth Amendment

The Constitution lists many rights of Americans. However, neither the Constitution nor the amendments list all of them. This would have been an impossible task because the nation, society, and the world keep changing. Instead, the Framers included the Ninth Amendment. The amendment says:

> The enumeration in the Constitution, of certain rights, shall not be construed to deny or disparage others retained by the people.

In other words, just because a right is not listed in the Constitution does not mean that the people do not have it. The Ninth Amendment places a limit on government power. Government may not claim that the people have only the rights listed in the Constitution.

Many Supreme Court decisions have dealt with these additional rights. For example, in *Escobedo* v. *Illinois*, the Supreme Court determined that accused persons have the right to remain silent during questioning. In *Gideon* v. *Wainwright*, the justices ruled that accused persons have the right to be represented by an attorney.

Putting It All Together

The Bill of Rights protects many of the basic freedoms we enjoy as Americans. However, we have other rights not protected by it. In your notebook, list some of these rights and how they are protected.

Freedom of Religion

Thinking on Your Own

Freedom of religion is very important in a society that includes many different religious beliefs. What problems could arise if the government favored one religion over others?

Many colonists and later immigrants came to America to have greater freedom to practice their religion. Many colonists and later immigrants came to these shores to escape religious persecution. The first two clauses of the First Amendment to the Constitution deal with religion.

The Establishment Clause

The First Amendment begins: "Congress shall make no law respecting an establishment of religion." This is known as the **Establishment Clause**. Great Britain had established, or made, the Church of England its official religion. Many citizens of the new United States wanted to make sure this did not happen here. They did not want the government to support any one religion. Thomas Jefferson said the Establishment Clause set up "a wall of separation between church and state."

The Supreme Court has heard many cases involving the place of religion in American life. Most of these cases involved the separation of church and state. For example, should religious symbols be placed on government property?

In 2005, the Court handed down two important decisions. Hanging copies of the Ten Commandments in county courthouses in Kentucky was declared unconstitutional. However, a monument of the Ten Commandments on the grounds of the Texas state capitol was not unconstitutional. The monument was in a 17-acre park along with other monuments.

---

focus your reading

Why was the Establishment Clause added to the Constitution?

Explain the issues involving religion and education.

Describe what the Free Exercise Clause guarantees.

words to know

Establishment Clause

Free Exercise Clause

Religion and Education

Not everyone favors separation of church and state or the Supreme Court's interpretation of the Establishment Clause. The biggest area of disagreement involves education. Most lawsuits have dealt with (1) aid to parochial schools, (2) release time, (3) school prayer and Bible reading, and (4) student religious groups.

Parochial schools are those run by religious organizations.

Parochial schools are schools run by religious or church groups. The kind of aid that governments can give to parochial schools has been the subject of several cases decided by the Supreme Court. The Court's decision in *Lemon* v. *Kurtzman* was especially important. This case laid the basis for the Court's decisions in later lawsuits about aid to parochial schools. The Court ruled in *Lemon*, first, that the aid must have a nonreligious purpose. Second, it must be neutral toward religion. The aid cannot be used to promote religion or harm it. Third, there cannot be an "excessive entanglement" of religion and government. These three factors are known as the "Lemon test." The justices use this test in ruling on new parochial aid cases.

**Landmark Supreme Court Case:
Aid to Parochial Schools**

Lemon v. *Kurtzman* (1971): Private schools in Pennsylvania were repaid from government funds for teachers' salaries, books, and other classroom materials.

The Court decided that the law allowing the payments was unconstitutional. The payments directly helped the schools by reducing their costs. This, in turn, helped the religious groups that ran the schools. The state closely monitored the program. This violated the third factor of the Lemon test. The monitoring involved the government in the business of the religious groups.

The Court has not struck down all laws involving state aid to parochial schools. Among the laws upheld were

- state payments to parochial schools to administer standardized tests required by the state

- lending of some materials and equipment, such as projectors, computers, and software, to parochial schools for nonreligious uses

- a Minnesota law that allows parents to deduct certain costs to send their children to parochial schools. The Court said that the tax deduction was available to all families. If parents send their children to public schools, they do not pay for tuition, textbooks, or transportation directly. Allowing parents of parochial schoolchildren to deduct these costs from their taxes makes the system equal.

- an Ohio law that allows parents in Cleveland to use school voucher payments to send their children to private schools. The Court ruled that the goal of the law was to aid low-income children. Otherwise, the children would remain in low-performing schools. The justices said that the goal of the vouchers was to aid the children, not the schools.

The second area of disagreement about religion and education has been release time. Students in public school are "released" from class to attend religious instruction. In 1948, the Court held that teaching religion courses in public school classrooms was unconstitutional. In 1952, the Court heard another release time case. This time, the Court ruled that students could be released from class to attend religious instruction. However, the courses had to be given in some place other than in the public school.

One of the most heavily debated issues is school prayer and Bible reading. The Supreme Court has ruled seven times since 1962 against prayer and Bible reading in schools. School buildings are public—government—buildings, and teachers are paid by the government. Allowing teachers to say prayers or read from the Bible in school buildings amounts to support of religion.

The Supreme Court has, however, upheld the use of public schools for student-led religious groups. In 1984, Congress passed the Equal Access Act. Most public high schools receive some kind of federal funding. According to the 1984 law, these schools must allow student-run religious groups to meet in the school. In 1990, the Court declared the law constitutional. The Court said that the schools may not lead such groups. However, the schools must allow religious groups the same freedom to use the school as any other student club, such as the school newspaper or debate team.

Free Exercise of Religion

The First Amendment has a second clause about religion. It states that Congress shall not pass any law "prohibiting the free exercise" of religion. This is known as the **Free Exercise Clause**.

Under the Free Exercise Clause, government may not limit what people believe. However, the Supreme Court has upheld government limits on what people practice as religion. For example, in 1879, the Court upheld the conviction of a Mormon for having two wives. Federal law bans polygamy—having more than one spouse at a time. The man claimed that the law violated the Free Exercise Clause. The Supreme Court disagreed. It ruled that Congress may pass laws that uphold social duties and public order.

In other rulings, the Court has found that

- parents must allow children to be vaccinated even if vaccination is against their religion.

- an Orthodox Jew on active duty in the air force may not wear his yarmulke.

- a person can be denied state unemployment benefits if fired for taking drugs as part of a religious ceremony.

However, the Court has upheld the right of Jehovah's Witnesses not to salute the U.S. flag. Saluting the flag violates their religious beliefs. The Court declared that the flag is a patriotic symbol. People do not have to go against their religious beliefs to show patriotism. There are other ways to develop and express patriotism.

Students may choose not to salute the American flag based on religious beliefs.

Putting It All Together

Is separation of church and state helpful or harmful to the nation? With a partner, make a T-chart. On one side, list reasons why you think it is helpful. On the other side, list reasons why you think it is harmful. Then decide on an answer to the question. Write a paragraph to state and explain your answer.

LESSON 3 Freedom of Speech and the Press

Thinking on Your Own

What do you think "freedom of speech" and "freedom of the press" mean? Discuss these terms with a partner. Then write a definition of each freedom in your notebook.

The First Amendment guarantees freedom of speech and freedom of the press. Speech is the spoken word. When the Constitution was written, "the press" meant the printed word: newspapers, books, and pamphlets. Today, the press is just one part of the **mass media**. Freedom of the press now extends to movies, radio, television, cable, and the Internet. Does freedom of the press extend to blogs and podcasts? The Supreme Court has yet to hear any cases involving these uses of the Internet.

Why are freedom of speech and freedom of the press important? After all, ideas do not need to be protected when most people agree with them. A democracy works best when all ideas—even unpopular ones—are discussed and thought about. For example, protests against the Vietnam War were very unpopular in the mid-1960s. By the late 1960s, the nation had turned against the war. The protests had forced many Americans to think about the war in new ways.

focus your reading

Summarize why speech is regulated.

When may prior restraint be used?

Discuss the major issues for freedom of the press.

words to know

mass media

pure speech

symbolic speech

seditious speech

defamation

slander

libel

fighting words

student speech

prior restraint

shield laws

commercial speech

Freedom of Speech

According to Supreme Court decisions, there are two types of speech. **Pure speech** is the spoken word. Pure speech may be a conversation between two people or a speech delivered to a crowd of 2,000.

Symbolic speech combines actions and symbols—with or without words—to express ideas. The Supreme Court has held that burning the U.S. flag to protest the Vietnam War was symbolic speech. As such, it was protected under the First Amendment. The Court also struck down a later federal law that made it a

crime to burn the flag. The ruling was very clear. Congress may not pass a law to limit the expression of an idea just because society does not like the idea.

Limits on Free Speech

Free speech is important to a free nation. However, government has the right to limit speech that is harmful. One type of speech that is limited is **seditious speech**. This is any speech that encourages the overthrow of the government or attempts to disrupt it.

The "clear and present danger" rule is the test for these cases. According to this rule, a person can be punished for using words that promote criminal acts. The Supreme Court has used this rule to test cases brought under the Smith Act of 1940. This sedition law was passed just before World War II. It has

Seditious speech is not allowed if it promotes violent action.

three major parts: it is a crime to encourage the overthrow of the government, to hand out material promoting the overthrow, or to belong to a group that promotes the overthrow. In its rulings, the Court has noted a difference between asking people to believe in something and encouraging them to act on that belief. Speech is protected when it only encourages people to believe something. However, speech is not protected when it encourages violent actions.

Landmark Supreme Court Case: "Clear and Present Danger" Rule

Schenck v. United States (1919): During World War I, Congress passed the Espionage Act of 1917. It forbade the speaking, writing, printing, or publishing of anything against the government. Charles Schenck was the general secretary of the Socialist Party. He was convicted of printing and mailing leaflets to 15,000 draftees. The leaflet urged them to refuse to report for military service. Schenck claimed that he was protected by the First Amendment.

The Supreme Court ruled against him. The Court agreed that in peacetime, Schenck would be protected. However, in wartime, his "speech" represented a "clear and present danger" to the nation. The Espionage Act was constitutional because Congress had the right to protect the nation.

Other kinds of speech that are not protected by the First Amendment are

- **defamation**: false words that damage a person's good name, character, or reputation

- **slander**: spoken defamatory speech

- **libel**: written defamatory speech

- **"fighting words"**: speech that is so insulting that it would cause a person to hit another

- **student speech**: two types of student speech within schools

  - indecent or vulgar speech

  - speech in school newspapers, plays and musicals, and similar school-related and school-supported activities

People who are the object of **defamation** may sue in civil court for money damages. However, in various rulings, the Supreme Court has limited the right of public figures to sue. The Court's concern is that such lawsuits might keep people from criticizing government officials.

The Supreme Court has also ruled that school officials may censor **student speech**. Students may not say or do anything in school that school officials consider improper. In other words, school officials may determine what students may or may not discuss in school newspapers or express in other school activities.

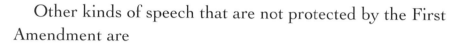

stop and think

Do you agree or disagree with the limits on the protection of student speech? Discuss the question with a partner. Make a T-chart to list pros and cons of the issue. Then write a persuasive essay giving reasons to agree and disagree with the limits on student speech. Conclude your essay with your personal opinion.

Freedom of the Press

A free press is an important tool in a democracy. It offers a place for people to voice their views about government. A free press enables reporters to investigate and report on government and business wrongdoing.

Freedom of the press means that there is no prior restraint on what is published. **Prior restraint** forbids the expressing of ideas before they are expressed. Doing this is censorship. How can something be forbidden before it occurs? The government could make up a list of what may or may not be expressed, either in writing or speaking. However, the Constitution forbids prior restraint.

The ban on prior restraint, however, is not complete. The Supreme Court has ruled that prior restraint is allowed in wartime. It is also permitted if the publication (printed or spoken) is obscene, meaning vulgar, or encourages violence. Student speech comes under the Court's test of prior restraint.

Free Press Issues

One of the biggest issues facing a free press is confidentiality, or secrecy, of sources. Many people will talk to reporters only if their names are kept secret. One of the most famous confidential sources was Deep Throat, the source for information about President Richard Nixon and the Watergate scandal. Mark Felt, the deputy director of the FBI during Watergate, revealed himself to be Deep Throat in 2005. You can understand why he did not want his name known in 1972.

Sometimes reporters are called to testify before grand juries that want to know the sources of stories the reporters wrote or researched. Reporters usually refuse to testify. They claim First Amendment protection. They fear that if they reveal their sources, no one will talk to them in the future.

The Supreme Court has ruled that reporters have no such right. The First Amendment does not protect a reporter's refusal to testify. The Court suggested a remedy, however. If reporters want special protection, then **shield laws** need to be passed. Some 30 states have passed laws to shield reporters and their sources. However, Congress has not passed a federal shield law.

Judith Miller, a *New York Times* reporter, was jailed for 85 days in 2005 for refusing to reveal a source.

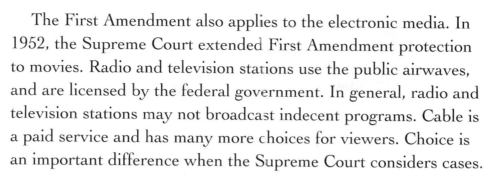

The First Amendment also applies to the electronic media. In 1952, the Supreme Court extended First Amendment protection to movies. Radio and television stations use the public airwaves, and are licensed by the federal government. In general, radio and television stations may not broadcast indecent programs. Cable is a paid service and has many more choices for viewers. Choice is an important difference when the Supreme Court considers cases.

The Telecommunications Act of 1996 replaced many of the regulations about radio and television in place since 1934. The act also attempted to regulate cable and the Internet. However, the Supreme Court struck down some parts of the law. The Court ruled that the Internet was protected by the First Amendment.

These decisions do not mean that Congress can do nothing. Congress can attempt to limit content on the Internet and cable in the future. However, any new laws must address the specific issues that the justices found unconstitutional.

Commercial Speech

Commercial speech is speech for business purposes. Advertising is an example of commercial speech. Until the 1970s, commercial speech was not considered protected speech. However, a series of Supreme Court rulings beginning in 1975 changed this view. It has struck down state or federal laws that banned

- listing prescription drug prices in ads
- listing liquor prices in ads
- radio and television ads for casinos

However, federal and state governments may ban certain kinds of advertising. False and misleading ads, and ads for illegal goods or services are banned. For reasons of public health and safety, for example, ads for cigarettes have been banned from radio and television.

Putting It All Together

Review the definitions you wrote in Thinking on Your Own. Write a paragraph to explain freedom of speech and a paragraph to explain freedom of the press. Share your work with a partner. Ask how you might improve your paragraphs to make them clearer to the reader.

Freedom of Assembly and Petition

Thinking on Your Own

The authors of the Bill of Rights believed the right to hold and attend public meetings was essential to democratic government. Do you agree? Create a bulleted list of reasons in your notebook to support your opinion.

Freedom of assembly and the right to petition allows people to gather together in private and in public places. The right of people to make their views known to public officials is also guaranteed. People may write petitions, letters, and ads to government officials. They may also lobby lawmakers and take part in marches, parades, and demonstrations. The right to assemble is one of the reasons people can form political parties, interest groups, and professional associations.

During the war in Iraq, demonstrations were held by those who were against the war (top) and those who supported the war (bottom).

Remember the principle of incorporation from Lesson 1. The Fourteenth Amendment applies to all the freedoms explained in Lessons 2 and 3. Because of the Fourteenth Amendment, these freedoms are protected from actions by state and local governments. The Fourteenth Amendment also protects the rights to assemble and petition government.

Freedom of Assembly

The First Amendment guarantees the right to assemble peacefully. However, people cannot just get together in the street and decide to march on city hall. The Supreme Court has allowed limits in order to ensure public order and safety. For example, in 1941, the Court ruled that states and cities

may require a permit for a demonstration, march, or parade. The purpose, however, cannot be to limit freedom of assembly. The permit is meant to control traffic flow and allow others to use the streets.

Regulations for protests and parades are known as time, place, and manner regulations. Rules may set the when, where, and how the protest may be carried out. For example, a permit might state that the march must begin at 10 A.M. and end by 1 P.M.; marchers must assemble at 12th Street and must walk east on Maple Street to city hall; there can be no bullhorns.

Time, place, and manner regulations must be specific and applied evenly to all groups. However, the content of a protest or demonstration may not be regulated. The rules regulating assemblies must be **content neutral**.

In 1977, the National Socialist Party, a white supremacist group, was allowed to march in Skokie, IL, a predominantly Jewish community.

Freedom of Assembly Issues

The Supreme Court has ruled that freedom of assembly does not extend to private property. For example, a group may not take over a shopping mall to hold a demonstration. A shopping mall is not like a public street with stores. Shopping malls are businesses owned by companies. However, the Court has upheld the right of peaceful petition in shopping malls. Individuals may approach shoppers to sign petitions.

Public property is property that people usually think of as places to demonstrate. These include streets, sidewalks, parks, and public buildings. The Supreme Court has upheld the right to assemble in public places. However, issues still arise about how to apply the freedom of assembly. Two questions in particular have come before the Court. Does the Constitution require the police to

Picketing is the walking back and forth of striking workers at a business. If the picketing is peaceful, it is protected. If it incites violence, it is not.

stop and think

How have the courts limited the right of assembly? List these limits in your notebook and work with a partner to decide whether you agree or disagree with each. As you read about the freedom of association, think about whether that right should also have limits. Explain your opinion in a one-sentence statement.

Gregory v. *City of Chicago* (1969): Dick Gregory, an African-American entertainer and activist, organized a march in Chicago. The march protested segregation in Chicago schools. The protesters had a permit and police protection as they marched five miles from city hall to the mayor's house. There, they marched in front of the house. About 1,000 people gathered to watch. After a while, the crowd began to throw rocks and eggs. They also shouted insults at the marchers. The police feared a riot. They ordered the protesters to end the demonstration and leave. The protesters refused. The police arrested them. Gregory and several others were convicted of disorderly conduct.

Gregory and the other protesters appealed. The Court sided with them. The protesters were peacefully exercising their First Amendment right. Because the protesters acted peacefully, they could not be charged with disorderly conduct. It was the crowd that had become disorderly.

allow a demonstration to continue if it has caused violence? When can the police order an end to a demonstration? The ruling in *Gregory* v. *City of Chicago* helped to answer these questions.

Freedom of Association

Freedom of assembly grants, or allows, a right of association. People may gather with others who share their views, interests, and concerns. These concerns may include working to create political, economic, and social change.

Organizations such as the American Medical Association routinely hold meetings for their members.

The right goes back to a Supreme Court ruling in 1958. The state of Alabama demanded that the Alabama chapter of the National Association for the Advancement of Colored People (NAACP) turn over its membership list. The NAACP refused and was fined. It appealed and the Supreme Court ruled in its favor. The Court said that association with others who support the same ideas is a guaranteed right.

Putting It All Together

Why is freedom of assembly important in a democracy? Use the information from the lists you created to write a paragraph to answer the question.

LESSON 5 Rights of the Accused

Thinking on Your Own

What happens when a police officer arrests a suspect? Think of an arrest that you have watched on a television program or movie or one that you imagine. Answer the question by writing a bulleted list in your notebook.

Due process is guaranteed by both the Fifth and Fourteenth Amendments. The Fifth Amendment states that the government may not take from any person "life, liberty, or property, without due process of law."

The Fourteenth Amendment picks up these words. It extends due process to state governments. In its decisions, the Supreme Court has applied each of the guarantees discussed in this lesson to the states.

What exactly is due process? The best way to define **due process** is that the government must act fairly and obey the rules of law. Due process is especially important to people in the criminal justice system.

> ### focus your reading
>
> List the rights a person has at the time of arrest.
>
> What rights protect a person who is on trial?
>
> What does the Constitution say about punishment?
>
> ### words to know
>
> due process
> search warrant
> probable cause
> exclusionary rule
> good faith exception
> self-incrimination
> bail
> preventive detention
> double jeopardy
> capital punishment

Rights at the Time of Arrest

Because of the Fourth Amendment, police cannot just go into a home or business and search it. They must have a **search warrant** issued by a judge. A police officer must swear under oath that there is probable cause. **Probable cause** means the reasonable possibility that evidence of a crime or criminal is in the place. However, the Supreme Court ruled that the police

Constitutional Protections for the Accused

Stage of the Criminal Justice System	Section of the Constitution	Protection
Gathering Evidence	Fourth Amendment	Protection against "unreasonable search and seizure"
Arrest and Questioning	Fifth Amendment Sixth Amendment	Right to remain silent Right to have an attorney
Jailing Before Trial	Eighth Amendment	Protection against "excessive bail"
Trial	Sixth Amendment Fifth Amendment Article III, Section 2, and the Sixth Amendment Sixth Amendment	Right to a "speedy and public trial" Protection against "double jeopardy" Trial by jury Right to question witnesses
Punishment	Eighth Amendment	Protection against "cruel and unusual punishment"

do not need a warrant if they see someone in the act of breaking the law. They can search and arrest a person at the scene of a crime.

What if the police conduct an illegal search? Can the evidence be used in a trial? In a 1914 ruling, the Supreme Court developed the **exclusionary rule** for such cases. The general answer is "no." However, as the Court continues to hear illegal search-and-seizure appeals, it continues to work on the exclusionary rule. For example, in a 1984 case, the Court developed the **good faith exception**. The police had asked for and received a search warrant based on probable cause. The warrant was later found to be incorrect. The Court upheld the conviction. It said the police had acted in good faith in believing that their warrant was correct.

The Supreme Court has found that students on school property do not have the same Fourth Amendment protections.

New Jersey v. *T.L.O.* **(1985):** A student was suspended and tried in juvenile court for having marijuana. The marijuana was found when the assistant principal searched her purse. He thought she had been smoking cigarettes in the restroom. He found the cigarettes as well as the marijuana.

The Supreme Court ruled that school officials do not need a search warrant or probable cause. However, school officials must have a reasonable belief that the search will find that the student has broken school rules. In later drug testing cases, the Court has ruled in favor of drug testing. No probable cause is needed to test students who want to take part in extracurricular activities.

The Fifth and Sixth Amendments offer protections to people suspected of or arrested for crimes. The Fifth Amendment guarantees that they do not have to incriminate themselves. **Self-incrimination** means giving testimony against oneself. A person does not have to help the police prove his or her guilt. The Miranda rule, which is read to suspects and those being arrested, states: "You have the right to remain silent. Anything you say may be used against you in a court of law." The Fifth Amendment also protects people from being pressured, tortured, or beaten into confessing.

The Miranda rule also states that the person "has the right to have an attorney present during questioning." Because of two other rulings, an arrested person must be represented by an attorney. If the person cannot afford an attorney, the court must appoint one. This is the result of *Escobedo* v. *Illinois* and *Gideon* v. *Wainwright*.

The Eighth Amendment does not state that everyone arrested for a crime must be allowed bail. **Bail** is money that a defendant deposits with the court as a promise to appear for trial on the appointed day. The judge in the case sets the amount of bail. The Eighth Amendment says only that the amount may not be "excessive." If it is feared that a person may commit another crime, a judge may decide not to set bail. This is called **preventive detention**. The Supreme Court has ruled that this is legal.

> **stop and think**
>
> Review the bulleted list you wrote for Thinking on Your Own. Did the police officer involved follow the law? If not, what should the officer have done? Add or remove items from your list. Share your answers with a partner.

Rights Related to Trial

The Sixth Amendment provides two protections once a person is arrested for a crime. The first is a guarantee of a "speedy, public trial." The government must bring an accused person to trial quickly. Today, the public part of the guarantee often involves media coverage. Local crimes often lead off the nightly television news and make front-page headlines. The courts have to balance the public's and media's desire for news with the defendant's right to a fair trial. The Supreme Court has ruled that the media has no special right to cover a trial.

People accused of a crime are guaranteed a lawyer.

The second protection is the right to confront witnesses during the trial. The attorney for a defendant has the right to question anyone who testifies against the defendant.

The Sixth Amendment also reinforces an earlier section of the Constitution, Article III, Section 2. This guarantees a person's right to a trial by jury.

Youth Court

Many local courts are overburdened by criminal cases. One solution for juvenile crimes is youth court, also called peer, teen, or student court. Youth court is only for first-time offenders under the age of nineteen. They must be accused of minor crimes only, such as trespassing and truancy.

In about half of youth courts, everyone involved is a teenager: the judge, jury, lawyers, and the bailiff, who swears in witnesses. Volunteers from seventh to twelfth grade take part in the program. The jury foreperson, judge, bailiff, defense attorneys, and prosecutors receive ten hours of training for their roles. They serve for a year and take turns at the different court jobs. In many youth courts, former defendants must be jurors at least once.

Most hearings take less than an hour. Jurors determine sentences. Sentences usually involve community service, writing a letter of apology, taking a victim-awareness class, and touring the local jail.

More than 1,000 youth courts have been set up. They hear more than 100,000 cases a year. Youth courts have impressive records. Students who go through youth court are more likely to stay out of trouble than students who go through the regular juvenile justice system.

The Fifth Amendment protects a person from **double jeopardy**—being tried twice for the same crime. There are some limits to this protection, however. Suppose a jury cannot agree on a verdict. The defendant may be tried for the crime again. Sometimes a crime is both a federal offense and a state offense. A person may be tried for the crime in both a federal and a state court. A crime may include several acts. For example, a person counterfeits CDs and sells them. The person can be charged and tried for both counterfeiting and selling fake goods.

Punishment

The Eighth Amendment prohibits "cruel and unusual punishment." Most Eighth Amendment cases that reach the Supreme Court involve **capital punishment**. This is another term for the death penalty. The death penalty is a heavily debated topic. Many human rights advocates say that it violates human rights. They point to the high numbers of minorities on death row. They also note the number of people who have later been found innocent of the crime of which they were convicted. However, supporters of the death penalty say that it keeps others from committing murders. It can also provide some end to the grief of victims' families.

Capital punishment remains a topic of much discussion in the United States.

Since the 1970s, the Supreme Court has made several important rulings related to the death penalty. The death penalty may be used only if the crime is murder. The penalty must be used fairly. It cannot be used more for one type of defendant than for others.

Recent Court rulings have refused to allow the death penalty for the mentally retarded and those under eighteen. The Court also decided that juries, not judges, must decide on whether to sentence a convicted killer to death.

Putting It All Together

Work with a partner. Imagine that you are reporters for the local television station. You get a call that the police are going to raid an illegal betting operation. You go along on the raid. Then you follow what happens until the end of the trial. Write a summary for your audience when the trial is over. Explain the action the police took before the raid, the arrest, the bail hearing, and the trial.

Participate in Government

Apply for a Green Card

A green card is officially known as a Permanent Resident Card. It is an official form of identification. It shows that a person is a lawful permanent resident (LPR) of the United States. The person is living and working here legally. In order to get a job in the United States, a person must show proof of citizenship or a green card.

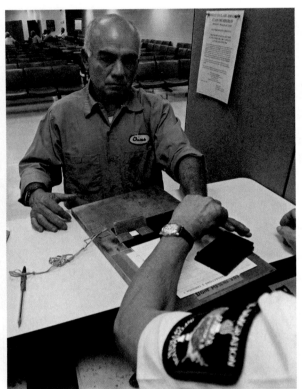

A Permanent Resident Card must be renewed every ten years

A green card is usually issued for two or ten years. A two-year card gives a person conditional permanent resident status. Certain conditions must be met before the two years are over. Then the person may apply for a Permanent Resident Card. Permanent cards expire at the end of ten years and must be renewed.

The U.S. Citizenship and Immigration Services Web site is a great tool for people wishing to become LPRs. The site provides information on how to apply. Among the ways are immigration through a family member or employment. Among those eligible are husbands or wives, unmarried children, married children, brothers and sisters, and parents of U.S. citizens or LPRs already living in the United States.

There are also special classes for refugees and asylum seekers. Refugees are people who have fled their countries because of war or famine. Asylum seekers fled because they feared jail or murder for their political views.

To Find Out More About Applying for a Green Card:

• Check the U.S. Citizenship and Immigration Services Web site (USCIS) for forms, fees, and addresses of CIS office.

Skill Builder

Identify Point of View

A person's point of view is shaped by his or her family, religion, education and reading, friends, personal experiences and time period.

For example, consider probable cause and the searching of bags. Should people's bags be searched before they get on an airplane? Before the 1980s, the answer would have been "no." Then airplane hijackings began and that point of view changed.

It is not always easy to determine point of view. To help you identify point of view, follow these steps:

1. Identify the author or the speaker. Learn about the person's background. If the person belongs to an organization, try to find out if the group supports conservative or liberal causes.

2. Identify the argument or issue. Find the main idea and supporting details of the piece of writing or speech.

3. Identify the facts and other information used to support the argument. Distinguish facts from opinions.

4. Examine the kinds of words and phrases that the author or speaker uses. Do some words and phrases seem more favorable to one side of the issue or the other?

5. State the person's viewpoint in your own words.

Use the following excerpt to answer the questions.

I consider the foundation of the Constitution as laid on this ground: That "all powers not delegated to the United States, by the Constitution, nor prohibited by it to the States, are reserved to the States, or to the people."

— Thomas Jefferson, Secretary of State, February 1791.

1 What do you know about the writer?

2 What point or argument is he making? What information does he use?

3 Write a sentence stating the writer's point of view about the powers of Congress.

Chapter

14 CIVIL RIGHTS: EQUAL JUSTICE

Getting Focused

Skim this chapter to predict what you will be learning.

- Read the lesson titles and subheadings.
- Look at the illustrations and read the captions.
- Review the vocabulary words and terms.

Civil rights are the rights of everyone to equal protection of the laws. Discrimination based on race, religion, gender, or ethnic origin is against the law. The Fifth and Fourteenth Amendments protect us from discrimination by government or by any other group or individual.

What are the Fifth and Fourteenth Amendments about? Write down as much as you can remember about both amendments. Then check your ideas against the amendments.

Women's rights (top left), civil rights (top right), Native American rights (bottom left), and rights of those with disabilities (bottom right) have all been the focus of demonstrations.

Equal Protection Under the Law

Thinking on Your Own

What does the term "civil rights movement" mean to you? Write a paragraph in your notebook to explain what the civil rights movement was and who was involved.

Equal protection under the law is guaranteed by the Fourteenth Amendment. The amendment declares that a state may not "deny to any person within its jurisdiction the equal protection of the law." Jurisdiction means authority or rule. Equal protection is also guaranteed under the due process clause of the Fifth Amendment.

Why is the guarantee of equal protection needed? The nation has a long history of discrimination against various groups. **Discrimination** is the unfair treatment of people. Discrimination may be based on race, gender, ethnic origin, age, mental or physical disability, or religion.

> ### focus your reading
>
> What tests do courts apply to decide if a law is discriminatory?
>
> List the groups that have had to fight for their civil rights.
>
> ### words to know
>
> discrimination
>
> rational basis test
>
> strict scrutiny
>
> fundamental rights
>
> intermediate scrutiny
>
> segregation

Classifications and Judicial Tests

Not all different treatment is discriminatory. Governments may pass laws based on distinctions among groups. This means that governments may set up classifications that recognize differences among groups. For example, a state government may classify students at its state university as in-state and out-of-state. The state government may then charge out-of-state students more to attend the state university.

The laws of the United States prohibit age discrimination.

In its rulings, the Supreme Court has developed three tests to determine if a law is discriminatory. The basic test is the **rational basis test**. Is there a reasonable relationship between the classification and an acceptable government purpose? For example, the states can set the legal drinking age at twenty-one. It is assumed that people under twenty-one are not mature enough to drink responsibly. To refuse alcohol to all blue-eyed people regardless of age is not a reasonable law. There is no relationship between eye color and responsible drinking. The rational basis test is applied to laws dealing with age, disability, income, and similar categories.

The second test is called **strict scrutiny**. This test is applied to laws based on race or national origin. Courts ask if the classification meets a "compelling public interest." They also ask if there is no other way to achieve that goal. For example, the Supreme Court has upheld affirmative action laws based on race. The Court recognizes the need to make up for years of discrimination against African Americans. It has also determined that affirmative action laws are required to achieve this goal.

In addition, the Supreme Court uses the strict scrutiny test for cases involving **fundamental rights**. These include the Bill of Rights, the right to vote, and the right to travel freely between states.

Possible discrimination against women comes under **intermediate scrutiny**. This lies between rational basis and strict scrutiny. The Supreme Court has thrown out any law based on the idea that women are weak or inferior to men. For example, the Court ruled that the states may not keep women from serving on juries. The Court has also upheld laws that seek to correct past injustices against women. The Court has upheld equal athletic programs for men and women under Title IX of the 1972 Education Act. The Court asks if the gender distinction serves an important government objective. The distinction must also be substantially, or largely, related to achieving the goal.

stop and think

The Supreme Court uses three tests to rule about discrimination. Create a T-chart to explain the three rules mentioned in this lesson. In the left column, list the rule. In the right column, list the facts. Work with a partner to complete the chart.

The Fight for Civil Rights

Everyone's civil rights have not always been protected. In 1866, Senator Charles Sumner led a group in Congress who strongly supported passing a civil rights bill. The law, if enacted, would have protected slaves from Southern Black Codes. By the 1870s, **segregation**, or the separation of whites and African Americans, was the law throughout the South. In *Plessy* v. *Ferguson*, the Supreme Court ruled that "separate but equal" was constitutional. It was almost 60 years before the Court overturned this decision. This time, it ruled that separate schools were inherently unequal, in *Brown* v. *Board of Education* in 1954.

The civil rights movement began with African Americans, as early as 1900. The National Association for the Advancement of Colored People was founded in 1909. Its lawyers filed the lawsuit that became the landmark case *Brown* v. *Board of Education*.

The decision in *Brown* was soon followed by the Montgomery bus boycott of 1955–1956. The bus boycott resulted from Rosa Parks's refusal in Alabama to give up her seat on a bus to a white man. In 1957, the governor of Arkansas refused to allow African-American students to enter Little Rock Central High School. President Eisenhower called out federal troops to enforce integration.

By the 1960s, civil rights leaders such as Dr. Martin Luther King, Jr., were leading marches and protests against segregation. Protesters were beaten and jailed. Some were murdered for their work.

By the early 1970s, many other groups were following their lead. Hispanics and Native Americans staged protests against discrimination. Women held marches and lobbied for equal rights and reproductive rights. Those with physical and mental disabilities and their supporters demanded education, jobs, and housing. In the 1980s, gay and lesbian activists were also marching for equal rights.

Immigrant rights remain a topic of debate in the United States today.

Putting It All Together

Write a paragraph in your notebook describing the role the Supreme Court plays in guaranteeing equal protection under the law. Does it always ensure that all groups are treated equally?

Federal Civil Rights Laws

Thinking on Your Own

Before reading the lesson, create a five-column chart in your notebook. Label column one, "What I Know About Civil Rights Laws"; column two, "What I Want to Know About Civil Rights Laws"; column three, "What I Learned About Civil Rights Laws"; column four, "What I Still Want to Know"; and column five, "How I Will Learn This." Fill in the chart as you read.

The civil rights movement pushed Congress to act. In 1957, Congress passed the first civil rights law in many decades. Additional civil rights laws were passed in 1960, 1964, and 1968. Congress also passed a series of important voting rights acts—in 1965, 1970, 1975, and 1982.

The laws touched many parts of U.S. life. To vote in some southern states, people had to pay a poll tax. The tax discriminated against African Americans because many were poor farmers. The poll tax was banned. Employers and labor unions are now barred from discriminating against workers because of race, color, gender, religion, physical disability, or age.

It became a federal crime to deny anyone service in a public place because of race, color, religion, or national origin. Restaurants, hotels, buses, and movie theaters are examples of public places.

Homeowners are barred from refusing to sell a house to someone because of race, color, religion, national origin, gender, or disability. Landlords are barred from refusing to rent to someone based on the same categories.

---

focus your reading

Why is there conflict over affirmative action?

Explain how the Supreme Court judges laws based on gender differences.

What kinds of things are protected by the right to privacy?

words to know

quota system

reverse discrimination

A civil rights commemoration in Philadelphia, MS

Affirmative Action

The civil rights laws made illegal all present and future discrimination. However, past discrimination had left its effects on U.S. society. What could be done about these effects? The federal government adopted a policy of affirmative action to answer this question. Affirmative action gives special consideration to African Americans, members of other ethnic groups, and women for employment and admission to colleges and universities. State and local governments and all federal agencies must follow this policy. All schools that receive federal aid and all employers doing business with the federal government must also follow it.

Affirmative action policies allow colleges and universities to show special consideration when enrolling ethnic groups and women.

The policy was first used in 1965. President Lyndon Johnson signed an executive order to use affirmative action in awarding federal contracts to businesses. Many employers and schools set up **quota systems** to try to fulfill the policy. They set aside a certain number of jobs or admissions openings for ethnic groups and women.

Not everyone was, or is, pleased with the policy. Some people say it is **reverse discrimination**. It discriminates against those who are not members of minority groups or women. The first major challenge to affirmative action occurred in 1978, when the Supreme Court ruled that Allan Bakke, a white male, had been unfairly denied admission to medical school as a result of affirmative action.

Landmark Supreme Court Case: Affirmative Action

Regents of the University of California **v.** *Bakke* **(1978):** Allan Bakke, a white male, applied to the medical school of the University of California at Davis. He was denied admission. The school had set aside 16 of its 100 openings for nonwhite students. Bakke claimed reverse discrimination and sued. His lawsuit charged the school with violating the equal protection clause of the Fourteenth Amendment.

The Supreme Court agreed that Bakke had been unfairly denied admission to the medical school. The Court ruled that race may be among the factors used in making affirmative action decisions. However, race may not be the only factor. Strict quota systems are unconstitutional.

Since the Bakke case, other affirmative action lawsuits have reached the Supreme Court. With each decision, the Court has rethought the policy. By the mid-1990s, the Court had narrowed the use of affirmative action. In a decision in 2004, the Court stated that it hoped that in 25 years, affirmative action would no longer be necessary. However, for the time being, affirmative action still needed to be enforced.

stop and think

Discrimination on the basis of various classifications, or differences, is illegal. What are those differences? Reread the introduction to the lesson. With a partner, make a list of the classifications.

Women's Rights

Gender has often been the basis of laws. The purpose of these laws may have been to protect women. However, the end result was often discriminatory. For example, a law against women working at night kept them from high-paying assembly-line jobs. This law discriminated against women while benefiting men.

However, the Supreme Court did not overturn any laws based on gender until 1971. In *Reed* v. *Reed*, the Court struck down an Idaho law. It gave fathers preference over mothers in handling the estates of their children. The Court ruled the law violated the equal protection clause of the Fourteenth Amendment.

Why was this law overturned when earlier laws were not? The nation was undergoing vast changes in the 1960s and 1970s. Views about women's roles were changing. As you read in Chapter 12, the Court in general reflects the opinions of the nation.

Since 1971, the Court has overturned a number of gender-based distinctions. For example, girls cannot be barred from joining Little League teams. Membership in men-only clubs and community service groups must be opened to women. Women must be paid the same retirement benefits as men. However, not all gender-based distinctions are unconstitutional. For example, the Court has approved the male-only draft for military service.

Although women may serve in the armed forces, only men can be drafted.

Right to Privacy

Congress has written several laws related to personal privacy. In 1974, it passed the Family Educational Rights and Privacy Act. Among other things, the act gives parents the right to see their children's school files. Students who are eighteen years of age and older may inspect their own files.

In 1996, Congress updated the Fair Credit Reporting Act. This law regulates the collection and distribution of information about people's credit. Using the Internet for browsing and shopping has complicated protecting personal information. Sites now regularly collect information about the people who visit them.

At age eighteen, students are able to review their education files with school counselors.

The Supreme Court has also recognized a person's right to privacy. In various cases, the Court has used the Bill of Rights and the Fourteenth Amendment to support the right to privacy. Decisions in cases about abortion and the sharing of personal information without someone's knowledge have been based on the right to privacy.

Putting It All Together

Fill in the chart that you began at the start of this lesson. Then write a summary of this lesson. Share your summary with a partner. Ask if you covered all the main points. If not, ask what you need to include in a revision. Revise your summary.

LESSON 3

U.S. Citizenship

Thinking on Your Own

Think about what it means to be a citizen of the United States. Write a letter to a friend in your notebook to explain what it means to be a U.S. citizen.

Most of the people who live in the United States are **citizens**. A person is a citizen of the United States either by birth or by naturalization. Naturalization is the process of becoming a citizen. A person who is born in another country, is still a citizen of that country, and lives in the United States is known as an alien, or a noncitizen. Noncitizens must go through naturalization to become U.S. citizens. By the early 2000s, about 12 percent of the U.S. population was born somewhere else. Of these 33 million people, more than 12 million were naturalized citizens.

U.S. Immigration Policy

At some time or another, all American families came from somewhere else. Since 1776, more than 70 million immigrants have come to the United States. Immigrants have made many significant impacts on the country. Cesar Chavez, for example, was the son of Mexican immigrants. He dedicated his life to improving the working conditions of migrant farm workers. Chavez, who died in 1993, was awarded the Presidential Medal of Freedom by President Bill Clinton in 1994. The work he did through the United Farm Workers union dramatically improved the lives of migrant farm workers.

The policy of the United States toward immigration has changed over time. Before 1882, no limits were placed on immigration. In 1882, Congress passed the Chinese Exclusion Act to ban Chinese people from immigrating to the United States. Another law that was passed that year barred people with mental illness and disabilities, convicts, and the poor from entering the United States.

The Immigration Acts of 1921 and 1924 and the National Origins Act of 1929 set up a quota system for immigrants. Only a certain number of people from each nation were allowed to immigrate. The number depended on how many people from that nation had settled in the United States by 1890. Most people had come from northern and western Europe. Far fewer people had come from southern and eastern Europe. As a result, the quotas for southern and eastern European nations were very small. In addition, people from Asia and Africa were barred from immigrating.

Ellis Island served as the gateway to the United States for thousands of immigrants during the late 1800s and early 1900s.

In 1965, the quota system ended. The Immigration Reform Act of 1965 set the total number of immigrants from the Eastern Hemisphere at 170,000. The total from the Western Hemisphere was set at 120,000. The earlier acts had limited immigration from all places to 165,000. However, the new act set up a **preference system**. People whose skills would be useful to the nation were given top priority. Nuclear scientists, for example, fell into this category. The second group was unmarried adult children of U.S. citizens. Third were husbands, wives, and unmarried children of permanent residents.

Between 1965 and the mid-1980s, **undocumented aliens**, also called undocumented immigrants, came to the nation in ever greater numbers. They entered the country without proper papers such as a passport, visa, or entry permit. To try to stop illegal immigration, Congress passed the Immigration Reform and Control Act of 1986. It had two major parts.

First, the act gave some undocumented aliens the opportunity to become citizens. Without papers, they would never be able to apply for citizenship. An undocumented alien must have entered the country before 1982 and lived here

Immigration laws govern who is admitted to the United States.

continuously. Undocumented aliens who met these conditions could apply for amnesty. **Amnesty** is a pardon, or forgiveness, for a crime granted by the government. With amnesty, many became lawful, temporary residents.

Second, the 1982 act made it a crime to hire undocumented aliens. Now employers are required to make sure that their workers are either citizens or in the nation legally.

In 1990, a new Immigration Act rewrote the quota system. Immigration is now set at 675,000 people a year. The preference system continues in effect. Family members of citizens and of permanent residents make up about one-third of immigrants each year. Another 140,000 places are given to people who have jobs waiting for them here. In addition to the 675,000 immigrants, the 1990 act also allows the nation to admit refugees fleeing war and persecution.

Since the attacks of 9/11, immigration laws are more strongly enforced. Federal government agencies dealing with immigration are now part of the Department of Homeland Security.

stop and think

Create a timeline based on the information about U.S. immigration policy. Share your timeline with a partner.

Rights of Noncitizens (Aliens)

Federal law has several categories of aliens. Undocumented aliens are only one category. A **resident alien**, or a **lawful permanent resident** (LPR), is someone who has moved permanently to the United States. A **nonresident alien** is someone who is in the country only for a short period. Foreign tourists and foreign students are nonresident aliens. A **refugee** is a person fleeing persecution. During the 1990s and early 2000s, the United States admitted refugees from war-torn nations in Africa and eastern Europe.

Lee Shong, a Hmong refugee from Laos, smiles as she arrives at the Sacramento airport in June 2004.

The Supreme Court has ruled a number of times about the rights of aliens. Noncitizens, or aliens, have almost all the same rights as citizens. However, aliens may not vote and usually do not serve on juries. They do not have the same freedom of movement as citizens. Noncitizens must notify the Customs and Enforcement Service when they move within the country. They have no obligation to join the armed forces. Yet around 30,000 were serving in the military in the early 2000s.

Aliens have the same duties as citizens. They must pay taxes and obey the law. They must also do nothing to harm the country. An alien who has committed a serious crime may be **deported**. The person is then returned to his or her country of origin. Illegal entry into the United States is also a reason for deportation. The Supreme Court has ruled that in deportation cases, rights such as the right to a court hearing do not apply. Deportation is a civil matter, not a criminal matter.

Citizenship

Most U.S. citizens are citizens because they were born in the United States. People born in U.S. territories such as Guam, Puerto Rico, and the U.S. Virgin Islands are also U.S. citizens. Children born to immigrants to the United States, including undocumented aliens, are also citizens. Anyone else gains U.S. citizenship through naturalization. Read the feature on page 267 to find out how a person becomes a naturalized citizen.

At one time, being born in the United States was not enough to be a citizen. A person had to be white. In 1857, the Supreme Court ruled that African Americans were not citizens. In *Scott* v. *Sandford*, the Court said that neither free nor enslaved African Americans were citizens.

As part of the naturalization process, applicants must answer questions and take a test.

In 1868, Congress made sure that this argument could never be used again. It approved, and the Northern states ratified, the Fourteenth Amendment. This amendment grants citizenship to "all persons born or naturalized in the United States." It further declares that "no state shall make or enforce any law" that denies the rights of citizenship to anyone.

Citizenship grants rights to those who hold it. These rights are the subject of this chapter. Citizenship also sets up certain responsibilities. Among the duties of responsible citizens are

- to know their legal rights
- to respect the law
- to become informed voters
- to work at the polls on Election Day
- to join groups that work for causes they are interested in
- to write to elected officials to state their views

In other words, responsible citizens take part in the political life of the nation.

Putting It All Together

The oath that new citizens take is one very long sentence. With a partner, paraphrase, or rewrite, the oath so that it is easier to understand. As you write, turn each clause, or new idea, into one or two sentences.

Oath of Affirmation for New Citizens

To become a citizen, a person must meet certain requirements. When a person is judged ready to become a citizen, the person must take the following oath of allegiance:

"I hereby declare, on oath, that I absolutely and entirely renounce and abjure all allegiance and fidelity to any foreign prince, potentate, state, or sovereignty of whom or which I have heretofore been a subject or citizen; that I will support and defend the Constitution and the laws of the United States of America against all enemies, foreign and domestic; that I will bear true faith and allegiance to the same; that I will bear arms on behalf of the United States when required by law; that I will perform noncombatant service in the Armed Forces when required by law; or that I will perform work of national importance under civilian direction when required by law; and that I take this obligation freely without any mental reservation or purpose of evasion: So help me God."

Participate in Government

Become a Naturalized Citizen

How does a person become a naturalized U.S. citizen?
The following lists the steps to naturalization.

1. A person must:

   - be at least eighteen years of age.

   - have entered the nation legally.

   - have lived in the United States for at
     least five years. (It is three years for
     husbands and wives of citizens.)

2. A person must

   - file a petition for naturalization.

   - pay an application fee.

   - be interviewed by an immigration official.

   - have two witnesses testify to the person's character.

   - be able to read, write, and speak English. (Anyone over
     fifty years of age who has lived in the United States for
     twenty years does not have to meet this requirement.)

   - be of "good moral character."

   - support the Constitution and the United States.

   - know basic information about the history and
     government of the United States.

   - take the oath of affirmation.

A person must
pass a citizenship
test to become a
U.S. citizen.

A lawful permanent resident must meet the first three items
on the list. Then he or she may apply for citizenship. The
person files an application and pays a fee. Citizenship and
Immigration Services (CIS) runs a background check. CIS is
looking for a criminal history. The agency also makes sure the
person is not a risk to the nation's security. Next, the person
has an interview with CIS and takes the citizenship test. If the
application is approved, the person joins other new citizens in a
naturalization ceremony.

Skill Builder

Recognize Bias

Bias is strong feeling for or against a person or issue without facts to support that feeling. Bias is an emotional reaction based on opinion. Another word for bias is *prejudice*.

Usually, bias is against a person or issue, rather than in support of someone or something. An example was the refusal of districts to integrate schools in the 1950s and later. This refusal was based on the bias of whites against African Americans.

Voters can also be biased for or against candidates and government policies. For example, some voters are biased against having a woman as president. Some do not think that a woman could be tough enough. Others do not think that women are smart enough. The fact that women run the governments of other nations does not change their minds. People with a bias may refuse to accept any facts that conflict with their viewpoint.

To determine bias:

1. Identify the issue.

2. Identify the arguments that are made about the issue.

   - Are the arguments based on fact or opinion? Can the arguments be proven to be true or false? If not, then the arguments are based on opinion.

3. Identify the speaker or writer.

   - To what political party or other group does the person belong?

   - What is the viewpoint of this organization on the issue?

   - What else do you know about the person or group?

Complete the following activity.

Two friends are arguing about whether a woman should be elected president. With a partner, take the two sides in the argument. Write a dialogue that presents arguments for and against having a female president. After you are finished, reread the dialogue. Underline any statements that show bias on either side of the argument.

6 UNIT

TAKING PART IN GOVERNMENT

- Join a political party.
- Campaign for candidates.
- Donate money to a public interest group.
- Attend League of Women Voters candidate nights.
- Become an informed voter.
- Write your member of Congress or your local council member to let him or her know your opinion on issues.
- Vote.

These are just some of the ways that ordinary citizens can take part in government. This unit will explain more about the political party system and voting. You will also learn about influences on public officials and public policy.

Chapter

15 POLITICAL PARTIES

Getting Focused

Skim this chapter to predict what you will be learning.

- Read the lesson titles and subheadings.
- Look at the illustrations and read the captions.
- Review the vocabulary words and terms.

Create a table with three columns. Label the first column "Democratic Party." Label the second column "Republican Party." Label the third column "Third Parties." In columns one and two, list the positions each party has taken on major issues that you know about. In column three, list anything you know about a third party or the history of third parties in the United States.

The 2004 Democratic National Convention (left) was held in Boston, MA. The 2004 Republican National Convention (right) was held in New York, NY.

Purpose of Political Parties

Thinking on Your Own

Why do you think nations have political parties? What do you think political parties do? Make a list in your notebook of activities that you know political parties carry out.

Republican, Democratic, Libertarian, Conservative, Green—how many political parties are there in the United States? Most people would say two. A **political party** is an organized group of people who share common values and goals. Members of political parties try to get their candidates elected to office.

The Democratic and Republican Parties are the most powerful. Most people who belong to a party belong to one of them. However, the nation has a number of other political parties. These are known as third parties. Some third parties have played important roles in our nation's electoral history.

How does a person join a political party? All a voter has to do is say, "I am a Republican" or "I am a Democrat." There are no membership dues, though political parties may ask their supporters for contributions. However, no one has to donate money to join a political party.

| focus your reading |

Describe the functions of the political parties.

What types of party systems exist in different countries?

Who are independent voters?

| words to know |

political party

multiparty system

coalition

one-party system

Voters can register as members of a political party or as independents.

Functions of Political Parties

The Constitution does not mention political parties. George Washington even warned against setting up political parties. However, modern political parties serve five major functions, or roles.

First, political parties nominate candidates for public office. Party officials look for members who will appeal to voters. Candidates must be honest and trustworthy. They must be qualified to do the job if elected. Candidates must also be good campaigners and support the major policies of their political parties.

Senator Dianne Feinstein reads California's roll call at the Democratic National Convention in Boston in 2004.

Second, political parties play a role in governing the nation. Remember that Congress is organized along party lines. So are state legislatures. Like legislators, the president and state governors are elected with the support of a political party. The president and governors depend on legislators elected by their party to get laws written and passed. The president and state governors fill top-level jobs in executive departments with their own party members.

Third, political parties educate the public about issues. Candidates for office mail out brochures describing their positions on issues and send press releases to the media. Candidates take part in debates, give interviews, and speak to groups. Their campaign organizations pay for ads and Web sites. The goal of these activities is to educate and inform the public about a candidate—and his or her party's—views.

Remember that a candidate generally supports the views of his or her party. Parties also serve as reliable labels for candidates. They help voters make up their minds about candidates. For example, the Republican Party claims to be for lower taxes. A candidate who is a Republican is therefore likely to promise tax cuts. A voter who thinks this is important will vote for a Republican candidate.

Fourth, the political party not in power becomes the "loyal

Debates such as this one between Johnny Byrd, Mel Martinez, and Bill McCollum during the 2004 campaign in Florida help voters understand the positions of each candidate.

opposition," or watchdog, of government. The party that loses the presidency—or governorship—is known as the party out of power. For example, when Bill Clinton, a Democrat, was president, the Republican Party was out of power. As the watchdog, the party out of power criticizes the actions of the party in power. It also offers alternatives to the president's policies.

Fifth, political parties reduce conflict. The nation is made up of people with many different points of view on issues. Political parties provide ways for people to work together—in and out of government. Political parties also provide for the peaceful transfer of power from one election to the next.

Political parties alone perform the first two roles and the last one. Other groups, such as the media, also educate the public about policy issues. Public interest groups, too, act as watchdogs over government actions. Environmental groups, for example, issue press releases about proposed laws.

stop and think

Review the list of activities you wrote for Thinking on Your Own. Add to or cross out items based on what you just read. Share your list with a partner. Decide which activities relate to the various roles of political parties.

Types of Party Systems

The United States has basically a two-party system. The Republican and Democratic Parties are much more powerful than any third parties. These two have far more money and members than the other parties combined. For example, in 2005, Republicans held 55 of the 100 seats in the U.S. Senate. Democrats held 44 seats, and one senator was an independent. Only about a dozen nations have a two-party system.

Most nations have a multiparty system. In a **multiparty system**, there are several major and minor parties. Each party wins some offices, including seats in the national legislature.

Italy is an example of a nation with a multiparty system.

Often, a major party must partner with a minor party to put together a majority in the legislature. The partnership is known as a **coalition**. Leaders of the minor party are appointed to the cabinet. Many European nations and emerging democracies have multiparty systems.

A few nations have **one-party systems**. The party and the government are the same. The leaders of the party are the leaders of the government. The only candidates are ones that the party approves. The former Soviet Union was a one-party nation. Today, China, Vietnam, Cuba, and North Korea have one-party systems. Like the former Soviet Union, the Communist Party dominates each.

Ross Perot ran as an independent in the 1992 presidential campaign.

A Word About Independents

Between one-quarter and one-third of all registered voters are independents. They belong to no organized political party. Independents, too, can play a major role in deciding which candidate is elected. Their votes have become increasingly important since the 1990s. The two major parties have about the same number of members. As a result, candidates, especially for president, need to appeal to independents in order to win.

Putting It All Together

What if no one belonged to a political party? Discuss the question with a partner. Make notes as you talk. Then use these notes to write an essay titled "What If No One Belonged to a Political Party?"

Beginnings of U.S. Political Parties

Thinking on Your Own

Suppose you were going to start a political party in the United States today. Think about the government policies that are important to you. List five policies in your notebook. Then write a sentence to explain why each policy should be supported.

Political conflict began early in President George Washington's first administration. His secretary of the treasury, Alexander Hamilton, proposed a plan to improve the nation's credit. It included creating a Bank of the United States. Secretary of State Thomas Jefferson and Congressman James Madison were outraged. The Constitution, they argued, did not give Congress the power to set up a bank. A majority in Congress voted for Hamilton's bank, but the issue divided the nation's political leaders. By 1797, two political parties had developed. One was the Federalist Party, and the other was the Democratic-Republican Party.

focus your reading

What were the main issues that divided political parties before the Civil War?

Explain how power has shifted between the major parties since 1932.

Describe the role third parties have in U.S. politics.

words to know

third party

single-issue party

ideological party

splinter party

From Washington to Lincoln

Supporters of Hamilton's policies became the Federalists. They believed in a strong central government and a loose interpretation of the Constitution. The supporters of Jefferson and Madison called themselves Democratic-Republicans. They were strict constructionists, and favored a weak central government.

The Federalists were able to elect John Adams as president in 1796. However, by 1800, the Federalists had lost many

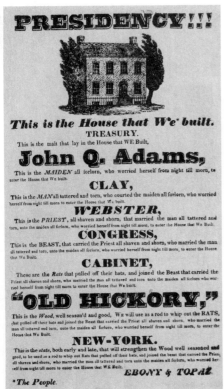

This is the House that We' built.

TREASURY.

This is the malt that lay in the House that WE Built,

John Q. Adams,

This is the MAIDEN all forlorn, who worried herself from night till morn, to enter the House that We built.

CLAY,

This is the MAN all tattered and torn, who courted the maiden all forlorn, who worried herself from night till morn, to enter the House that We built.

WEBSTER,

This is the PRIEST, all shaven and shorn, that married the man all tattered and torn, unto the maiden all forlorn, who worried herself from night till morn, to enter the House that We Built.

CONGRESS,

This is the BEAST, that carried the Priest all shaven and shorn, who married the man all tattered and torn, unto the maiden all forlorn, who worried herself from night till morn, to enter the House that We Built.

CABINET,

These are the Rats that pulled off their hats, and joined the Beast that carried the Priest all shaven and shorn, who married the man all tattered and torn, unto the maiden all forlorn who worried herself from night till morn to enter the House that We Built.

"OLD HICKORY,"

This is the Wood, well season'd and good, We will use as a rod to whip out the RATS, that pulled off their hats and joined the Beast that carried the Priest all shaven and shorn, who married the man all tattered and torn, unto the maiden all forlorn, who worried herself from night till morn, to enter the House that We Built.

NEW-YORK.

This is the state, both early and late, that will strengthen the Wood well seasoned and good, to be used as a rod to whip out Rats that pulled off their hats, and joined the beast that carried the Priest, all shaven and shorn, who married the man all tattered and torn unto the maiden all forlorn, who worried herself from night till morn to enter the House that We Built.

EBONY & TOPAZ.

*The People.

The 1828 race for president was the first to use a nationally organized political party. These efforts allowed Andrew Jackson to defeat John Quincy Adams.

supporters, and Jefferson's party was far stronger. Jefferson was elected president in 1800 and again in 1804. The Democratic-Republican Party won every presidential election until 1828.

By the election of 1828, the Democratic-Republican Party had split into the Democratic Party and the National Republican Party, or Whigs. A national bank and tariffs divided the Democratic-Republican Party along regional lines. Tariffs are taxes on goods brought into the country. In general, northern members of the party favored the national bank and tariffs. Western and southern members were against tariffs and the national bank. In time, the issue of slavery would also split the nation politically.

The modern Democratic Party traces its history back to Jefferson's Democratic-Republican Party. From 1828 until the 1850s, the Democratic and Whig Parties were the two major parties. However, the Whigs were able to elect only two presidents.

By the 1850s, slavery dominated U.S. politics. The Whig Party had collapsed. Several smaller parties tried to appeal to former Whigs and anti-slavery Democrats. Among them was the Free Soil Party. It wanted to ban slavery from the new territories to protect white workers.

The modern Republican Party was founded in 1854. It was the most successful of the new parties and quickly picked up supporters. By 1860, its candidate, Abraham Lincoln, won the presidency.

Modern Political Parties

After the Civil War, the Republican Party was the dominant party. It was the party that saved the Union and ended slavery. It also supported high tariffs and free homesteads in the West.

President Franklin Roosevelt addressing Congress in 1935

In the northern states, businessmen, farmers, and many laborers voted Republican. So did most African Americans in states that allowed them to vote. The Democratic Party was strongest in the South and Midwest. Between 1860 and 1932, the Democrats won only four presidential elections.

One of those presidents, Woodrow Wilson, won because the Republican Party split in the 1912 election. Former president Theodore Roosevelt and his supporters left the Republican Party over the party's choice of presidential candidate, President William Howard Taft. They founded the Progressive Party, also known as the Bull Moose Party. As a result, Roosevelt and Taft divided the Republican vote. Democratic candidate Woodrow Wilson was able to win.

A shift in power occurred in the 1932 election. The nation was in the depths of the Great Depression. The policies of Republican president Herbert Hoover were not working. Voters elected Democrat Franklin D. Roosevelt. During President Roosevelt's New Deal era, the Democrats supported labor unions, price supports for farmers, and Social Security. Between 1932 and 1968, only one Republican was elected president, Dwight Eisenhower, a World War II general and hero.

The power shifted again between 1968 and 1992. Republicans held the White House for 20 of those 24 years. Voters turned to Democrat Jimmy Carter in 1976 after the crimes of the Nixon presidency. Carter failed to win reelection against Republican Ronald Reagan in 1980. Reagan was the most conservative president since the early 1920s. He won the votes of Democrats unhappy with their party's social policies, as well as the votes of traditional Republicans. By the late 1980s, more and more southerners were voting Republican.

Then Democrat Bill Clinton won the 1992 and 1996 elections. A southerner, he was able to pick up support in the South. He also appealed to moderates in both parties. In addition, a third-party candidate, Ross Perot, may have taken some votes away from the Republican candidate, President George H. W. Bush.

President Ronald Reagan was sworn into office in 1981 and became one of the most conservative presidents since the early years of the twentieth century.

A contested election in 2000 put a Republican back in the White House. George W. Bush defeated Al Gore after the U.S. Supreme Court ruled against counting contested ballots in Florida.

Third Parties

While U.S. politics is dominated by two major parties, third parties also play a role. **Third parties** are also called minor parties. A third party develops when a group of people believes that the major parties are not dealing with some important issue.

There are three types of third parties. The **single-issue party** arises to deal with a single social, economic, or moral issue. The Free Soil Party was a single-issue party.

An **ideological party** wants to change society rather than solve a single problem. The Socialist, Socialist Worker, Socialist Labor, and Communist Parties want to do away with private ownership. They want the government to control all business. The Libertarian Party, on the other hand, wants to do away with most government control. Ideological parties win few votes, but they tend to last for a long time.

A **splinter party** breaks off from a major party. Splinter parties are often based on a politician's personal popularity. When the candidate fails to win office, the party collapses. As in the 1912 election, splinter parties can make a difference in an election. For this reason, they are sometimes called "spoilers." They spoil the outcome for one group.

It is possible that the 2000 election could have turned out differently without a third-party candidate. The Green Party candidate, Ralph Nader, ran on a platform of protection for the environment, health care for everyone, campaign finance reform, and similar policies. He won 2.8 million votes, or 2.7 percent of the total cast. Most experts believe that without Nader, most of these votes would have gone to the Democrat, Al Gore.

Theodore Roosevelt ran for president as a member of the Bull Moose Party in 1912.

Putting It All Together

With a partner, create a timeline of major political parties in the United States. On your timeline, indicate which parties dominated time periods before the Civil War and since the Civil War.

Organization of Parties

Thinking on Your Own

Do you belong to a social group or club? What are the titles of the officers of the clubs? What does each officer do? Write a paragraph in your notebook to explain how a club is set up.

As you just read, anyone can join any political party, or choose not to join a party. In some states, a person must declare a political party to vote in a primary election. **Primary elections** choose the candidates from each party who will run in the general election. A voter does not have to belong to a party to vote in a general election.

Political parties are loosely joined groups of people with similar views on issues. Many people do nothing more than vote for their party's candidates. Others actively work for their party, especially at the local level. Working for a political party is one way to influence what government does.

The National Party

Every four years, Americans watch as the national parties carry out one of their most important duties. The parties hold their **national conventions**. The conventions have only two tasks. They nominate the party's presidential and vice-presidential candidates, and they write the party's platform. A **platform** states the party's position on various issues. It is a promise of what the party will do if elected. For example, the platform may state that the party will reform the nation's health-care system.

During the 1936 presidential campaign, the Democratic Party provided convention attendees with tickets and a party handbook that explained the party's position.

Between conventions, the national party is run by the **national committee**. This committee is headed by the national chairperson. The president selects the national chair for his or her party, and the committee approves the choice. The national committee of the party out of power picks its own chair. The job of the chairperson is to run the party organization on a day-to-day basis.

The national committee is made up of a man and a woman from each state. They are often large donors to the party or important politicians. The national committee handles disagreements among different groups within the party over the party's positions on issues. The national committee also raises money for campaigns. Another task, especially for the party out of power, is getting media coverage. The party wants to keep reminding the public what they are doing and what the opposing party is not doing.

Each national party also has a Senate campaign committee and a House of Representatives campaign committee. These congressional campaign committees raise money for House and Senate races. They also recruit candidates to run for office. The chairs and members of the committees are elected by fellow senators or members of the House.

stop and think

Draw a diagram to show how national parties are set up. Leave enough space to list what each part does. Work with a partner to create and fill in your diagram. Then as you read, create a similar diagram for state parties.

The State Party

State law and a party's own rules determine how political parties are organized on the state level. A **state central committee** runs the party at the state level. Committee members are usually elected from local parties and usually

elect the party state chair. However, in some states, a state party convention chooses the state chair.

The state party has several duties. The major effort of the state party is to get statewide candidates elected to state government and to Congress. It raises campaign funds to support statewide candidates. Some of the funds may also be given to county and local candidates.

Many areas require that campaign workers remain at least 100 feet from a polling place.

The Local Party

Each county within a state has a **county committee**. Local parties elect its members. A county chair runs the committee. In some states, the county chairs are very powerful. Candidates running for office in a state need their support. The county chairs may actually choose which candidates the party will back. County chairs also recommend people for appointment to judgeships and jobs in state executive departments.

There are several different local party structures. The **precinct** is the smallest unit of elective government. Everyone in a precinct votes at the same polling place. A voting precinct contains from 300 to 600 people. In a very large city, a single apartment building may be a precinct.

The precinct may also be the smallest unit of the local political parties. In that case, each precinct has a volunteer precinct captain for each political party. The job of the precinct captain is to organize party members to work in election campaigns. One of the tasks is to get members out to vote. Several precincts are combined into **wards**. Ward leaders coordinate the work of precinct captains, especially during election campaigns. Some cities also have political clubs. They focus on a certain section of a city or on electing a particular candidate.

Political clubs often support local candidates and promote issues of community importance.

In some areas of the country, there are no precincts. Instead, cities, towns, townships, and villages are divided into districts for voting. The local political parties in those areas are organized into district or township committees.

Putting It All Together

Suppose a person wants to become active in a local political party. Where should the person start? How far could the person go in the party? Create a flowchart that shows a person's progress through different levels of a political party, ending at the national level. Work with a partner to be sure you do not skip a step.

Passing Judgment on a Party's Policies

In the following excerpt, President John F. Kennedy describes how the party system works. He was speaking to national and state Democratic committees at the White House in 1963.

"**Our Founding Fathers did not realize that the basic fact which has made our system work was outside the Constitution. And that was the development of political parties in this country so that the American people would have the means of placing responsibility on one group, that group would have a chance to carry out its program, and the American people would have an opportunity to indicate their dissatisfaction by going to an alternative.**"

—President John F. Kennedy, 1963

reading for understanding

1. Explain what the president means by "outside the Constitution."

2. What is the "alternative" that President Kennedy mentions?

3. What is the process that President Kennedy is describing?

Participate in Government

Join a Political Party—or Not

The two major political parties are the Democratic Party and the Republican Party. There are also a number of minor parties.

When you register to vote, you will be asked how you want to register. Do you want to register as a Republican, a Democrat, an independent, or for some other party? To help you decide, you should do some research and some thinking.

To Find Out More About the Parties:

• Check the Web sites of the national parties.

• Contact your local election board to find out if you can vote in primaries if you are an independent. You can find the phone number in the white pages of the phone book.

• Check the phone book for the number of any minor party you may be interested in learning more about.

To decide how to register, think about the following questions.

• Are you a liberal, conservative, or moderate on public policy issues?

• Do you believe in a strict or loose interpretation of the Constitution?

• Can independents vote in primaries in your state?

Democrats tend to be loose constructionists and liberal. The party supports civil rights, women's rights, and government aid for health care, education, housing, and the environment. Republicans tend to be strict constructionists and conservative. The party supports tax cuts and less government aid to individuals, local communities, and the states. Independents may hold more liberal views on some issues and more conservative views on others.

Remember to register when you turn eighteen!

Skill Builder

Recognize Propaganda

Propaganda is the spreading of information, beliefs, and ideas to influence people for or against an issue or person. Propaganda does not always tell the whole truth. It is usually biased.

Advertising is a form of propaganda. Advertisers may exaggerate claims about their products. Candidates for public office also use propaganda to get people to vote for them. There are seven major propaganda techniques that are used in political campaigns.

- **Card stacking**: The candidate gives only the positive side of his or her record. This is the most popular technique.

- **Labeling**: A candidate pins an unflattering name on an opponent. In 2004, John Kerry was labeled a "flip-flopper."

- **Glittering generality**: The candidate speaks in broad terms about what he or she will do to solve problems. Richard Nixon promised "peace with honor" in the Vietnam War but never said how he would achieve this.

- **Plain folks**: Although worth millions of dollars, a candidate acts like an ordinary citizen.

- **Testimonial**: Movie actors, singers, and other famous people may publicly support a candidate. People who admire the celebrity may vote for the candidate.

- **Transfer**: A candidate uses a patriotic symbol, such as the American eagle, on ads. The hope is that voters will associate the candidate with patriotism and vote for him or her.

- **Bandwagon**: A candidate urges voters to vote for him or her because "everyone else is."

To analyze propaganda, look for these techniques in campaign ads, brochures, and Web sites.

Complete the following activities.

1 With a partner, design an ad that uses one of the techniques.

2 Think of a recent political campaign. Write a paragraph and explain any examples of propaganda that you remember.

Chapter

16 ELECTIONS, VOTING, AND VOTER BEHAVIOR

Getting Focused

Skim this chapter to predict what you will be learning.

- Read the lesson titles and subheadings.
- Look at the illustrations and read the captions.
- Examine the tables.
- Review the vocabulary words and terms.

Every four years, voters elect a president. Every two years, they elect members of the U.S. House of Representatives. Elections that occur between presidential elections are known as off-year elections. Voters also elect their U.S. senators, their state's governor, members of the state legislature, their mayor, members of the local school board, and more. In a democracy such as ours, all levels of government are freely elected.

Choose a recent election. It could be for a local, state, or federal office. Make a bulleted list with facts about the election, such as candidates, issues, the winners, and so on.

The democratic process allows citizens to participate in government through voting, political party activities, and electoral campaigns.

Nominating Candidates

Thinking on Your Own

Suppose you want to run for class president. You are going to self-announce your candidacy. This is a way that people let others know they want to be elected to a certain office. Write a press release in your notebook announcing your candidacy. In it, explain why you are running and what issues you think are important.

To **nominate** a candidate means to select a candidate to run for office. There are four ways that candidates have their names placed on ballots. They are the (1) caucus, (2) convention, (3) direct primary, and (4) petition. Which one a person uses depends on the office he or she is seeking. A candidate for town council may get on the ballot by petition. A presidential nominee from a major party is chosen at a national nominating convention.

Caucus and Nominating Conventions

The earliest method for choosing candidates was the caucus. Party leaders met and decided who would run for office. By the 1820s, however, voters were complaining that caucuses were undemocratic. As a result, parties developed the nominating convention.

A **nominating convention** is a public meeting of party members to choose candidates for office. By 1832, the major parties were using nominating

Ross Perot self-announced his candidacy for president in both the 1992 and 1996 elections.

> ### focus your reading
>
> Explain the difference between a caucus and a nominating convention.
>
> What are the different kinds of primaries?
>
> How is the petition an example of direct democracy?
>
> Describe how the major parties nominate presidential candidates.
>
> ### words to know
>
> nominate
> nominating convention
> party bosses
> general election
> direct primary election
> closed primary
> open primary
> petition
> proportional representation primary
> winner-take-all primary
> preference primary

conventions to choose presidential candidates. By the 1840s, nominating conventions were also used for state, county, and local offices. Party members in the precinct or district elected delegates to a county convention. At the county convention, the delegates chose candidates to run for county offices. The delegates also elected delegates to the state convention. This convention chose candidates for statewide offices.

Conventions soon became as undemocratic as the old-style caucus. In many areas, party leaders known as **party bosses** chose the delegates. They, in turn, made sure the bosses' candidates were chosen to run in elections. In the early 1900s, primary elections replaced conventions in many areas.

Caucuses and conventions did not stop. Both are still used in a number of states. However, there are changes. In a modern caucus, party leaders do not make the choices. Instead, members of a political party meet in their districts or precincts on caucus day. They discuss the qualifications of the candidates and then vote. Whoever wins the most votes becomes the party's candidate in the general election. The **general election** is the election in the fall that determines who will hold the office until the next general election.

The Iowa Caucus takes place around the state.

Primary Elections

Today, most states use **direct primary elections** to select party candidates. In these elections, several candidates from the same party campaign against one another. Voters cast their ballots on primary election day. The person with the most votes will run against candidates for that office from other parties.

There are two types of direct primary. The **closed primary** is limited to registered members of political parties. Each party has its own ballot. Republicans may vote only for Republican candidates. Democrats may vote only for Democrats. New Jersey uses the closed primary.

Hillary Clinton campaigning for the Senate in 2000

In an **open primary**, any registered voter may vote for any candidate. This means that independents may vote. However, the voter must choose which party he or she wants to vote in. A voter may not vote for a Republican for mayor and a Democrat for governor. Texas is one of the 23 states that use the open primary.

Petition

The petition is another way for a candidate to get on the ballot. A **petition** is a paper that states that a person wishes to run for a

Petitions are one means of putting a candidate's name on the ballot.

particular office, such as town mayor. A certain number of voters must sign the petition and it must be filed with the board of elections. The voters must live in the area that will be served by the candidate if elected. The number of signatures needed varies, based on the office. A person running for governor needs more signatures than a person who wants to be a city council member.

Nominating Presidential Candidates

Nomination for president is somewhat different from nominations for other offices. Presidential candidates have to compete for delegates to the national convention. The 2004 Republican convention had 2,520 delegates. The Democratic convention had 4,348. The national committee of each party gives each state committee a certain number of delegates. The voters decide who those delegates will be and whom they will support. In presidential primaries, voters do not vote for the candidates. Voters cast their ballots for delegates who support the candidates.

Most states use presidential primaries to choose delegates. However, Iowa uses the caucus system. About one-quarter of the states hold conventions.

Create a concept web to show how candidates are selected. Label the large circle "Nominating Candidates." Then add smaller circles and connect them with lines to the large circle. In each circle, write one way that a candidate is nominated. Share your web with a partner. Add one detail to each circle.

There are three kinds of presidential primary: (1) proportional, (2) winner-take-all, and (3) preference. Each state has its own laws for setting up its primary. Remember that depending on the state, the primary may be open or closed. In some states, each candidate is awarded delegates in proportion to the number of votes cast. For example, if Candidate A gets 70 percent of the votes, then 70 percent of the delegates will represent Candidate A at the convention. This is known as a **proportional representation primary**. The Democratic Party uses this type of primary. In the **winner-take-all primary**, which is used by the Republican Party in most states, the candidate who gets the most votes gets all the delegates.

Franklin Roosevelt, in 1932, was the first presidential candidate to address a party convention.

A few states use a **preference primary**. Voters do not vote for delegates. Instead, they vote to show which candidate they prefer. Party conventions later choose the delegates. The number of delegates for each candidate is based on the number of votes each receives. However, most preference primaries are only advisory—the party is not bound by the results of the primary. Most award their delegates on the basis of winner-take-all.

Putting It All Together

Suppose your school held nominating conventions for student council president. Which type of primary do you think would be the most fair to candidates? Remember that each type of presidential primary may be open or closed. Discuss the question with a partner. Make notes as you talk. Then write a paragraph to explain which type of primary you think is most fair. Be sure to explain your reasons.

LESSON 2

Elections and Election Campaigns

Thinking on Your Own

Think about a recent political campaign in your community, state, or in the nation. Perhaps the mayor or governor was running for office. Perhaps it was the year when members of the U.S. House of Representatives were being elected. In your notebook, list five things that you remember about the candidates and the campaign.

The right to vote freely is basic to democracy. Citizens exercise this right on Election Day. For candidates, that day is the end of their campaign for public office. Depending on the office, the campaign may have lasted as long as two years and cost millions of dollars.

focus your reading

What levels of government regulate elections?

What are the different ways that candidates may finance their campaigns?

Describe how the use of soft money is limited.

How are the president and vice president elected?

words to know

political action committee

hard money

soft money

popular vote

electoral vote

Regulating Elections

Most elections in the United States choose state or local officials. As a result, most laws that govern elections are state laws—not federal laws. However, federal laws regulate federal elections. These laws, in turn, impact state election laws. For example, Congress has the power to set the date for the election of members of Congress. This date is the first Tuesday following the first Monday in November. As a convenience and a cost saver, many state and local elections are held on the same day.

In 2002, Congress passed the Help America Vote Act. It requires changes in how states carry out elections. This law

Polling places can be in schools, firehouses, libraries, or other community buildings.

was passed as a result of the ballot and voter registration problems in the 2000 presidential election. Among the sections of the law, all states must upgrade their voting machines by 2006. Poll workers must be better trained to deal with voter registration problems on Election Day. Voter registration files must be computerized.

Financing Elections

Campaigns for local and state offices tend to begin during the year the election will be held. In recent years, presidential races have begun as early as two years before the election. Even races for Congress start as much as one year early. Long campaigns require a great deal of money to rent offices, pay campaign workers, and run ads on television and radio and in newspapers. Campaigns also finance Web sites.

Where does the money come from? Contributions come from private donors and from public money. In 1971, the Presidential Election Campaign Fund Act set up public funding for presidential campaigns. Taxpayers may check off a box on their income tax form to direct $3 of their tax to the fund. In 1975, Congress set up the Federal Election Commission (FEC) to oversee campaign finance law. Campaigns must report donations to the FEC.

Howard Dean's 2004 campaign for president was the first to use the Internet for soliciting campaign contributions.

Candidates may use the money for primary and caucus campaigns. The money may also be used by the national parties to help pay for their national convention. Presidential candidates may also apply for funds for the general election campaign. The federal fund matches campaign contributions dollar for dollar. In a recent campaign, this amounted to $76 million for each of the major party candidates. However, if a candidate accepts the federal money, he or she may not spend money over this amount. If the candidate does not accept the funds, he or she may spend as much money as he or she wishes.

Campaign money can lead to abuses. Donors of large amounts often expect favors in return for their money. As a result, Congress has passed a number of campaign finance laws. The table on page 294 shows the limits for contributions to candidates in federal elections.

Limits on Giving to Campaigns for Federal Office			
Primary Election	**General Election**	**Political Action Committee**	**National Party**
No more than $2,000 to a single candidate	No more than $2,000 to a single candidate	No more than $5,000 to one PAC in a year	No more than $95,000 during two years between congressional elections

There are also other restrictions. Corporations and labor unions may not give money directly to candidates. However, their political action committees may. A **political action committee** (PAC) is a political organization formed by special-interest groups such as companies and labor and professional organizations. The American Medical Association (AMA) and the National Rifle Association (NRA) are examples of special-interest groups. Each has a PAC.

PACs may not give more than $5,000 to a single candidate in an election or a total of $10,000 to a candidate for a primary and a general election. PACs set up by professional groups get their money from donations by their members. If the PAC is set up by a corporation, the corporation's employees donate the money.

Hard Money and Soft Money

Donors and candidates found a way around the campaign finance laws. The laws regulated **hard money**. This is money raised and spent by the candidates for Congress and the White House themselves. However, the laws said nothing about **soft money**. This is money raised and spent for party-building activities. These include registering voters and get-out-the-vote activities on Election Day.

By the 1990s, the two major parties were raising millions of dollars in soft money. There were no laws to govern how much soft money could be raised. Although soft money was supposed to be used only for party building, the parties found ways to use the money to help their candidates.

In 2002, Congress passed the Bipartisan Campaign Reform Act. The goal of the law is to ban soft money. However, by the 2004 presidential election, the parties and their supporters had found a way around the new law. Donors were setting up Section 527 organizations to raise and spend money to support their party's candidates. A Section 527 organization is similar to a PAC, except it is not regulated by the FEC. Instead, it is governed by the Internal Revenue Code.

Presidential Elections

From studying the Constitution, you know that voters do not elect the president and vice president. Voters choose electors who meet in December as the Electoral College. They choose the president and vice president. On the Monday after the second Wednesday in December, the electors in each state meet in their state capitols to vote. The votes are sent to Congress.

On January 6, the Senate and the House count the votes in a joint session. The candidate who has the majority of the electors' votes is declared president.

Of course, by then the nation already knows the outcome. On election night, newscasters keep a running count of both the popular vote and the electoral vote. The **popular vote** is the number of votes cast by citizens. The **electoral vote** is the number of votes that the states and the District of Columbia have in the Electoral College. Each state's electoral vote is the sum of its two senators plus the number of its members in the House. The District of Columbia gets three electoral votes.

January 6 is the date when a joint session of Congress meets to officially count the electoral votes in a presidential election.

In all, there are 538 electoral votes. To become president, a candidate must get 270 votes. Sometimes, a candidate may win a huge number of electoral votes. For example, in 1980, Ronald Reagan defeated President Jimmy Carter by 489 votes to 49. Elections may also be much closer. In the 2000 election, George W. Bush won 271 votes to 266 for Al Gore. In the popular vote, Gore won 500,000 more votes. However, it is the electoral vote that counts in the election for president, not the popular vote.

Putting It All Together

How is a presidential election similar to and different from other elections? Discuss this question with a partner. Take notes as you talk. Then create a Venn diagram to show the differences and similarities. Refer to the notes you made in the Thinking on Your Own activity at the start of the lesson for ideas.

People in the News

Antonio Gonzalez (1957–   )

Antonio Gonzalez is president of the Southwest Voter Registration Education Project (SVREP). It was founded in 1974 and is the largest and oldest nonpartisan Latino voter participation organization in the nation. SVREP is based in Los Angeles but works with Latino communities across the country.

Gonzalez joined SVREP in 1984. He had graduated from the University of Texas at San Antonio and done graduate work at the University of California at Berkeley. His family was not rich. His father emigrated from Mexico and loaded trucks for a living.

Gonzalez began as a community organizer for SVREP. He put together voter participation activities. By the time he became president of the organization in 1994, there were five million Latinos registered to vote. In ten years, Gonzalez's efforts have almost doubled the number. SVREP ran hundreds of voter-registration and get-out-the-vote campaigns in 14 states to achieve this goal.

It is not just presidential elections that motivate Gonzalez and SVREP. They work to get Latinos involved and voting in local and statewide elections. Gonzalez believes that Latinos must participate in politics. Otherwise, they will not be able to solve the problems of their communities. SVREP's slogan is "Your Vote Is Your Voice."

Voting Rights and Voting Laws

Thinking on Your Own

Create an outline of this lesson in your notebook to help you study the information. Look at the subheadings and the vocabulary words. Be sure to include information from the table. Fill in the outline as you read the lesson.

The right to vote is guaranteed to all U.S. citizens today. However, this was not always the case. African Americans were not even considered citizens until 1868. Women were not allowed to vote until 1920. Native Americans were not granted citizenship until 1924.

As you read in Lesson 2, states set most election laws. State laws also govern voter qualifications. However, the Constitution has set limits on what states can do. The table on page 296 shows how these limits developed.

> ### focus your reading
>
> What groups have benefited from the expansion of the right to vote?
>
> What laws have been needed to expand voting rights for African Americans?
>
> ### words to know
>
> suffragists
> grandfather clause
> literacy test
> poll tax

The History of Voting Rights

During the early years of the United States, states had religious and property requirements for voting. The religious qualification was left over from the many colonies that wanted to live according to their religion. For that reason, a man had to be a member of the church to be able to vote. By 1810, religion was no longer a requirement for voting in any state. However, the property qualification continued until the mid-1800s. Only men who owned property and paid taxes on it could vote. As the population grew, fewer men owned land. They made their living as shopkeepers and factory workers. As a result, the property requirement was also eliminated.

By the mid-1800s, all white male citizens could vote. However, women could not vote. In the 1840s, suffragists began to campaign for the vote for women. **Suffragists** are people who supported the right to vote, especially for women. As tensions grew over slavery in the 1850s, suffragists put aside their own fight to work for an end to slavery. When the

Extending Suffrage

1810	End of religion as a qualification for voting
Mid-1800s	End of property qualifications
1870	Fifteenth Amendment makes it a crime to deny anyone the right to vote because of the person's race or color or because the person had been enslaved
1920	Nineteenth Amendment makes it a crime to deny women the right to vote
1924	Indian Citizenship Act gives Native Americans citizenship and the right to vote in federal elections
1961	Twenty-third Amendment gives the District of Columbia three electors for presidential elections
1964	Twenty-fourth Amendment bans the poll tax to keep poor African Americans from voting in elections
1965	Voting Rights Act of 1965 ends literacy tests and other tests used to keep African Americans from voting; law applies to local, state, and federal elections
1970	Voting Rights Act of 1970 expands the Voting Rights Act of 1965
1971	Twenty-sixth Amendment lowers the voting age to eighteen
1975	Expansion of the earlier Voting Rights Acts
1982	Another expansion of the earlier Voting Rights Acts
1993	Federal "Motor Voter" Law enables citizens to register to vote when they register their cars
2002	Help America Vote Act requires states to update their registration and voting systems

Civil War was over, women expected to get the right to vote along with African Americans. However, the Fifteenth Amendment made it a federal crime to deny the vote to any *citizen* because of race, color, or enslavement. The word *citizen* was understood to mean "men."

Women campaigned for another 50 years to get the vote. They did not succeed until 1920. The Nineteenth Amendment guaranteed women the right to vote.

During the 1960s, Congress passed major laws to end voting discrimination against African Americans.

The final expansion of voting rights was the Twenty-sixth Amendment in 1971. It lowered the voting age from twenty-one to eighteen for all local, state, and federal elections.

Congress has also passed other voting laws that affect the states. The "Motor Voter" Law of 1993 allows people to register to vote when they apply for a driver's license. After the problems with the 2000 presidential election, Congress passed the Help America Vote Act of 2002.

stop and think

How has the right to vote been expanded to different groups during the history of the United States? List each group that has gained the right to vote. Use the text and the table to make your list. Review your list with a partner. Add any groups you missed.

qualifications to vote

To vote, a person must be

- a native-born or naturalized citizen.
- at least eighteen years old.
- a resident of the state in which he or she wishes to vote. Residency requirements vary from state to state. It is typically 15 to 30 days.
- registered to vote. The exception is North Dakota.

Voting Rights Laws

The goal of the Fifteenth Amendment was to expand voting rights to African-American men. However, Southern lawmakers found ways to keep them from voting. Some states added a **grandfather clause** to their state constitution. Only men whose grandfathers had been free to vote before 1867 could vote. Because most African Americans had been enslaved, their grandfathers could not have voted. The U.S. Supreme Court ruled the grandfather clause unconstitutional in 1915.

During the 1960s, voter registration drives were held throughout the South.

The Voting Rights Act of 1965 outlawed the literacy test. Before 1965, whites as well as African Americans could be asked to pass a **literacy test**. However, whites could pass by writing their names. African Americans had to explain some point of law such as a section of the U.S. Constitution.

The **poll tax** was a fee of a few dollars that a person had to pay in order to vote. For poor farmers, this was a lot of money. The Twenty-fourth Amendment outlawed the poll tax.

By the 1960s, the civil rights movement was awakening Americans to the evils of segregation and racial discrimination. Congress reacted with major civil rights laws. One of them was the Voting Rights Act of 1965. This act was renewed and expanded in 1970, 1975, and 1982. Over the years, the laws have called for

- the federal government to register voters in districts where fewer than 50 percent of African Americans were registered or voted in the 1964 election.

- the federal government to register voters in districts with a history of discrimination against African-American voters.

- federal examiners to ensure that all votes are counted.

- federal approval for any change in voting laws or practices in areas with a history of discrimination.

- an end to the creation of election districts that lessen the influence of African Americans or other minority groups.

- ballots to be printed in the native languages of Hispanics, Native Americans, Asian Americans, and Alaskan natives in areas with more than 10,000 non–native English speakers.

By the late 1990s, more than 13,000 elected officials in the nation were African Americans. Between 1960 and the 1990s, the percentage of African-American registered voters doubled to 60 percent.

Putting It All Together

Write a summary of this lesson. Use the outline that you wrote in the Thinking on Your Own activity to help you. Share your summary with a partner. Revise your summary if needed.

Voter Behavior

Thinking on Your Own

Nonvoting is a big problem in the United States. Why do you think citizens do not vote in elections? Write a bulleted list in your notebook to explain your opinions.

In a recent presidential election, only 51.2 percent of registered voters cast their ballot. In a recent election for the U.S. House of Representatives, only 33.9 percent of registered voters voted. Why do some citizens vote in every election and some never vote? How do voters decide for whom to vote?

Influences on Voting Decisions

Influences on How a Person Votes

Personal Characteristics

Age
Ethnic Background
Income
Occupation
Education
Gender
Religion
Geography

Group Associations

Family
Friends
Co-Workers

Political Factors

Party Identification
Candidates
Issues

focus your reading

What factors influence how a person votes?

What is the profile of a regular voter?

Explain the reasons people give for not voting.

words to know

generalization
straight-ticket voting
political efficacy

There are three broad categories that influence voters. One category includes personal characteristics of the vote. The second is groups such as family. The third involves party identification and the particular election. The table at the left lists each category. In real-life decisions, the categories interact. Personal characteristics and group associations combine. Together, they influence how a person views the candidates and issues.

The following descriptions are **generalizations**. They show how voters in general are influenced. They may or may not apply to any single person.

"Let's try voting for the greater of the two evils this time and see what happens."

Former California governor Gray Davis at a Democratic campaign rally

In general, younger voters tend to vote Democratic. For most elections between 1960 and 2000, voters under thirty voted for Democratic candidates. African Americans have generally voted Democratic since the New Deal in the 1930s. Before that, they generally voted Republican, because Lincoln had been a Republican. Historically, immigrant groups have voted Democratic. However, since the mid-1990s, Latinos are voting Republican in larger numbers.

Voters who make higher incomes—$100,000 or more—tend to vote Republican. Doctors, lawyers, and business executives tend to vote Republican. This fits with the incomes of these jobs. A large number of college graduates tend to vote Republican. High school graduates tend to vote Democratic. Women tend to vote based on issues. More women vote for candidates who support abortion rights and health-care coverage, and who are against war. Based on these issues, slightly more women vote Democratic.

Protestants tend to vote Republican. Catholics and Jews tend to vote Democratic. In general, this matches the support that ethnic groups give the two parties. More immigrants are Catholic than Protestant.

Since the 1970s, southerners and westerners have been voting more heavily for Republicans. The Northeast and Midwest are generally more Democratic. Voters still tend to vote Democratic in large cities. Voters in small cities, the suburbs, and rural areas tend to vote Republican.

Most voters support the policies of one or the other of the major parties. As a result, they naturally tend to vote for that party's candidates. This is known as **straight-ticket voting**. In the last 40 years, candidates and issues have become more and more important to voters. They can cause voters to jump to the other party.

stop and think

Write profiles of the typical Democratic voter and the typical Republican voter. Work with a partner. Then discuss what could make a typical voter support a candidate from the other party.

Voters and Nonvoters

The regular voter is the voter who votes in most, if not all, elections. Regular voters share certain characteristics. They tend to be college graduates with higher incomes and over forty-five. Those sixty-four and older have the highest rate of voting. More women than men vote regularly.

Married people are more likely to vote than single people. People who have lived in the same place for a long time are more likely to vote than those who move around. People who attend religious services regularly are also more likely to vote.

Millions of citizens, however, fail to vote in each election. They skip local, statewide, and national elections. In a recent presidential election, 100 million people—about one-half of the eligible population—did not vote. Why? Around the world, people fight and die for the freedom to vote. Why do millions of Americans give up their vote at every election?

Some people move right before an election and do not meet the residency requirement. Some people just never get around to registering. Others do not vote because they believe that little will change regardless of which party is in power. Some do not vote because they are happy with the current government and see no reason to take the time to vote.

Others do not vote because many nonvoters lack a sense of political efficacy. **Political efficacy** is the idea that a person can influence government by voting. Those who have a sense of political efficacy are more likely to vote.

Political scientists describe the average nonvoter as male, under thirty-five, single, and with a low level of education. Nonvoters generally work at unskilled jobs. However, there is one factor that outweighs all others in determining whether a person will vote. That factor is a sense of political efficacy.

Putting It All Together

Create a T-chart. Label one column "Voter." Label the other column "Nonvoter." Work with a partner to complete the T-chart and fill in information about each group. How can people develop a sense of political efficacy? Write a statement describing one thing a person could do to feel that his or her voice will be heard.

Participate in Government

Join an Interest Group

An interest group is a group of people with common concerns who join together to influence government policy. There are different kinds of interest groups. Some accept members based on their shared economic interests or work. The Farm Bureau was organized for farmers. The American Dental Association accepts only dentists. Actors Equity accepts only actors.

However, there are some interest groups that anyone can join. These are the interest groups for special causes, such as the Audubon Society. People who want to protect birds join the society. National organizations like the Audubon Society often have state chapters that sponsor programs for members.

Not all interest groups are national. Some are local. The Sourlands Planning Council, for example, works to preserve the Sourland Mountains in central New Jersey. Local groups like this one are often nonprofit volunteer organizations. These groups have either no paid staff or a part-time paid director. The work is done by volunteers. To join, people pay small yearly dues. To get money to run programs, members hold fund-raisers like raffles.

These organizations are generally nonprofits. They pay no taxes to federal, state, and local government. Contributions to them are tax deductible. A taxpayer may claim any money donated to them as deductions on his or her income tax.

Joining interest groups that work to improve life is a good way to use free time. It gives people a good feeling to know they have helped others.

To Find Out About National, State, or Local Interest Groups:

- Check the local paper for news of meetings of groups.

- Check the Web for groups that deal with issues that interest you. See if they have state or local chapters.

Skill Builder

Interpret Political Cartoons

The goal of a political cartoonist is to make people think about an issue. A political cartoonist has a point of view. He or she may be for or against the issue and wants readers to agree with that point of view. The bias is usually easy to see.

Political cartoonists use symbols and caricatures to make their point. A symbol is a person or object that stands for something else. The usual symbol for the Democratic Party is a donkey. An elephant stands for the Republican Party.

A caricature is an exaggerated detail about a person. For example, cartoonists often exaggerate physical features of presidents. For a man in his seventies, President Ronald Reagan had a lot of hair. Cartoonists drew him with even more hair.

To analyze political cartoons:

1. Identify the topic of the cartoon and any figures.

2. Read any labels.

3. Identify what is happening in the cartoon.

4. Identify the point of view of the cartoonist.

Complete the following activities.

1 Who are the figures in the cartoon?

2 What does the text tell you about the topic?

3 What are the people doing in the cartoon?

4 What message is the cartoon sending?

Chapter
17
INTEREST GROUPS, PUBLIC OPINION, AND MASS MEDIA

Getting Focused

Skim this chapter to predict what you will be learning.

- Read the lesson titles and subheadings.
- Look at the illustrations and read the captions.
- Review the vocabulary words and terms.

After skimming the chapter, work with a partner to answer the following questions: What is this chapter about? What questions does this chapter answer? What questions do I still have about this chapter?

Mass media has a significant impact on public opinion.

Interest Groups

Thinking on Your Own

Suppose you want to get your local government to turn an empty lot in your neighborhood into a playground. How could an interest group, made up of like-minded neighbors, help you accomplish this?

The American Association of Retired Persons (AARP), the National Rifle Association, the National Association of Manufacturers, and the American Medical Association are among the thousands of interest groups in the United States. An interest group is a group of people with common concerns who join together to influence government policy. This may sound like a political party. However, there are important differences between interest groups and political parties.

Political parties nominate candidates for public office. Interest groups do not nominate candidates. However, they often work for or against candidates during elections. For example, an interest group that favors public transportation may back, or support, candidates who will vote in favor of more money for railroads. Interest groups generally focus on one or just a few issues. Political parties work for solutions across a range of issues.

focus your reading

Explain how interest groups apply pressure to government.

What is the goal of economic interest groups?

Describe some special causes that interest groups support.

What is the difference between a public-interest group and other types of interest groups?

words to know

special interest

labor union

public-interest group

Organization of Interest Groups

Professional administrators manage most interest groups. Membership depends on the group. Unions are made up of union members. Professional groups are made up of doctors, lawyers, or accountants, for example. Other types of interest groups consist of people who share a common concern about civil rights, the environment, women's rights, or another issue.

Farmers protested high farm prices in Washington, D.C., during 1977.

Interest groups can be very powerful. Political Action Committees (PACs) and Section 527 groups of large national organizations raise millions of dollars during elections. These political arms of interest groups raise money for the campaign. These groups then expect the candidate, if elected, to support and vote in their favor on laws. A candidate may claim that his or her opponent is the "tool of special interests." Interest groups are the **special interests** that politicians sometimes complain about. In reality, few candidates today are elected without the support of at least some interest groups.

In addition to contributing to election campaigns, interest groups pressure government officials in other ways. Members testify at government hearings for or against proposed laws. Groups take out ads in newspapers and on television, cable, and radio to let officials know their views. Members write letters to their lawmakers. Sometimes they demonstrate in front of the legislature.

stop and think

You are still working to turn the empty lot into a playground. As you read, decide which kind of interest group described in this lesson would best be able to help you accomplish this goal. Write your answer in your notebook.

Economic Interest Groups

There are four categories of economic interest groups: (1) business and trade groups, (2) labor unions, (3) farm-related groups, and (4) professional associations. These groups are concerned about government policies that affect how they do business and how much money they earn. They lobby for and against government regulations and tax policies.

Each type of interest group may have a different view of the same public policy. As a result, groups sometimes clash. For example, the insurance industry wants Congress to rewrite a federal law about malpractice cases. These are lawsuits against doctors for the way they treated patients. The insurance trade group wants Congress to put a cap, or limit, on damages awarded in these lawsuits. Trial lawyers oppose the cap because they earn money on such cases. Both interest groups lobby Congress to protect their own interests.

A trade group, or trade association, is made up of companies in the same industry. For example, the National Restaurant Association is made up of people who work in the restaurant business. Business groups such as the Chamber of Commerce include many different kinds of companies.

Labor unions represent people who work in the same job or the same industry. The AFL-CIO is the umbrella group made up of over 50 separate unions. These unions include the Retail Clerks International Union and the American Federation of State, County, and Municipal Employees. There are also independent unions such as the Fraternal Order of Police and the International Longshore and Warehouse Union. Issues that concern union members include the minimum wage, Social Security, tax credits for day care, and similar economic and social policies.

United Farm Workers president Arturo Rodriguez negotiated a pledge with Lucky stores that gave workers the right to organize.

Farm groups include the American Farm Bureau and the National Farmers Union (NFU). The Farm Bureau represents the interests of large farm owners. The NFU represents small farmers. In addition, producers of certain commodities are also organized into interest groups. Groups such as the American Meat Institute lobby state and federal government for regulations that favor their product over others.

Professional groups are groups such as the American Medical Association for doctors and the American Bar Association for lawyers. There are also much smaller groups, such as the National Science Teachers Association. Professional groups deal mostly with regulations related to their profession. For example, state bar associations determine how many hours of continuing education lawyers in their state must take each year. However, professional groups also lobby government about issues of importance to them.

Interest Groups for Special Causes

In addition to economic interest groups, there are hundreds of other groups. Some are organized around environmental issues. These include the Sierra Club, the Audubon Society, and the National Wildlife Federation. Others, such as the National Women's Political Caucus and the National Organization for Women, support women's rights. Some support the civil rights of different groups, such as the National Association for the Advancement of Colored People and the Mexican American Legal Defense Fund. There is also the Children's Defense Fund.

Some issues create groups on both sides. Abortion and gun control are two such issues. The National Right-to-Life Committee protests abortion. The National Abortion and Reproductive Rights Action League supports a woman's right to choose it. Handgun Control, Inc., supports background checks on gun purchasers. The National Rifle Association opposes them.

The Sierra Club (top), the American Legion (center), and the National Organization for Women (bottom) are all interest groups that lobby the government to promote their causes.

Public-Interest Groups

A **public-interest group** works for public policies that will benefit all or most Americans. Whether people belong to the public-interest group does not matter to these organizations. The groups work for Americans in general, rather than just for their members. Common Cause is an example. It works for openness and fairness in the political system.

Putting It All Together

Create a table to organize information about interest groups. Make three columns, titled "Type of Group," "Purpose," and "Example." Which kind of interest group did you decide could best help you with your playground plan? Discuss your answer with a partner and include it in your notebook.

Influencing Public Policy

Thinking on Your Own

Interest groups try to influence public policy. Do you know of others who try to do this? How do they work?

You just read about some ways that interest groups try to influence government. However, the most successful way is by lobbying lawmakers. **Lobbying** is making direct contact with lawmakers, their staffs, and government officials for the purpose of influencing the passage of laws and regulations.

> **focus your reading**
>
> Who are lobbyists?
>
> Describe how lobbyists work.
>
> Why have Congress and state legislatures passed laws to regulate lobbyists?
>
> **words to know**
>
> lobbying

Lobbyists are the people who work to sway public officials toward a particular opinion. Lobbyists get that name from the days when they would wait in the lobbies of Congress to speak to members of the House of Representatives or senators. Successful lobbyists are paid hundreds of thousands of dollars a year for their work. This means that interest groups with large numbers of members or members who are wealthy have the most influence. These organizations can afford to hire the best lobbyists.

Who Lobbyists Are

Some lobbyists set up their own businesses in Washington, D.C. Interest groups hire them on contract to work for them. Other lobbyists are employees of large organizations such as the major labor unions or the Chamber of Commerce. Lobbyists are not limited to trying to influence Congress. Interest groups also use lobbyists to persuade state lawmakers and officials to support their side of issues.

"WHO SAYS THE AMERICAN PEOPLE AREN'T SAVING ENOUGH?"

Lobbyists are often former government employees. They may have worked for executive departments or been senators or members of the House. These people know from the inside how government works. They have friends in agencies and among lawmakers. This closeness between lobbyists and officials can cause concerns about favoritism. As a result, federal law bars members of Congress from becoming lobbyists for at least one year after leaving Congress.

Public relations experts also work as lobbyists. An important job of lobbyists involves public relations. Sometimes lobbyists are lawyers or former reporters. Lobbyists work to make sure that the public images of, or ideas about, the groups they represent are favorable.

stop and think

What advantages do groups that can afford to hire lobbyists have over ordinary citizens? Discuss this question with a partner and write an answer in your notebook.

How Lobbyists Work

Lobbying is a huge industry. In a recent year, more than 14,000 lobbyists were registered with the federal government. By one estimate, more than two dozen groups work to protect Alaska's environment. On the other side, oil companies and their allies work to expand drilling in Alaska. Lobbyists represent all these groups.

Lobbyists use a variety of methods. First, they try to meet with lawmakers or public officials to tell their side of the issues. Lobbyists may make appointments to see lawmakers or officials in their offices. If the lobbyist knows a person well enough, the lobbyist may entertain the person at lunch or dinner. The federal government and state governments set limits on the amount and type of gifts that government officials may take from lobbyists.

The chairmen and CEOs of SBC, Inc.; AT&T; MCI, Inc.; and Nextel testify before Congress.

As you read in Chapter 16, PACs and Section 527 groups raise money for candidates. A campaign contribution does not mean the person will vote the way the interest group wants. However, it probably means the lobbyist for the group will get an appointment with the official.

Second, lobbyists provide information to government officials. As you read in the chapter on Congress, lobbyists testify before committees. They also provide reports that their interest groups have prepared. At times, lobbyists help write the bills that come before Congress. This occurs for about half of all bills.

Third, lobbyists also use the members of the organizations that hire them. They ask members to write letters and e-mails to lawmakers in support of or against bills.

Fourth, lobbyists use the media to get their message to the public. They provide information for magazine and newspaper articles favorable to their side. They recruit well-spoken supporters to appear on television and cable news shows.

Regulating Lobbying

In the past, lobbyists and public officials were guilty of abusing their power. Officials took bribes from lobbyists. Lobbyists gave false testimony before committees. However, Congress and many states have moved to end these abuses.

In 1995, Congress passed the Lobbying Disclosure Act. It strengthened earlier regulations. All lobbyists and organizations that work to influence Congress must register with the federal government. They must list their clients and explain all their lobbying activities. Each lobbyist and group must file these reports twice a year.

A meeting of Florida lobbyists

Putting It All Together

Create a two-column chart. In the left column, list the methods lobbyists use to influence government. In the right column, evaluate these methods. Do they strengthen or weaken a democratic government? Then write a paragraph that summarizes your chart.

Forming and Measuring Public Opinion

Thinking on Your Own

The news media often reports the results of public opinion polls. You have your own opinions about public issues. Why do you take those positions and not others? Do other people influence your opinions? If so, who? What do you know about public opinion polls and polling? Write three statements in your notebook about public opinion polls and polling.

What is public opinion? **Public opinion** is the ideas and attitudes that a significant number—or large amount—of Americans have about government and political issues. The phrase "significant number" is important. There is no single public agreement in this country about any political issue. This helps to explain why there is a need for political parties.

Even within the two major parties, however, members hold different opinions about issues. Some Republicans do not believe that the federal government should set education standards. However, the No Child Left Behind Act does exactly that. It was proposed by a Republican president, George W. Bush, and supported by a majority of Republican members of Congress.

Public opinion reflects what most people who express their opinions believe. This is why the phrase "significant number" is important. Politicians look for consensus, or a general agreement, on an issue by a large number of people.

focus your reading

What influences a person's attitudes about government and political issues?

Explain how politicians measure public opinion.

Describe the process of scientific polling.

words to know

public opinion

political socialization

midterm election

scientific poll

universe

sample

random sample

margin of error

How do politicians determine public opinion? To be considered part of public opinion, a person must express his or her views. This expression can be spoken or written. It can also be expressed by marching in a protest and by voting. The outcomes of elections tell politicians whether voters support certain policies or not. Even before elections, opinion polls can tell politicians much about how the public thinks.

How Attitudes About Government Are Shaped

What a person thinks about government is shaped by many factors. The Ideas to Remember box lists the major factors that influence political attitudes. These factors are similar to the ones that influence voting behavior. The process of shaping one's ideas and attitudes about government is called **political socialization**.

The first and possibly most important factor is family. Parents' views about government and their political party, if any, greatly influence people. More than two-thirds of adults belong to the same political party as their parents.

The second influence is school. Schools teach basic civic values. Children learn to say the Pledge of Allegiance. Courses teach about the nation's political system. U.S. history courses teach about the clash of ideas and the resulting compromises. These experiences and knowledge help to shape people's ideas about what government should do.

Public opinion after Hurricane Katrina in 2005 led to the resignation of FEMA director Michael Brown.

A peer group is a person's circle of friends. Friends tend to have similar views. Constant contact among friends reinforces those views. There is no one with a different opinion to challenge those views.

Some members of the public are more concerned about some issues than others. These issues, therefore, have a greater influence on their political views. For example, a voter in his or her sixties will be more interested in laws affecting Social Security than a thirty-year-old.

The mass media is any form of communication that reaches a large number of people. Television, cable, blogs, radio, newspapers, magazines, CDs, movies, videos, and books are the major media. They both reflect public opinion and help to shape it. The aftermath of Hurricane Katrina in 2005 is an example. The media showed hours of video and printed pages of stories and photos about the lack of federal response for the victims in New Orleans. The public responded with food, water, money, and clothes for the victims. It also turned sharply against the Bush administration. The media then reported this shift.

The media, especially television networks, covers the president's activities daily. He or she uses this coverage to promote policies and programs. This is a major help to the president and his or her party in shaping public opinion. Other federal officials, as well as state and local officials, also use the media to get their ideas out. Personal contact and mailings to constituents—members of an elected official's district—are other ways they get their views in front of the public.

Events also shape the public's view of the proper role of government. Before the Great Depression, the federal government had a limited role in people's lives. However, the suffering of people during the Depression changed many people's views. They came to believe that only the federal government had the resources to help pull the nation out of the Depression. During the civil rights movement, many

stop and think

Draw a table with three columns. Label the first column "Factors Influencing Political Attitudes." Label column two "Explanation." Label column three "Example." Work with a partner to fill in the details for each column.

Americans turned to the federal government to force states and communities to end discrimination. However, times change and with them, people's views. Public opinion swung the other way in the 1980s. As President Ronald Reagan said, "Government is not the solution to our problem. Government *is* the problem."

Measuring Public Opinion

Politicians monitor public opinion in a number of ways. Their staffs read their mail and e-mail to learn what constituents think about issues. Members of Congress make regular trips home to talk with their constituents. The president often announces a new program by visiting the state that will benefit from it. At these stops, he or she meets with local and state officials. Sometimes ordinary citizens are invited to meet with him or her. State and local officials also meet both formally and informally with voters. All of these methods are known as personal contact.

The results of elections also tell politicians about public opinion. The election held between presidential elections is called a **midterm election**. In the midterm election of 1998, voters increased the number of Democrats in the House of Representatives. This was considered a message to Republicans. Since the 1950s, voters in midterm elections had never increased the number of House members from the president's party.

The media both shapes public opinion and reports it. Politicians read papers and watch television news just like voters. They can easily see if their political message is getting out to people. Politicians also listen to interest groups. However, they are aware that interest groups represent only a portion of the public. They do not speak for the general public, only for their members.

Scientific Polling

A better way to read public opinion is scientific polling. A **scientific poll** asks voters for their opinions about candidates, issues, and government policies. However, pollsters do not just ask any voter any question. The word *scientific* is important.

Many voter polls take place outside polling places after voters have cast their ballots.

First, pollsters choose a **universe**. This is the group of people the pollster wants to study. It may be all voters in New York City or all voters in New York City between ages twenty-five and fifty. Second, pollsters select a **sample**. This is a small group of the universe. Usually, pollsters question about 1,500 people to determine how the general public feels about an issue. The sample is called a **random sample**. Everyone in the universe has an equal chance of being selected.

The third step is writing the questions to ask voters. This is a very important step because the questions must be carefully worded. They cannot lead people to give a certain answer. Suppose the question was "Would you vote to give aid to developing nations?" Most people would answer "yes." Suppose the question was "Would you vote to give aid to developing nations if it meant raising taxes?" The answer then is not so easy to answer. It is a better question, however. It will show how strong or weak support is for aid to developing nations.

The fourth step is conducting the poll. Most interviews today are done over the telephone. They can last from three to 15 minutes, depending on the number of questions. If the questions are too long, the person being interviewed may become confused. Too many choices for the answer may also be confusing. These are all problems that pollsters recognize. However, telephone polls are relatively inexpensive and a fast way to test issues and candidates.

The final step is analyzing all the data from interviews. The answers are fed into computers. Pollsters analyze the results and report their findings. They always indicate the **margin of error**. This percentage is a measure of the poll's accuracy. Suppose the results are accurate "plus or minus 3 percentage points." This means that 3 percent more or 3 percent fewer people in the poll universe may agree with a statement.

Putting It All Together

In your notebook, write a summary paragraph about public opinion. It should 1) define public opinion, 2) explain how opinions are formed, and 3) describe how public opinions are measured. Share your paragraph with a partner.

What Polls Say About the Undecided Voter

Reports of opinion polls generally focus on which candidate is leading. However, there is also the category of undecided voters. These are the people who have not made up their minds about whom to vote for. Larry Hugick, chairman of Princeton Survey Research Associates, addressed the importance of undecided voters in the following excerpt from a news article.

Primary Source

reading for understanding

1. What will probably happen if the final poll shows a tight race with a large number of undecided voters?

2. Explain what is meant by "gone that far."

3. Do you agree with Mr. Hugick's reasoning about why undecideds vote for the challenger?

"Mr. Hugick's favorite last-minute indicator concerns the lingering undecided voters.... [I]f the final poll [before the election] is 48 percent to 48 percent, with 4 percent undecided, it is probable that the [challenger] will pick up enough of that vote to come out on top....

"'What it seems is that if you are undecided at the very end, you are more likely just trying to figure out if you want the guy to stay in office. If you have gone that far, you probably really want a change.'"

—Robert Strauss, "As Far as Political Polls, N.J. Owns the Pole Position," *The New York Times*, October 31, 2004.

Mass Media

Thinking on Your Own

Review the definition of *mass media* in the Glossary. How many forms of mass media have you used in the past week? Make a list in your notebook.

The media, or mass media, is an important influence on U.S. politics. Most Americans get their news about government and political issues from television, newspapers, radio, and magazines. Since the 2004 election, the Internet has grown in importance as a source of information.

You have read about some of the ways that the media influences political socialization and public opinion. The media also influences the public agenda and presidential elections. The media covers the activities of Congress and the decisions of the Supreme Court.

focus your reading

How does the media influence the public's view of issues?

Why has the media become so important in presidential elections?

Describe how the media interacts with Congress and the Supreme Court.

words to know

public agenda

The Media's Influence on the Public Agenda

The **public agenda** is a list of societal problems that both political leaders and the general public agree need government attention. Over the years, these issues have included health care for the elderly and the poor, civil rights for African Americans, and protection of women's rights. The federal government responded with Medicare and Medicaid to provide health care. The Civil Rights Act of 1964 and the Voting Rights Act of 1965 ended racial discrimination. Women's rights are protected through Title IX and other laws, regulations, and Court rulings. Each time, the media puts these issues before the public.

The media's choice of what to show and what not to show helps set the public agenda. When the media focuses on an issue, people begin to think about it. People absorb information through the perspective of their own bias—conservative, liberal, or moderate. The media usually does not make people think about issues in a certain way. However, the media does get people to think and talk about issues.

Sometimes this results in shifts in people's attitudes and values. Television, cable television, and video and photos posted on the Web can have a great impact on people. Even before the time of cable and bloggers, television coverage of the war in Vietnam caused a shift in attitude in the country from prowar to antiwar. This shift affected the 1968 presidential election. Democratic president Lyndon Johnson chose not to run for reelection. Republican candidate Richard Nixon won. One reason was Nixon's campaign promise to get the United States out of Vietnam. Political leaders pay attention to what the media is saying.

The Media's Influence on Presidential Elections

Presidents use the media to explain and promote their policies and programs to the American public. Reporters are assigned to cover the president. The media also plays a role in who becomes president.

A good example is the 1960 presidential election. Vice President Richard Nixon had the advantage of being vice president. John Kennedy was a senator from Massachusetts. The 1960 election was the first presidential election that included televised debates. Nixon sweated heavily under the hot lights and looked nervous. Kennedy looked confident and at ease. Those who listened to the debate on radio thought Nixon won. Those who watched it on television believed Kennedy won. Kennedy went on to win the election. Many thought it was because of his performance in the debates.

The 1960 presidential debate

Bill Clinton campaigning on television in 1991

There are three ways that television shapes presidential elections. First, little-known candidates can make an impact on voters. Second, candidates' television ads reach more people than ads in newspapers. Third, television networks put more resources into covering the front-runners in primaries.

Bill Clinton's campaign for president in 1992 is a good example of how television can influence elections. In 1988, Governor Bill Clinton of Arkansas had delivered a speech at the Democratic National Convention. He used this speech to begin building name recognition around the nation and won the election.

The Media and Congress and the Supreme Court

Most media coverage for members of Congress is done in their home state or district. Most also have a press secretary whose job it is to get news coverage of the member's activities.

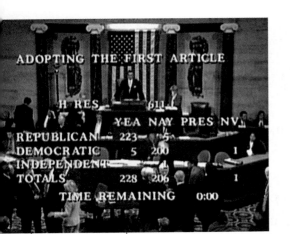

C-SPAN broadcasts daily from the houses of Congress.

Back in Washington, most work of Congress is done in committee meetings and hearings. Some hearings get news coverage because of the topic of the hearings. Since 1986, C-SPAN has broadcast the daily sessions of the House of Representatives and the Senate.

Some state and local courts allow cameras to broadcast trials. The federal court system does not. However, reporters attend daily sessions and report what happened. The media also reports on the hearings that take place before the Supreme Court and then on the Court's decisions.

Putting It All Together

Create a concept web to show the groups with which the media interacts. Draw a large circle in the center of a sheet of paper. Label the circle "The Media." Draw smaller circles for each group with which the media interacts.

Participate in Government

Analyze Public Opinion Polls

Polls measure the public's opinion about an issue at a point in time. They are a snapshot of what Americans think. Not every American can be asked the questions. As a result, scientific sampling is used to find a representative group of people.

It is important to know the following information about any poll you hear or read about:

1. when the poll was taken

2. who was asked the questions

3. how large the sample was

4. what the margin of error is

5. what the questions were

Newspaper articles about poll data should provide this information. A long article about an important issue may have a separate box titled something like "How the Poll Was Conducted." It should tell you items 1 through 4. The article may also reprint some of the most important questions. If the article is brief, look for the same information in the body of the article.

> **The national poll was conducted by Research Polls, Inc., from Friday night through Monday night. The telephone poll reached 1,251 adults. The responses of racial, ethnic, or gender groups were not separated out. The margin of sampling error is plus or minus 3 percentage points.**

Knowing when a poll was taken is important. It tells you how fresh the issue was in people's minds. Before an election, pollsters conduct polls right up to two or three days before the election. They hope to find out if any last-minute events have changed voters' minds.

To Be an Informed Poll Reader:

- Read the complete news article to find out how the poll was conducted.

- Check the Web site of the polling organization or the newspaper or television news program to find out more about the poll.

Skill Builder

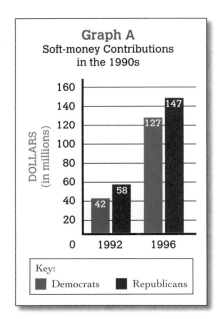

Graph A
Soft-money Contributions
in the 1990s

Key:
■ Democrats ■ Republicans

Analyze a Bar Graph

A bar graph shows data about different subjects at the same time. Graph A is the typical bar graph. The quantity, or amount, is listed along the left, or vertical, axis of the graph. The subjects are shown along the bottom, or horizontal, axis. The time period may be given in the title, or along the side or bottom of the graph.

Sometimes, poll data is shown on a different kind of bar graph. The results of a few questions are pulled out of the survey. The question is stated and the results are placed on a horizontal graph. This type of bar graph is used to show percentages of responses. Graphs B and C are examples of this type of graph.

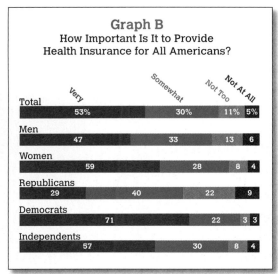

Graph B
How Important Is It to Provide
Health Insurance for All Americans?

To read a bar graph:

1. Read the title of the graph.

2. Examine each axis to learn the subjects.

3. Examine the labels and the data.

4. What can you determine about the relationships between bars?

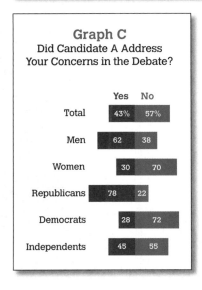

Graph C
Did Candidate A Address
Your Concerns in the Debate?

Complete the following activities.

1 How much soft money was raised (a) by the Republicans in 1996? (b) by the Democrats in 1992?

2 Did more men than women answer "yes" to the question in Graph C?

3 What were the four answers that people could have given to the question in Graph B?

UNIT 7

PUBLIC POLICY

Public policy is the goals that government sets for itself in order to solve problems. The national government sets public policy for the nation as a whole. The state and local governments set public policy at the state and local levels.

The executive branch of the federal government turns public policy into public programs. Congress passes the laws that set up the programs. These laws lay out the goals and describe what is to be done. The executive departments and agencies are responsible for putting these laws into practice. They create the operations that make the laws work on a day-to-day basis. How is all this paid for? Most money to fund programs comes from taxes.

Chapter 18

FINANCING GOVERNMENT POLICIES

Getting Focused

Skim this chapter to predict what you will be learning.

- Read the lesson titles and subheadings.
- Look at the illustrations and read the captions.
- Examine the map, table, and graphs.
- Review the vocabulary words and terms.

Taxes pay for government programs, such as defense and Social Security. Make a list of all the government programs that you know about. Then indicate which program you believe should receive more or less tax support by placing a plus (+) or a minus (-) beside each.

Policies related to federal taxation and spending are decided by lawmakers in Washington, D.C.

Taxing and Borrowing

Thinking on Your Own

Make two lists from the Words to Know for this lesson. In one list, include the words you already know. In the other, list those you do not know. Then use each word that you know in a sentence. Write the sentence in your notebook.

Taxes are payments by individuals and businesses to support the activities of government. The power of the federal government to tax comes from Article I, Section 8, of the Constitution and from the Sixteenth Amendment. Article I states that the government may levy and collect "Taxes, Duties, Imposts, and Excises to pay the Debts and provide for the common Defence and general Welfare." In 1895, the United States Supreme Court ruled that Congress could not tax incomes. The Sixteenth Amendment, ratified in 1913, gave Congress that power. In a recent year, the federal government collected almost $1.8 billion in taxes. This was about $6,690 per person.

Types of Taxes

Congress decides what to tax and what the tax rates should be. The first pie graph on page 329 shows how much money each tax raises. The second pie graph shows how the government spends the money.

Residents in a Manhattan post office rush to file their tax returns before the midnight deadline on April 15.

Income taxes are **progressive taxes**. They are based on a person's or business's ability to pay. The president of a corporation pays at a higher rate of taxation than a teacher. Current rates for the personal income tax range from 10 to 35 percent.

Types of Taxes Collected by the Federal Government

Tax	Definition	Explanation
Individual income tax	Tax on a person's income minus exemptions and deductions	An **exemption** is for a person who depends on the person being taxed for food, clothing, and shelter. Children are the main exemptions. Exemptions are also called **dependents**. Deductions include interest on mortgage payments and state and local taxes that a person pays.
Corporate income tax	Tax on a corporation's income minus expenses and deductions	Expenses and deductions are the cost of doing business.
Social insurance taxes	Taxes collected from employees and employers to pay for major social programs; also known as **payroll taxes** and social insurance taxes	The major social programs are Social Security, Medicare, and the unemployment compensation program. The taxes are taken from a worker's pay. The employer pays a similar amount.
Excise taxes	Taxes on the manufacture, transportation, sale; or use of goods and performance of services	Examples of goods and services that are taxed are gasoline, tires, cigarettes, liquor, airlines, and long-distance telephone calls.
Customs duties	Taxes on goods brought into the country for sale; also called tariffs	Customs duties are used to raise money for the government. They can also be used to protect U.S. businesses. For example, a high duty is placed on imported shoes or grain. This raises the price to U.S. buyers. High customs duties are also called **protective tariffs**.
Estate tax	Tax on the property and wealth over $1.5 million of a person who dies	The tax applies to less than 3–5 percent of estates. The tax does not apply to estates left by spouses to each other.
Gift tax	Tax on gifts above $11,000 to any one person given in any one year	This tax is meant to keep people from getting around the estate tax. Before this tax, they could give away all their money and property so there was nothing left to tax when they died.

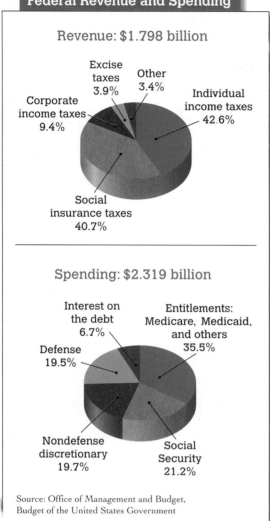

Federal Revenue and Spending

Revenue: $1.798 billion

- Excise taxes 3.9%
- Other 3.4%
- Corporate income taxes 9.4%
- Individual income taxes 42.6%
- Social insurance taxes 40.7%

Spending: $2.319 billion

- Interest on the debt 6.7%
- Entitlements: Medicare, Medicaid, and others 35.5%
- Defense 19.5%
- Nondefense discretionary 19.7%
- Social Security 21.2%

Source: Office of Management and Budget, Budget of the United States Government

Many individuals and companies can use **tax credits** to lower their taxes. For example, families can receive a tax credit to help pay for day care. There are also tax credits for businesses. For example, companies that hire and retrain workers receive a tax credit.

Social insurance taxes are **regressive taxes**. Everyone is taxed at the same rate. However, the taxes take more out of the paychecks of lower-wage earners. Suppose one worker earns $200 a week. Another worker earns $2,000 a week. They both pay $50 in social insurance taxes. The worker who earns $200 loses a larger portion of his or her salary in taxes.

stop and think

Play "What Am I?" with a partner. Write a definition for each type of tax. Use information from the text as well as the table. End each definition with the question "What am I?" Take turns giving definitions and asking the question.

Social insurance taxes go into special trust accounts in the Treasury. Money is taken out of the accounts to pay Social Security, Medicare, and unemployment compensation benefits as needed. The other taxes go into the general fund to pay for government services.

Federal Borrowing

Most taxes are used to raise money to pay for government services. However, in most years since the 1950s, the federal government has run a deficit. A **deficit** occurs when the amount of money spent is more than the amount of money collected. In the years 1998–2001, there was a **surplus**. More money was collected than the government spent. Beginning in 2002, tax cuts and the war in Iraq created a yearly deficit.

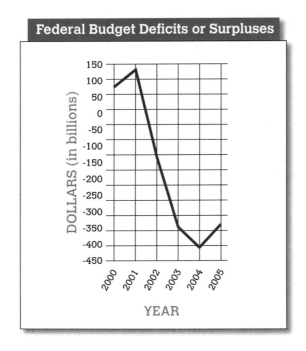

Federal Budget Deficits or Surpluses

What happens when the government spends more than it takes in? It borrows money just as individuals, families, and businesses do. However, the government does not borrow from banks or credit unions. The Treasury Department sells treasury notes and bonds to investors. These papers promise that the government will pay back the money. Like other debtors, the government must pay interest on the money it borrows.

The result of all this borrowing is the **national debt**. By 2005, the national debt was more than $7.9 trillion. People don't agree about the national debt. Some people are concerned about the size of the debt. They fear that it will make it harder for Americans in the future to have a good life. Others believe that the national debt is good for the economy. They argue that using borrowed money for investment, such as infrastructure projects, has a positive effect on the economy.

Putting It All Together

Make a two-column chart in your notebook. Title one column "Taxes" and the other "Debt." In the first column, list the types of taxes the government imposes. In the second column, explain how the government borrows money and goes into debt.

The Federal Budget

Thinking on Your Own

A government, like many individuals and families, has a budget. It lists the amount it can spend for various items or purposes. In your notebook, make a list of the items that you would include in the federal government's budget. Compare your list with that of a friend.

Each year the federal government creates a budget for itself. The budget describes how the federal government will "provide for the general welfare" of the nation. Article I, Section 9, Clause 7, of the Constitution gives Congress the power to appropriate money. **Appropriate** means to set aside money for certain uses. In 1921, Congress passed the Budget and Accounting Act. This law directs the president to begin the budget-making process.

Each February, the president sends Congress a proposed budget. This budget is more than just numbers. It lays out what the president considers to be important policies and proposes amounts of money to pay for them. Without money, policies cannot be carried out. However, there are limits to what the president can propose.

> ### focus your reading
>
> What is the difference between controllable and uncontrollable spending?
>
> What is the president's role in developing the budget?
>
> How does Congress interact with the president in making the budget?
>
> ### words to know
>
> appropriate
> controllables
> uncontrollables
> entitlement
> discretionary spending
> continuing resolution

Controllable and Uncontrollable Spending

The president and Congress have control over about only 30 percent of the yearly budget. This 30 percent is known as **controllables**. The other 70 percent is called uncontrollables. **Uncontrollables** are spending that is required by laws or by earlier obligations. Payment of interest on the national debt is

Senator Edward Kennedy (D-Massachusetts) holds a press conference to discuss veterans' benefits.

an uncontrollable expense. So are payments for Social Security, federal workers' pensions, veterans' benefits, Medicare, and Medicaid. These are also known as **entitlements**.

Examine the second pie graph on page 329. In a recent year, 56.7 percent of the budget went to entitlements. Another 6.7 percent paid interest on the debt. That left 36.6 percent for all other spending. Subtract spending for the Defense Department. About 17.1 percent was left. In dollars, that was about 400 million for controllable, or **discretionary spending**. On top of that, Congress borrowed another $500 billion.

That is a lot of money. However, consider how it has to be divided. It must fund the work of the other 14 executive departments. It also supports more than 150 independent agencies, government corporations, and commissions, as well as Congress and the president. That is why the budget process is long and difficult.

The President's Role in Budget-making

The budget process takes about 18 months. It starts in February of the year before the budget will go into effect. For example, the budget process for October 2007 through September 2008 began in February 2006. The federal government's budget year runs from October of one year through September of the next year.

The executive departments, independent agencies, and regulatory commissions work out their budgets. These are sent to the Office of Management and Budget (OMB) in the Executive Office of the President (EOP). The OMB reviews each budget request. Often, the OMB holds hearings with the heads of the various groups. These officials must justify their budget requests.

The Director of the OMB and the Council of Economic Advisers (CEA) then take the budget to the president. They advise him or her on how the individual budgets do or do not match his or her policy agenda, or plans. They also discuss how the requests may affect the deficit, borrowing, and taxes.

The president must sign budget bills into law.

After this meeting, the budget requests are returned to the various groups. They must then revise their requests. Usually, the revised budgets are lower than what the groups first wanted.

The final budgets from the executive branch are put together in one budget package. This package is then delivered to Congress by the first Monday in February of the year the budget will go into effect.

Congress's Role in Budget-making

When a budget arrives in Congress, it is sent to the Senate and the House Budget Committees. Each committee reviews the budget with the help of the Congressional Budget Office (CBO). Congress set up the CBO in 1974 to get independent advice. Because of the CBO, Congress does not have to rely on the president's data. The CBO does its own analysis of the budget.

The House and the Senate Budget Committees draft a concurrent resolution on the budget. It estimates the total revenue and spending for the budget year. Both houses must pass the resolution by May 15. In September, the two budget committees draft a second resolution. This one sets binding, or required, limits on spending. Federal departments, agencies, and commissions may not spend above these limits.

In the meantime, the House and the Senate Appropriations Committees and their subcommittees review the president's budget. They ask officials from executive departments and agencies to testify about their budget numbers. Outside experts, including lobbyists, also testify. These committees write the actual bills that appropriate funds for government activities.

In all, Congress votes on 13 appropriations bills each year. The business of the government is broken down into 13 areas. As you learned in Chapter 7, if one house makes changes in a bill, the bill must go to a conference committee. Committee members try to resolve the differences. Then both the Senate and the House must vote again on the bill.

Some federal funds are allocated for space research, such as for the Mars Exploration Rovers.

The deadline for passing the budget is October 1. The new budget year begins on October 1. However, all 13 bills are not always approved by then. If a bill is not passed, the agencies funded by the bill will have no money. They would have to shut down. To keep this from happening, Congress passes a **continuing resolution**. When the president signs it, agencies can continue to operate. However, they receive their funding at the same rate as the previous budget. When the appropriations bill is passed, the agencies will get the money in the new budget.

In reality, the budget is not necessarily the final amount of money the government receives. Emergencies may occur during the year. The president must then ask Congress for more money. For example, the war in Iraq required additional budget requests each year. In 2005, billions of dollars were added to the budget to help victims of Hurricane Katrina and Hurricane Rita.

Putting It All Together

Create a chart to show the budget-making process. Label each step. Share your chart with a partner. Discuss the chart to be sure that each label is clear.

Managing the Economy

Thinking on Your Own

Turn each of the subheadings in this lesson into questions in your notebook. As you read, write the answers to the questions.

The first pie graph on page 329 shows where government revenue comes from. The second pie graph shows where it goes. The "wheres" indicate what the president and Congress think are the nation's most important issues. These issues become the basis for public policy.

One issue that the nation always faces is economic growth. For various reasons, the nation's economy goes through good times and bad times. In good times, most people have jobs. They are able to borrow money at low or moderate interest rates. In bad times, unemployment is high and so are interest rates. Should the government try to influence the economy to improve? Most Americans answer "yes" to this question. However, there is less agreement on how the government should do this.

focus your reading

What is monetary policy?

How does the Federal Reserve regulate the economy?

words to know

fiscal policy

monetary policy

Federal Reserve System

nonpartisan

discount rate

reserve requirement

Fiscal Policy

Fiscal policy uses government spending and taxing to influence the economy. The biggest tool of fiscal policy is the federal budget. It determines how much the government will take in and how much it will spend.

During the Great Depression, President Franklin Roosevelt used the federal budget to speed up the economy. He persuaded Congress to add millions of dollars to the budget. This money provided loans to businesses and farmers. It also created relief

The Civilian Conservation Corps was one means used by the federal government to stimulate the economy during the Great Depression.

programs and jobs for the poor and unemployed. The economy improved, but the national debt grew as well.

Starting in the 1980s, Republican presidents and Congress used a different strategy. They did not use tax money to create jobs. Instead, they cut taxes. They wanted taxpayers to keep more of their income. They thought if taxpayers had more money, they would spend more. This would create jobs and improve the economy. The result was reduced government programs and an increasing national debt.

The solution appeared to be careful spending combined with deficit reduction. This enabled President Bill Clinton to cut the yearly deficit to zero in 1999. The result was a balanced budget. However, the cost of wars in Afghanistan and Iraq, fighting terrorism, and tax cuts ended balanced budgets by 2003.

Monetary Policy and the Federal Reserve

Monetary policy controls the supply of money in the economy and the cost of borrowing to influence the economy. Neither the president nor Congress controls monetary policy. The **Federal Reserve System**, or Fed, controls monetary policy.

The Federal Reserve System is "the bankers' banks." The nation is divided into 12 Federal Reserve Districts. There is a main Federal Reserve Bank and branches in each district. A Board of Governors oversees the Fed. These seven economists or bankers are chosen by the president and confirmed by the Senate. They serve for 14 years. The chairperson of the Board of Governors is chosen by the president and serves a four-year term. However, the Fed is **nonpartisan**—meaning that its Board acts independently of political pressure from either the president or Congress.

The Fed controls the nation's monetary policy in three

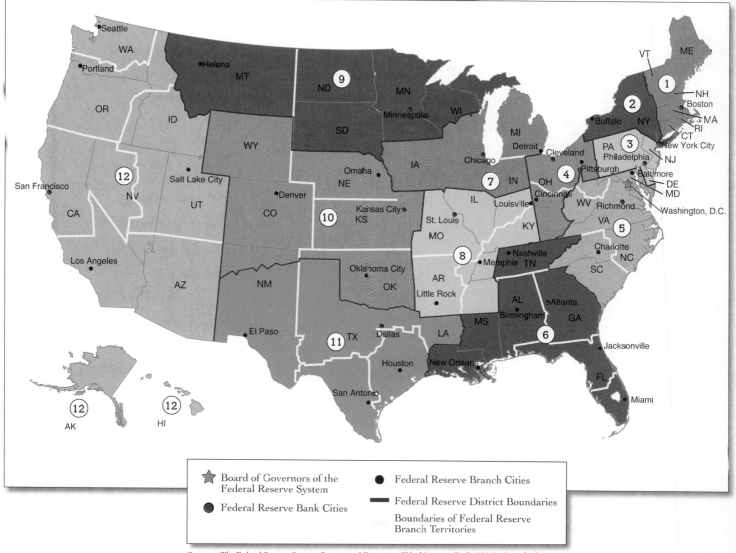

Board of Governors of the Federal Reserve System

Federal Reserve Bank Cities

Federal Reserve Branch Cities

Federal Reserve District Boundaries

Boundaries of Federal Reserve Branch Territories

Source: *The Federal Reserve System: Purposes & Functions* (Washington, D.C. 1994). Board of Governors of the Federal Reserve System.

ways. First, the Fed may raise or lower the **discount rate**. This is an interest rate. Member banks pay this rate on loans from the Fed. A lower discount rate costs member banks less to borrow the money. They, in turn, charge their customers lower interest rates on loans. This helps economic growth. The higher the discount rate, the less member banks borrow. The result is less money to lend customers. The economy slows down.

The Federal Reserve Bank in Washington, D.C.

Second, the Fed may raise or lower the reserve requirement of member banks. The **reserve requirement** is the amount of money that member banks must keep in the main Federal Reserve banks. The reserve is a percentage of the money deposited in the member banks by customers. If the reserve rate is low, member banks can lend more to customers. This means there is more money in the economy to produce and buy goods and services. The economy grows. If the reserve rate is increased, member banks have less money to lend.

Third, the Fed may buy and sell government securities such as bonds and T-notes on the open market. By buying them, the Fed puts money into the economy. By selling them, the Fed takes money out. Investors rush in to buy up the securities. The result is less money in the economy.

Putting It All Together

Create a concept map to show how the economy is managed. Draw a large circle and label it "The Economy." Then draw two smaller circles connected to it. Label one "Fiscal Policy." Label the other "Monetary Policy." Share your map with a partner. Ask your partner to check to make sure you have included all the important information.

Making Money: The U.S. Mint and the Bureau of Engraving and Printing

If the federal government runs low on money, it cannot just make new money. It must sell bonds and notes to investors. However, the federal government does print and coin new money regularly. Bills and even coins wear out from continuous use.

They are also lost, rolling into storm drains and behind seat cushions.

The U.S. Mint produces all the nation's coins. The headquarters of the U.S. Mint is in Washington, D.C. Other plants are located in Philadelphia, Denver, San Francisco, and West Point, New York. The U.S. Mint is also responsible for protecting the nation's gold supply. At Fort Knox, Kentucky, $100 billion of gold is stored under guard by the Mint.

The Bureau of Engraving and Printing (BEP) produces the nation's paper money. It also prints documents for other government departments. These include treasury notes, alien identification cards, and naturalization certificates. The BEP has facilities in Washington, D.C., and Fort Worth, Texas.

Participate in Government

File Your Income Tax

Once you begin to work, you will need to file a federal tax return each year. You probably will have to file a state tax return, too. Only a couple of states do not have personal income taxes. Depending on your community, you may also have to pay a city income tax.

People known as tax protesters claim that the federal income tax is unconstitutional. They make many different arguments against the federal income tax and refuse to file tax returns. However, the Internal Revenue Service (IRS) prosecutes tax protesters. In every case, the courts have found tax protesters guilty of tax evasion, or failure to pay taxes. Their arguments are not based on the law. They are based on their desire not to pay taxes. As this chapter explains, taxes are used for programs to benefit the "general welfare," or good, of the people.

Federal and state tax returns are due every year on April 15. Both citizens and resident aliens who work in the United States must pay taxes. Tax forms are available online. Taxes may also be filed online. If you are due a refund, you often will receive it faster if you file online.

During the year, file all of your financial records in one place. This makes it easier to find information when it is time to prepare your tax return. File receipts and records in separate envelopes or folders. Then you will not have a mound of paper to sort through.

To File Your Return:

- Gather your records. Get your W-2 form from your employer.

- Fill out the return. Get help from the IRS online or by phone.

- Mail the return or file it online by midnight on April 15.

Skill Builder

Analyze a Pie Graph

A pie graph shows parts of a whole. It illustrates how much of the whole each slice, or segment, represents. Usually, pie graphs illustrate percentages. The entire pie is 100 percent.

To Read a Pie Graph:

- Read the title of the graph, so you know what it is about.

- Read the labels for each segment.

- Compare the parts of the circle to find the relation each has with the other.

- Draw conclusions about the information and the relation among the parts.

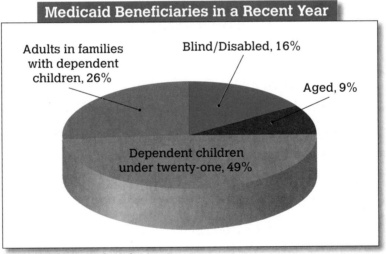

Medicaid Beneficiaries in a Recent Year

Adults in families with dependent children, 26%

Blind/Disabled, 16%

Aged, 9%

Dependent children under twenty-one, 49%

Source: Health Care Funding Administration

Use the pie graph to answer the following questions.

1 What is the graph about?

2 Which group gets the largest percentage of funding?

3 Which group gets the second-largest percentage of funding?

4 Who benefits from Medicaid funding?

Chapter 19

DOMESTIC POLICY: EDUCATION, HOUSING, TRANSPORTATION, AND SECURITY

Getting Focused

Skim this chapter to predict what you will be learning.

- Read the lesson titles and subheadings.
- Look at the illustrations and read the captions.
- Examine the graph.
- Review the vocabulary words and terms.

Domestic policy is policy that relates to government regulations and programs in the United States. Foreign policy relates to U.S. interactions with other nations. Social Security, Head Start, and running veterans' hospitals are examples of domestic policy. So are fining companies for polluting the air and screening passengers' bags in airports. What other domestic programs do you know of? List at least five.

President George W. Bush signed an appropriations bill for Hurricane Katrina relief in September 2005. Domestic policy is one of the responsibilities of the president.

Business and Labor

Thinking on Your Own

In your notebook, write a paragraph that includes as many of the Words to Know as you can. As you encounter these words in your reading, check to see if you used them correctly.

Promoting U.S. businesses at home and abroad is one of the tasks of the federal government. Also, the federal government has another role in relation to business. Since the late 1800s, the federal government has actively regulated business activities. The result is a **mixed market economy**. The economy is based on the private ownership of goods and services. However, the government both promotes and regulates the workings of private enterprise.

focus your reading

Explain how the federal government promotes U.S. businesses.

How does the federal government regulate U.S. businesses?

Describe the relationship between the federal government and labor.

words to know

domestic policy

mixed market economy

free trade

trust

monopoly

deregulate

bargain collectively

union shop

Promoting Business

At various times in the nation's history, the government has supported either free trade or protectionism. **Free trade** means low tariffs, or customs duties, on goods brought into the country for sale. At other times, the government has used high tariffs to keep imports out. High tariffs protect U.S. businesses. Tariffs used to protect U.S. businesses are known as protective tariffs.

In recent years, the United States has placed fewer restrictions on imports from other countries. In 1994, Canada, the United States, and Mexico joined in the North American Free Trade Agreement (NAFTA). Barriers to trade among the three partners will end over a period of 15 years. In 2005, President George W. Bush signed into law the Central

American Free Trade Agreement (CAFTA). It is similar to the NAFTA and focuses on trade with Central American nations.

The federal government provides three major types of subsidies, or financial supports, to businesses. The first is tax credits. Like families, businesses are given tax credits in exchange for certain activities. For example, businesses may subtract the cost of training workers under the Welfare to Work Program.

The federal government also offers loans to businesses at low interest rates. Small businesses, especially minority- and women-owned businesses, greatly benefit from this service.

Workers assemble circuit boards at a manufacturing facility in Nevada.

Small businesses and giant corporations also benefit from the third major way the government supports businesses. The government provides masses of information free to companies. Otherwise, they would need to pay for this research. This is a major job of the Department of Commerce, which supports the interests of U.S. businesses.

The Small Business Administration (SBA) is an independent agency of the executive branch. It aids small businesses in direct ways. It offers help with all areas of starting and running small businesses. All this aid is free.

stop and think

Make a three-column chart in your notebook. Title one column "Promoting Business," another "Regulating Business," and the third "Protecting Workers." List three ways that the government promotes business. As you read ahead, include three items in each of the other two columns.

Regulating Business

The Commerce Department was not set up until 1913. However, the federal government's power to regulate commerce, or business, rests in the Constitution. Article I, Section 8, Clause 3, is known as the Commerce Clause. It says that Congress shall have the power "to regulate commerce with foreign nations, and among the several states . . . ."

In the United States, the Industrial Revolution began in the early 1800s. By the 1880s, a few giant companies controlled major areas of the economy. **Trusts** combined several corporations into a single business. The purpose was to end

Poor working conditions, such as in this tailors' shop in New York City, led to regulations for businesses during the late 1800s.

competition in an industry. As a result, they could set any prices they wanted for their goods and services. They could also drive out of business suppliers who would not sell to them cheaply. They paid their workers poorly and did nothing to make their factories, mines, and railroads safe for workers.

In an effort to end these abuses, Congress passed the Interstate Commerce Act in 1887. It was the first law regulating businesses. It set limits on what railroads could charge to carry freight. Other antitrust laws were the Sherman Antitrust Act in 1890 and the Clayton Antitrust Act in 1914. The Antitrust Division was set up in the Justice Department to enforce antitrust laws. Antitrust laws have three goals. The first is to prevent monopolies from occurring. A **monopoly** is the control of an industry or most of an industry by one company. The second is to break up any monopolies that do exist. The third is to restore competition in the industry.

In addition to antitrust laws, there are other kinds of laws that affect how businesses operate and what they can and cannot do. These are regulatory laws. Since the 1930s, Congress has passed many laws regulating businesses. For example, cars must have airbags. A television or cable company may not own all the television or cable stations in a city. Prescription drugs cannot be sold unless they are approved by the Food and Drug Administration. The Security and Exchange Commission licenses and oversees stockbrokers.

However, regulating business is not popular with all Americans. Some believe that it raises the price of goods and services. Others claim that it hinders competition. Every industry has its own concerns. Carmakers want fuel efficiency standards relaxed. Manufacturers want clean air and water laws weakened.

Beginning in the 1970s, the federal government began to **deregulate** some industries. A number of regulations were removed from the banking, television and cable, airline, railroad, and trucking industries. Deregulation has worked better in some industries than in others. For example, since

the airlines were deregulated in 1978, several of the large airlines have declared bankruptcy. They have cut jobs and services in order to keep flying. Some airlines have gone out of business. The result is cheaper fares in cities with several airlines. However, a number of cities have lost all airline service or have very limited service. Fares in these cities remain as high or higher than they were when several airlines served them.

Labor

Today, laws protect workers. Laws regulate working hours, ensure safe working conditions, and set the minimum wage. This was not always the case. In the late 1800s, government supported business owners, not workers. The courts even used the Sherman Antitrust Act against labor unions. The Supreme Court ruled that unions were an attempt to limit the activities of businesses.

Workers organized into local unions as early as the 1790s. By the 1860s, national unions were struggling to survive.

Consumer Protection

One regulatory agency that directly affects Americans daily is the Consumer Product Safety Commission (CPSC). It is an independent regulatory commission. The CPSC was set up in 1972 to protect consumers from dangerous products. Some 15,000 consumer products are under the CPSC's review. Its employees investigate injuries caused by products such as power tools, cribs, and microwaves.

In the 30 years since CPSC began, the injury and death rate from consumer product accidents has gone down 30 percent. The CPSC sets required product-safety standards. If products do not meet these standards, the CPSC orders their recall.

People can find free and low-cost information about consumer concerns from the Consumer Information Center (CIC). Each year the CIC publishes a free "Consumer Action Handbook." The handbook offers information about how to solve consumer complaints and where to file complaints. Among the CIC's most popular publications are ones on how to save money, how to protect against identity theft, and how to choose the best wireless telephone service. To help consumers find what they need, the CIC publishes a free catalog of publications.

A demonstration by the CPSC about the dangers of window blind drawstrings.

Unions organized against the NAFTA during the 1990s.

However, business owners refused to recognize unions. Unions wanted to negotiate contracts with business owners. Employers did not want to guarantee wages or spend money on making workplaces safer.

By the early 1900s, Americans' views of business and labor were changing. Congress and the Supreme Court reflected these changing views. Journalists known as muckrakers were exposing how badly companies treated their workers.

The result was new laws and new Court rulings. Congress set up the Department of Labor in 1913 to aid workers. The Clayton Antitrust Act of 1914 states that unions are not conspiracies, or plots, to limit business activities. In 1935, Congress passed the Wagner Act. It guarantees workers the right to organize unions in workplaces and to **bargain collectively**. This means to negotiate a contract between a union and a company.

The act also set up the National Labor Relations Board (NLRB). When a group of workers wants to start a union in their workplace, the NLRB oversees the election. A majority of workers have to vote to join the union before one can be started. The NLRB also hears complaints about supposed unfair labor practices by employers.

By the late 1940s, some Americans thought that labor unions had too much power. In 1947, Congress passed the Taft-Hartley Act. The Taft-Hartley Act set up a 60-day cooling-off period before a union could strike. The union had to notify the company that it would strike. The idea was that during this time, the union and the company could reach an agreement. It ended the closed shop, but allowed the **union shop**. Only union members can be hired in a closed shop. Nonunion members may be hired in a union shop. However, they must then join the union.

Putting It All Together

How does the federal government interact with business and labor? Write a summary paragraph to answer this question. Use the lists you made in the Stop and Think activity. Exchange your paragraph with a partner. Ask your partner if your paragraph includes all the main points of the lesson. If not, which ones did you miss?

Agriculture, the Environment, and Energy Resources

Thinking on Your Own

The environment includes the air, water, land, trees, plants, animals—the natural world around us. Environmentalists believe that every generation has a responsibility to take care of the environment for the next generation. What do you think about this belief? What if it means higher prices for things like gasoline, cars, and food? Write a paragraph in your notebook to explain your answer.

S ince the early 1800s, the United States has more than doubled its territory. As the nation expanded, so did the role of the federal government. The Agriculture Department was set up in 1862 to help farmers. Congress set up the Environmental Protection Agency in 1970. It was created because of concern about the environment. The Energy Department was set up in 1977 because of the oil shortages of the mid-1970s. With each new department or agency, the federal government took on a new policy-making role.

focus your reading

Explain why the federal government became involved in farm policy during the 1930s.

Why were environmental laws passed?

Describe some of the issues involved in energy policy.

words to know

global warming

Employees of the Department of Agriculture helped farmers develop new ways of farming.

Modern Farm Policies

The original purpose of the Agriculture Department was to help farmers become better farmers. Department agents showed them new equipment and new ways to farm. By the 1920s, farmers were producing more than the nation needed. They could not sell the surplus overseas, because foreign nations had little money to pay for imports after World War I. The result was declining prices for U.S. farm goods.

The United States provides food relief to many African nations.

By the time of the Great Depression, thousands of farmers had lost their land. Like other Americans in need, farmers appealed to the government for help. By the early 1930s, Americans had realized that they had no control over a worldwide economic depression. In the 1932 election, they rejected President Herbert Hoover and elected Franklin Roosevelt.

Roosevelt began a series of actions to aid all Americans. For farmers, he used the principle of supply and demand. Farmers were paid to produce less than they had in the past. As a result, the supply of certain farm goods, such as corn, wheat, and hogs, was limited. This raised the price that farmers could charge for these products.

Since the 1930s, the federal government has continued to aid farmers. In 1996, though, Congress passed the Federal Agricultural Improvement and Reform Act to end many of the earlier programs. The Commodity Credit Corporation (CCC), however, continues to aid farmers in many ways. The CCC helps farmers find markets and makes it easier to sell farm goods overseas. It provides research on prices and the best time to sell. The CCC also buys farm products for food assistance programs in the United States and overseas. This includes food for school lunch programs, the armed forces, veterans' hospitals, and correctional institutions.

stop and think

In your notebook, make a list of federal government policies that have helped agriculture. As you read ahead, list other policies that show how the role of the federal government has expanded in recent years.

The Environment

The CCC also oversees conservation programs through the Natural Resources Conservation Service. These programs include overseeing the national forest system and soil conservation districts. Their goal is to protect, or conserve, the environment.

Before the 1950s, the federal government was not involved in environmental policy. In the 1950s, Americans began to see the damage caused to the environment by businesses, communities, and farms. Factories released pollution into the air from smokestacks. Communities disposed of sewage in rivers and lakes. Farmers let chemical fertilizers and pesticides run off into streams and rivers. The air over cities was unhealthy to breathe. Sources of drinking water were unsafe.

The bald eagle is protected by the Endangered Species Act of 1973.

By the 1960s, groups had organized and were lobbying for environmental laws. In 1970, Congress passed the first Clean Air Act and the Water Quality Improvement Act. The Endangered Species Act of 1973 requires the federal government to protect the animals, birds, and other wildlife, including plants that are on the list of endangered species.

In 1970, Congress set up the Environmental Protection Agency (EPA). Its mission is to make sure that environmental laws are obeyed. Since 1970, Congress has passed additional environmental protection laws. The EPA then writes regulations to enforce these laws. For example, in 2000, the EPA set standards for clean exhaust from buses and heavy trucks.

Superfund Environmental Protection Agency workers clean a site near Houston, Texas.

Not everyone agrees with environmental protection policies. Many of these environmental regulations require costly changes in how companies, communities, and farmers do business. The result is often a debate over the strictness of new environmental laws and regulations.

Energy Resources

Global warming cuts across environmental and energy issues. **Global warming** is the warming of Earth's surface. It is occurring because of growing levels of carbon dioxide and other greenhouse gases in the atmosphere. Carbon dioxide is produced when fossil fuels—coal, oil, and natural gas—are burned. The carbon dioxide acts like insulation. It collects in Earth's atmosphere and traps the energy from the sun under the atmosphere. This extra heat warms Earth. The only way to stop global warming is to produce less carbon dioxide.

However, developing nations and the United States rarely support efforts to reduce carbon dioxide. Developing nations claim that such changes will cost too much money. U.S. politicians have argued that such efforts will put too much of a cost burden on businesses. Environmentalists in the United States continue to lobby politicians to pass laws to cut carbon dioxide. They want tougher clean air regulations and more money to research other energy sources.

During the 1970s, long lines at gas stations were the result of oil crises.

In 1973 and 1974, Arab nations refused to sell oil to the United States. The United States had decided to support Israel against its Arab neighbors. The Department of Energy was created in 1977. Since then, various presidents and Congresses have tried to shape a national energy policy. But, competing groups and political beliefs make shaping a national energy policy difficult. During the 1980s, policy-makers urged energy conservation. People bought smaller, more fuel-efficient cars. A national highway bill set the speed limit on interstate highways at 55 miles per hour. During the 1990s, small cars gave way to less fuel-efficient sport utility vehicles (SUVs). The speed limit was raised to 65 miles per hour.

Putting It All Together

Review the paragraph you wrote at the beginning of the lesson. Do you still agree with what you said? If not, revise your paragraph. If you still agree, write another paragraph to explain why. Share your writing with a partner. Discuss your viewpoints and try to reach an agreement about the environment.

Health and Social Service Programs

Thinking on Your Own

Should the federal government provide benefits to the elderly, widows or widowers and dependent children, and those with disabilities? Or should people save enough to take care of themselves and their families? In your notebook, write your opinion using what you already know.

The federal government's social welfare programs began during the Great Depression. **Social welfare programs** provide benefits to individuals, especially those in need. During the Great Depression, many people lost everything they had. Parents went without food so their children could eat. State and local governments and private charities did what they could. However, the problems were too great and too widespread. Only the federal government had the power to help so many people across so many states.

Franklin Roosevelt was elected president in 1932 on his promise to end the Depression and help people. He pushed programs through Congress that created jobs and aided farmers. He also proposed a program to pay benefits to retired people, widows and their children, and people with disabilities. It was the first of many social welfare programs that Congress has passed since 1935.

focus your reading

What are the social insurance programs?

List and describe the major public assistance programs.

How does the federal government promote public health?

Describe the benefits provided to veterans by the Department of Veterans Affairs.

words to know

social welfare program

entitlement program

public assistance program

Social Insurance Programs

Roosevelt's proposal was the basis of the Social Security and unemployment insurance programs. Social Security is an entitlement program. **Entitlement programs** must be funded

People wait in line at a California unemployment office.

every year. Workers and employers contribute to the program through payroll taxes. Social Security pays a monthly benefit to retired people, people with disabilities, and widows or widowers of workers and their dependent children. The Social Security Administration is an independent federal agency.

Unemployment insurance is also an entitlement program. However, only employers pay the tax. The money is paid to the federal government, which returns it to the states. Benefits vary from state to state. Workers who are laid off from their jobs apply for weekly payments. The money helps them with basic living expenses until they can find a new job.

Medicare is the third social insurance program. It was set up in 1965. An earlier effort to pass a law to help retirees with medical costs was defeated. However, by the 1960s, health-care costs were rising. They were becoming a burden to many retired people. There was enough pressure to push Congress to pass the new bill.

Medicare pays part of the cost of hospital care for retired people and people with disabilities. It is funded by payroll taxes on workers and employers. Those eligible for Medicare may also pay a small amount for Medicare B. This is insurance coverage for doctors' visits, X-rays, and some other services. Like Social Security and unemployment insurance, Medicare is an entitlement program.

Public Assistance Programs

Public assistance programs are different from social insurance programs. They pay benefits to people who do not contribute to the programs. They are known as "means-tested" programs. People who qualify do not have the means, or money, to pay for them. Taxes pay to fund public assistance programs. The major public assistance programs are Medicaid, food stamps, Supplemental Security Insurance (SSI), and Temporary Assistance to Needy Families (TANF).

Medicaid was signed into law in 1965. It pays hospital, nursing home, and medical costs for those who qualify. States administer the program and pay part of the cost. The federal government, however, provides most of the money. Benefits vary from state to state, but they cannot go below a certain level.

The food stamp program was set up in 1964. It provides debit cards that can be used to buy food. The cards are given to people whose income falls below a certain limit.

stop and think

Create a table to compare and contrast social insurance and public assistance programs. Label the columns across the top "Name of Program," "Description," "Who Benefits," "Funding," "Entitlement/Not an Entitlement." Work with a partner. Be sure to give the table a title. Fill in the table. Then write three sentences that make comparisons or contrasts about the information in the table.

SSI provides cash payments to people who are elderly, have disabilities, or are blind. To qualify, their income must be below a set level. The program began in 1974. The federal government administers SSI and funds it with tax money.

Social Security payments assist in the living expenses of people age sixty-five and over.

TANF is a new program. It was signed into law in 1996 and takes the place of a previous welfare program. TANF is also known as Welfare to Work. It offers two years of job training, child care, and health care in return for an agreement to find work. If a person does not go to work within two years, he or she loses all benefits. The lifetime limit for collecting welfare is five years. The federal government pays for the program, but it is administered by the states.

The CDC promotes flu shots as part of its mission to keep Americans healthy.

Public Health

The Department of Health and Human Services also runs programs related to the health of the general public. Four of these agencies are the National Institutes of Health (NIH), the Centers for Disease Control (CDC), the Office of Public Health Preparedness (OPHP), and the Food and Drug Administration (FDA).

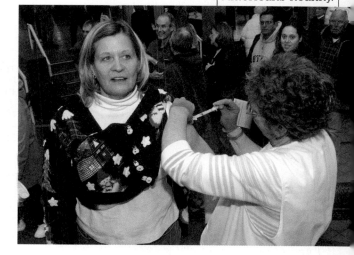

The NIH conducts research on health issues and provides grants to other researchers. The CDC educates the public about infectious diseases such as flu and AIDS. It also conducts research on these easily spread diseases. Its mission is to stop their spread. The OPHP was set up after the terrorist attacks of September 11, 2001, because of the nation's concern with terrorism. Its mission is to direct the response to health emergencies, especially bioterrorism. The FDA approves the sale of all prescription drugs and medical devices used in the nation. Companies must conduct thorough tests on their products before the FDA will approve them.

Aid to Veterans

The Department of Veterans Affairs (VA) also carries out health and human service policies. It provides benefits to veterans and their families, including widows, widowers, and dependent children. Supporting veterans is national policy. There is little or no disagreement over this.

The GI Bill was enacted after WWII to help veterans to pay for college after serving in the armed forces.

The VA provides health care for veterans in VA hospitals and clinics. In a recent year, more than five million people were treated through the VA health-care system. The VA also administers several financial programs for veterans. These include cash benefits for veterans who were disabled by injury or disease while in the service. Veterans may also receive education and training benefits. Since 1944, more than 20.4 million veterans have used the GI Bill of Rights and later laws to attend college and acquire other educational training. The VA also offers low-cost home loans and life insurance to veterans.

Putting It All Together

What are the nation's social policies? Do you agree with what the federal government does about social issues? Work with a partner to answer these questions. Identify each social policy mentioned in the lesson and give an opinion.

LESSON 4

Education, Housing, Transportation, and Security

Thinking on Your Own

The federal government supports programs for education, housing, transportation, and security. Choose one area. In your notebook, list five programs in your community that you think the federal government does or should support.

Federal aid to education began in the 1860s. Congress passed the Morrill Land Grant Act during the Civil War. Among other things, it offered land to states to build colleges to teach agricultural and mechanical arts. Over 70 land grant colleges have been built. Many state universities, such as Texas A&M, began this way.

Today, the federal government supports education in many ways. It also sets policies for housing, urban development, transportation, and security.

Federal Aid to Education

Federal aid to elementary and secondary education is a recent development. Historically, support for public schools has been a state and local responsibility. In 1953, Congress created a cabinet-level Department of Health, Education, and Welfare. Federal aid for K–12 students dates from the Elementary and Secondary Education Act passed by Congress in 1965. It provided funds for schools that had students living in poverty.

---

focus your reading

How does the Department of Education impact students and school districts?

Describe the role of the Department of Housing and Urban Development.

How has September 11, 2001, affected the mission of the Department of Transportation?

words to know

equal access

financial aid

school vouchers

charter schools

urban renewal

public housing

mass transit

The Department of Education, created in 1980, ensures **equal access** to education for all students. It guarantees that schools do not discriminate on the basis of race or gender. The department also collects national statistics on education.

A major responsibility of the Department of Education is to set policies on **financial aid**. The department gives financial aid to school districts. Federal aid to K–12 schools makes up about 9 percent of state and local budgets for these schools. Since 2001, states have been required to test students in grades three through eight in reading, math, and science. Their federal aid depends on obeying the No Child Left Behind Act.

Some student loans are forgiven when people agree to teach in areas that require more teachers.

Two other topics in education are school vouchers and charter schools. **School vouchers** give money to parents of children in low-performing public schools. The parents use the money to send their children to private schools. **Charter schools** are public schools. However, they do not have to obey all the rules and regulations of public schools. They are also free to experiment with different kinds of curricula. Charter schools are typically opened in large cities with many underperforming schools.

The federal government also provides financial aid to college and graduate students. Students receive money based on financial need. Pell Grants do not have to be paid back. There are also Perkins and Stafford Loan programs. They require the payment of interest as well as the original loan amount. The payment period is extended over ten years.

stop and think

Create a concept web for the Department of Education. Draw a large circle in the center of your paper. Label it "Department of Education." Draw and label smaller circles for each activity the department does. Connect these smaller circles with lines to the large circle. Work with a partner.

Aid to Housing and Urban Areas

In a recent year, the budget of the Department of Housing and Urban Development (HUD) was $38 billion. This money was spent on programs such as grants for community planning and development, lead hazard control, public housing, and loan programs for home ownership.

The federal government has been involved in housing policy since the Great Depression. In 1934, Congress created the Federal Housing Administration (FHA) and passed the National Housing Act in 1937. The purpose of both was to help builders and potential homeowners. The FHA continues to guarantee bank loans to builders and middle- and low-income home buyers. The FHA also runs housing programs for the homeless.

The "urban development" part of the department's title refers to programs to help cities. In the 1950s and 1960s, many large cities in the Northeast and Midwest had become run-down. People who could afford to were moving to the suburbs. Businesses followed. Parts of cities became filled with empty and decaying buildings. The people who were left became poorer and poorer.

Many housing projects, such as these in Chicago, are being replaced with affordable, low-income housing.

The federal government stepped in with money for **urban renewal**, or rebuilding. Issues arose, however, about how the money was used. Often, poor people were forced out of their homes, which were then torn down. Office buildings and apartments for middle-income and wealthy people took their place.

HUD also helps cities through its public housing policies. HUD provides aid to local governments to set up and operate public housing programs. In the beginning, **public housing** took the form of high-rise apartment buildings for low-income families. Problems with crime, drugs, and poor maintenance halted the building of these projects. Low-rise apartment buildings and townhouses are now built in some areas as public housing. The majority of public housing money is spent on rent subsidies. Low-income families pay a part of the rent themselves. A federal grant pays the rest.

Transportation Programs

The mission of the Department of Transportation (DOT) is to ensure "a fast, safe, efficient, accessible, and convenient transportation system that meets our vital national interests and enhances the quality of life of the American people." The DOT does this in a number of ways.

The DOT runs labs that test the safety of cars and trucks. It publishes the results of these rollover and crash test studies. These reports keep consumers informed about the safety of cars and trucks they might be thinking of buying.

The Federal Aviation Administration (FAA) sets standards for airline safety. Its mission is to provide the safest, most efficient aerospace system in the world. It also aids in the investigation of airline crashes and issues reports on their causes. The National Transportation Safety Board (NTSB) is an independent federal agency that investigates every aviation accident in the United States. It also investigates significant railroad, highway, marine, and pipeline accidents.

The Department of Transportation conducts tests on vehicles in the United States to ensure consumer safety.

The most direct impact of the DOT comes through federal spending on highways and mass transit. Trains, buses, and subways are **mass transit**. Unlike cars, they transport large numbers of people at one time. The federal government has been aiding state highway building since 1916. The greatest boost to highway construction began in 1956. In that year, Congress passed the Federal-Aid Highway Act. The federal excise tax on gasoline, tires, and similar goods is given to states to build and improve the national highway system. There are 45,000 miles of multi-lane highways that join most of the nation's major cities.

Mass transit, on the other hand, suffers from a lack of funding. A few rapid transit rail lines, like San Francisco's BART (Bay Area Rapid Transit), have been built. However, these projects cost millions of dollars. States and cities look to the federal government for help for at least some of the cost.

Homeland Security

A major change in domestic policy came after September 11, 2001. The terrorist attack on the United States showed how at risk the nation was. As a result, President George W. Bush proposed the creation of a Department of Homeland Security. The mission of the department is to "prevent and deter terrorist attacks against and respond to threats and hazards to the nation." The department ensures safe and secure borders, welcomes lawful immigrants and visitors, and promotes the free flow of commerce.

The new department combined 22 agencies from existing executive departments. For example, the Secret Service, Coast Guard, airport baggage screeners, and border patrol officers became employees of the new department. The main focus of the department is terrorism. However, it is also responsible for the government's response to natural disasters. Its Federal Emergency Management Agency (FEMA) provides aid after major floods, tornadoes, and hurricanes.

Americans welcomed the new department when it was created. However, disagreements have arisen over how it does its job. Immigration officers have increased arrests of undocumented aliens. Often, these arrests are of people who have lived, worked, and raised families in the United States peacefully for years. Critics claim that these people pose no threat to the country.

Controversies have also arisen over the Patriot Act, which allows the government to search out terrorists without giving them some of the protections of the Bill of Rights. Supporters say it is needed to track down terrorists. Others claim it threatens people's civil liberties. Critics claim the act endangers the freedom of all Americans.

Critics also claim that more money should be spent on securing the nation's harbors. Millions of tons of cargo come through U.S. ports daily. Little of it is inspected. Big cities like New York want more money for security. In a recent budget, New York City received what amounted to $5 a person. Western states like Wyoming received $33 a person.

Like all policy disagreements, these will be solved through the give-and-take of public discussion and elections. Not everyone will be happy with the solutions. However, everyone will have a chance to make his or her ideas known at election time.

Putting It All Together

Imagine you are a member of Congress. There is $100 million to divide among housing, transportation, and homeland security. How much would you give to (1) public housing, (2) highway repairs, (3) mass transit, and (4) improvements to harbor security? Explain in two or three sentences how you decided on the amount given to each program.

Participate in Government

The Census: Fill It Out and Be Counted

Every ten years, the U.S. Census Bureau counts every American—or tries to. The Constitution requires that a census, or count, of residents be taken every ten years. The first census was in 1790. U.S.

marshals went from house to house counting people. They found that the new nation's population was 3.9 million. It is now close to 300 million and growing.

Today, census forms are mailed to every household in the nation. Most forms are "short forms." They contain just a few questions about age, gender, ethnic group, race, and similar topics. One person is supposed to fill out the form for everyone living in the home. About one in six forms is a "long form." It asks a long list of questions. They deal with topics such as disability, income, occupation, number of rooms in the house, value of the home or monthly rent, and number of cars. The long form attempts to get a summary of certain characteristics of the nation's households.

Some people lose their census forms. Others just forget to fill them out. Still other people do not like to give information to the government. To get as accurate a count as possible, the Census Bureau hires people to visit households that have not returned their form.

Why is it important to fill out the census form when it arrives in the mail? Many government programs depend on population information. The census provides data that is used

- for redrawing districts for members of the House of Representatives and for state lawmakers.
- for distributing federal funds for programs such as Medicaid and aid to education.
- for planning where to build schools, roads, and other government facilities.

Be counted—fill out the census form when it comes!

Skill Builder

Analyze a Line Graph

A line graph shows information about a topic over a period of time. Usually, the time is shown along the bottom, or horizontal axis, of the graph. The quantity, or amount, is given along the left side, or vertical axis, of the graph. The line or lines on the graph show the ups and downs of the topic. A graph key explains what each line represents.

By reading a line graph, you can determine if there is a trend, or pattern, over time. Understanding you decide how important something is over time. A line graph may show a rising federal deficit.

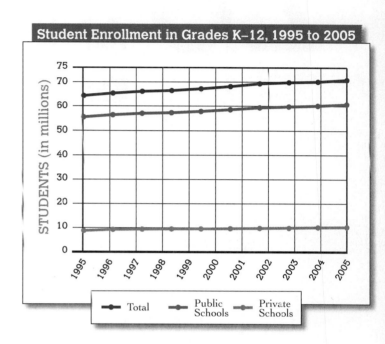

To Read a Line Graph:

- Read the title of the graph to see what it is about.

- Examine the vertical, or side, axis to determine the quantity.

- Examine the horizontal, or bottom, axis to determine the time period.

- Read the key if there is more than one line on the graph.

- Examine the line (or lines) on the graph. Does the line go up or down steadily over time? Does the line zigzag over time?

Study the graph and then answer the following questions.

1 What is the title of the graph?

2 What do the lines represent?

3 Does the number of students ever decrease?

4 Do the numbers move steadily, or do they zigzag?

Chapter 20

FOREIGN POLICY AND NATIONAL DEFENSE

Getting Focused

Skim this chapter to predict what you will be learning.

- Read the lesson titles and subheadings.
- Look at the illustrations and read the captions.
- Examine the tables and Time Box.
- Review the vocabulary words and terms.

On many days, foreign policy issues seem to take over the news. The president spends a great deal of time dealing with other nations. List at least four foreign policy issues that you know the current president is dealing with.

The president of the United States is responsible for setting foreign and domestic policy agendas. In this role, the president regularly meets with other world leaders, such as during this meeting of NATO members.

U.S. Foreign Policy

Thinking on Your Own

Read the Time Box on page 365. Choose one entry. Write at least three things in your notebook that you already know about that event.

Foreign policy is all the strategies and goals that guide a nation's dealings with other countries. It includes trade treaties like the NAFTA and treaties that limit nuclear weapons. It includes military actions such as peacekeeping as part of the North Atlantic Treaty Organization (NATO). Diplomats such as ambassadors, however, carry on most foreign relations. These people are representatives of the government who deal directly with other nations.

focus your reading

What are the goals of U.S. foreign policy?

Explain how U.S. foreign policy has changed over time.

How has internationalism affected U.S. foreign policy?

words to know

foreign policy

alliances

isolationism

globalization

The Goals of U.S. Foreign Policy

Five basic goals underlie all U.S. foreign policy. Some of these goals, such as national security, date back to the beginning of the United States. Others, such as world peace, are more recent.

National security: The nation's borders and territories must be kept safe from invasion or control by other countries. This is the meaning of national security. The first interest of all U.S. foreign policy is to keep the nation safe.

Trade: The economy of the United States is based on the ability to buy and sell freely in other nations. U.S. businesses buy and sell more than just finished goods such as cars. They buy and sell natural resources, as well as services. In return, U.S. businesses sell their services overseas.

World peace: For much of the twentieth century, the United States acted as the world's peacemaker. After World War I, it tried to get other nations to stop building weapons. During World War II, the United States worked to get other countries to establish the United Nations.

U.S. soldiers served as peacekeepers in Bosnia during the 1990s.

Democracy: The United States is the oldest constitutional democracy in the world. It serves as a model to other nations. The United States also has a long history of helping others fight undemocratic governments. For example, Communist governments in Eastern Europe collapsed in the late 1980s. Many of the new governments received U.S. economic aid and political help to set up democracies.

Humanitarianism: This is concern for the welfare of humanity. Both the U.S. government and private citizens respond to world crises. The outpouring of aid to the tsunami victims in South Asia in 2004 is an example.

U.S. officials see world peace, democratic nations, and a concern for humanity as ways to ensure the nation's security.

stop and think

Create a concept map to represent the goals of U.S. foreign policy. Work with a partner. Decide what to label the central circle and the smaller circles for the goals. Add another smaller circle to each goal with an example from the text and from class discussion.

U.S. Foreign Policy Over Time

President George Washington warned the United States to stay out of foreign **alliances**. He believed that having partnerships with other nations could be dangerous. The next few presidents agreed with Washington. They thought the nation was still too weak to fight another war. As a result, the nation followed a policy based on **isolationism**. It did not become involved in world affairs, particularly those of Europe.

In 1823, President James Monroe warned Europe to stay out of the Americas. This is called the Monroe Doctrine. In truth, the United States was still not powerful enough to defeat European nations. Monroe knew that the United States could rely on Great Britain to help enforce this policy. Great Britain had territories in the Americas and wanted to keep other nations out, too.

In the 1890s, the United States began to look overseas. As a growing industrial nation, it needed inexpensive raw materials and overseas markets. In 1898, it went to war against Spain. As a result, the United States acquired Cuba, Puerto Rico, Guam, and the Philippines. These islands provided natural resources, markets, and coaling stations for American steamships.

Many Americans did not want to be pulled into World War I. However, by 1917, it looked as though Germany would win. The United States then entered the war. President Woodrow Wilson declared that the United States would make the "world safe for democracy."

World War I resulted in a huge loss of life and was very costly. In the 1920s and 1930s, the United States stopped intervening in the affairs of other nations. It did not want to get caught in the war that seemed to be building in Europe. When Japan bombed U.S. forces at Pearl Harbor in 1941, the United States entered World War II against Japan, Germany, and Italy.

After World War II, the United States remained involved in world affairs and kept its place as a world power. For the next 45 years, it waged a Cold War against the Communist Soviet Union and People's Republic of China. No actual wars were fought against these nations. But each side supported other groups in pro-Communist and anti-Communist conflicts. The Korean and Vietnam Wars were the longest and most costly. During this time, the United States, the Soviet Union, and China also built massive nuclear weapons.

The Cold War thawed somewhat during the 1970s. However, President Ronald Reagan toughened foreign policies toward Communist nations in the 1980s.

⏳ Time Box

U.S. Foreign Policy

1789–1823
  Isolationism

1823
  Monroe Doctrine

1823–1890s
  Expansion of the U.S. across the continent

1898–1914
  U.S. as a world power

1914–1917
  Return to isolationism

1917–1919
  World War I

1920s–1930s
  Return to isolationism

1939–1945
  World War II

1945–1989
  Cold War; Korean War; Vietnam War; nuclear weapons

1969–1970s
  Détente

1980s
  Return to a hard line against the Communist Soviet Union

1989
  End of the Cold War

1990s–present
  Globalization and fighting terrorism

President Ronald Reagan and Soviet president Mikhail Gorbachev shake hands during a meeting in 1988.

Communism collapsed in Russia and Eastern Europe in the late 1980s and early 1990s. Most of the new governments were democratic. In the 1990s, China became more open to private enterprise. However, it remains Communist.

U.S. Foreign Policy Today

U.S. foreign military policy is focused on fighting terrorism. The first terrorist attack on U.S. soil was a bombing of the World Trade Center in New York City in 1993. Between then and 2001, terrorists carried out other attacks on U.S. interests such as the U.S. Navy ship the USS *Cole*. On September 11, 2001, terrorists flew planes into the World Trade Center in New York City and the Pentagon in Washington, D.C.

Since the attacks of September 11, 2001, the federal government has waged a "war on terrorism." President George W. Bush sent troops into Afghanistan looking for the terrorists who were responsible for planning the attack. The United States and European nations help one another track down and arrest terrorists. It is a fight that will go on for many years.

Economic Foreign Policy

U.S. economic foreign policy is focused on globalization. **Globalization** is the interaction among people, companies, and governments of different nations. International trade is one force behind globalization. Another is investment. Technologies such as computers, robots, and the Internet aid globalization. U.S. trade policies aid U.S. companies as they buy and sell in the world market.

Globalization offers jobs and wages to many people who would have none. However, many workers in developing nations work in unsafe and unhealthy factories. Critics of globalization believe the United States should do more to improve conditions in other nations.

Putting It All Together

Work with a partner. Create a table with five columns. Label each column with a foreign policy goal. Then classify the events in the Time Box by goal. You may write an event in more than one column. With a partner, discuss any differences between your tables.

Shared Powers

Thinking on Your Own

As you skim the lesson, make an outline of it in your notebook. Remember to include the subheadings. Start each section of your outline with the most important information. As you read, fill in the details of the outline.

The president is the chief architect of U.S. foreign policy. The Departments of State and Defense and the Office of National Intelligence, an independent agency, advise the president. Congress also has a role in foreign policy.

Influences on Policy-makers

Like all policy decisions, foreign policy is influenced by outside factors. Both public opinion and interest groups influence foreign policy. In the early 1960s, the public supported the Vietnam War. As the war dragged on and the human and money costs mounted, the public turned against the war. In 1968, President Lyndon Johnson decided not to run for reelection. It seemed certain he would lose. He had become unpopular because of the war. Richard Nixon won the 1968 election because he promised to end U.S. involvement in the conflict.

Groups with an interest in foreign policy include unions and trade and farm associations. Special-interest groups such as human rights organizations also try to influence U.S. foreign policy. Some **economic interest groups** lobby Congress to protect their

focus your reading

List three of the outside influences on foreign policy decision-making.

How do the president's roles affect foreign policy?

Who are the president's chief foreign policy advisers?

Explain how the president and Congress interact in making foreign policy.

words to know

economic interest group

human rights group

ambassador

intelligence

hot spot

Antiwar protesters demonstrated against the Vietnam War in May 1971.

members. Others want free trade to make U.S. goods less costly for other nations to buy. Unions and some trade and farm groups want high tariffs to make imports more expensive. **Human rights groups** want U.S. foreign policy to punish nations whose policies violate people's human rights. These groups want the United States to withhold support from the governments that fail to act against human rights abuses. The president and Congress must weigh these competing foreign policy goals.

The President's Foreign Policy Roles

Article 3, Sections 2 and 3, of the U.S. Constitution lists the powers and duties of the president. Among these are diplomatic and military responsibilities. As head of state, the president represents the United States to the rest of the world. The president often takes an active role in world affairs. For example, both presidents Jimmy Carter and Bill Clinton tried to make peace between Israel and its Arab neighbors.

Israeli Prime Minister Yitzhak Rabin, President Bill Clinton, and PLO Chairman Yasser Arafat in 1993

The president is also chief diplomat for the nation. In this role, the president receives **ambassadors**—official representatives—from other countries. The president can also break off diplomatic relations with other nations. This occurs only over serious disagreements. For example, President Dwight Eisenhower broke off relations with Cuba after the Communists came to power there. On the other hand, President Bill Clinton reestablished diplomatic relations with Vietnam in 1995.

The president is commander in chief of the military. It is the president who decides when and if U.S. troops will be sent into battle zones. Although the president can use the military around the world, Congress must be notified of such a decision.

Foreign Policy Advisers

Foreign policy is about more than terrorism and war. Foreign policy also involves issues such as trade and energy resources. As a result, most executive departments have foreign policy issues. However, the Departments of State and Defense play the major roles in foreign policy decisions.

stop and think

List three foreign policy issues. Choose one to write about. State your position on the issue in one sentence. Write three reasons to support your position. Use this information as the basis for a letter to the president. Write your letter. Share it with a partner. Ask your partner if your letter is clear. How could you make it clearer? Also ask your partner to proofread your letter.

The Department of State runs all diplomatic activities of the government. The secretary of state is an expert in foreign affairs. He or she represents the United States in discussions and negotiations with high-level officials of other nations. The State Department employs thousands of area experts. These people gather and analyze **intelligence**, or information, about political events in different areas of the world.

Secretary of State Condoleezza Rice, Defense Secretary Donald Rumsfeld, and President George W. Bush in 2005.

The secretary of defense is responsible for all branches of the armed forces—army, navy, air force, and marines. The strength of the U.S. military is important in deciding whether to send troops to some world hot spot. A **hot spot** is an area of political tension and violence. The Defense Department also has intelligence experts.

reading for understanding

1. What is needed for economic growth?
2. Explain what is needed to improve public services.
3. Describe what foreign aid must do.

The following is from a speech given by a member of the U.S. Agency for International Development in 2005. It states the agency's and the U.S. government's view of the proper role of foreign aid.

Primary Source

"**Without trade, there can be no sustained economic growth. Without economic growth, there will be no increase in tax revenues to support improved public services. Without growth and services, there will be no increase in wealth and reduction in poverty. Unless foreign aid contributes to economic growth, it is failing to achieve its primary mission.**"

—Andrew S. Natsios, Administrator,
U.S. Agency for International Development, July 20, 2005

After the attacks of September 11, 2001, a national commission studied the government's intelligence system. The commission determined that a better system might have uncovered the September 11, 2001 plot. As a result, the Office of National Intelligence was created in 2005. This independent agency directs the work of 15 other government agencies that gather intelligence. The mission of the office is to make the 15 agencies work more efficiently and share information.

Congress and the President

Article I, Section 8, of the U.S. Constitution lists the powers of Congress. Declaring war and ratifying treaties relate directly to foreign policy. However, Congress can use its budget and confirmation powers to make foreign policy. It can approve part of or more than what the president asks for foreign aid. It can hold up or refuse to confirm a presidential nominee.

The president, not Congress, sets the direction for foreign policy. The president decides whether to send troops as part of a United Nations peacekeeping mission. Congress approves and funds programs proposed by the president. However, sharp differences can arise. The war in Iraq began with bipartisan support. However, when no weapons of mass destruction were found in Iraq, Democrats began to speak out against the war.

The president has certain advantages over Congress in foreign policy. The president is the head of state and therefore the only person who speaks for the United States in dealings with other nations. The president has the benefit of reports from all the government intelligence agencies. Much of this is classified, or secret. Congress may not be allowed to see all of what the president sees. Therefore, Congress does not have all the information to make decisions about foreign policy.

If the president feels it necessary, Congress can be bypassed. Instead of signing a treaty with a nation, an executive agreement can be issued. Unlike treaties, executive agreements do not have to be approved by Congress.

The Senate Foreign Relations Committee routinely holds hearings on foreign policy issues.

Putting It All Together

Use your outline to write a summary of this lesson. Share your summary with a partner. Revise your summary if needed.

Tools of Foreign Policy

Thinking on Your Own

Examine the photographs in this lesson. Choose one photograph. Describe the photograph in a paragraph in your notebook. Who is shown? What are they doing? Include any information you already know about the topic.

America's foreign policy is a mix of programs and actions. Military force is one tool, but the United States uses it carefully. The nation has declared war only five times in its history. However, it has frequently sent troops to aid allies, protect the innocent, and preserve freedom.

The goal of U.S. foreign policy is to protect national security by means other than war. Defense and economic agreements combined with foreign aid are two methods. The United States is also a member of the United Nations and other organizations that work to keep world peace.

> **focus your reading**
>
> What is the purpose of the alliances and pacts to which the United States belongs?
>
> What is the goal of foreign aid?
>
> What groups are part of the United Nations?
>
> **words to know**
>
> internationalism
>
> regional security alliances

Alliances

After World War II, the United States did not return to a policy of isolationism. It adopted **internationalism**. The nation became deeply involved in world affairs. Soon after the war, the United States sent billions of dollars in aid to Europe to rebuild and to fight communism. This aid included food, machines, and weapons. The United States was also a founding member of the United Nations. In addition, the United States entered into **regional security alliances** with nations in different parts of the world.

The following table shows the major U.S. defense alliances. Each alliance commits its members to defend one another. Suppose the Soviet Union had attacked France in the 1950s. All NATO members would have been duty-bound to defend France.

U.S. Foreign Policy Alliances

Defense Alliances	Economic Alliances
North Atlantic Treaty Organization (NATO; United States, Canada, and 17 European nations, 1949)	Organization of American States (OAS, 1948)
Rio Pact (United States, Canada, and 32 Central, Caribbean, and South American nations, 1947)	North American Free Trade Agreement (NAFTA; United States, Canada, Mexico, 1994)
ANZUS (Australia, New Zealand, United States, 1951)	World Trade Organization (WTO, 1996)
Japanese Pact (1951)	Central American Free Trade Agreement (CAFTA: United States and Central American nations, 2005)
Philippines Pact (1951)	
Korean Pact (United States and South Korea, 1953)	

Three of the pacts shown on the table are between the United States and a single nation—Japan, the Philippines, and South Korea. In addition to these three, the United States has defense pacts with 50 other nations. The United States agrees to defend these nations if they are attacked.

The table also shows major economic agreements that the United States has signed. The WTO is an international organization. Its goal is to make trade among nations easier and fairer. It sets trade regulations and settles trade disagreements among nations. The NAFTA and the CAFTA have eased trade between the United States and the nations of North and Central America.

stop and think

Why are defense and trade agreements good foreign policy? Discuss this question with a partner. Draw a T-chart. Label one column "Defense." Label the other column "Economic." List your reasons in the T-chart. Share your T-chart with another pair. Try to come to agreement on the best three reasons for each type of agreement.

Foreign Aid

Foreign aid is military and economic assistance to friendly nations. The aid may be in the form of money, food, seeds, equipment, technology, and advisers. Money is given either as loans or grants. Grants do not have to be paid back. There is one condition to any grant or loan, however. The money must be used to buy U.S.-made goods.

The United States contributes to the United Nations World Food Programme.

Most economic aid programs are run through the U.S. Agency for International Development (USAID). It is part of the State Department. The goals of economic aid programs are humanitarian and economic. Foreign aid provides developing nations with food, medical care, and educational programs. These fulfill the humanitarian goal of U.S. foreign policy.

Because the developing nations must buy U.S.-made goods, foreign aid helps the U.S. economy. This is a short-term result. However, the long-term purpose is to grow the economies of developing nations. As their economies improve, these nations will be able to buy more U.S. goods over time.

Most military aid programs are run through the Defense Department. In addition to weapons, military aid includes sending military advisers. They help friendly nations train and build up their armed forces.

Foreign aid became an important part of U.S. foreign policy after World War II. For many years, the United States used it to help nations fight communism. Since World War II, the United States has spent more than $500 billion in foreign aid. In the beginning, most of the aid was economic. Between 1948 and 1952, the United States gave $12.5 billion to 16 nations in Western Europe to rebuild.

Military aid is provided by the United States to many countries around the world.

Since the 1950s, much of the aid has been military. Instead of Europe, the aid has flowed to nations in the Middle East, Asia, and Latin America. At first, it was used to support friendly governments from Communist takeovers. Since the 1990s, the aid has been focused on the fight against terrorism. Israel has also received large amounts of foreign aid in its 60-year conflict with its Arab neighbors.

International Organizations

The United States is a founding member of the United Nations (UN). The first session met in 1945. That first session had 50 member nations. Today, the UN has 191 member nations.

The UN Charter is similar to a constitution. It states the purpose of the organization and its rules. The goal of the UN is to maintain friendly relations among nations. The General Assembly is the main body of the UN. It debates issues and makes recommendations to the Security Council. All member nations have a vote in the General Assembly.

The Security Council is made up of five permanent member nations and ten nations selected by the General Assembly. These ten serve on the council for two-year terms. The United States, along with Great Britain, France, Russia, and China, are the permanent members. The United States takes a leading role in Security Council discussions and votes. It is also often the lead nation in carrying out the council's decisions. For example, the Security Council voted in 1950 to defend South Korea from an invasion by Communist North Korea. The United States provided most of the troops and equipment for the Korean War. The United States also took the lead in the war in Iraq in 2003.

The United Nations Food and Agriculture Organization and the World Food Programme provide assistance to developing nations around the world.

The International Court of Justice (ICJ) is the judicial branch of the UN. The court has 15 judges who serve for nine-year terms. The General Assembly and Security Council select the judges. The court hears cases between member nations and provides legal advice to other groups within the UN.

Major Groups Within the United Nations

Agency	Purpose
Food and Agriculture Organization (FAO)	Provides assistance to increase food production
International Monetary Fund (IMF)	Promotes international trade
International Bank for Reconstruction and Development (World Bank)	Makes loans to developing nations to • invest in projects • promote trade • repay debts to developed nations
United Nations Educational, Scientific, and Cultural Organization (UNESCO)	Promotes international exchanges of educational, scientific, and cultural information
World Health Organization (WHO)	Provides assistance to developing nations to • set up health services • promote health education, nutrition, and sanitation • fight epidemics

The UN does not have a president or prime minister. A secretary general manages the huge bureaucracy that runs the UN on a day-to-day basis. The secretary general is elected for a five-year term by the General Assembly.

The table on this page lists some important agencies within the United Nations. The United States is often the major supporter in these groups. For example, the World Bank is always headed by an American nominated by the U.S. government.

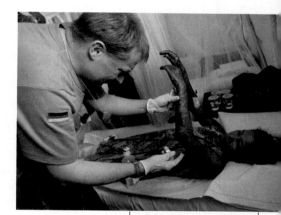

After the tsunami of 2004, the World Health Organization provided medical assistance to those affected by the disaster.

Putting It All Together

Create a concept web to illustrate how the United States puts its foreign policy goals into action. Draw a large circle and label it "U.S. Foreign Policy." Draw smaller circles for each tool it uses. Connect these with lines to the large circle. Add smaller circles and lines with examples. Work with a partner.

Participate in Government

Register for Selective Service

The Selective Service System (SSS) is the way the United States registers young men for possible service in the army. It is not the same as the draft. A draft actually calls up young men for service. The draft was ended in 1975.

Who must register with the SSS?

- all male U.S. citizens between ages eighteen and twenty-six living in or outside the United States

- all male legal permanent residents between ages eighteen and twenty-six

- all undocumented male aliens between ages eighteen and twenty-six

- all men between ages eighteen and twenty-six who hold U.S. citizenship as well as citizenship in another country. It does not matter whether they live in the United States.

Foreign men who are in the United States on student or visitor visas do not have to register. Neither do men who work for a foreign government in the United States.

Men have from 30 days before to 30 days after their eighteenth birthday to register. A male noncitizen who becomes a resident of the United States must register within 30 days. If the man is older than twenty-six, he does not have to register.

Registration is easy. The SSS Web site has a form that can be submitted online. Post offices have copies of the form. The Federal Student Financial Aid (FAFSA) form has a SSS checkbox. If a student checks this box, the Department of Education sends the necessary information to SSS. Some high schools have SSS registrars who will register male students.

Those who do not register are breaking the law. Failing to register carries a fine of up to $250,000 and five years in jail. In addition, those who do not register cannot get federal student loans and grants. Registering is a condition for U.S. citizenship for men between the ages of eighteen and twenty-six. Only those who register are eligible for federal job training programs and for federal jobs.

Skill Builder

Problem-solving and Decision-making

Identifying a problem and deciding what to do about it are two important citizenship skills. Government officials need these skills and so do ordinary citizens.

Suppose there is no traffic light within six blocks of the elementary school. Cars speed through stop signs. Children crossing the street on their way to school are in danger. What can citizens do?

First, they have to identify the problem—too many fast-moving cars. Then, they have to study solutions. They decide on one and present it to the city council. The city council agrees. However, the job of the citizens' group is not over. Members have to determine if the solution has fixed the problem.

To help you identify problems and make decisions, follow these steps:

1. Identify the problem.

2. Gather information about the problem.

3. List as many solutions as you can think of.

4. Review the advantages and disadvantages of each solution.

5. Decide on your solution.

6. Put your solution/decision into practice.

7. Review and evaluate your decision after a period of time.

Complete the following activities with a partner.

1 Think of a problem in your community. Go through steps 1 to 5 to reach a possible solution. Then think of a way to evaluate your solution.

2 Write a letter to the mayor about the problem and your solution. State the problem. Then state your solution. Describe how everyone will be able to tell if your solution is working.

UNIT 8

STATE AND LOCAL GOVERNMENT

State governments are older than the federal government. The Framers used the states as the model for the federal government. As a result, there are many similarities between the federal and state governments. The states have constitutions and executive, legislative, and judicial branches. The federal and state governments have some of the same powers, such as the power to tax. However, only the states have certain powers, such as the power to set up school districts.

The authority to found local governments comes from state government. Local governments have executive, legislative, and judicial branches. Local governments also have powers similar to the states, such as the power to enforce laws and tax citizens.

Chapter
21 STATE GOVERNMENT

Getting Focused

Skim this chapter to predict what you will be learning.

- Read the lesson titles and subheadings.
- Look at the illustrations and read the captions.
- Examine the tables.
- Review the vocabulary words and terms.

State governments have a constitution and executive, legislative, and judicial branches. What do you think the purpose of each of these is for a state? Think about their purposes for the federal government. Then write a sentence to describe the purpose of a constitution and of executive, legislative, and judicial branches in state government.

State governments provide many services to residents, including education, social programs, and recreational areas, such as Jedediah Smith Redwoods State Park in California.

State Constitutions

Thinking on Your Own

In the United States, states as well as the national government have constitutions. Why are state constitutions necessary in a federal system of government? What would you call a system of government that lacked state constitutions? Discuss this question with a partner and write your answer in your notebook.

Every state constitution serves the same purpose for the state that the U.S. Constitution does for the federal government. State constitutions

- create the structure for state government: executive, legislative, and judicial

- create the structure for local government, such as county, parish, city, township, and borough

- describe the powers and duties of each unit of local government

- identify the ways that the state and the local governments may raise and spend money

- set up state agencies, boards, and commissions

focus your reading

Explain how state constitutions are alike and how they are different.

How can state constitutions be amended?

Why is there a need for constitutional reform in the states?

words to review

limited government

popular sovereignty

separation of powers

checks and balances

Bill of Rights

judicial review

amendment

ratified

State agencies, boards, and commissions are independent. For example, all states have state boards of education. They oversee the schools within the state and make education policy for the state.

The U.S. Constitution is the supreme law of the land. State constitutions and state law may not conflict with the U.S. Constitution. This is a very important fact.

The Basics of State Constitutions

Limited government and **popular sovereignty** are common to both state constitutions and the U.S. Constitution. In other words, the government may not set policy or act if the people do not wish it to do so. The government operates within limits that the people set for it.

The Framers also borrowed the three branches of government, **separation of powers**, and **checks and balances** from the state constitutions. The federal and state governments all have executive, legislative, and judicial branches. Each branch has its own powers and duties. The state constitutions set up ways that the three branches check and balance each other's powers.

Each state constitution has a **Bill of Rights**. Most have guarantees similar to the U.S. Bill of Rights. However, a few list additional rights. For example, the right to self-government and to be free from discrimination based on race or gender may be included.

State constitutions, like the U.S. Constitution, describe the process for amending the constitution.

There are two other characteristics that most state constitutions have in common. State constitutions tend to be long and detailed. This is not true of the U.S. Constitution, which gives only a broad outline of what the federal government should be.

Common Characteristics of State Constitutions

State constitutions are based on the principles of

- Limited government
- Popular sovereignty

State constitutions create a system of state government that includes

- Separation of powers
- Checks and balances
- Judicial review

State constitutions describe

- The structure of state government: executive, legislative, and judicial branches
- The structure of local governments
- The powers reserved for each branch of the state government and to local governments
- A Bill of Rights
- The process for changing the state constitution

stop and think

Create a two-column chart to show the similarities and differences between the U.S. Constitution and state constitutions. Work with a partner to complete your chart.

Former California governor Jerry Brown (left) during a 1978 news conference discussing Proposition 13— a law that changed property taxes

Amending State Constitutions

Like the U.S. Constitution, state constitutions can be amended. Approved **amendments** are ratified by the voters. Delaware, however, requires the legislature to ratify amendments. There are three basic ways to amend state constitutions.

First, the state legislature may propose an amendment. In most states, an amendment is proposed and voted on in one session of the legislature. In a few states, an amendment must be approved in two different sessions. This gives lawmakers a chance for second thoughts.

Second, a legislature may call a constitutional convention. The voters must approve the need for it. A constitutional convention is usually used to revise the constitution or to write a new one.

Third, the voters may propose amendments in 18 states. Voters must sign a petition asking for the amendment to be placed on the ballot. If the petition drive succeeds, the amendment is voted on at the next general election.

Constitutional Reforms

The first state constitutions were written in the years right after 1776. Only 17 states have proposed and **ratified** new constitutions. This means that the constitutions are all close to or over 100 years old.

Age is not necessarily a problem. The U.S. Constitution is more than 200 years old. However, state constitutions have grown significantly in length. Unlike the U.S. Constitution, state constitutions have acquired many amendments.

"GUILTY? DO YOU REALIZE HOW THAT WOULD LOOK IF I DECIDE TO RUN FOR POLITICAL OFFICE?"

Many constitutions are filled with sections that are no longer enforced. New amendments have taken the place of these old sections. In addition, the constitutions are filled with details such as what subjects should be taught in school.

Putting It All Together

Refer to your chart from the Stop and Think activity. Work with a partner to add information from the last two subheadings in this lesson. Refer to Chapter 3, if necessary, to add information about the U.S. Constitution.

Legislative, Executive, and Judicial Branches

Thinking on Your Own

Draw three columns in your notebook. Label them "Federal Legislature," "Federal Executive," and "Federal Judiciary." Then list three facts about the federal government in each column. As you read, think about how the federal and state governments are similar and how they are different.

Like the federal government, state governments have legislative, executive, and judicial branches. Like the branches of the federal government, they act as checks on each other's power. However, they are different from the federal branches in various ways.

focus your reading

Describe the organization and duties of state legislatures.

Explain the roles and duties of a state governor.

What are the organization and duties of state court systems?

words to know

unicameral

line item veto

pardon

parole

commute

reprieve

opinions

misdemeanor

The Legislature

The legislature is the lawmaking body in each state government. In addition to the power to make laws, the legislature has the power to tax, to borrow money, and to spend money. The purpose of the powers of the legislature is to promote the general well-being of the state's citizens.

Nebraska is the only state with just one house in the state legislature. Nebraska's legislature is **unicameral**. The other 49 states have two houses. The lower house is usually called the assembly. The upper house is usually called the senate. Legislatures with two houses are bicameral.

Qualifications for members of state legislatures vary from state to state. In general, a person must be at least twenty-one years old to be elected to the lower house and twenty-five to be elected to the upper house. The person must also live in the district from which he or she is elected. Each state sets its own requirement for how long a person must live in the district before running for office.

State legislative districts are drawn by the state legislatures. Every ten years after the U.S. census, states review their population and redraw districts as needed. In 1964, the Supreme Court ruled that districts must be based on population. Before this, many states drew legislative districts based on area. Now, state legislative districts must have about the same number of people in every district.

Four states hold elections for the state legislators in odd-numbered years. The other 46 states hold them in even-numbered years, when members of the U.S. House of Representatives and the U.S. Senate are also elected. State legislators serve for two- or four-year terms. Most members of state assemblies serve two-year terms. Most senate terms are four years.

At one time, many state legislatures met every other year or for one or two months each year. Today, 44 state legislatures meet every year. The sessions have also become longer. The legislators face many more complex issues than they did in the past. Issues range from how to finance education to whether to tax sales over the Internet. If necessary, state governors may also call the legislatures back into special session. In about two-thirds of the states, legislators themselves may call special sessions.

In about half the states, the leader of the upper house is the lieutenant governor. This position is similar to the vice president of the United States. The senators in these states also choose a president pro tempore. He or she oversees the upper house when the lieutenant governor is absent. In the other half of the states, state senators choose their own presiding officer. This person is also called the president pro tempore.

The presiding officer in the lower house is called the speaker. The majority party in the house chooses the speaker. About 99 percent of all state lawmakers are either Democrats or Republicans. Fewer than 100 are independents or members of minor parties.

Like Congress, state legislatures do much of their work in committees. The presiding officers choose committee chairs and members of all committees. This is different from the way Congress chooses committee members and chairs. However, the way bills are passed is similar. Review the diagram on page 140 to see how a bill becomes a law.

Review the diagram on page 140 to see how a bill becomes a law.

The table on page 386 lists basic information

The table on page 387 lists the

Review the diagram on page 140

stop and think

Review the three-column chart that you made at the beginning of this lesson. Draw a line under the lists for the federal government. Prepare to make new lists for each branch of state government. First make a list of three facts for state legislative branches. As you read ahead, add three facts for each of the remaining two columns.

Only members of the legislature may introduce bills, which are then sent to committees to consider. People other than members of the legislature usually write the bills. Interest groups write the majority of bills. The governor's office, state agencies, and local governments also send bills to state legislators to introduce. Only about one-quarter of all bills end up in the governor's office for signature. Like the president, governors may veto a bill. Usually, a two-thirds vote in both houses will override a governor's veto.

The Executive Branch

The governor is the chief executive and chief administrator of state government. In the past, the position had limited power. Often, a governor was limited to one term in office, and terms were often only two years. However, since the mid-twentieth century, the position of governor has been greatly strengthened. The reason is the same as the one that caused state legislatures to have longer sessions. States must deal with more issues today than they did even 50 years ago.

The table on page 386 lists basic information about the election and term of office of governors. Governors do not have the same amount of power as the president. Governors share their power with other officers of the executive department. The table on page 387 lists the other major officers and their duties. Generally, states have all four positions. Most states fill them through elections rather than by appointing people.

Rod R. Blagojevich (center) ran on the Democratic ticket for governor of Illinois and was elected in 2002.

State Governors

Qualifications	Must be • a U.S. citizen • at least twenty-five years of age (or thirty in some states) • a resident of the state for a period of time (usually five years)
Election	Most states hold elections for governor in even-numbered years.
Term of Office	Most terms are four years. More than half the states limit governors to two terms.

Governors have executive, legislative, and judicial powers. As the executives of their states, all governors

- carry out the laws passed by the legislation

- appoint and remove nonelected officials to state government

- supervise the work of the many agencies within the state government

- are commander in chief of the state's National Guard

- promote their state's business and industry

In most states, governors also

- propose the state budget

Governors' legislative powers include

- proposing legislation

- vetoing legislation

- calling a special session of the legislature to deal with an urgent issue

Most governors have the **line item veto.** They may reject part of a bill without rejecting the entire bill. Usually, the line item veto is used only in budget bills. Governors cut out money for programs they want to end. Legislatures may override a line item veto if they can gather enough votes.

Governors have more limited judicial powers. About one-quarter of all state judges are appointed by governors. Most of a governor's judicial powers have to do with people convicted of crimes. Governors may **pardon**, or release, a person from the consequences of a crime. This is different from a parole. A **parole** releases a person from jail without having served a complete sentence. Governors may also grant paroles. In addition, they may **commute**, or lessen, a sentence. They may also grant a **reprieve**, or postponement of an execution.

The Judicial System

Each state has its own system of laws. These laws are based on the shared tradition of English law. As a result, the laws are similar. In addition, no state law can conflict with the U.S. Constitution and the law that has developed from it. The purpose of the state court systems is to interpret and apply state and local laws. Courts that hear cases in cities and towns are part of the state court system. The table on page 388 shows the number and types of courts in a typical state court system.

About 75 percent of all state judges are elected. Most of the other judgeships are filled by appointment. Usually the governor selects those judges. However, the legislature appoints judges in two states.

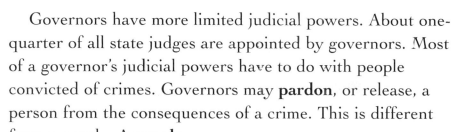

Other State Executive Officers

Title	Duties
Lieutenant Governor	• Presides over the senate • Succeeds the governor if the governor dies, resigns, or is removed from office
Attorney General	• Represents the state in lawsuits • Offers legal advice to the governor, other state officers, agencies, and the legislature • Provides formal written opinions, or interpretations, of state law, including state constitutional law; these have the force of law within the state
Secretary of State	• Oversees all state records and public documents • Records all official acts of the governor and legislature • Supervises election laws
State Treasurer	• Collects taxes • Pays the state's bills

Types of Courts in a State Court System

State Supreme Court	• Highest court in a state • Reviews decisions of lower state courts on appeal • Decisions are final unless some issue of U.S. constitutional law is involved. Those cases can be appealed to the U.S. Supreme Court.
Court of Appeals	• Accepts appeals of decisions in lower state courts • Hears arguments by lawyers • Not a trial court • Most decisions are final. Appeals can be brought only on how the law was applied.
General Trial Courts (titles vary by state: district, circuit, county, superior, court of common pleas)	• Hear cases from one or more counties • Divided into criminal and civil courts Criminal court: • Hears cases or accepts guilty pleas from defendants • Sentences guilty defendants Civil court: • Hears cases involving damages, such as a lawsuit over ownership of property or for money for badly done home repairs Most decisions are final. Appeals can be brought only on how the law was applied.
Juvenile Courts	• Hear cases involving those under eighteen • Focus on rehabilitation in sentencing • Depending on crime and circumstances, those under eighteen can be tried in adult court.
Municipal Courts	• Used mostly in large and medium-sized cities • Divided into different types: civil, criminal, traffic, small claims
Magistrate's Courts (also known as police courts)	• Used in cities • Presided over by a judge • Similar to rural justice courts • Hear cases involving **misdemeanors**, or minor crimes, such as traffic violations, vandalism, or shoplifting
Justice Courts	• Similar to city magistrate's courts • Presided over by a justice of the peace • Mostly in smaller towns and rural areas • Hear cases involving misdemeanors

Judges can be removed from office in one of three ways. They can be defeated at reelection time. They can be impeached and tried for illegal or unethical conduct or for incompetence. A state disciplinary board can also investigate judges. The board reports to the state supreme court. Suppose a judge is accused of favoring corporations in civil cases. A civil case involves a disagreement between two or more persons or organizations. No crime has been committed in a civil case. The disciplinary board investigates. The charges are found to be true. The board then recommends that the state supreme court suspend the judge. The state supreme court can also remove a judge.

Putting It All Together

Return to your lists of facts for the legislative, executive, and judiciary branches of government. In your notebook, write a paragraph for each column that summarizes how state and federal governments are similar and how they are different.

Ming Chin (1942–   )

Ming Chin's parents were immigrants from China. They settled in Oregon as potato farmers. Chin and his seven brothers and sisters worked on the family farm. A good student, Chin graduated from the University of San Francisco in 1964 with a degree in political science. Three years later, he earned a law degree from the university's law school. Chin later received a bronze star for his service in the Vietnam War.

Chin entered public service when he returned from the war. He served as a deputy district attorney for Alameda County in northern California. In 1973, he moved to private practice and handled civil law cases. However, in 1988, Chin returned to public service. He was appointed Alameda County Superior Court judge. In 1990, the governor appointed Chin to the First District Court of Appeals for the state of California. Chin is a hard worker who takes a great interest in the details of the cases that the court hears.

Public Policy at the State Level

Thinking on Your Own

What do you know about public policy at the federal level? What areas of public policy do you think states deal with? In your notebook, make a list of state public policy issues that you believe confront state lawmakers. As you read, check your list against the lesson.

Governments put public policy into practice by providing services. Some federal programs are joint activities with states. Medicaid and unemployment insurance are two of these joint programs.

State governments also provide a number of services. Some services are handled directly by the states. Some are handled by their local government unit. Some are activities of both the state and local governments. Education is one example of a joint responsibility.

Regulating and Promoting Business

In the late 1800s, giant corporations were very powerful. They were free to pay workers what they chose and to charge what they wanted for their goods. They could also use dishonest practices to force competitors out of business.

Beginning in the 1880s, the federal government began to regulate big business. States also started to pass laws to limit the actions of businesses. At first, the regulations only

---

focus your reading

Explain how states both regulate and promote business.

What is the role of the states in providing for public safety?

How do states provide for education and the well-being of their people?

Describe the issues involved in transportation and the environment for the states.

words to know

corrections

outsource

environmental impact statement

Regulating Businesses

Generally, states regulate most business practices within their borders. The following are just a few of the things states do:

- Set the rates that insurance companies may charge
- Administer licensing exams for doctors, lawyers, and other professionals
- Set rates that public utilities may charge
- Set rules for landlords and renters
- License health-care facilities such as nursing homes and hospitals
- Require accurate advertising and fair sales practices
- Set limits on working hours and jobs for those younger than sixteen years of age
- Protect the right of workers to join unions if they wish

guaranteed competition. However, by the early 1900s, both the federal government and the states began to protect workers and consumers. The box to the left shows just some of the areas in which state governments regulate business.

States must respect each other's civil laws. This requirement is set out in the "full faith and credit" section of the U.S. Constitution, Article IV, Section 1.

Many states have an agency that tries to attract new businesses to the state or to keep businesses. Often, the governor will lead the effort. When he was governor of Arkansas, Bill Clinton went on several trade missions to countries such as South Korea to explain why their businesses should build plants in Arkansas. He also succeeded in getting some large Arkansas companies to remain in the state.

To get companies to build in a state or remain there, they may be offered tax credits and reduced taxes. In the long run, these special tax breaks result in more jobs and more tax revenue for state programs.

Governor Arnold Schwarzenegger (R-California) on an overseas trip promoting the state of California

Providing for Public Safety

Every state has a code, or set, of criminal laws. Actions such as murder, burglary, forgery, robbery, drunk driving, and the sale of illegal drugs are prohibited by state law. Both local police forces and the state police enforce these laws.

Each state has a state police force. Their names vary. In Texas, they are known as Texas Rangers. In California and Florida, they are the highway patrol. In Illinois, they are state

**The following
are some of the
responsibilities of
states to ensure the
safety of their
residents:**

- Create and enforce a code of laws
- Operate a corrections system
- Fund, build, and maintain a system of roads
- License car and truck drivers
- Set speed limits
- Require safety inspections of motor vehicles
- Police the highways

troopers. The major job of the state police force is to patrol the state's highway system. They can also be called in to investigate crimes. In rural areas, the state police typically act as the local police force.

Each state also has a **corrections**, or prison, system. A state agency such as the Bureau of Corrections runs prisons, prison farms, and juvenile facilities. More than one million people are now incarcerated in state prisons.

Because of the cost, some states have **outsourced** the job to private companies. Instead of the state hiring employees and maintaining the prisons, they hire private companies to do the work. These companies build new prisons at their expense rather than the taxpayers'. They are then paid to run the prisons. The idea is that these companies will be more efficient and save taxpayers' money.

stop and think

Suppose you are the governor of a state. You want to persuade a corporation from another country to locate in your state. In your notebook, write a letter to the corporation's president explaining the services that your state government provides that benefit businesses.

Providing for Education and the Public Welfare

Every state has a system of public education that includes kindergarten through graduate school. Public education from kindergarten through grade 12 is the responsibility of state and local government. School districts are created by the state but run by local governments. The box at the top of page 393 lists many of the ways that states typically oversee K–12 public education.

Funding for K–12 public schools comes from a combination of federal, state, and local governments. The federal government provides about 9 percent of funding for K–12 schools. The amount of state funding varies. Some states fund more than half the cost of the schools. Other states provide much less.

**States typically
regulate the following:**

- Number of days in the school year
- Courses that are required to graduate from high school
- Number of years students must go to school
- Grade-level testing, including an exit test from high school
- Content standards and/or frameworks for content and skills
- Minimum teacher salaries
- Teacher qualifications
- Tax rates that districts may charge for education
- The amount of money that districts may borrow

In general, funding for K–12 schools comes from local property taxes. The amount of tax is based on the value of property. Funding for schools has brought about a number of lawsuits. Supporters of schools in big cities have sued their states over the property tax system. Their goal is to make school funding fairer between cities and suburbs. As a result, some property tax systems have been declared unconstitutional by state supreme courts. Texas, for example, had to redesign its system. New Jersey has to provide additional money for 30 urban school districts.

Florida State University is one of many state-funded universities in Florida.

Each state also has a system of public higher education. This includes universities, technical schools, and community colleges. California's higher education system is the largest in the nation. Tuition at these state-supported schools is typically lower for in-state students than for out-of-state students. State funding for these schools has increased greatly and has put an additional strain on state budgets.

In addition to education, states provide for the public welfare. This includes public health and assistance to the needy. Chapter 19 describes the role of the states in Medicaid and Temporary Assistance to Needy Families (TANF). The box to the right lists just a few of the public welfare services of states.

**State Public
Welfare Services**

**States typically do the
following in the area
of public welfare:**

- Administer Medicaid
- Administer Temporary Assistance to Needy Families (TANF)
- License doctors and dentists
- Require vaccinations for children
- Operate hospitals and clinics, and oversee group homes for those with mental illness
- Operate facilities for those with developmental disabilities
- License private facilities for those with developmental disabilities
- Regulate the sale of medications
- Enforce antipollution laws
- Inspect workplaces for safety

Protecting the Environment

States did little to protect the environment until the 1980s. Before that, most environmental laws were federal. In the 1960s, the federal government passed several laws to clean up air and water pollution. The states began passing and enforcing tough antipollution laws in the 1980s.

For example, in most states, a company has to produce an **environmental impact statement** in order to begin a major building project. The statement is really a report. The company must study and report on how its project will affect the environment. In states with this law, federal, state, and local government agencies must also file impact statements before beginning major projects.

The Environmental Protection Agency is responsible for monitoring pollution and other environmental hazards.

The States and the Environment
Among state responsibilities for the environment are the following:

- Set limits on air and water pollution
- Regulate the size and placement of roadside billboards
- Set aside public land for conservation and recreation
- Require environmental impact statements
- Regulate certain kinds of land use that harm the environment, such as strip mining

States require companies to pay for cleaning up major chemical spills. In the past, the federal government has helped to pay for the cleanup of long-term polluted areas. The Superfund and Brownfields were two such state programs. Often, the companies that created the problems have moved or are no longer in business. States also have major conservation laws to help save natural resources such as land, rivers, and wildlife.

Putting It All Together

Review the subheadings in this lesson. Then write a paragraph that summarizes the role state governments play in our federal system of government. Share your paragraph with a partner.

Financing State Government

Thinking on Your Own

Suppose you are on your state budget committee deciding how to spend the state's revenues. What categories do you think are included in a state budget? In other words, what items does a state budget have to fund? In your notebook, make a list of categories.

States need money to fund all their different programs. Like the federal government, states raise money by taxing residents. States also have other sources of revenue. A major source is the federal government. States may also borrow money.

Sources of Revenue

States have two types of revenue: taxes and non-taxes. Most states have a sales tax. This tax is a percentage of the price of an item. For example, Virginia's general sales tax is 5 percent. A $1.00 pen in Virginia really costs $1.05. The extra 5 cents is sales tax. The general sales tax covers a range of goods, from paper and pens to furniture. Both the tax rate and the range of goods vary from state to state. The sales tax in Illinois is 6.25 percent.

A second type of sales tax is the excise tax. The federal government collects an excise tax on items such as cigarettes and gasoline. States may also levy excise taxes on the same goods. As a result, anyone who buys gasoline is paying both state and federal excise taxes.

focus your reading

Explain how the states produce revenue.

Describe how state budgets are developed and passed.

words to know

inheritance tax

progressive

proportional

categorical grant

block grant

Most states do not tax food goods but do tax paper goods and cleaning supplies.

Most states have both an individual income tax and a corporate income tax. The taxes may be progressive or proportional. Income taxes make up about 30 percent of state tax revenue. Sales tax accounts for about 50 percent.

The rest of state tax revenue comes from estate and inheritance taxes and licensing fees. Estate tax is tax on the money and property a person leaves at death. Those who inherit, or get, the money and property may have to pay an **inheritance tax**. The tax rate and the amount that is taxed vary from state to state.

In addition, states collect fees for driver's licenses, hunting and fishing licenses, and marriage licenses. States also collect fees for registering cars. People may think all these are licensing fees, but they are really taxes.

Non-tax sources of revenue are borrowing, state lotteries, and federal grants. States borrow money by selling bonds to the public. Bonds are investments that repay the amount of the bond, plus interest, by a certain date. States often sell bonds to fund large construction projects such as bridges and highways.

> **Types of Taxes**
>
> - Sales tax is a regressive tax. Sales tax takes a larger percentage of the pay of people with lower incomes. People with lower incomes are affected more than people with higher incomes.
> - Income taxes are progressive or proportional.
>   - A **progressive** tax uses different rates for different levels of income. People with lower incomes pay a lower rate than people with higher incomes.
>   - A **proportional** tax is a flat tax. Everyone is taxed at the same rate. People earning millions of dollars pay the same tax rate as people earning minimum wage.

A majority of states have lotteries. Often, states use lottery earnings to fund certain programs. For example, Florida uses its lottery money to support multiple public education programs.

Many states use the lottery as a means of generating revenue for government-sponsored programs.

The federal government returns money to the states through grants. In the past, most grants were **categorical grants**. States received the money for very specific purposes such as to fund school lunch programs. The states had to add money of their own for the programs. In addition, the federal government had very specific guidelines the states had to follow as they managed a grant.

stop and think

Create a table of the revenue sources that states have. List and explain each source. Work with a partner.

Today, most grants are **block grants**. Instead of being given for specific programs, the grants are awarded for more general purposes. For example, block grants are given to states for homeland security and public health. There are fewer guidelines with block grants than there are with categorical grants.

Budget Process

Like the federal government, every state government has a budget. State budgets reflect decisions about public policy. Each state budget answers these questions: Which programs should receive money? How much money should they receive? The answers are based on what the people and the government of the state think are most important.

The budgeting process in the states is similar to the process in the federal government. Each state agency prepares a budget estimate. The executive budget office reviews the estimates. The state agencies make changes and submit their final budgets. The executive budget office then prepares the final budget for the entire state government. The governor presents this to the state legislature.

Nevada governor Kenny Guinn works on the state budget with staff members.

The legislature holds hearings and reviews the budget. When both houses agree on the budget numbers, they pass the state's budget. The governor may either sign or veto the budget. Remember that in some states, the governor may veto just certain line items in the budget.

If the governor signs the budget, it goes into effect. If the governor vetoes all or part of the budget, it goes back to the legislature. Lawmakers either change the budget to agree with what the governor wants, or vote to try to overturn the governor's veto. Once the budget is passed and signed, the governor oversees spending by the state government.

Putting It All Together

Create a diagram to show how a state makes and passes a state budget. Work with a partner. First, list the steps. Then decide how to show them on a diagram. Finally, draw and label the diagram.

Participate in Government

Get a Driver's License

To drive legally in the United States, a person must have a valid driver's license. States set the basic requirements for obtaining a driver's license. Generally, a person may apply for a first driver's license at age sixteen. Some states set the age at seventeen. A few states also allow for farm licenses at fifteen.

A person begins the process by applying for a learner's permit. This entitles a person to drive with a licensed driver in the car in the passenger's seat. In addition to this requirement, states may also limit the learner to driving only during daylight hours.

States also may require a student driver to take and pass a driver's education course in school or from a private driving school. A person must also pass a vision test, a test of the state's driving regulations, and a road test. An applicant must also state any disability that might impact driving a car.

In 2005, the U.S. Congress passed the Real ID Act. This act requires that everyone applying for a driver's license show a number of pieces of identification. These are then checked against federal databases. The act is meant to reduce the number of fake driver's licenses. People applying for a new driver's license must show

- a photo identification such as a passport.
- a birth certificate.
- a Social Security card.
- proof of residence such as a phone bill.

To Find Out More About Getting a Driver's License:

- Call your state department of motor vehicles (DMV).
- Check the white pages in the phone book for the nearest DMV.
- Go online to your state's Web site and click on the DMV's page.

Skill Builder

Read a State Legislative Map

A state's legislative map shows the legislative districts for the state's legislature. The map may show the districts for the upper house, which is typically called the senate. The map may be of districts for the lower house. In most states, the lower house is called the house of representatives.

The state legislative map on this page shows districts for Florida's upper house, the senate. Florida has 40 senate districts and 120 house districts. Unlike U.S. senators, state senators represent only parts of a state. U.S. senators represent all voters in a state, so states are not divided into two U.S. Senate districts.

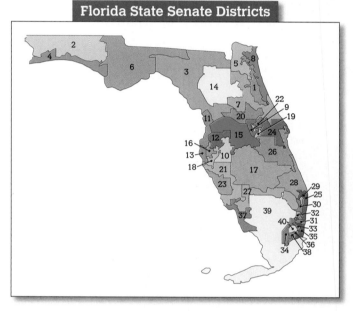

Florida State Senate Districts

Florida's senate districts do not match its county borders. They are made up of several counties and even cities. The districts for Florida's lower house, or its house of representatives, are also arranged this way.

Answer the following questions about this map.

1 What do the numbers in dark type represent?

2 How are district borders shown on the map?

3 How many senate districts are there at the southern tip of Florida?

4 How many senate districts are there along the eastern coast?

5 Why would there be so many districts in one area and so few in another?

Chapter

22 LOCAL GOVERNMENT

Getting Focused

Skim this chapter to predict what you will be learning.

- Read the lesson titles and subheadings.
- Look at the illustrations and read the captions.
- Examine the diagrams.
- Review the vocabulary words and terms.

What county or parish do you live in? Do you live in a village, city, town, or township? Who is the chief executive of your community? Answer these questions and list as many facts as you can about your local government.

Local governments include cities, towns, villages, parishes, counties, townships, and other forms of locality.

Types of Local Government

Thinking on Your Own

Read the subheadings in this lesson. What would you like to know about each topic? For each subheading, write two questions in your notebook that you would like answered as you study this lesson. After you study the lesson, answer your questions.

Local governments are created by the state. They exist only because the state allows them to exist. This is known as a unitary system of government. Unitary government is one in which all government power is held by the state. The state uses its power to set up lesser governments. The state constitution lists the powers that local governments may have. In other words, states have a centralized form of government.

County Government

Imagine that a state is a pyramid. At the top is the state government. Below it are county governments. At the base are towns, townships, special districts, and municipalities, or cities. In most states, the largest territorial and political unit is the **county**. In Louisiana, this government unit is called a parish and in Alaska, a borough. Connecticut and Rhode Island do not have counties.

Counties vary in size and number from state to state. Delaware has three counties. Texas has 254 counties.

---

focus your reading

What do county governments do?

Explain how towns, townships, and municipalities are the same and how they are different.

What are the possible forms of government in municipalities?

words to know

county

township

town meeting

selectperson

special district

municipality

mayor-council form

strong-mayor system

weak-mayor system

commission form

council-manager form

Bexar County Courthouse in San Antonio, Texas

The populations of counties also vary greatly. Los Angeles County has nine million people. A typical county has 50,000 or fewer.

A board generally governs counties. In some states, members of the county board are called supervisors. In others states, they are called freeholders. They may also be called commissioners. Generally, people are elected to the boards by the voters, rather than appointed. The typical term of office is four years. A county board may have as few as three or as many as 80 members. The typical board has between five and 15 members.

County boards have both executive and legislative powers. The most important legislative powers are the powers to levy taxes, determine how the money will be used, pay out money, and borrow money.

Using their executive powers, county boards administer programs and oversee county departments. In some states, the members of the county board oversee departments directly. In other states, the voters elect the heads of departments. In this case, the department heads report to the board. Among the departments are the county jail, county school board, county board of elections, county parks and recreation, and county social services such as the county home for the aged and the county hospital.

Some Duties of County Governments

In general, counties have the following jobs:

- Levy and collect county taxes
- Maintain law and order
- Build and maintain the county jail and other correctional facilities
- Build and repair county roads
- Administer elections
- Issue marriage, fishing, and hunting licenses
- Record mortgages and deeds
- Provide for the poor and needy in the county
- Oversee recreational areas and facilities

Towns, Townships, and Special Districts

Towns and townships are more important than counties in New England. In the Midwest, county and town or township governments share duties. The word *town* is used in New England and *town* or *township* in the other areas. The town or **township** includes a small center of houses and businesses and the surrounding rural areas. Townships may be very large and include several centers.

MARTA, Atlanta's mass transit system, includes trains and buses.

New England towns are the models of direct democracy. Once a year, citizens of a town meet to vote on tax rates and spending. They also elect town officers at the annual meeting. This yearly **town meeting** dates back to the beginning of the Massachusetts Bay Colony. Between meetings, the town's **selectpersons**, or officials, make decisions and run the government day to day. The selectmen and selectwomen make up the town board.

A **special district** is an independent unit of local government that deals with one function. A school district is a special district. There are 13,522 school districts in the United States and 35,356 other special districts. Compare that with 3,034 county governments, 16,506 towns and townships, and 19,372 municipalities, or city governments. As you can see, there are more special districts than other kinds of local government.

Why are there so many special districts? They are created when no other local government can take care of an issue. Special districts often cross the borders of several counties, towns and townships, or cities. This is often the reason why transportation networks are special districts. Two such districts are Chicago's RTA-Metro and New York's PATH. They each connect a large city and its suburbs. A great variety of special districts exist. Some provide water and sewage services. Others are soil conservation or reforestation districts.

stop and think

Use the statistics on this page to create a bar graph with a partner. Use the lines on a sheet of notebook paper as the sections on your graph. Label your graph "Number of Local Governments in the United States." After your graph is completed, write three sentences about the data on your graph.

City Government

Municipality is another word for a city. Cities vary in size. They can be as small as 50,000 people or as large as Houston, Texas, with almost two million. Regardless of size, cities have one of three forms of government: mayor-council, commission, or council-manager.

About half of all cities use the **mayor-council form**. It is the oldest form and the one that most large cities use. The mayor and the city council are both elected. The mayor has executive power and the city council has legislative power. The typical city council has ten members. All voters in the city may vote for all council members. They are not elected by district in most cities.

There are two forms of the mayor-council form. One is known as the **strong-mayor system**. The strong-mayor model gives the mayor a great amount of executive power. The strong mayor may

- prepare the city budget.
- veto city council laws and regulations.
- hire and fire department heads and other high-ranking officials of the city government.
- propose legislation and regulations to the council.

The strong-mayor system is often the model used in large cities such as Houston, San Diego, Detroit, and Dallas. The mayor in this system is typically elected for a four-year term.

The other model is called the **weak-mayor system**. It is most often found in smaller cities. The typical term for the mayor in this system is two years. Executive power is shared with department heads and council members. The mayor in this system

- may share budget responsibility with the council, or the council may have budget responsibility.
- may or may not have veto power over council laws.
- shares appointment and firing duties with the council, or the council may have complete power.
- has limited ability to propose legislation to the council.

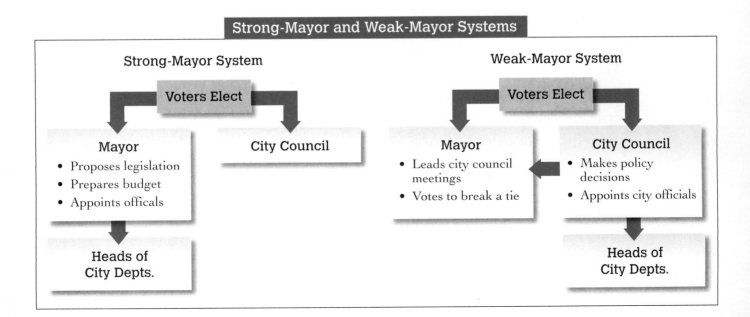

Strong-Mayor and Weak-Mayor Systems

Strong-Mayor System

Voters Elect

Mayor
- Proposes legislation
- Prepares budget
- Appoints officals

City Council

Heads of City Depts.

Weak-Mayor System

Voters Elect

Mayor
- Leads city council meetings
- Votes to break a tie

City Council
- Makes policy decisions
- Appoints city officials

Heads of City Depts.

The **commission form** of city government is run by a group of elected officials known as commissioners. They have both executive and legislative powers. Most city government commissions have five members. Each member heads a department such as the department of public safety. The members also meet as a group to propose and pass legislation for the city. They make all decisions about public policy. One member is elected by fellow commissioners to act as mayor. He or she leads council meetings and attends ceremonies such as groundbreakings for new buildings.

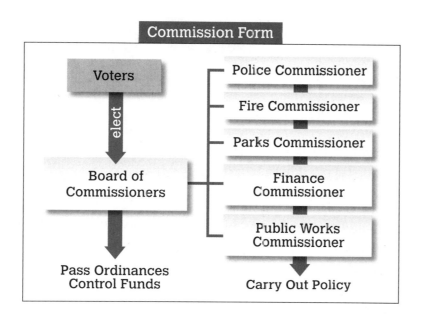

Commission Form

Voters

elect

Board of
Commissioners

Pass Ordinances
Control Funds

Police Commissioner

Fire Commissioner

Parks Commissioner

Finance
Commissioner

Public Works
Commissioner

Carry Out Policy

The commission form began in Galveston, Texas, in 1900. Few cities use the commission form today. One problem is the lack of leadership. No single person heads the city government. As a result, there is no one whose job it is to get commissioners to cooperate and compromise. Commissioners may look out for their own departments rather than for the good of the city. This can result in larger budgets than necessary because commissioners try to get as much money as they can for programs for their departments. For these reasons, few cities today have a commission form of government.

The **council-manager form** separates executive and legislative duties. The council makes policy decisions and passes laws and regulations for the city. The council is usually made up of five to nine members. The city manager is the chief executive of the city. However, he or she is not elected by the voters. They elect the council members and the council hires the city manager. The council also has the power to fire the city manager if he or she does not do a good job.

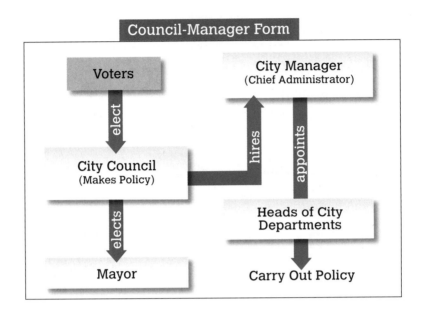

The city manager prepares the budget and sends it to the council for a vote. He or she does not have veto power over decisions of the council. It is part of his or her job to recommend policy to the council.

The city manager also hires and fires city workers. The city manager is a professional administrator. He or she is trained to run a city government on a day-to-day basis. Many city managers have college degrees in public service or municipal management. About 40 percent of cities use the council-manager form.

Putting It All Together

Make a three-column chart in your notebook. Title the columns "Mayor-Council," "Commission," and "Council-Manager." Under each column, include at least one strength and one weakness of that form of government. Then decide which form would be best for the city in which you live.

Public Services

Thinking on Your Own

Imagine you are founding a community. What kinds of government services would your community need? Think about what you know about the community in which you live. In your notebook, list as many government services as you can for your new community.

What services does your local government provide? It can be hard to answer this question. However, knowing how your tax dollars are spent is important. The federal, state, and local governments all contribute to many of the same services. For example, the federal government provides money for schools. That money is passed through the state government to your local school district. Your state also provides money to your school district. The major part of school funding comes from your local community.

focus your reading

Describe the services local governments provide for educational, cultural, and recreational activities.

Explain how zoning laws affect communities.

How do local governments provide for public safety and transportation?

What social services and public health activities do local governments support?

words to know

zoning

metropolitan area

suburb

Educational, Cultural, and Recreational Services

One of the jobs of local government is to provide education. School districts are local government units called special districts. Local tax revenue pays for the majority of education expenses.

Voters elect a local school board to run the school district. One of its most important decisions is the hiring and firing of the superintendent of schools for the district. This person manages the day-to-day operations of the school district. He or she is responsible to the board.

Local control is a key part of public education in the United States. Local control means that the local community wants to determine what is taught in its schools. Since the early 2000s, the federal No Child Left Behind Act has raised concerns in many districts. The act requires testing in math, reading, and science in grades three through eight. Local and state governments have to pay for these tests.

Another issue is how local districts raise money to fund schools. Property taxes are the major source of school funding. This leads to great inequality among school districts. Wealthy districts are able to spend more on their schools than poorer districts.

In addition to education, local communities also support cultural and recreational activities. Playgrounds, parks, playing fields, pools, and skating rinks are some of the places that local governments fund. Museums and zoos may also be owned and managed by local government. Sometimes counties and cities provide money and tax credits to private companies to build stadiums and arenas in their area.

Laura Bush greets the cast and crew at a theater program for disadvantaged youth in Los Angeles.

The Duties of School Boards

Typically, school boards have the following duties:

- Hire and fire the superintendent
- Approve the hiring and firing of other school officials including principals and teachers
- Prepare the school district's budget
- Approve the curriculum, programs, and facilities plans
- Set the tax rate to be collected for the district

Zoning

Zoning is the way that local governments regulate land use and construction within their borders. How land is used affects cities, towns, and townships. It can also affect counties and special districts. For example, if a large section of forest is turned into homes, the local school district can suddenly find itself with 500 more students than it had the year before. The local transportation system can suddenly be carrying an extra 1,000 passengers a day. The water and sewage special districts are also affected.

Property taxes can be greatly impacted by the decisions made by zoning boards.

Local communities have a set of zoning laws. These describe what can be built in the community, and where. Some areas are reserved for houses only. Some areas are zoned only for businesses. Some are zoned for houses and businesses. The zoning laws also describe the permitted height and width of buildings. These are determined by the size of the plot of land the building will be built on.

To make sure that the zoning laws are obeyed, local governments have zoning boards. Members of zoning boards are usually appointed, not elected. Their job is to plan for growth in their community. They review permits for building. They may approve, reject, or ask for changes to the builder's plans. The zoning board also recommends changes in local zoning laws to the council or commission.

Public Safety and Transportation

Two very important services of local governments are fire and police protection. After education, police account for the largest part of the local government budget. Even most small towns have a regular police force.

Large cities have professional, full-time firefighters. Small towns and townships usually have a volunteer fire department. When a fire occurs, volunteers leave their jobs and rush to the fire. Small cities may have a mix of professional and volunteer firefighters.

The United States is a nation of cars. They drive on 45,000 miles of federal highways, four million miles of state highways, and 650,000 miles of local streets. Taxpayers pay for building and repairing all these roads. They also support the nation's mass transit system of railroads, subways, and rapid transit lines. Mass transit is transportation that carries large numbers of people. The fares that people pay to use mass transit also support it.

The "L" train is part of the mass transit system in Chicago, Illinois.

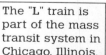

Many commuters who live in large metropolitan areas such as San Francisco and Chicago depend on mass transit to get around. A **metropolitan area** is a large city and its surrounding area. The surrounding area is called the **suburbs**. Both environmentalists and local governments encourage people to use mass transit instead of their cars. First, mass transit saves gasoline. Second, it pollutes the environment less. Third, fewer cars on the road mean less wear and tear on the roads. This saves taxpayers money. Fourth, mass transit is more efficient. A single subway car can carry up to 100 people at a time.

Social Services and Public Health

The federal and state governments provide money to local governments for certain social services. For example, money to aid those with developmental disabilities may be passed to local governments. Some cities also run their own hospitals. They accept patients with limited means to pay. Cities may also run homeless shelters and help food kitchens feed the hungry. Federal money for housing and for job training is also passed to cities.

Some large cities have their own water supplies. Las Vegas, for example, uses water from the human-made reservoir of Lake Mead. Special water districts are sometimes set up among several local communities to ensure a supply of fresh water.

Local governments also arrange for sewage and sanitation services. Some cities have their own sewage treatment plants. Some communities set up special districts to dispose of sewage. It is important to keep sewage from draining into sources of water such as streams and rivers. Sanitation includes picking up trash and garbage from homes and businesses and keeping the streets clean.

Depending on the community, homeowners and business owners may pay fees for water, sewage disposal, and sanitation services. In other communities, some or all of these may be part of the local taxes. These services all cost money to provide.

Putting It All Together

Review the list you made for Thinking on Your Own. Compare it to the services mentioned in this lesson. Did you leave out any essential services? If so, add them to your original list.

Cleaning up after New Year's Eve celebrations is one of the responsibilities of the New York City Department of Sanitation.

LESSON 3

Funding Local Government

Thinking on Your Own

What do you remember about types of federal and state taxes? Draw a three-column chart in your notebook. Label the columns "Federal," "State," and "Local." Using what you remember, fill in the first two columns. As you read this lesson, fill in the third column.

Providing services costs money. Local governments must raise money to provide services. Taxes, fees, and fines are three ways that local governments raise money. They also receive money from the federal and state governments for certain programs.

Property Taxes

A **property tax** is tax on property. The property may be land and buildings or personal property such as jewelry, cars, stocks, and bonds. Usually, local governments tax only land and buildings. Property taxes provide about 75 percent of all local tax revenue. They are an important source of revenue for school districts.

The value of property for tax purposes is decided by a **tax assessor**. He or she makes an **assessment** of property in the community every two or four years. The assessor determines the value of the property. The tax rate is then applied to this value. The result is the amount of tax the owner must pay. Homeowners can dispute this estimate.

There are a number of issues related to property taxes. First, people in school districts with increasing numbers of children pay high taxes to build new schools. People without children or retired people consider this unfair. Second,

Property taxes are a continual issue for homeowners.

property taxes are regressive. People with lower incomes pay a higher part of their incomes in property taxes. This also impacts retired people who live on limited incomes.

Third, property taxes can result in unequal services among communities. Wealthy communities can afford more and better services than poorer communities. This is especially true of older, big cities. Their suburbs are much wealthier. In fact, using property taxes to fund schools has been found unconstitutional in some states. The state courts have told local governments to find fairer ways to fund schools.

stop and think

As you read, list each form of revenue that cities have. Decide how a tax or other source of revenue can be fair or unfair in the way it affects people. As you read, rearrange your list of revenues so the most fair is at the top.

Biography

Shirley Clarke Franklin (1945–)

Shirley Franklin took office as mayor of Atlanta, Georgia, in 2002. She was the first African-American woman to lead a major southern city.

The city was facing an $82 million budget deficit. Franklin proposed a 1.5 percent increase in the sales tax and a 50 percent increase in property taxes. She cut 1,000 city jobs. Franklin also cut her own salary by $40,000. The city council agreed to pass the tax increases.

Franklin showed great political courage in raising taxes. People do not like having their taxes raised. However, Franklin was able to convince Atlantans that it had to be done. Under her leadership, the city was on its way to balancing its budget. By 2005, the city had a budget surplus, and city services had improved greatly.

Franklin was born in Philadelphia. She graduated from Howard University in 1968 and earned a master's degree from the University of Pennsylvania. In 1978, she became Atlanta's commissioner of cultural affairs. In 1982, she was appointed the city's chief administrative officer/city manager. To gain the 1996 Summer Olympics for Atlanta, Franklin served as senior vice president of the Atlanta Committee for the Olympic Games. In 2005, she was awarded the John F. Kennedy Profile in Courage Award.

Other Sources of Revenue

In addition to property taxes, local governments have other ways to raise revenue. A local income tax is paid in addition to federal and state individual income taxes. A local sales tax is usually a low rate. For example, the sales tax in Texas is 6.25 percent. Dallas has a sales tax of 2 percent. Consumers pay both the state and the local sales tax when they make purchases.

Traffic fines and fines for other violations are revenue for local governments. Fees for building permits and licenses also raise revenue. Sometimes a local government will pass a special assessment on homeowners and business owners. For example, homeowners in an area without sidewalks may be assessed if the town decides to put in sidewalks.

Local governments often rely on many sources of revenue, such as fines issued in traffic court.

Local Governments' Sources of Revenues

- Property tax
- Individual income tax
- Sales tax
- Fines
- Fees for certain services
- Special assessments
- Borrowing

Some local governments also run businesses. For example, they may own and operate parking lots and garages. They may provide funding for a stadium and be paid rent from those who use it.

States allow local governments to borrow money by selling bonds. However, states usually regulate the terms of the borrowing. They may set a limit on how much the local government may borrow. Local governments borrow money to build government office buildings, new firehouses, or moneymaking buildings like convention centers and arenas.

Putting It All Together

Without taxes, the government could not provide services. Few people like to pay taxes. Should the government provide all these services or provide fewer services? This is the problem that all lawmakers face. Write a three-paragraph essay to explain your ideas about the kinds of services that government should or should not provide. Share your essay with a partner. Try to come to an agreement.

Participate in Government

Volunteer for a Local Government Commission

Local governments may govern a city of eight million people like New York City. Local governments may also run a 500-person village in New England or a 16,000-person township in Indiana. Regardless of the size, local governments manage many different services for their citizens. Paid employees and elected officials do most of the day-to-day work of local governments. However, communities also have committees made up of volunteers who provide many services.

What kinds of volunteer committees serve communities?

- Planning boards oversee the growth of the communities so that they grow in orderly ways. Too many new buildings and homes can put a strain on schools, water and sewer systems, and other local services.

- Zoning boards recommend whether requests for new buildings should be approved. They also recommend changes to zoning laws.

- Shade tree committees oversee the care and replacing of trees.

- Community parks and recreation committees make sure that parks, playgrounds, and playing fields are maintained. They may also recommend the purchase of new areas for recreation.

Volunteering for local government committees is very important to a community. Volunteers save taxpayers money. They also provide a way for ordinary citizens to have a voice in their community's government.

To Find Out More About How to Join a Committee:

- Contact the local government office in your community.

Skill Builder

Writing or Speaking Persuasively

Suppose you hear on the news that your community is going to close down an after-school sports program. What do you do? You can complain to your friends, family, and neighbors, or you can complain to the city council. Rather than just complain, you can also persuade the council to keep the program running.

To present a well-organized speech, you have to research your facts and write out your speech. There are certain things you should include in any persuasive speech or piece of writing.

To speak or write persuasively,

- introduce the topic, or main idea, in your first paragraph.

- tell what you want done in the second paragraph.

- in the body of your speech, letter, or essay, develop your ideas about why your position is the right one.

- answer objections about your position in the main part of your speech, letter, or essay.

- restate your main idea in your conclusion, and ask your listeners or readers to take the action that you want.

Practice your speech in front of a mirror. Write out the important points on note cards. You do not need to memorize your speech. However, you need to know it well enough to be able to speak using just your note cards.

Complete the following activity with a partner.

Imagine that an after-school sports program is going to be closed. It serves both boys and girls and provides a variety of sports as well as homework help. The money that had been used for it has been moved to programs for senior citizens.

1 List reasons why the program is important to students.

2 List one objection that the city council might raise about keeping the program open.

3 Use the information from your answers to questions 1 and 2 to write a speech to deliver before the city council. Your speech requests that the after-school program remain open.

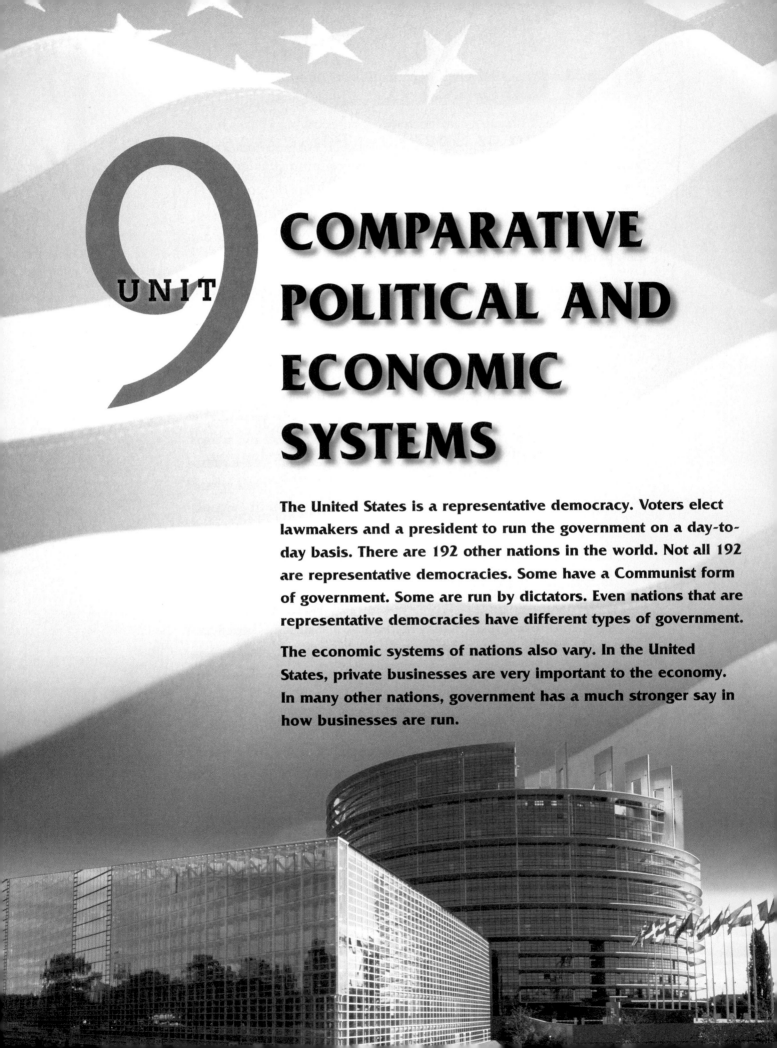

UNIT 9

COMPARATIVE POLITICAL AND ECONOMIC SYSTEMS

The United States is a representative democracy. Voters elect lawmakers and a president to run the government on a day-to-day basis. There are 192 other nations in the world. Not all 192 are representative democracies. Some have a Communist form of government. Some are run by dictators. Even nations that are representative democracies have different types of government.

The economic systems of nations also vary. In the United States, private businesses are very important to the economy. In many other nations, government has a much stronger say in how businesses are run.

Chapter

23 MODERN POLITICAL SYSTEMS

Getting Focused

Skim this chapter to predict what you will be learning.

- Read the lesson titles and subheadings.
- Look at the illustrations and read the captions.
- Review the vocabulary words and terms.

If you and your family are native-born Americans, write down the names of three nations. Write one fact about each nation and its government. To help you, think about what you have seen on television or cable news, or what people are talking about. Did you or your family come from another country to the United States? If so, write down as many facts as you can remember about that country and its government.

Japan's prime minister, Yoshiro Mori, meets with U.S. president George W. Bush in the Oval Office.

Democratic Governments

Thinking on Your Own

Many nations in the world today have democratic governments. However, such governments are not all alike. One democratic nation today has a queen. Another has 40 political parties. Some do not have separation of powers. Write a brief paragraph in your notebook explaining how governments so very different can still be democratic.

Democracy is rule by the people. In a representative democracy, voters elect others—representatives—to govern for them. The voters give their representatives the power to make and enforce laws for the community, state, or nation.

A democratic nation has the following characteristics: free elections, political parties, a constitutional government, an independent judiciary, and usually a capitalist, or market, economy. Even with these five characteristics in common, democracies vary in organization.

Britain's Queen Elizabeth II makes a speech during the State Opening of Parliament.

Great Britain

Great Britain is a constitutional monarchy and has a parliamentary government. Queen Elizabeth II is the current British monarch.

A **parliamentary government** is one in which an elected assembly has both legislative and executive powers. In Great Britain, this elected assembly is called Parliament. Its members pass the nation's laws and choose the prime minister and the cabinet. The prime minister is the leader of the executive branch of government. The cabinet consists of the officials who head the departments of the executive branch. They are all members of Parliament.

Parliament is bicameral. It has an upper house, called the House of Lords, and a lower house, called the House of Commons. The House of Lords is made up of 733 members of the nobility and bishops of the Church of England. The Commons has 646 members who are elected by voters. Each member represents one district.

The House of Lords has limited power over lawmaking. It can delay bills sent to it by the Commons, but it cannot reject bills. The Commons can override a veto by the House of Lords by passing a bill for a second time. The bill then becomes law. The House of Lords may amend bills. However, the Commons may reject the changes by the House of Lords. All money bills must begin in the Commons.

Most bills are introduced by the prime minister or members of the cabinet. Bills are sent to one of ten standing committees. Unlike standing committees in the U.S. Congress, these standing committees do not have particular areas of responsibility. For example, there is no energy committee or homeland security committee. Any committee can review any bill. Committees review bills, hold hearings, and revise bills as needed. The committees then send the bills back to the House of Commons for a vote. Unlike the U.S. Congress, all bills must be reported back to the full house for a vote. They cannot be killed or pigeonholed in committee. The House of Lords has no standing committees.

British prime minister Tony Blair answers questions during a session of Parliament in 2002.

There is no required term of office for members of Parliament. This also means that there is no required term of office for the prime minister. However, according to British law, an election must be held at least once every five years. The prime minister generally calls for an election when his or her party seems most likely to win a majority of seats in Parliament.

However, if the prime minister loses the confidence of the Commons, he or she calls for a general election. "Losing the confidence of the Commons" means losing its support for the government's policies. This happens if the Commons votes down some important bill favored by the prime minister.

Great Britain's court system has several levels. County courts hear civil cases. Minor criminal cases are heard in magistrates' courts. Serious criminal cases are heard in Crown Court. There are also appellate courts. The highest appellate court is made up of Law Lords. British courts do not have the power of judicial review.

Russia

From 1917 until 1990, the Soviet Union had an authoritarian government. Russia was the largest of the 15 republics that made up the Union of Soviet Socialist Republics, commonly known as the Soviet Union. The officials who headed the government had absolute control over the people. Free elections did not exist. Whoever ran the Communist Party ran the government. The constitution protected the system of government. It did not guarantee the rights of the people.

The government also controlled the economic system. All means of production—land, buildings, factories, and machinery—belonged to the government. This is known as a **command economy**.

stop and think

Create a table to compare and contrast the British government with that of the United States. Work with a partner. List the branches of government down the left side of your table. Label the columns "Branches of Government," "British Government," and "U.S. Government." Use Chapters 5 through 12 if you need to review facts on the U.S. government. When you have finished your table, write at least five sentences to compare or contrast the two governments. Share and discuss your statements with another student.

In 1985, Mikhail Gorbachev came to power as head of the Communist Party. He began a program of reform that became known as *glasnost*, or openness. He eased some of the limitations on political and economic life. The economic restructuring was known as *perestroika*. He also allowed some freedom of expression and political opposition. By the end of 1991, the Soviet Union collapsed and many of the republics declared their independence.

Mikhail Gorbachev

In 1993, the Russians wrote a new constitution. It set up a federal system with a democratic form of government. The constitution also lists and guarantees a number of rights for the people. Among these are freedom of speech, press, and movement. The Communist Party is now one of 40 political parties in Russia.

The government is divided into executive and legislative branches. Each has its own powers. The executive branch is headed by a president. He or she is elected by the voters for a four-year term. The Russian president also names the prime minister. This official is similar to the U.S. vice president. The Duma must approve the prime minister.

The **Duma** is the lower house of the Federal Assembly. The Duma has 450 members who are elected from districts. The upper house is the Federation Council and has 178 members. Each of Russia's 89 regions elects two members to the Council. Members of both houses serve four-year terms.

The Duma and the Council make laws for the nation. However, the Duma may override Council vetoes. A vote of both houses can also override a presidential veto.

Russia also has a court system of several levels of courts. At the top is the Constitutional Court. It has 19 members who are elected by voters for 12-year terms. This court has the power of judicial review.

Mexico

Mexico's constitution was written in 1917. The Mexican constitution set up the organization and form of the government. It also lists many rights and guarantees for the people, especially the poor.

Mexico is a democracy with a federal system. It is made up of 31 states and a federal district. The federal district is Mexico's capital, Mexico City. Each state has a governor, a constitution, a legislature of a single house, and a system of courts. Each state may pass laws for people living within its borders. Each state may also levy and collect taxes. States also receive funding from the federal government.

The federal government has three branches. The executive branch is headed by a president elected for one six-year term. He or she chooses the cabinet members, known as the Council of Ministers. The president is commander in chief and appoints the heads of the armed forces. It is also the responsibility of the president to recommend legislation to the legislature.

Vincente Fox, National Action Party candidate, during the 2000 Mexican presidential election

The legislature is called the Congress of the Union. The upper house is the Chamber of the Senate and the lower house is the Chamber of Representatives. The Senate has 128 members, two from each state and two from the federal district. Senators are elected for six-year terms. The Chamber of Representatives is made up of 500 members who serve for three-year terms. Voters in districts elect 300 deputies. The other 200 are chosen from the many political parties. The number of seats that each party receives is based on the percentage of votes the party received in the national election. Senators and deputies may not run for two terms in a row.

The Congress meets for only four months each year. As a result, the Congress is considered weak. It does not have much influence on national policies.

Mexico has both state and federal court systems. State courts hear cases that deal with state criminal and civil laws. Each state has levels of courts: trial, appeals, and a state supreme court. The federal system has district and circuit courts and a Supreme Court.

Putting It All Together

Create a three-way Venn diagram to show the differences and similarities among the governments of Great Britain, Russia, and Mexico. Work with a partner. When you have finished, write an essay of three paragraphs explaining how these governments are different.

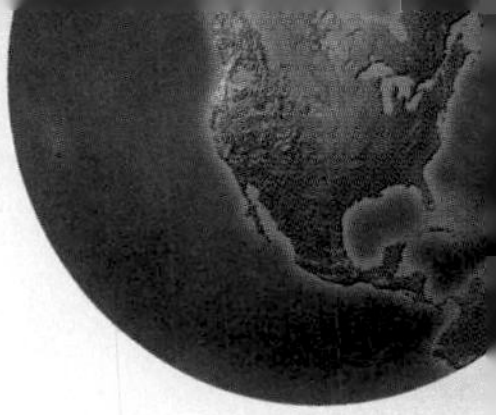

Authoritarian Governments

Thinking on Your Own

Stalin, Mussolini, and Hitler were twentieth-century dictators. They ruled with absolute power in Russia, Italy, and Germany. What do you know about their leadership methods? In your notebook, write at least two facts about how each of these dictators ruled.

The Soviet Union collapsed in 1991. However, it was not the last authoritarian government. A number of these governments still exist today. Only a few are Communist. Today, most authoritarian governments are led by military officers or are civilian governments supported by the military. Many authoritarian governments include the word *republic* in their name. A republic is a representative democracy. Calling itself a republic helps to disguise the authoritarian nature of the government.

focus your reading

Describe how the Communist Party controls the government of China.

Explain how a junta controls a government.

How do nations shift from authoritarian to democratic?

words to know

theocratic republic

junta

martial law

ethnic groups

There are also a few monarchies. Saudi Arabia and Jordan are both headed by monarchs. Jordan, like Great Britain, is a constitutional monarchy. However, in Saudi Arabia, the king is the sole ruler. There is no constitution and the rights of citizens are limited. This is especially true for women.

Iran is a **theocratic republic**. It has a constitution based on a strict interpretation of Islam. Citizens vote for candidates for public office. However, the rights of citizens, especially women, are limited.

People's Republic of China

The largest Communist nation today is the People's Republic of China (PRC). Other Communist governments include Vietnam, Laos, and Cuba.

Communists came to power in China in 1949 under the leadership of Mao Zedong. They had been fighting the non-Communist government since the 1920s. When the Communists took control, they set up a command economy. Mao died in 1976. Since then, Chinese leaders have eased economic controls. Most Chinese still live in poverty. Since the 1980s, the Chinese government has encouraged small businesses and investment by foreign companies. However, the Communists have not eased political controls.

The PRC's constitution does not guarantee rights. Unlike the U.S. Constitution, the PRC's constitution is not the basis of China's law. The Chinese constitution describes how the government is to be set up. It also states the policies the nation is to follow. The current constitution was written in 1982. It sets goals to modernize the nation and to become a world industrial power by the twenty-first century.

The Wangfujing shopping district in Beijing, China

The Chinese constitution describes the duties of the National People's Congress and the State Council. The National People's Congress has about 3,000 deputies. The members are elected by local people's congresses, or assemblies, for five-year terms. The National People's Congress has little power. Its role is to approve policies developed by the Communist Party. The Communist Party is the real power in the PRC. For example, the constitution states that the National People's Congress elects the president of the PRC. In reality, the Communist Party's highest officials, called the politburo, determine who will be president. The National People's Congress just approves this person.

The president nominates the premier, and the National People's Congress approves this person. The premier heads the State Council, which is similar to the cabinet or Council of Ministers in other nations. The State Council manages the bureaucracy in the executive branch of the government.

The National People's Congress meets once a year for two weeks. The Standing Committee of the Congress deals with legislative business the rest of the year. The Standing Committee as of 2003 had 175 members.

The government of the PRC is unitary. All power flows from the national government to local governments. Local governments could not exist if the national government did not allow them to exist. The PRC has 22 provinces, which are similar to states. There are also five independent regions that are under the control of the Chinese government.

stop and think

Imagine that the Chinese people decided to have a truly republican form of government. What changes would they have to make in their government to become a republic? Discuss the question with a partner. Make a list in your notebook of the changes that would be required.

The Chinese court system has local courts called the people's courts. They hear both civil and criminal cases. The Supreme People's Court oversees the local courts.

People protested in favor of free speech and freedom of the press in Tiananmen Square in Beijing, China, in 1989.

Dictatorships

A dictatorship may be run by a single person or by a small group. Usually, the group consists of military officers. In this case, the dictatorship is called a **junta**.

Over time, various governments in Latin America have been taken over by juntas. For example, in the twentieth century, juntas ruled in Chile, Guatemala, El Salvador, Paraguay, and Peru. Military officers have seized control of governments from elected civilian officials. Usually, the junta is supported by wealthy landowners. The civilian governments are overthrown because they attempt to help the poor. The goal of the juntas is to end reforms by the civilian governments. The military officers and wealthy citizens want to ensure that they will not lose their power and wealth.

Cuban president Fidel Castro

Aung San Suu Kyi won the Nobel Peace Prize in 1991 for resisting the Myanmar junta.

Once in control of the government, the junta usually suspends the constitution. It rules by **martial law**, or military law, not by the guarantees of the constitution. Elections are either eliminated or staged. Only candidates backed by the junta can run for office, or the junta makes sure that opposition candidates lose. Juntas often use kidnappings, torture, and murder to silence opponents. The national legislature may be disbanded. If it is allowed to continue, it can pass only laws the junta approved.

Juntas also occur in other parts of the world. For example, a military junta has been in power in Myanmar since 1962. The last election for a national legislature was held in 1990. However, the junta has never allowed the legislature to meet.

In Syria, a single ruler, Hafez al-Assad, came to power in 1971. The military had seized power in 1963. All political parties except al-Assad's party, the Socialist Ba'ath Party, were banned. Al-Assad ruled with the support of the military until his death in 2000. The military now supports his son Bashar as president.

North Korea is also ruled by the son of a previous dictator. In 1953, Kim Il Sung became the leader of North Korea. The Chinese and Soviet Communist governments supported him with foreign aid and weapons. Kim Il Sung introduced a command economy into North Korea and banned all opposition. After his death, his son Kim Jong Il became president. A national legislature, called the Supreme People's Assembly, passes legislation and oversees the judiciary. However, Kim Jong Il really holds all the power himself.

The North Korean government controls all aspects of business, including this biscuit factory in Hyesan, Korea.

Governments in Transition

Communist nations collapse because they do not benefit ordinary citizens. Dictatorships work for the group in power, but not for the majority of people. Since the end of the twentieth century, more and more people have fought for democratic governments. The nations of Eastern Europe were quick to end their Communist governments once the Soviet Union collapsed. In some cases, the nations of Eastern Europe forced out their Communist governments even before the Soviet Union collapsed. This occurred in Poland and in the former nation of Czechoslovakia.

Iraqis wait in line to vote during the 2005 elections.

Changing to a democracy is not easy for a nation. Groups in power fight to keep their power. This can be seen in the difficulties in setting up democratic governments in Nigeria, Sudan, and Somalia. Often, in African nations, the fight is not between wealthy landowners and the poor. It is between **ethnic groups**, or tribal groups. One group does not want to share power with another. This was also true in the former nation of Yugoslavia and in the new nation of Bosnia and Herzegovina in eastern Europe. Ethnic and religious groups in these nations fought one another for control.

Ethnic conflict has also caused problems in Iraq since the removal of Saddam Hussein. Backed by the Iraqi military, he seized power in 1979. In 2003, a force of U.S. and British soldiers aided by other nations invaded Iraq. Hussein fled and was later captured. The coalition forces assisted the Iraqis in writing a constitution and setting up a democratic government. However, bitter rivalry still exists between the two major groups in Iraq, the Shiites and the Sunnis. The opposing groups turned the country into a battleground of insurgents.

Putting It All Together

This lesson has presented information about several authoritarian governments. While these governments have much in common, they also are different. Make a two-column list in your notebook. In one column, list what these governments have in common. In the second column, list how each authoritarian government is different from the others.

Issues of Global Security

Thinking on Your Own

What does the phrase "global security" mean to you? Brainstorm what the phrase means with a partner. In your notebook, write whatever ideas come to mind. After you study this lesson, review your list. Add topics to your list. Cross out any topics that apply only to one country.

Today, trade, travel, and communications connect the nations of the world more than ever before. Nations are no longer isolated from one another. Together, the global community faces many issues. Some issues, like global warming, threaten the environment. Others, like the movement of factory jobs to poorer nations, are economic issues. Terrorism, regional wars, civil wars, and nuclear weapons are issues of global security. They threaten the safety of all nations.

> **focus your reading**
>
> Describe what is being done to end terrorism.
>
> Why are regional wars fought?
>
> What is being done to end the spread of nuclear weapons?
>
> **words to know**
>
> terrorism
>
> weapons of mass destruction
>
> civil war
>
> nuclear proliferation

The world's nations have taken steps to protect their security. In 1945, they founded the United Nations (UN). The goal of the UN is to work for world peace. The United States was one of the original founders. The United States also belongs to regional security associations such as the North Atlantic Treaty Organization (NATO). The goal is to protect the security of member nations through cooperation.

Terrorism

Terrorism is a political strategy that uses violence against people or property to achieve a goal. Often the goal is to force a change in government or society.

On September 11, 2001, militant Islamic fundamentalists hijacked four airplanes. They flew two airplanes into the World Trade Center towers in New York City, one into the Pentagon in Washington, D.C., and the fourth into a field in Pennsylvania. Investigations have shown that the attacks were planned by Osama bin Laden and his terrorist group, Al-Qaeda. He founded Al-Qaeda after the Gulf War in the Middle East. The United States has kept troops in Saudi Arabia since the war ended in 1991. The kingdom is considered holy by Muslims. Bin Laden's original goal was to force the United States to remove its troops. However, the goal of Al-Qaeda and its allies has shifted. They want to end all non-Islamic influences in the Middle East. They want to set up governments based on Islamic religious law throughout the region.

In 2003, the United States and its allies invaded Iraq. One goal was to remove the dictator Saddam Hussein. The other was to end his program to build **weapons of mass destruction**. These are chemical, biological, and nuclear weapons that can kill large numbers of people. After the invasion, the United States discovered that Iraq had already destroyed its weapons of mass destruction. Many Americans concluded that Iraq had not been a serious threat to our national security.

Police investigate a bombing at a Bali nightclub in 2002.

Once Hussein was overthrown, the United States and its allies also wanted to help the Iraqis set up a democratic government. The invasion and occupation of Iraq led to attacks by insurgents against the American forces and their allies. The insurgency was led by supporters of Saddam Hussein and Islamic fundamentalist fighters. Some of the fighters came from other Islamic nations in the Middle East. The insurgents used roadside bombs and suicide bombers to kill allied troops and Iraqis who worked with them. Many Iraqi citizens disliked their violent methods, but shared the insurgents' goal of getting foreign troops out of Iraq.

There are four types of terrorist organizations. One is made up of Islamic militants who want to end U.S. and European influences in the Middle East. They fought the allies in Iraq

United Airlines Flight 175 was one of four airplanes used by terrorists during the attacks of September 11, 2001.

and took their campaign of terror to Europe. They bombed trains in Madrid and London and planned similar acts in other nations including the United States. However, counterterrorism agencies in European nations and the United States shared information. This cooperation halted a number of plots.

Another is made up of terrorists such as HAMAS. Their goal is to create a nation for Palestinians. They are Arabs who left their lands when Israel was created in 1948. Israel was set up as a homeland for Jews. Islamic militants want to destroy Israel and take back the land. However, the conflict eased somewhat in late 2005. Israel gave up the West Bank region to Palestinians as part of their future nation.

Other terrorist groups want to create their own nations. For example, Chechnya is a region in Russia. In 1991, it declared itself independent. The Russian government did not recognize its independence. Since then, Chechen rebels and Islamic fundamentalists have attacked several sites in Russian cities, including a theater in Moscow and a school in Beslan. The goal of the rebels is to set up their own government. They want it based on Islamic law.

Terrorists also operate in Latin America. For example, the *Sendero Luminoso*—the Shining Path—fought for many years to overthrow the government of Peru. However, in 1992, the democratically elected president took action against the rebels. He also began a series of reforms to aid the poor. Conflict continued throughout the 1990s. In 2003, the last Shining Path leader was caught.

The United Nations has 19 global and regional treaties relating to terrorism. Many of these date to the 1970s. After the terrorist attacks of September 11, 2001, the UN adopted Resolution 137. All nations that signed the resolution agree to fight terrorism. The UN also set up a Counter-Terrorism Committee. The committee's job is to make sure that UN member nations cooperate in the fight against terrorism.

stop and think

Create a T-chart with the label "Types of Terrorist Groups" in the left column. Label the right column "Examples." Fill in both columns. Share your T-chart with a partner. Discuss what a nation might do to end terrorism within its borders.

Regional Wars and Civil Wars

Regional wars are wars that break out in a particular part of the world. The Arab-Israeli wars of 1948–1949, 1956, 1957, and 1973 are examples of regional wars. So is the Indian-Pakistani war of 1971 over the region of Kashmir. Both nations claim the area. The claims are still not settled. Regional wars often break out over border disputes.

Sudanese refugees wait at a feeding center in Bahai, Chad.

Regional wars threaten global security. Other nations besides the original ones can be drawn into the fighting. Each side has allies that may come to the aid of the nations that are at war. For example, in 1990, Iraq invaded Kuwait. Saddam Hussein wanted Kuwait's rich oil fields. The United States is an ally of Kuwait. It demanded that Iraq withdraw. When it did not, President George H. W. Bush established a coalition, or group, of 13 nations to fight Iraq. Iraq began sending missiles against Israel. However, no Arab allies joined Iraq. Within six weeks, the coalition had invaded and defeated Iraq.

Civil wars can also draw other nations into the fighting. A **civil war** is a war in which groups within a nation battle for power. The Korean War, for example, began when North Korea invaded South Korea in 1950. The United States came to the aid of South Korea. The Chinese Communists supported North Korea. Both China and the United States sent troops, weapons, and other supplies. The war dragged on for three years and ended without a victory for either side. A peace treaty still has not been signed. In the meantime, the United States keeps troops in South Korea as part of the UN's peacekeeping forces.

UN peacekeepers patrol in Bosnia in 1995.

Other regional security associations also send peacekeepers when civil war breaks out. For example, after the collapse of communism in eastern Europe, some nations split apart. Serbia and Montenegro declared independence from Yugoslavia. The Serbian province of Kosovo, however, wanted to unite with Albania. A civil war broke out. NATO sent troops into Kosovo to put down the rebellion. The peacekeepers remain in Kosovo.

A mushroom cloud rises above an atomic bomb test near Alamogordo, New Mexico, in 1945.

Nuclear Proliferation

Nuclear proliferation is the spread of nuclear weapons to nations that do not have nuclear capabilities. It is one of the greatest dangers to global security. The United States was the first nation to develop a nuclear bomb. Today, Russia, China, France, and Great Britain are also known to have nuclear weapons. India, Pakistan, and Israel are suspected of having them. Experts also suspect that Iran and North Korea either have nuclear weapons or are capable of building them. South Africa destroyed its nuclear weapons in 1991.

In 1970, the Nuclear Nonproliferation Treaty (NPT) went into effect. Since then, 189 nations have joined the treaty. India, Pakistan, and Israel have not. North Korea withdrew in 2003. The other nations with nuclear weapons (NWS) have all agreed to the treaty. According to the NPT, NWS will not help nations without nuclear weapons (NNWS) to develop them. NWS also will not sell nuclear weapons to NNWS. NWS agree to their own complete disarmament, or getting rid of nuclear weapons. For their part, NNWS have agreed not to develop or buy nuclear weapons.

The International Atomic Energy Agency (IAEA) was created by the United Nations to make sure that nations obey the NPT. The IAEA helps NNWS carry out programs that use nuclear materials for peaceful uses. For example, nuclear material is used to create energy in nuclear power plants. The IAEA also polices member nations to make sure that they do not use their nuclear materials to build weapons.

Nations that want to hide their nuclear programs can refuse to allow IAEA inspections. In the early 2000s, Iran's leaders refused to allow IAEA inspectors to work in Iran. However, the IAEA and the NPT have succeeded in keeping nuclear weapons out of the hands of many nations. Experts believe that without their efforts, 28 nations would have nuclear weapons today.

Putting It All Together

What do you think is the greatest threat to global security? Discuss the question with a partner. Make a table with three columns. Label each column with one of the threats discussed in this lesson. List reasons that explain why each topic is a serious threat to the world. Decide which threat you think is most serious. Write a paragraph to explain your reasoning.

Mohamed ElBaradei and the IAEA

Mohamed ElBaradei (1942–   ) is the head of the International Atomic Energy Agency (IAEA). The IAEA is the UN agency that polices the use of nuclear materials around the world. Dr. ElBaradei is an Egyptian lawyer and diplomat. He was named

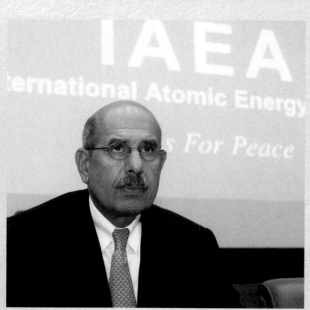

head of the IAEA in 1997. The IAEA was involved in the search for weapons of mass destruction in Iraq before the U.S.-led invasion in 2003. The IAEA is also part of the discussion about potential nuclear weapons in Iran and North Korea.

In 2005, Dr. ElBaradei and the IAEA were awarded the Nobel Prize for Peace. This important award recognized the work of the IAEA to "prevent nuclear energy from being used for military purposes." The award also praised the IAEA for its efforts "to ensure that nuclear energy for peaceful purposes is used in the safest possible way."

Participate in Government

Use Government Resources

Do you

- want to see if the Secret Service has any job openings?

- need a federal income tax form?

- want to apply for a passport but do not know what documents you need?

- want information about Independence Hall for a report?

The United States government provides all kinds of information and resources—in print and online. In Chapter 19, you read about some of the booklets and reports that the Consumer Information Center publishes.

After each census, the Department of Commerce publishes booklets and reports about the nation's population. Basic statistics are updated in yearly reports. These reports provide an interesting view of the nation. Much of the information is now available online.

The National Park Service, the National Archives, the Presidential Libraries, the Library of Congress—all these agencies have sites that offer an abundance of information for students, teachers, and all Americans. Information can be downloaded for free or ordered online to be shipped for a small fee.

The White House, Congress, the Supreme Court, and all the departments of the executive branch have Web sites. These contain the history of each agency, biographies of officials, and the duties and responsibilities of each agency. These sites also post job openings. The Court's Web site contains its decisions.

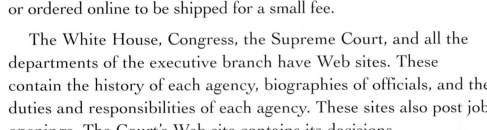

To Find Out What Resources Are Available from the Federal Government:

- Using a search engine, find the Web site of an agency, department, or branch of government.

- Explore the site to see what is available.

Skill Builder

Synthesize Information

The author of this textbook consulted many sources in writing the book. He synthesized the information, which means he put together pieces of information into something new. To synthesize means to "bring together separate pieces or parts."

Whenever you buy a CD on the advice of several friends, you synthesize information. One person says you should buy it for this reason. Another friend says you should buy for that reason. You hear it played on the radio and decide you like it. The DJ offers another reason why it is a great CD to own.

Being able to synthesize information is a good skill for school, too. When you write a research report, you have to synthesize information from different sources.

To synthesize information, follow these steps:

1. Choose the sources you will use.

2. Find the main idea and supporting details for the information that you find.

3. Look for links between the information.

4. Put the information together based on those links.

Complete the following activities.

1 Chapter 3 and Lesson 1 of Chapter 21 discuss constitutional government. Chapter 3 talks about the U.S. Constitution, and Chapter 21 describes state constitutions. Work through Steps 2 and 3 to compare the U.S. Constitution to state constitutions. To help you, create a table comparing them. Use information from both chapters to fill in the table.

2 Use the table as the basis for a three- or four-paragraph essay about the similarities between the U.S. Constitution and state constitutions.

Chapter

24 MODERN ECONOMIC SYSTEMS

Getting Focused

Skim this chapter to predict what you will be learning.

- Read the lesson titles and subheadings.
- Look at the illustrations and read the captions.
- Examine the map and tables.
- Review the vocabulary words and terms.

All nations have one of three types of economic systems. In a traditional economy, people barter, or exchange, goods and services. Someone with extra eggs may exchange them with someone with extra wheat. In a command economy, the government tells people what to make, how much to make, and for whom to make goods and services. In a market economy, buyers and sellers decide what to make, how much to make, and for whom.

Which kind of economy do you think the United States has? Give examples to support your answer.

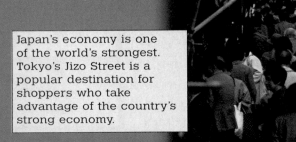

Japan's economy is one of the world's strongest. Tokyo's Jizo Street is a popular destination for shoppers who take advantage of the country's strong economy.

LESSON 1

Capitalist and Mixed Economies

Thinking on Your Own

Many people choose to start their own businesses. Why do you think people want to work for themselves? Make a list in your notebook of reasons why you think people start their own businesses.

Capitalism is based on the market system. Buyers and sellers make their own choices about what to produce, how much to produce, and for whom. The capitalist system is also called the **free enterprise** and the **private enterprise** system.

Capitalism

Capitalism has five basic characteristics. First is private ownership. Individuals and private companies own the factors of production. Farmers own their land. Businesses own their factories and machinery. Workers own their labor and sell it to whomever they wish. That is, no one tells workers in a capitalist system for whom to work.

The second characteristic is individual initiative. *Initiative* means the ability to get things done on one's own. Entrepreneurs have a great deal of individual initiative. They are willing to start businesses using just their ideas and whatever capital they can put together. In a capitalist system, everyone has the freedom to start a business. Bill Gates, who started Microsoft, is an example of a very successful entrepreneur.

Every economic system has the following basic resources. They are called the **factors of production**.

- Natural resources: This includes all natural resources found on or in land and in water in rivers, lakes, and ponds. It includes air, soil, iron, coal, and similar resources.
- Labor: Labor is human resources, meaning workers.
- Capital: **Capital** is the means of production. It includes money, factories, and machinery used to produce other goods and services.
- Entrepreneur: An **entrepreneur** organizes the other factors of production in order to produce goods and services. This person risks his or her capital to own and run a business.

Competition is one factor that forces businesses to close their doors.

Competition is the third characteristic of a capitalist system. Anyone may start a business. As a result, any industry will have a number of businesses competing for buyers of their goods or services. They compete on the basis of high quality, low price, and good service. Businesses try to sell the best quality with the best service at the lowest prices. For example, a number of companies sell computers. The company that sells low-priced computers of good quality and provides good service will take the largest share of the computer market.

The fourth characteristic is profit. Profit is the difference between the amount of money a business takes in and the cost of running the business. An entrepreneur goes into business to make a profit. This is his or her reward for risking capital. However, in a capitalist system, there is also the risk of not making a profit and actually losing all of one's capital. For example, Wang Laboratories was one of the original computer industry giants. It was started by one man, Dr. An Wang. At first, the company made huge profits. Later, when there was more competition, the company went bankrupt.

Businesses of all sizes are often forced to find new and different ways to attract customers.

Freedom of choice is the fifth characteristic of a capitalist system. Sellers decide for themselves what they will produce and for whom. They also set their own prices for their goods and services. Price is based on the cost of production and what the competition is charging. Workers sell their labor. They choose the jobs they will take and the wages they will accept. If a better job comes along, workers can decide to quit their present job and take the new one. Buyers decide for themselves what they will buy and how much they are willing to spend. The government is not part of these decisions.

A Mixed Economy: The United States

The government is not involved in the capitalist economy. It plays no role in economic decision-making. Today, there are no pure capitalist systems. Instead, nations like the United States have **mixed economies**. Government is involved in setting economic and social policies. Such decisions are not left entirely to individuals.

First, government at the federal, state, and local levels regulates private enterprise. For example, the federal government regulates business activities that affect the environment and public health. Congress has passed clean water and air acts and pure food and drug laws. The executive branch enforces these laws. State and local governments require licenses for certain kinds of businesses such as day care centers.

Second, government has taken on responsibility for many social policies that affect the economy. Since the 1930s, the federal government has provided a safety net of programs for the elderly, the poor, and those with disabilities. These programs include Social Security, Medicare, and Medicaid. State governments participate in Medicaid. They also administer unemployment insurance for laid-off workers.

Delivering mail is one of the responsibilities assumed by the U.S. government.

Third, most of the factors of production are privately owned in a mixed economy. However, government provides funding for some resources, such as roads, highways, and bridges. The federal government also provides funding for public corporations such as the postal service. State and local governments may operate water and power companies. They also run regional transportation systems like bus and subway lines.

Other Nations with Mixed Economies

Most nations in Europe have mixed economies. So do Canada, Japan, Singapore, Taiwan, South Korea, Australia, and New Zealand. However, the nations vary in how much government intervenes in the economy.

England provides socialized medical care for the country's citizens.

For many years, Great Britain had government ownership of large industries such as the railroads. In recent years, the government has been privatizing businesses, or turning ownership over to private companies. Medical care is free. The elderly get government pensions. The fees for public colleges and universities are very low. When the government tried to raise fees in 2005, the public protested.

Japan's government, on the other hand, does not provide much funding for social programs. It does protect Japanese companies from foreign competition, however. High tariffs, or import fees, make goods coming into Japan more costly than Japanese-produced goods.

In recent years, eastern European nations such as Poland and Hungary have privatized many of their businesses. Beginning in the late 1980s, the governments of eastern Europe were no longer controlled by Communists. As a result, these nations have moved toward mixed economies.

Putting It All Together

"In a mixed economy, government becomes involved in private enterprise." Work with a partner to explain this statement. Discuss what you think the statement means. Make a list of the ways that government regulates and also helps businesses.

Socialism and Developing Nations

Thinking on Your Own

Suppose you were part of a committee to develop a plan for the economy of a new nation. Your country is poor, but it has many natural resources. It has few factories, though. There is also a large population of workers, but they have few skills. They are mostly farmers. What would your country need to do to develop its economy? Look at the illustrations in this lesson. Think about the question. In your notebook, write at least five things your country would have to do to improve its economy.

Many of the nations in the Southern Hemisphere are **developing nations**. Their economies are based on farming and the export of natural resources. Many of their citizens live in poverty. These nations were once part of European colonial empires. Latin America's nations gained their independence in the 1800s. African nations did not gain independence until the mid- or late twentieth century. A number of these nations have chosen to develop Socialist economies.

focus your reading

Describe what the characteristics of socialism are.

How are Latin American nations modernizing their economies?

In what ways are African nations improving their economies?

words to know

developing nation

socialism

nationalization

central planning

industrialization

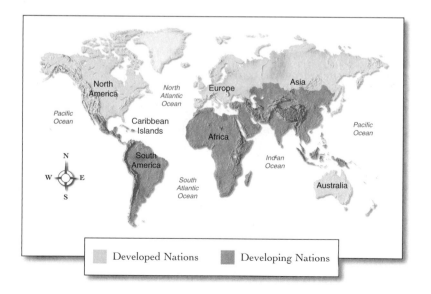

Developed Nations   Developing Nations

Socialism

Socialism is an economic system in which the government owns the basic means of production and decides how resources should be used. The government also provides social services such as health care and welfare. The basic principle of socialism is that all members of society should share equally in the benefits of economic activity.

Socialism may be democratic, or it may be authoritarian. For example, Great Britain, France, Sweden, and Germany are democratic nations. Each has Socialist political parties, however. When these parties are voted into national office, they approve programs that distribute more of the nation's resources to poorer citizens. For example, providing free medical care for everyone is a Socialist-supported program.

Like the United States, the Argentinian government provides education for all children.

Socialism has four characteristics: nationalization, guarantee of the public welfare, high taxes, and a centrally planned economy. However, great differences exist among Socialist governments. There are differences in how many of these characteristics are present and how strongly they are followed.

The first characteristic of socialism is **nationalization**. The central government takes over certain industries, such as transportation and steel. These are often the most important companies and have thousands of workers. In a democratic nation such as France, the Socialist government pays the owners of the companies for the loss of their businesses. In authoritarian nations, the government does not pay the owners.

Guarantee of the public welfare is the second characteristic. Socialist governments seek to ensure that the basic needs of all citizens are met. These include free or low-cost medical and dental care; low-cost public housing; free schooling, including a university education; pensions for the retired and those with disabilities; and unemployment payments.

These benefits, however, cost money. As a result, high taxes are a third characteristic of socialism. Taxes are the chief means Socialist governments use to fund benefits. People may pay as much as 50 or 60 percent of their income in taxes. The idea is to even out the distribution of wealth among a nation's citizens.

stop and think

Create a three-column chart to list the four characteristics of socialism. List the characteristics in one column. In the second column, explain each characteristic. In the third column, give an example of each one. Work with a partner to create your chart.

The fourth characteristic is **central planning**. A centrally planned economy is one in which the government decides how resources will be used. In a market economy like the United States, sellers decide what resources they need, how to get what they need, and what to produce. They also decide to whom to sell their goods and services. In a centrally planned economy, government bureaucrats make decisions about what will be produced and for whom. They decide which industries will be able to buy what resources. They also decide how much of any good or service will be produced. A nation with strict central planning has a command economy. Most Socialist nations, however, allow some private companies to operate.

Health care is lacking in many regions of the developing world, such as in Kinshasa, D.R.C.

Developing Economies

The governments of many developing nations have chosen socialism. There are some practical reasons for this.

First, when African nations became independent, they had few locally owned companies. Even in Latin America, foreign investors owned and ran many of the large businesses. Nationalizing foreign businesses puts control of these businesses in local hands. The idea is that their resources can be used to benefit the nation, rather than foreigners.

It does not always work that way. An example is Chile in the early 1970s. Salvador Allende, a Socialist, was elected president in 1970. He nationalized foreign-owned businesses. However, the economy worsened. In 1973, military leaders overthrew him. They set up a dictatorship and welcomed back foreign investors.

Second, a goal of governments in developing nations is to improve the economy. They believe that this, in turn, will raise the standard of living of their citizens. Most governments see industrialization as the way to achieve this. **Industrialization** is the growth of industries such as manufacturing. Central planning enables these governments to direct capital—money and natural and human resources—toward industrialization.

Infrastructure is often lacking in developing countries, including Haiti.

In Kenya, mechanics receive government training.

Problems of Socialism in Developing Nations

Unfortunately, socialism comes at a cost to developing nations. So many resources may be used to produce goods for export that agriculture is overlooked. Nigeria and other nations have to import food.

Another problem is the growth of government bureaucracies. Central planning requires large numbers of bureaucrats. However, bureaucracy can become so large that it is a drain on the nation's resources. Taxes increase for salaries of the bureaucrats. Decision-making is slowed down.

Nationalization is also an issue. Developing nations need money to industrialize. Foreign companies are unlikely to put money into nations that may nationalize their businesses.

Putting It All Together

Create a concept web about socialism. Label the center circle "Socialism." Label the smaller circles "Advantages" and "Problems." Work with a partner to add details.

Biography

Wangari Maathai (1940—   )

Wangari Maathai is the first environmentalist to win the Nobel Peace Prize. She is also the first African woman to win it. The award was presented to her in 2004. It recognized her work for "sustainable development, democracy, and peace." Sustainable development is economic development that uses natural resources to meet present needs without endangering supplies for the future.

Maathai began her environmental work in 1977 in her native Kenya. In that year, she founded the Green Belt Movement (GBM). Logging and development had stripped the country of its trees. Since 1977, the GBM has planted more than 30 million trees. More than 100,000 people have found work with the GBM, planting and taking care of the trees.

In the 1990s, Maathai and the GBM turned to politics. They opposed the dictatorship of Kenya's president, Daniel arap Moi, who finally banned the GBM. Maathai was beaten and jailed repeatedly over the years. In 2002, Moi was banned from running for office again and a freely elected government took over. Maathai was named Assistant Minister for Environment, Natural Resources, and Wildlife.

Communist Systems

Thinking on Your Own

Communist economic systems are another alternative to capitalist or mixed economies. Skim this section and list three characteristics of a Communist system in your notebook. Check the accuracy of your list as you read this lesson.

In the 1920s, the Communists took over the government of Russia and formed the Soviet Union. They introduced a new form of government and a new economic system. These were based on the ideas of Karl Marx.

Marx was a German philosopher. He believed that there are only two classes—owners and workers. The owners of land, factories, buildings, and the like, are capitalists. According to Marx, they grow rich while their workers suffer. Workers must revolt against the capitalists. They must seize all factors of production and set up a dictatorship of the proletariat. *Proletariat* means "the people." The Russian Revolution of 1917 was the first step. Communists acting in the name of the people overthrew the czar and seized power. They set up a Communist state.

focus your reading

What are the characteristics of a Communist economy?

Explain what caused the collapse of Soviet communism.

How have the Chinese adapted their economy to capitalism?

words to know

collectivization

commune

Characteristics of Soviet Communism

Communism has four basic characteristics. First is the role of the Communist Party. The party controls the government. Party leaders make all major political and economic decisions for the nation.

The U.S.S.R. used propaganda posters to promote collective farming.

A collective farm in Vilshanka, Soviet Union

Communist nations have centrally planned economies. This is the second characteristic. The national government makes all economic decisions. It decides what will be produced and by whom. It decides which companies and farms will get what resources, including the number of workers.

Government bureaucrats draw up very detailed economic plans. Each farm is given a quota of certain crops and animals to raise. Each factory is given a quota of goods to produce. For example, a factory may have a quota of 500 tractors a month to produce. If the factory falls short, the managers could be punished. Ever-larger numbers of bureaucrats are hired by the government to develop these plans and see that they are carried out.

The third and fourth characteristics, collectivization and government ownership, are related. The government owns all means of production, from trains and buses to housing and stores. **Collectivization** is the process of taking over privately owned property. For example, in the 1930s, the Soviet Union collectivized small farms. The government seized all farms in an area and joined them into a single government-owned collective.

stop and think

How did the Communists in the Soviet Union put Marx's ideas into practice? Discuss the question with a partner and make a list of ideas. As you read further, list reasons for the collapse of communism in the Soviet Union.

Why Communism Collapsed in Russia

From the 1930s through the 1970s, the Soviet economy grew steadily. However, the growth masked a number of problems. For example, there was a lack of goods for ordinary people to buy. Government planners focused on building weapons and machinery. They were not concerned with producing refrigerators, furniture, and stylish clothes.

Agriculture also suffered under central planning. Farmers in a market economy earn their money by selling their crops. In the Soviet Union, many farmers were paid wages. It did not matter how large their harvests were or if they harvested their crops on time. As a result, there were often food shortages. By the 1980s, the problems were leading to unrest. Both economic growth and productivity had slowed greatly.

Mikhail Gorbachev became head of the Communist Party and the Soviet Union in 1985. He tried to reform the Communist political and economic systems. Central planning was relaxed. The bureaucracy's size was cut. Managers were allowed to make decisions about their factories. Farmers were given land on government-owned farms to grow crops. However, change was difficult. In the end, Gorbachev's efforts were unsuccessful. Shortages worsened. Prices rose for goods that were available. Unemployment also rose.

Long lines in grocery stores were common during the Communist era in Soviet Russia.

At the same time, eastern Europeans were rebelling against their Communist-dominated governments. This led to rebellions among the other Soviet republics. In 1991, the Soviet Union collapsed. The 15 republics became independent nations. A new president of Russia replaced Gorbachev.

Since the early 1990s, Russia has attempted to build a democratic nation and a market economy. It has been difficult. The Russians have no history of democratic government or civil rights and liberties. Before the revolution in 1917, the nation was a monarchy ruled by the czar. Many of the same people who ran the Communist government in the 1980s are still in power. By the early 2000s, the government had strengthened its power over the rights of citizens.

It has not been any easier to improve the economy. The economy of czarist Russia was based on agriculture. The Communists forced the nation to adopt central planning and to industrialize. There is no history of private enterprise. As a result, moving to a market economy has been difficult.

Shifts in Chinese Communism

Mao Zedong and his Communist followers seized power in China in 1949. Like the Communists in Russia, Mao founded a Communist political and economic system in the People's Republic of China (PRC). Like the Soviet Union, the Chinese economy was based on central planning and government ownership of property. Small farms were combined into large government-owned **communes**. Private enterprise was not allowed. Mao's goal was to modernize China. However, his efforts at raising the standard of living failed.

Beijing has slowly introduced concepts from a market economy.

After Mao's death, Deng Xiaoping became head of the Communist Party and the government in 1977. Deng relaxed much of the central planning put in place by Mao. He and his successors have slowly shifted China to more of a market economy. Many government-owned businesses have been sold to entrepreneurs. Other entrepreneurs are opening their own small businesses. Many businesses are owned and managed by their workers. Foreign companies and foreign investors are welcome to do business in China. China has become an economic giant.

However, political control has not eased. The Communist Party still runs the government and people's rights are limited. No one may oppose the government.

Putting It All Together

Working with a partner, imagine that one of you lived in the Soviet Union and the other in China under Mao. How might central planning have affected each of you as a worker and a consumer? Make a T-chart. Label one side "Soviet Union." Label the other "PRC." Work with a partner to list ideas about how central planning would affect you as a worker or consumer in each of these nations. Discuss how life in the Soviet Union and the PRC is different from life in the United States.

Global Economic Issues

Thinking on Your Own

The United States imports goods from many parts of the world. In your notebook, list at least five items you buy that U.S. companies import and sell in the United States.

Globalization is the integration of economic activities across national borders. Globalization creates a single world market through the free flow of goods, services, labor, and capital. The globalization of the economy began centuries ago.

In the 200s B.C., merchants carried goods along the Silk Road. The trade route stretched from China through the Middle East to the Roman Empire. In the 1400s, European explorers opened trade routes between Asia and Europe. In the 1500s, the Americas joined the international trade network.

Globalization has increased the spread of Western goods around the world.

focus your reading

Explain how technology impacts the interdependence of nations.

How can nations both limit and encourage international trade?

What economic issues does globalization present for developing nations?

words to know

technology
trade barrier
quota
subsidy
free trade

Since the mid-1800s, the interdependence of economies has increased dramatically. Technology and government policies drive globalization. **Technology**— the use of science in business and industry—includes the ability to move raw materials and goods quickly and cheaply. First, it was the invention of the clipper ship in the mid-1840s. These fast sailing ships sped raw materials and goods around the world. In the late 1800s, even faster steamships replaced clipper ships. Then came railroads, trucks, and airplanes to move goods and passengers within countries and across borders.

Technology also includes the ability to send information quickly. The inventions of the telegraph and telephone made it possible to send information quickly from place to place. Computers and the World Wide Web make it possible to send huge amounts of data cheaply and quickly.

Government Policies and International Trade

All the speed in the world will not expand world trade if government policies block it. There are several ways that governments can put up **trade barriers**.

Some nations use tariffs, or taxes on imports, to make them more costly than locally produced goods. The goal is to protect local businesses and jobs from foreign competition. Governments also use quotas to limit foreign-made goods. A **quota** allows only a certain amount of a good, such as tuna, to be brought into a country during a certain time period.

International trade has increased in recent years and allowed a greater flow of goods around the world.

Subsidies are government payments to the producers of a good or service. They encourage local production by increasing the amount of money that the producer receives. However, the European Union (EU) has fined the United States in recent years for its use of subsidies for U.S. farmers. The EU charged that the subsidies gave U.S. farmers an unfair price advantage in the world market. They did not have to charge as much for their crops and still made a profit. Other nations have also been fined for using subsidies.

The European Union is one of the regional organizations that have been formed to promote freer trade. The table on page 451 shows some of the other major groups. Their purpose is to reduce trade barriers among member nations.

Major Regional Trade Groups
Common Market for Eastern and Southern Africa (COMESA)
Economic Community of West African States (ECOWAS)
Asia Pacific Economic Cooperation (APEC)
Association of South East Asian Nations (ASEAN)
European Union (EU)
Caribbean Community and Common Market (CARICOM)
Central American Free Trade Agreement (CAFTA)
North American Free Trade Agreement (NAFTA)

In 1948, the United States and 22 other nations created the General Agreement on Tariffs and Trade (GATT). The goals included lowering tariffs and quotas. The goal was **free trade**, or trade without barriers. By 1994, 110 countries were operating under GATT rules. In that year, they agreed to create the World Trade Organization (WTO). It is a permanent agency that enforces trade rules and settles trade disputes. It also encourages world trade by developing nations.

stop and think

Play "What Am I?" with a partner. Write a definition for each term introduced so far in this lesson. End the definition with the question "What am I?" Take turns with a partner asking and answering questions.

Issues for Developing Nations

About 126 of the world's 191 nations are developing nations. Their populations total more than 5 billion. This equals five-sixths of the world's people. However, these nations have only 20 percent of the world's resources.

Developing nations face many problems in improving their economies and the standard of living of their people. Listed here are some of the major problems.

- Population growth

Developing nations tend to have higher rates of population growth than developed nations. This creates a drain on food resources, health care, and education. Some countries have set policies to limit population growth. In an effort to cut population growth, the Chinese government limits families to one child.

Diseases such as cholera are still of concern in many developing nations, such as Peru.

● Poor health

People in developing nations often suffer from a lack of sanitation, education about good health practices, and medical care. They may live in poverty without enough food to eat and, in many countries, without clean water to drink. As a result, life expectancy is about half of what it is in developed nations. Diseases such as AIDS can infect millions. Polio, which was wiped out in developed nations years ago, has appeared in Africa again.

● Civil wars and military rule

Many of the developing nations are torn by civil wars. Often, military rulers step in and seize power. In the 1970s and 1980s, half of Africa's nations were led by military dictatorships. Many are still ruled by dictators. Instead of using resources to develop the economy, these governments use their resources to support the military. Nations such as Somalia and Sudan are still caught up in civil war. Little economic development can take place when people are not safe.

● Lack of capital and the burden of debt

Somali refugees

Generally, developing nations were once part of European or U.S. colonial empires. Their colonial rulers used them as sources of raw materials. They did not invest large amounts of money in developing industry. When these former colonies became independent, they lacked the capital to build industries on their own. As a result, they began to borrow heavily from developed nations.

By the early twenty-first century, it was unlikely that some nations would ever be able to pay off their debts. This made it even harder to grow their economies. In 2005, Prime Minister Tony Blair of Great Britain led developed nations in creating a plan to forgive billions of dollars of debt from the poorest developing nations.

Putting It All Together

With a partner, discuss the economic issues facing developing nations. Choose the one that you think will be the hardest to solve. List at least three reasons for your opinion.

Participate in Government

Apply for a Passport

To travel between nations, a person, even an infant, needs a passport. A U.S. citizen needs a U.S. passport. These are available from the passport service of the State Department. There are passport offices in many cities where you can apply for and get a passport. U.S. Post Offices also offer this service.

Passports are valid for ten years. If a person has a valid passport, a renewal can be done online or by mail. However, if a person's passport expired more than 15 years ago, the person must go to a passport office or post office to reapply. If a person has never had a passport or it has been stolen, lost, or damaged, the person must apply in person for a new one.

Children younger than fourteen must apply in person for a passport. Both living parents or guardians must agree to the passport application. Minors between fourteen and seventeen must also appear in person. Parental consent may also be required.

To apply for a passport, a person needs

- a completed but unsigned application form. The person will have to sign the form in front of the passport clerk.

- proof of U.S. citizenship such as the expiring U.S. passport, certified birth certificate, naturalization certificate, or certificate of citizenship.

To Find Out More About Getting a Passport:

- Visit the State Department Web site and look for information on passports.

- Ask your local post office for information.

Skill Builder

Make Comparisons and Contrasts

To compare information is to look for how things, people, or events are the same. To contrast information is to look for how things, people, or events are different.

Tables are very useful for comparing and contrasting information. This textbook uses a number of tables to help you see the similarities and differences between and among things related to government. For example, the table on page 34 shows the two competing plans and the compromises that resulted in the U.S. Constitution.

When you talk or write about comparisons and contrasts, there are certain words and phrases that make your meaning clear. They act as signals for your meaning.

Similarities	Differences	
as well as	although	instead
both	even though	on the other hand
in common	but	unlike
in comparison	however	while
like	in contrast	yet
same		
similar		
too		

Complete the following activities using comparison and contrast words to signal similarities and differences.

1 Examine the table on page 34. (a) Write two sentences that compare the two plans with the U.S. Constitution. (b) Write two sentences that contrast the two plans with the U.S. Constitution.

2 Read the sections on capitalism, pages 437–439, and socialism, pages 442–444. (a) Write two sentences that compare capitalism and socialism. (b) Write two sentences that contrast them.

Appendix
Supreme Court Cases and Historical Documents

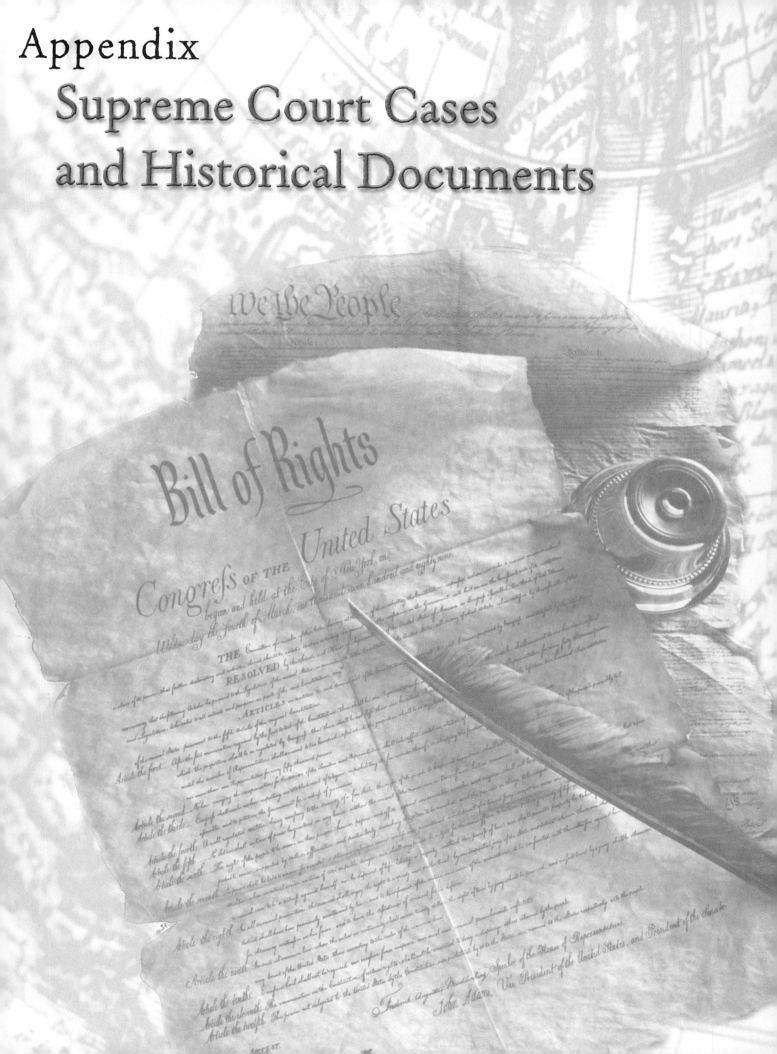

Summaries of Important Supreme Court Cases

Interstate Commerce—*Gibbons v. Ogden* (1824)

Background: Aaron Ogden was licensed to run steamboats to and from New York. His was the only company licensed by New York State to operate this service. Thomas Gibbons obtained a federal "coasting license" to operate a steamboat business in the area. He claimed the federal license allowed him to land his boats in New York City. Ogden sued Gibbons for violating his license.

Decision: The Supreme Court ruled in favor of Gibbons. The Court declared that the federal regulations were superior to the state's regulations. The decision was based on the Supremacy Clause of the Constitution. Because of this decision, Congress regulates business activities that take place between states.

School Prayer and the Establishment Clause—*Engel v. Vitale* (1962)

Background: New York State schoolchildren were required to recite a short prayer each day before school. The prayer was not based on a specific religion, but said, "Almighty God, we acknowledge our dependence upon Thee." The State Board of Regents, which oversees education in the state, set the regulation. It also composed the prayer. A group of parents sued. They claimed the regulation violated the Establishment Clause of the First Amendment.

Decision: The Supreme Court agreed with the parents. The Regents' regulation was declared unconstitutional. The Court said that under the Establishment Clause, government had no right to write prayers and require people to say them.

Right to Counsel—*Gideon v. Wainwright* (1963)

Background: Sometimes defendants in criminal cases are too poor to hire a lawyer. The government appoints a lawyer to represent the defendant. However, in 1961, Florida state law only required an attorney if the state was asking for the death penalty. Clarence Gideon was tried in a Florida state court and found guilty of breaking and entering. He was sentenced to five years in prison. Gideon wrote his own appeal and filed it with the U.S. Supreme Court. He claimed that he had been denied a lawyer in violation of the Sixth Amendment's guarantee of due process.

Decision: The Court agreed with Gideon. It granted him a new trial. At his trial, he was represented by a court-appointed lawyer and acquitted. Court-appointed lawyers are paid by the government for their work. The Gideon Rule guarantees a court-appointed lawyer for anyone too poor to hire an attorney. However, to qualify, the person must be facing six months or more in jail if convicted.

Interstate Commerce—*Heart of Atlanta Motel v. United States* (1964)

Background: The Heart of Atlanta Motel was two blocks from the center of Atlanta and easily reached from two interstate highways and two state highways. It used billboards and highway signs to advertise. Residents of other states made up about 75 percent of its guests. The motel had always refused to rent rooms to African Americans. After the passage of the 1964 Civil Rights Act, the owner went to court to have the Act declared unconstitutional.

Decision: The Court ruled against the motel and upheld the constitutionality of the law. The Court based its decision on the Equal Protection Clause and the Commerce Clause. The Court said that Congress's power to regulate interstate commerce includes the power to regulate local activities that harm interstate commerce. This was one of the most important civil rights cases of the 1960s.

Rights of the Accused—*Miranda* v. *Arizona* (1966)

Background: Ernesto Miranda was arrested for kidnapping and sexual assault. He was interrogated by the police without an attorney present. The police did not tell him that he could have an attorney with him during questioning. He also did not ask for one. During questioning, Miranda signed a confession. He was tried and found guilty in state court. The confession was introduced as evidence. Miranda appealed his conviction. He said that his right against self-incrimination under the Fifth Amendment had been violated because he did not have the advice of an attorney during questioning.

Decision: The Court overturned Miranda's conviction. The Court said that the presence of an attorney is necessary to protect the rights of a person being questioned. Under the pressure of interrogation, a person may not fully understand his or her right to remain silent. The ruling set out what is known as the Miranda warning: (1) A person has the right to remain silent, and (2) the right to have an attorney present during questioning. (3) Anything the person says may be used against him or her in a court of law. (4) An attorney will be appointed if the person is too poor to hire an attorney. The ruling confirmed the right of a person to a fair trial in state courts.

Voting Age—*Oregon* v. *Mitchell* (1970)

Background: In 1970, Congress passed amendments to the Voting Rights Act of 1965. The changes in the law related to residency and literacy requirements. The new law also lowered the voting age from twenty-one to eighteen. President Richard Nixon signed the law, but said he did not believe that Congress could change the voting age. He believed that a Constitutional amendment was needed to lower the voting age. The president and the states of Oregon, Arizona, Texas, and Idaho filed lawsuits opposing the law. The issue was whether Congress had the power to change the voting age in state and local elections.

Decision: The Court ruled that Congress could lower the voting age for national elections. Article I, Section 4, and Article II, Section 1, give Congress this power. However, Congress may not change the voting age for state and local elections. This power is reserved to the states under Article I, Section 2 and the Tenth Amendment. Soon after the Court's ruling, Congress approved and sent to the states the Twenty-sixth Amendment. The states ratified the amendment and the voting age for all elections is now eighteen.

Right to Privacy—*Roe* v. *Wade* (1973)

Background: Texas, like other states, banned abortions. A woman using the name Jane Roe to protect herself sued the state of Texas for an abortion.

Decision: The Court struck down the law. It ruled that women have a Constitutional right to choose to have an abortion. This is part of the right to privacy and is guaranteed under several sections of the Constitution. The Court's ruling has three parts. (1) During the first three months of pregnancy, states cannot place limits on a woman's right to choose. (2) During the second three months, states may put some limits on how, where, and when abortions are carried out. This is because the state has an interest in protecting the health of the woman. (3) During the last three months, it is possible for a fetus to live outside the mother. The state then has an interest in protecting the fetus. At this point, the state may forbid abortions, except when necessary to protect the health of the mother.

This ruling is one of the Court's most controversial decisions. Several later Supreme Court cases have somewhat limited the justices' ruling in Roe, but the right to an abortion remains the law.

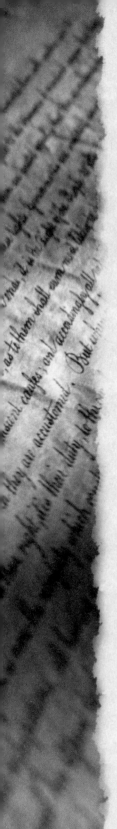

Separation of Powers—*United States v. Nixon* (1974)

Background: During the 1972 presidential election, there was a break-in at Democratic National Headquarters. The supposed burglars were caught with electronic eavesdropping equipment. They were going to plant the equipment in the Democratic offices. Through a series of investigations and hearings, it was discovered that the advisers close to President Richard Nixon had hired these men. During the investigations, a witness testified that the president had taped all conversations in the Oval Office. When the special prosecutor got a court order for the tapes, President Nixon refused to hand them over. He claimed executive privilege under Article II of the Constitution.

Decision: The Supreme Court ruled against the president. The Court said that only conversations related to the duties of the presidency are covered by executive privilege. In this case, due process was more important than the president's interest in maintaining the general principle of confidentiality for presidential conversations.

Women and the Draft—*Rostker v. Goldberg* (1981)

Background: The United States ended the military draft in 1973. Young men between the ages of eighteen and twenty-six no longer had to register for military service. In 1979, President Jimmy Carter asked Congress to restore military registration. The Soviet Union had invaded Afghanistan and the president wanted to be ready if a draft was needed. He requested that both men and women be required to register. Congress passed a bill to register only men. Several young men filed a lawsuit. They claimed that military registration of men only was discriminatory. It violated the due process clause of the Fifth Amendment.

Decision: The Supreme Court upheld the law. Congress could omit women from the draft because the goal of the draft was to call up troops that could be used in combat. Congress had determined after lengthy debate that women should not be used in combat. Therefore, a male-only draft was in line with this policy.

Drug Testing of Students—*Vernonia School District 47J v. Acton* (1995)

Background: The Vernonia School District regularly did random drug tests of student athletes. The tests were not based on suspicion of drug use or possession.

Decision: The Court ruled that these tests did not violate students' rights. The school district's interest in fighting drug abuse was greater than students' interests.

Line-Item Veto—*Clinton* v. *New York City* (1998)

Background: Many states allow their governor to veto parts, or lines, of the state budget. This is known as the line-item veto. Prior to 1996, the president did not have this power over the federal budget. He or she either had to veto the whole budget or sign it as Congress passed it. The president could not pick and choose what he or she wanted to approve in the budget. Presidents had long requested Congress to give them this power. In 1996, Congress finally passed the Line-Item Veto Act.

In 1997, President Bill Clinton used the line-item veto to reject parts of the federal budget. New York City and several hospitals in the city filed a lawsuit against the president. He had used the line-item veto to reduce Medicaid spending for New York State. This affected the hospitals and the city.

Decision: The Supreme Court ruled against the president. It said that Congress could not give the president powers not granted to him by the Constitution. By allowing the president to veto parts of the budget, Congress was giving the president the power to make budget decisions. Article I of the Constitution gives this power to Congress. If Congress wants to give the president the line-item veto, then the Constitution has to be amended. As a result, the president still does not have the line-item veto.

Affirmative Action—*Gratz* v. *Bollinger* / *Grutter* v. *Bollinger* (2003)

These two cases were heard in the same session of the Supreme Court.

Background: The University of Michigan awarded 20 points to applicants who belonged to an ethnic or racial group. The University of Michigan law school used race or ethnic background as one factor in its admission policy. The goal of both policies was to create a diverse student body. Two students who were denied admission because of these policies sued the University of Michigan and its law school.

Decision: In Gratz, the Court found that the undergraduate admissions policy was unconstitutional. The Court ruled that the policy violated the Equal Protection Clause.

The Court found in Grutter that the admissions policy was constitutional. Race was simply one factor that was considered in deciding whether to admit a student. Justice Sandra Day O'Connor wrote the majority opinion. In it, she said that the hope of the Court was that affirmative action policies would not be needed in 25 years.

The Federalist, No. 10

The Utility of the Union as a Safeguard Against Domestic Faction and Insurrection

November 22, 1787

James Madison wrote several of The Federalist Papers supporting ratification of the Constitution. In the excerpt below, Madison argues for the idea of a federal republic.

By a faction, I understand a number of citizens . . . who are united and actuated by some common impulse . . . adverse to the rights of other citizens. . . .

The inference to which we are brought is that the causes of faction cannot be removed and that relief is only to be sought in the means of controlling its effects. . . .

A republic, by which I mean government in which the scheme of representation takes place . . . promises the cure for which we are seeking. . . .

The two great points of difference between a democracy and a republic are: first, the delegation of the government, in the latter, to a small number of citizens elected by the rest; secondly, the greater number of citizens, and greater sphere of country, over which the latter may be extended.

The effect of the first difference is . . . to refine and enlarge the public views, by passing them through the medium of a chosen body of citizens, whose wisdom may best discern the true interest of their country, and whose patriotism and love of justice will be least likely to sacrifice it to temporary or partial considerations. . . .

The Federalist, No. 51

The Structure of the Government Must Furnish the Proper Checks and Balances Between the Different Departments

February 6, 1788

James Madison wrote several of The Federalist Papers supporting ratification of the Constitution. In the excerpt below, Madison argues for a system of checks and balances.

TO WHAT . . . , shall we finally resort, for maintaining in practice the necessary partition of power among the several departments, as laid down in the Constitution? The only answer that can be given is, . . . by so contriving the interior structure of the government as that its several constituent parts may, by their mutual relations, be the means of keeping each other in their proper places. . . .

. . . it is evident that each department should have a will of its own; and consequently should be so constituted that the members of each should have as little agency as possible in the appointment of the members of the others. . . .

It is equally evident, that the members of each department should be as little dependent as possible on those of the others. . . .

But the great security against a gradual concentration of the several powers in the same department, consists in giving to those who administer each department the necessary constitutional means and personal motives to resist encroachments of the others. . . . In framing a government which is to be administered by men over men, the great difficulty lies in this: you must first enable the government to control the governed; and in the next place oblige it to control itself.

But it is not possible to give to each department an equal power of self-defense. In republican government, the legislative authority necessarily predominates. The remedy for this inconveniency is to divide the legislature into different branches; and to render them, by different modes of election and different principles of action, as little connected with each other as the nature of their common functions and their common dependence on the society will admit. . . .

There are, moreover, two considerations particularly applicable to the federal system of America, which place that system in a very interesting point of view.

First. . . In the compound republic of America, the power surrendered by the people is first divided between two distinct governments, and then the portion allotted to each subdivided among distinct and separate departments. Hence a double security arises to the rights of the people. The different governments will control each other, at the same time that each will be controlled by itself.

Second. It is of great importance in a republic not only to guard the society against the oppression of its rulers, but to guard one part of the society against the injustice of the other part. Different interests necessarily exist in different classes of citizens. If a majority be united by a common interest, the rights of the minority will be insecure. There are but two methods of providing against this evil: the one by creating a will in the community independent of the majority — that is, of the society itself; the other, by comprehending in the society so many separate descriptions of citizens as will render an unjust combination of a majority of the whole very improbable, if not impracticable. . . .

Washington's Farewell Address

September 26, 1796

At the end of his second term as president, George Washington warned against the dangers of political parties and sectionalism. He also advised the nation against forming permanent alliances with other nations.

. . . Citizens by birth or choice of a common country, that country has a right to concentrate your affections. The name of American, which belongs to you in your national capacity, must always exalt the just pride or patriotism more than any appellation derived from local discriminations. With slight shades of difference, you have the same religion, manners, habits, and political principles. You have in a common cause fought and triumphed together. . . .

In contemplating the causes which may disturb our union it occurs as matter of serious concern that any ground should have been furnished for characterizing parties by geographical discriminations. . . .

No alliances, however strict, between the parts can be an adequate substitute. They must inevitably experience the infractions and interruptions which all alliances in all times have experienced. . . .

The great rule of conduct for us in regard to foreign nations is, in extending our commercial relations to have with them as little political connection as possible. . . .

I anticipate with pleasing expectation that retreat in which I promise myself to realize . . . the sweet enjoyment of partaking in the midst of my fellow citizens the benign influence of good laws under a free government—the ever-favorite object of my heart, and the happy rewards, as I trust, of our mutual cares, labors, and dangers.

The Seneca Falls Declaration

July 19–20, 1848

One of the first documents to express the desire for equal rights for women is the Declaration of Sentiments and Resolutions. It was issued in 1848 at the Seneca Falls Convention in Seneca Falls, New York. Lucretia Mott and Elizabeth Cady Stanton led the delegates in adopting a set of resolutions that called for women's suffrage and opportunities for women in employment and education. They formatted these resolutions after the Declaration of Independence.

When, in the course of human events, it becomes necessary for one portion of the family of man to assume among the people of the earth a position different from that which they have hitherto occupied, but one to which the laws of nature and of nature's God entitle them, a decent respect to the opinions of mankind requires that they should declare the causes that impel them to such a course.

We hold these truths to be self-evident: that all men and women are created equal; that they are endowed by their Creator with certain inalienable rights; that among these are life, liberty, and the pursuit of happiness; that to secure these rights governments are instituted, deriving their just powers from the consent of the governed. Whenever any form of government becomes destructive of these ends, it is the right of those who suffer from it to refuse allegiance to it, and to insist upon the institution of a new government, laying its foundation on such principles, and organizing its powers in such form as to them shall seem most likely to effect their safety and happiness. Prudence, indeed, will dictate that governments long established should not be changed for light and transient causes; . . . But when a long train of abuses and usurpations, pursing invariably the same object, evinces a design to reduce them under absolute despotism, it is their duty to throw off such government, and to provide new guards for their future security. . . .

The history of mankind is a history of repeated injuries and usurpations on the part of man toward woman, having in direct object the establishment of an absolute tyranny over her. To prove this, let facts be submitted to a candid word. . . .

Now, in view of the entire disfranchisement of one-half the people of this country, their social and religious degradation—in view of the unjust laws above mentioned, and because women do feel themselves aggrieved, oppressed, and fraudulently deprived of their most sacred rights, we insist that they have immediate admission to all the rights and privileges which belong to them as citizens of these United States. . . .

The Emancipation Proclamation

January 1, 1863

On January 1, 1863, President Abraham Lincoln issued the Emancipation Proclamation. This document freed all slaves in states under Confederate control. The Proclamation was a significant step toward the Thirteenth Amendment (1865) that ended slavery in the United States.

Whereas, on the 22nd day of September, in the year of our Lord 1862, a proclamation was issued by the President of the United States, containing, among other things, the following, to wit:

> That on the 1st day of January, in the year of our Lord 1863, all persons held as slaves within any state or designated part of a state, the people whereof shall then be in rebellion against the United States, shall be then, thenceforward, and forever free; and the executive government of the United States, including the military and naval authority thereof, will recognize and maintain the freedom of such persons and will do no act or acts to repress such persons, or any of them, in any efforts that may make for their actual freedom.

> That the executive will, on the 1st day January aforesaid, by proclamation, designate the states and parts of states, if any, in which the people thereof, respectively, shall then be in rebellion against the United States; and the fact that any state or the people thereof shall on that day be in good faith represented in the Congress of the United States by members chosen thereto at elections wherein a majority of the qualified voters of such states shall have participated shall, in the absence of strong countervailing testimony, be deemed conclusive evidence that such state and the people thereof are not then in rebellion against the United States.

Now, therefore, I, Abraham Lincoln, President of the United States, by virtue of the power in me vested as commander in chief of the Army and Navy of the United States, in time of actual armed rebellion against the authority and government of the United States, and as a fit and necessary war measure for suppressing said rebellion, do, on this 1st day of January, in the year of our Lord 1863, and in accordance with my purpose so to do, publicly proclaimed for the full period of 100 days from the day first above mentioned, order and designate as the states and parts of states wherein the people thereof, respectively, are this day in rebellion against the United States. . . .

And, by virtue of the power and for the purpose aforesaid, I do order and declare that all persons held as slaves within said designated states and parts of states are, and henceforward shall be, free; and that the executive government of the United States, including the military and naval authorities thereof, will recognize and maintain the freedom of said persons. . .

And upon this act, sincerely believed to be an act of justice, warranted by the Constitution upon military necessity, I invoke the considerate judgment of mankind and the gracious favor of Almighty God.

The Gettysburg Address

November 19, 1863

On November 19, 1863, President Abraham Lincoln delivered a short speech at the dedication of a national cemetery on the battlefield of Gettysburg. His simple yet eloquent words expressed his hopes for a nation divided by civil war.

Four score and seven years ago our fathers brought forth on this continent a new nation, conceived in liberty, and dedicated to the proposition that all men are created equal.

Now we are engaged in a great civil war, testing whether that nation, or any nation so conceived and so dedicated, can long endure. We are met on a great battlefield of that war. We have come to dedicate a portion of that field as a final resting place for those who here gave their lives that that nation might live. It is altogether fitting and proper that we should do this.

But, in a larger sense, we can not dedicate—we can not consecrate—we can not hallow—this ground. The brave men, living and dead, who struggled here, have consecrated it far above our poor power to add or detract. The world will little note nor long remember what we say here, but it can never forget what they did here. It is for us, the living, rather, to be dedicated here to the unfinished work which they who fought here have thus far so nobly advanced. It is rather for us to be here dedicated to the great task remaining before us—that from these honored dead we take increased devotion to that cause for which they gave us the last full measure of devotion; that we here highly resolve that these dead shall not have died in vain; that this nation, under God, shall have a new birth of freedom; and that government of the people, by the people, for the people, shall not perish from the earth.

John F. Kennedy's Inaugural Address

January 20, 1961

President Kennedy's Inaugural Address on January 20, 1961, set the tone for his administration. In his address Kennedy stirred the nation by calling for "a grand and global alliance" to fight tyranny, poverty, disease, and war.

We observe today not a victory of party but a celebration of freedom—symbolizing an end as well as a beginning—signifying renewal as well as change. For I have sworn before you and Almighty God the same solemn oath our forebears prescribed nearly a century and three-quarters ago.

The world is very different now. For man holds in his mortal hands the power to abolish all forms of human poverty and all forms of human life. And yet the same revolutionary beliefs for which our forebears fought are still at issue around the globe—the belief that the rights of man come not from the generosity of the state but from the hand of God.

We dare not forget today that we are the heirs of that first revolution. Let the word go forth from this time and place, to friend and foe alike, that the torch has been passed to a new generation of Americans—born in this century, tempered by war, disciplined by a hard and bitter peace, proud of our ancient heritage—and unwilling to witness or permit the slow undoing of those human rights to which this nation has always been committed, and to which we are committed today at home and around the world.

Let every nation know, whether it wishes us well or ill, that we shall pay any price, bear any burden, meet any hardship, support any friend, oppose any foe to assure the survival and the success of liberty.

This much we pledge—and more.

To those old allies whose cultural and spiritual origins we share, we pledge the loyalty of faithful friends. United, there is little we cannot do in a host of cooperative ventures. Divided, there is little we can do. . . .

Let us never negotiate out of fear. But let us never fear to negotiate.

Let both sides explore what problems unite us instead of belaboring those problems which divide us. . . .

Let both sides seek to invoke the wonders of science instead of its terrors. Together let us explore the stars, conquer the deserts, eradicate disease, tap the ocean depths, and encourage the arts and commerce. . . .

And so, my fellow Americans: ask not what your country can do for you—ask what you can do for your country.

My fellow citizens of the world: ask not what America will do for you, but what together we can do for the freedom of man.

Glossary/Index

Glossary terms and locations are shown in **bold type**.

and Russia, 430

September 11, 2001, terrorist attacks by, 429

Islamic militants, 429–430

Isolationism—a nation's policy of not becoming involved in world affairs, 364

Israel

Arab-Israeli wars and, 431

and Arab neighbors, 368

foreign aid for, 373

Islamic militants and, 430

Italy

multiparty system in, 275

World War II and, 365

J

Jackson, Andrew, 130, 278

federal employees and, 192–193

Supreme Court and, 229

James II (England), 17

Japan

bombing of Pearl Harbor by, 365

mixed economy in, 440

Japanese Pact, 371

Jay, John, as Federalist, 35

Jefferson, Thomas, 6

Bill of Rights and, 35

Declaration of Independence and, 22, 23

elections of, 278

on Establishment Clause, 237

Library of Congress and, 134

Jobs. *See also* Civil service system

of bureaucracy, 196–200

congressional help with, 146–147

John (England), Magna Carta and, 16

Johnson, Andrew, 122

Johnson, Lyndon B.

cabinet of, 160

filibuster against, 131

media and, 321

Medicare and, 197

presidential roles of, 175

public opinion on, 173

Vietnam War and, 367

Joint committee—a committee made up of members of both houses, 126, 127

Joint resolution—a decision passed by both houses of Congress that deals with a special case, 139

Jordan, 423

Journal (House and Senate), 141

Judges (federal), 208, 210

Judges (state), 387

removal from office, 389

Judicial branch (national), 33, 46–47, 203–229

under Articles of Confederation, 30

compromises over, 34

under Constitution, 61–62

courts and, 41

Judicial branch (state), 387–389

Judicial interpretation, of Constitution, 79–80

Judicial powers

of independent agencies, 197

of independent regulatory commissions, 191

Judicial proceedings, between states, 91

Judicial restraint—to refrain from reading into the Constitution things that the Framers never meant, 80

Judicial review—a principle that gives the courts the power to rule on the constitutionality of a law or action of local, state, or national government, 40, 42, 89, 213, 226–227

Judiciary. *See* Court(s)

Judiciary Act (1789), 213

Junta—a dictatorship that is run by a single person or by a small group that consists of military officers, 425–426

Jurisdiction—area of law that a court may hear cases about, 24, 47, 211

of federal courts, 211–212

Jury duty, 214

Justice courts, in states, 388

Justice Department, 186

counterterrorism agencies in, 199

Justices (Supreme Court), 210, 222–223

Juvenile courts, in states, 388

K

Kashmir, war over, 431

Kennedy, John F., on party system, 284

Kennedy-Nixon debate, media and, 321

Kenya, Maathai, Wangari, in, 444

Kim Il Sung, 426

Kim Jong-Il, 11, 426

King, Martin Luther, Jr., 232, 259

Korea. *See* North Korea; South Korea

Korean Pact, 371

Korean War, 365, 431

UN and, 374

Kosovo, 431

K-12 public education, in states, 392–393

Kuwait, 431

L

Labor Department, 186, 346

Labor union—a group that represents people who work in the same job or in the same industry, 309

bureaucratic influence by, 199

campaign funds and, 294

history of, 345–346

as interest groups, 308, 309

"Lame-Duck" Amendment, 72

Land

state regulation of use, 394

zoning of, 408–409

Land Ordinance (1785), 28

Landslide victory—a victory with a huge number of votes, 179

Latin America

developing nations in, 441

foreign aid to, 373

juntas in, 425

Laurens, Henry, 28

Law(s)

antitrust, 344

bureaucrat influence on, 197

civil rights, 260

colonial passage of, 21

Congress and, 43

enforcement under Articles of Confederation, 30

environmental, 349

equal protection under, 257–259

federal civil rights laws, 260–263

governing elections, 292–293

interpreting, 30

presidential enforcement of, 46

priority of federal over state, 119

process of bill becoming, 52–53, 110, 138–147

for public programs, 325

regulatory, 344

in Russia, 422

state, 387

struck down by Supreme Court, 226

written by bureaucrats, 197

Law clerks—a person who does most of the legal research for a Supreme Court justice, 218, 219

Law enforcement

by president, 46

by states, 88

Lawful permanent resident (LPR)—a resident alien, or someone who has moved permanently to the United States, 254, 266

Lawmaking, under Articles of Confederation, 30

Law of the Land, Constitution as, 38, 39, 64, 89

Lawsuits

filed by states against states, 93

over school funding, 393

Lawyer, right of accused to, 252

policy issues and, 275
political attitudes and, 316
presidential elections and, 321–322
public agenda and, 320–321
public opinion and, 306, 316, 317
Supreme Court and, 322

Mass transit—forms of transportation that transport a large number of people at one time, 358, 410

Mayflower Compact—a written plan for a government signed by the Pilgrims before they came ashore at Plymouth Rock, 18

Mayor-council form—a form of city government in which the mayor and the council are both elected, 403–404

McCollum, Bill, 274

McConnell, Mitch, 112

McCulloch v. *Maryland*, 89, 119

Media. *See* Mass media; specific media

Medicaid, 332, 352, 353

Medicare, 97, 197, 328, 329, 332, 352

Mercenaries, 25

Metropolitan area—a large city and its surrounding area, 410

Mexico
NAFTA and, 342
political system in, 422

Microsoft, 437

Middle East. *See also* Arab world; specific countries
foreign aid to, 373
terrorism in, 429

Midterm election—an election held between presidential elections, 317

Migrant farm workers, immigration policy and, 264

Militants, Islamic, 429–430

Military. *See also* Armed forces
bureaucratic influence and, 199
noncitizens in, 267
power over, 121
president and, 59, 79, 368
women in, 262

Military aid programs, 373

Military dictatorships, 425–426

Military force, as tool of foreign policy, 371

Military rule, in developing nations, 452

Militia, 66
congressional control over, 53

Miller, Judith, 244

Minority leader—a member of the House from the minority party who determines how his or her party will react to the majority party's programs, 109

in House, 109
in Senate, 112

Minority party—the party with the fewer number of seats in the Senate or the House during a term, 108

Minority whip—the minority leader's assistant, 109
in House, 109
in Senate, 112

Miranda v. *Arizona*, 226, 251

Mixed economy—an economy in which the government is involved in setting economic and social policies, 439
in other nations, 440
in United States, 439–440

Mixed market economy, 342

Moderate—one who has views that are somewhere in between a conservative's and a liberal's, 155, 222

Mondale, Walter, female running mate for, 154

Monetary policy—policy that controls the supply of money in the economy and the cost of borrowing to influence the economy, 336–338

Money supply, monetary policy and control of, 336–338

Monopoly—the control of an industry or most of an industry by one company, 344

Monroe, James, foreign policy of, 364

Monroe Doctrine, 364

Montesquieu, baron de, Declaration of Independence and, 23

Mormons, polygamy and, 240

Morrill Land Grant Act, education and, 355

"Motor Voter" Law (1993), 36, 299

Muckrakers, workers treatment and, 346

Multiparty system—a system where there are several major and minor parties, 275–276

Municipal courts, 388

Municipality—another word for city, 403–406

Mussolini, Benito, 11

Myanmar, 426

N

NAACP. *See* National Association for the Advancement of Colored People (NAACP)

Nader, Ralph, in 2000 election, 280

Nation, as state, 4

National Association for the Advancement of Colored People (NAACP)
Brown decision and, 228
right of association and, 248

National bank
regional views of, 278
Supreme Court on, 89

National capital, congressional control over, 53

National committee—a committee that runs the national party between elections, 282

National Constitution Center, Philadelphia, 80

National convention—a convention held every four years by political parties to nominate the party's presidential and vice-presidential candidates and write the party's platform, 272, 274, **281**, 290

National debt—money owed by the government as a result of spending and borrowing money, **330**

National defense, power over, 121

National Drug Control Policy, Office of, 165

National Emergencies Act (1976), as limit on presidential power, 133

National Farmers Union (NFU), 309

National government
commerce power of, 97
expansion of, 96–97
federalism and, 83
powers denied to, 85
powers given to, 84–85
power to tax, 97
states and, 41, 88–89
in United States, 10
war power of, 96–97

National Guard, congressional control over, 53

National Housing Act (1937), 357

National Institutes of Health (NIH), 353–354
scientists in civil service system, 193

Nationalist position—the opinion that the the national government is better suited to act for all the people in dealing with problems, **95**, 96

Nationalization—a characteristic of socialism in which the central government takes over certain industries, such as transportation and steel, 442
in developing nations, 444

National Labor Relations Board (NLRB), 190, 346

replacement of, 222–223

Release time, for parochial education, 239

Relief programs, in Great Depression, 335–336

Religion(s)
education and, 238–239
fighting among, 427
First Amendment on, 64
freedom of, 66, 233, 237–240

Reporters, confidentiality of sources for, 244

Representation, compromises over, 34

Representative democracy—where people elect representatives who govern in their place, 12

Representative government—a government in which people elect delegates to speak for them in the government, 17, 33
in colonies, 18
in constitutional monarchy, 11
guaranteeing in states, 88

Representatives. *See also* Congress (U.S.); House of Representatives
asking questions of, 115
committee membership of, 126
constituents aided by, 144–147
to U.S. Congress, 33

Republic, 423
theocratic, 423

Republican National Committee, fund-raising by, 149

Republican National Convention, in 2004, 272

Republican Party, 108, 273
characteristics of, 285
after Civil War, 278–279
elephant as symbol of, 108
founding of, 278
taxes and, 274
two-party system and, 275
voter characteristics in, 302
winner-take-all primary of, 291

Reserved powers—powers that belong exclusively to the 50 states, 86

Reserve requirement—the amount of money that member banks must keep in the main Federal Reserve Banks, 337–338

Resident alien—someone who has moved permanently to the United States, 266

Resolution 137 (UN), 430

Resolutions, congressional, 139

Revenue—income, 20
congressional power over, 53
federal, 329
local sources of, 411–413

state, 395–397

Revenue bills, 139

Reversal of Court decisions, 228

Reverse—overturn, 228

Reverse discrimination—to discriminate against those who are not members of minority groups or women, 261

Revolutionary War, 21
debts after, 30

Rice, Condoleezza, 169

Rider—an amendment to a bill that does not have anything to do with the subject of the bill, 139

Rights. *See also* Bill of Rights entries; Civil rights
of accused, 67, 249–253
in Bill of Rights, 18, 235–236
of citizenship, 268
fundamental, 258
of immigrants, 259
to life, liberty, and property, 67
of noncitizens, 266–267
privacy, 263
related to trial, 252–253
social contract theory and, 6
of states, 29, 91
at time of arrest, 249–251
to trial, 67

Rio Pact, 371

Roberts, John, 223

Rockefeller, Nelson, 122, 157

Rodriguez, Arturo, 309

Roe v. *Wade*, 225

Roosevelt, Franklin D., 130, 279
as economic planner, 177
election of 1932 and, 348
informal power of, 171–172
leadership by, 178–179
nationalist position of, 96
social welfare programs of, 351
Supreme Court and, 224

Roosevelt, Theodore, 130
election of 1912 and, 279, 280
presidential power and, 79

Rule of four—when four justices must agree to take a case, 218

Rules Committee (House), 110

Rules of procedure, in Congress, 51

Running mate, vice presidential candidate as, 156

Russia. *See also* Soviet Union
Chechen rebels in, 430
collapse of communism in, 366
communism in, 445–447
political system of, 420–422
after Soviet Union, 447

Russian Revolution (1917), 445

Saddam Hussein, 133, 175, 427, 429
Kuwait and, 431

Safety testing, by DOT, 358

Sales tax, 396
local, 413
in state, 395

Sample—a small group of the universe a pollster is using, in scientific poll, **318**

Sanchez, Linda, 104

Sanchez, Loretta, 104

Saudi Arabia, 423, 429
absolute monarch in, 11

Schenck v. *United States*, 243

School(s). *See also* Education
charter, 356
influence on political attitudes, 315
property taxes and, 411
unequal funding of, 412

School districts, 403, 407

School prayer, 239

School voucher—a grant of money to parents of children in low-performing public schools to be used for sending children to private schools, 356

Scientific poll—a poll that asks voters for their opinions about candidates, issues, and government policies, 318–319. *See also* Public opinion polls

Scott v. *Sandford*, 267

Search and seizure, 67

Search warrant—a warrant authorizing police to go into a business or home to search for unlawful possessions, 249–250

SEC. *See* Securities and Exchange Commission (SEC)

Second Amendment, 66, 78

Secondary education, federal aid to, 355

Second Continental Congress (1775), 19, 21, 22

Secretary general, of UN, 375

Section 527 organization, 295, 308

Securities and Exchange Commission (SEC), 190, 191, 344

Security. *See also* National security
global, 428–433

Security Council (UN), 374

Seditious speech—any type of speech that encourages the overthrow of the government or attempts to disrupt, 242

Segregation—the separation of whites and African Americans, 259
Plessy v. *Ferguson* and, 227

and treaties are the "supreme Law of the Land," 40, 64, 89

Supreme court (state), 388

Supreme Court (U.S.), 47, 208. *See also* specific issues and cases
  on affirmative action, 262
  appointing justices to, 210
  Bill of Rights interpreted by, 235
  Chief Justice and, 223
  civil liberties and, 229
  on death penalty, 253
  decision-making process of, 218–220
  election of 2000 and, 218, 280
  on freedom of association, 248
  on freedom of religion, 237
  on freedoms of press and speech, 241
  on implied powers of Congress, 119
  influences on, 221–225
  judicial review by, 213
  jurisdiction of, 212
  justices of, 47
  labor unions and, 345
  lawsuits by states against states heard by, 93
  limits on, 229
  national policy and, 226–227
  operations of, 216–229
  presidential authority and, 173
  on privacy rights, 263
  reversal of court decisions by, 228
  on rights of aliens, 267
  Roosevelt, Franklin D., and, 224
  on state aid to parochial schools, 238–239
  workers and, 346

Supreme Court Building, 216

Supreme Law of the Land. *See* Law of the Land; Supremacy Clause

Supreme People's Assembly (North Korea), 426

Surplus—more money is collected than spent, 329

Swing vote—the fifth and deciding vote, 220

Symbolic speech—speech that combines actions and symbols with or without words to express ideas, 242

Syria, 426

T

Taft, William Howard, election of 1912 and, 279

Taft-Hartley Act (1947), 346

Taguba, Antonio, 128

Tariff—a tax on imports, 209
  protective, 328, 342
  regional views of, 278

Tax-and-spend—Congress's power to

tax and authorize the spending of the income from taxes, 120

Tax assessor—a person that determines value of property for tax purposes, 411

Taxation
  Congress and, 43, 53, 139
  Constitution on, 56, 57
  education funding from, 393
  by national government, 97
  property taxes as, 411–412
  public programs and, 325, 326
  for road building and maintenance, 409
  in Socialist nations, 442
  state revenues from, 395–396

"Taxation without representation," 20

Tax Court, 208, 210

Tax credits—a credit used in order to lower taxes, 329
  for business, 343
  by states, 391

Tax cuts
  balanced budgets and, 336
  federal deficit and, 329

Taxes—payments by individuals and businesses to support the activities of government, 327
  under Articles of Confederation, 29
  colonial government and, 18
  on exports, 34
  government use of, 8
  levied on colonies, 20
  payroll, 328
  progressive, 328
  regressive, 329
  social insurance, 328
  types of, 327–329

Tax protesters, 339

Tax returns, filing, 339

Tea Act (1773), 20

Technology—the use of science in business and industry, 449–450
  bureaucratic influence and, 198
  globalization and, 366

Telecommunications Act (1996), 145

Television
  First Amendment and, 245
  impact of, 321
  presidential elections and, 322

Temporary Assistance to Needy Families (TANF), 352, 353

Tennessee Valley Authority (TVA), 188

Tenth Amendment, 67, 78, 85
  state powers and, 86

Terms—periods of time in which Congress meets, 103
  of Congress, 103
  of county officers, 402

for members of Parliament, 420
  for Russian president, 421
  of state legislators, 384
  for U.S. president, 58, 72
  for U.S. vice president, 58, 72

Territorial courts, 210

Territorial integrity, of states, 89

Territories, citizens in, 267

Terrorism—a political strategy that uses violence against people or property to achieve a goal, 428–430
  bureaucratic influence and, 199
  current foreign policy and, 366
  foreign aid and fight against, 373
  Homeland Security Department and, 187, 358–359

Texas, educational system in, 393

Texas Rangers, as state police, 391

Theocratic republic—a government that has a constitution based on a strict interpretation of religion, 423

Third Amendment, 66, 78

Third party—a party that develops when a group of people believe that the major parties are not dealing with some important issue, 273, 275, 279, **280**

Thirteenth Amendment, 49, 70, 78, 87
  limits to state power in, 87

Thomas, Clarence, law clerks of, 219

Three-Fifths Compromise, 33, 49, 70

Timelines, analyzing, 37

Title IX, of Education Act (1972), 197, 258

Town, 402–403

Town meeting—a meeting of a town's citizens to vote on tax rates and spending, 403

Township—an area that includes a small center of houses and businesses and the surrounding rural areas, 402

Township committees, 284

Trade. *See also* International trade
  Constitution on, 33–34, 56
  as foreign policy goal, 363
  global, 449
  international, 366
  power to regulate, 34
  regulation under Articles of Confederation, 29
  technology and, 449–450

Trade barrier—a block in international trade put in place by the government, 450

Trade Court, 208

Trade groups, as interest groups, 308,

487

Acknowledgements

Photo Credits

American Civics and Government Photo Credits

4 ©Associated Press. U.S. Senate; 5 ©JupiterImages Corporation; 7 (tl)©Image Bank/Getty, (tr)©Associated Press, AP, (br)©Associated Press, The Times of Trenton, (bl)©Royalty-Free/CORBIS; 9 ©Comstock Images/Getty/RF; 10 ©Associated Press, AP; 11 ©Hulton-Deutsch Collection/CORBIS; 13 ©Photodisc Green/Getty RF; 15 ©Dennis Degnan/CORBIS; 16 ©Bettmann/CORBIS; 17 ©Bettmann/CORBIS; 18 ©Bettmann/CORBIS; 20 ©Bettmann/CORBIS; 21 ©North Wind Pictures Archives; 22 ©Bettmann/CORBIS; 27 ©Library of Congress; 28 ©CORBIS; 30 ©The Granger Collection, New York; 31 ©Bettmann/CORBIS; 32 ©Bettmann/CORBIS; 35 ©Bettmann/CORBIS; 36 ©Associated Press, AP; 38 ©The McGraw-Hill Companies; 39 ©Bettmann/CORBIS; 42 (r)©Photodisc Blue/Getty, (l)©Photodisc Green, (m)©The McGraw-Hill Companies; 45 ©Associated Press; 47 ©Jason Reed/Reuters/CORBIS; 79 ©CORBIS; 80 ©Getty Images; 81 ©Getty Images; 83 ©Charles E. Rotkin/CORBIS; 85 ©Associated Press; 86 ©Bettmann/CORBIS; 87 ©Bettmann/CORBIS; 88 ©Bettmann/CORBIS; 89 ©Mike Lane, Cagle Cartoons; 91 ©Owen Franken/CORBIS; 92 ©David Butow/CORBIS; 93 ©AP; 94 ©AP; 96 ©AP; 97 ©Hazir Reka/Reuters/CORBIS; 98 ©AP; 99 ©Getty Images; 101 ©Panoramic Images/Getty; 102 ©Mike Theilder/Reuters/CORBIS; 103 ©Associated Press; 104 ©Reuters/CORBIS; 107 ©Bettmann/CORBIS; 108 (t)©Bettmann/CORBIS, (b)©Democratic National Committee; 109 (t)©Larry Downing/Reuters/CORBIS, (b)©Reuters/CORBIS; 110 (b)©Associated Press, (t)©Associated Press; 111 ©Brooks Kraft/CORBIS; 112 ©Associated Press; 113 (t)©Getty Images News, (b)©Associated Press; 114 ©Micah Walter/Reuters/CORBIS; 115 ©Photodisc Red/Getty/RF; 117 ©Associated Press; 118 ©AFP/Getty Images; 119 ©Charles O'Rear/CORBIS; 122 (t)©Bettmann/CORBIS, (b)©Associated Press; 125 ©Kat Wade/San Francisco; 126 ©Wally McNamee/CORBIS; 128 (t)©Associated Press, (b)©Jason Reed/Reuters/CORBIS; 129 ©Associated Press; 130 ©Associated Press; 131 ©Bettmann/CORBIS; 132 ©John Trevor; 133 ©Getty Images News; 134 ©Associated Press; 135 ©www.ca.gov; 137 ©Courtesy of the U.S. Government Printing Office; 139 ©Shaun Heasley/Reuters/CORBIS; 141 ©Associated Press; 143 (t)©Reuters/CORBIS, (b)©AFP/Getty Images; 144 (t)©Micah Walter/GNS/CORBIS, (b)©Getty Images News; 145 ©Associated Press; 146 ©Aaron Horowitz/CORBIS; 147 ©Associated Press; 148 ©Associated Press; 152 ©The McGraw-Hill Companies; 153 ©Hulton Archive/Getty; 154 ©Roger Ressmeyer/CORBIS; 156 (t)©Associated Press, (b)©Wally MaNamee/CORBIS; 157 ©Associated Press; 158 ©CORBIS; 160 ©Associated Press, ©Getty Images News, ©Associated Press, ©CORBIS; 162 ©Photodisc Green/Royalty Free/Getty; 163 (t)©Tim Thompson/CORBIS, (b)©Zack Seckler/CORBIS; 166 ©Reuters/CORBIS; 167 ©Associated Press; 169 ©Reuters/CORBIS; 170 ©Associated Press; 172 ©Associated Press; 173 ©Bettmann/CORBIS; 174 ©Osservatore Romano/Pool/Reuters/CORBIS; 175 (t)©Bettmann/CORBIS, (b)©Brooks Kraft/CORBIS, (m)©AP; 179 ©Associated Press; 180 ©Ralf-Finn Hestoft/CORBIS; 181 ©Bettmann/CORBIS; 182 ©AP; 184 ©Jim Sugar/CORBIS; 188 ©Associated Press; 189 ©Associated Press; 192 ©CORBIS; 193 (t)©Associated Press, (l)©Paul. A. Souders/CORBIS, (r)©Reuters/CORBIS; 194 ©www.osc.gov; 197 ©Bettmann/CORBIS; 198 ©Downing Larry/CORBIS Sygma; 201 ©www.opm.gov; 203 ©Taxi/Getty; 204 ©Rick Friedman/CORBIS; 205 ©Newsday/TMS Reprints; 208 ©Bettmann/CORBIS, ©Brooks Kraft/CORBIS, ©Bettmann/CORBIS; 209 ©www.gpo.gov; 211 ©Royalty-Free/CORBIS; 213 ©Bettmann/CORBIS; 214 ©Stone/Getty Images; 216 ©Reuters/CORBIS; 217 ©CORBIS; 218 (t)©Reuters/CORBIS, (r)©Cartoon Feature Syndicate, (b)©Najlah Feanny/CORBIS; 219 ©Getty Images; 220 ©AP; 221 (l)©www.wickimedia.org, (r)©Alan Schein Photography/CORBIS; 222 (t)©The New Yorker Collection 1992 J.B. Handelsman from cartoonbank.com, (b)©Markowitz Jeffrey/CORBIS Sygma; 224 ©Franklin Delano Roosevelt Library; 226 ©Kim Kulish/CORBIS; 228 ©Associated Press; 229 ©North Wind Picture Archives; 230 ©Ariel Skelley/CORBIS; 232 ©Bettmann/CORBIS; 233 (tl)©Digital Vision/Getty, (bl)©The McGraw-Hill Library, (tr)©The McGraw-Hill Library, (br)©The McGraw-Hill Library; 234 ©Ed Kashi/CORBIS; 235 ©Stone/Getty; 238 ©Digital Vision/Getty; 240 ©The McGraw-Hill Companies; 242 (t)©Bettmann/CORBIS, (b)©Bettmann/CORBIS; 244 ©AP; 246 (t)©Henry Ray Abrams/Reuters/CORBIS, (b)©AP; 247 (t)©Bettmann/CORBIS, (b)©The McGraw-Hill Companies; 248 ©AP; 252 (b)©Daemmrich Bob, (t)©Daemmrich Bob; 253 ©Daemmrich Bob/CORBIS Sygma; 254 ©AP; 256 (tl)©AP, (bl)©Bettmann/CORBIS, (tr)©Flip Schulke/CORBIS, (br)©Reuters/CORBIS; 258 ©Photodisc Red/Getty; 259 ©Najlah Feanny/CORBIS SABA; 260 ©Philip Gould/CORBIS; 261 ©Stone/Getty; 262 ©Aurora/Getty; 263 ©AP; 265 ©Bettmann/CORBIS; 266 (t)©Ramin Talaie/CORBIS, (b)©Christophe Calais/ In Visu/CORBIS; 267 ©AP; 268 ©AP; 269 ©David Butow/CORBIS Saba; 271 ©Barbara Davidson/Dallas Morning News/CORBIS; 272 (l)©Rick Friedman, (r)©Rick Wilking/Reuters/CORBIS; 273 ©Stone/Getty; 274 (t)©AP, (b)©AP; 275 ©Origlia Franco/CORBIS Sygma; 276 ©Wally McNamee/CORBIS; 278 ©Bettmann/CORBIS; 279 (t)©Bettmann/CORBIS, (b)©Bettmann/CORBIS; 280 ©CORBIS; 282 ©Bettmann/CORBIS; 283 ©Reportage/Getty; 284 (t)©www.mcmanudemocrats.com, (b)©Bettmann/CORBIS; 287 ©Brian Snyder/Reuters/CORBIS; 288 ©Robert Maass/CORBIS; 289 (t)©Erich Schlegel/Dallas Morning News/CORBIS, (b)©Ross Frank/CORBIS Sygma; 290 ©AP; 291 ©AP; 292 ©Robert Galbraith/Reuters/CORBIS; 293 ©Kevin P. Casey/CORBIS; 294 ©Jeff Parker; 295 ©AP; 298 (t)©The Granger Collection, (m)©Underwood & Underwood/CORBIS, (b)©AP; 300 ©Bettmann/CORBIS; 301 ©Cartoon Stock; 302 ©Kenneth James/CORBIS; 303 ©AFP/Getty Images; 305 ©www.cartoonstock.com; 306 © AP; 308 ©AP; 309 ©AP; 310 (t)©Bettmann/CORBIS, (m)©Mark E. Gibson/CORBIS, (b)©Katy Winn/CORBIS; 311 ©RJ Matson; 312 ©Michah Walter/Reuters/CORBIS; 313 ©AP; 315 ©Mike Lester; 316 ©Brian Snyder/CORBIS; 318 ©Jim Ruyman/Reuters/CORBIS; 321 ©Bettmann/CORBIS; 322 (t)©Reuters/CORBIS, (b)©AP; 325 ©The McGraw-Hill Companies; 332 ©AP; 333 ©AP; 334 ©Handout/Reuters/CORBIS; 336 ©CORBIS; 337 ©Joseph Sohm/ChromoSohm Inc./CORBIS; 338 (b)©James L. Amos/CORBIS, (t)©AP; 339 ©Photonica/Getty; 341 ©Paul Morse-White House/CNP/CORBIS; 343 ©Jim Sugar/CORBIS; 344 ©Bettmann/CORBIS; 345 ©AP; 346 ©Najlah Feanny/CORBIS Sygma; 347 ©CORBIS; 348 (t)©JA Giordano/CORBIS Saba, (b)©Greg Smith/CORBIS; 349 ©Photodisc Green/Getty; 350 ©Bettmann/CORBIS; 352 ©Joel Stettenheim/CORBIS; 353 (t)©Alison Wright/CORBIS, (b)©AP; 354 ©Bettmann/CORBIS; 356 ©Iconica/Getty; 357 ©Frank Polich/Reuters/CORBIS; 358 ©Tim Wright/CORBIS; 360 ©Getty Images; 362 ©Kevin Lamarque/Reuters/CORBIS; 364 ©AP; 366 ©Bettmann/CORBIS; 367 ©Wally McNamee/CORBIS; 368 ©Reuters/CORBIS; 369 ©AFP Getty Images; 370 ©Getty Images; 372 ©Bettmann/CORBIS; 373 (t)©AP, (b)©Time Life Pictures/Getty Images; 374 ©Handout/Gerald Bourke/Reuters/CORBIS; 375 ©AP; 376 ©Stone; 377 ©Darrell Gulin/CORBIS; 380 ©AP; 383 ©Cartoonstock; 384 ©AP; 385 ©AP; 389 ©AP; 391 ©Getty Images; 393 ©David G. Houser/CORBIS; 394 ©Erich Schlegel/Dallas Morning News/CORBIS; 395 ©Stone; 396 ©AP; 397 ©AP; 399 ©Buddy Mays/CORBIS; 402 ©Richard Cummins/CORBIS; 403 ©Franz-Marc Frei/CORBIS; 408 ©AP; 409 ©AP; 410 ©AP; 412 (t)©Time Life Pictures/Getty Images, (b)©Getty Images; 413 ©Douglas Kirkland/CORBIS; 416 ©K. Hackenberg/zefa/CORBIS; 417 ©Ron Sachs/CNP/CORBIS; 418 ©Reuters/CORBIS; 419 ©Reuters/CORBIS; 420 ©Peter Turnley/CORBIS; 424 ©Victoria Valiterra/Clasos/CORBIS Sygma; 424 ©Liu Liqun/CORBIS; 425 (t)©Bettmann/CORBIS, (b)©Rafael Perez/Reuters/CORBIS; 426 (t)©Reuters/CORBIS, (b)©Gerald Bourke/World Food Programme/Reuters/CORBIS; 427 ©Erik deCatro/Reuters/CORBIS; 428 ©AP; 430 ©Reuters/CORBIS; 431 ©Lynsey Addario/CORBIS, ©AP; 432 ©Bettmann/CORBIS; 433 ©Herwig Prammer/Reuters/CORBIS; 436 ©Tom Wagner/CORBIS Saba; 438 (t)©Gail Mooney/CORBIS, (b)©Jon Feingersh/zefa/CORBIS; 439 ©Henry Diltz/CORBIS; 440 ©Martin Jones; 442 ©Pablo Corral V/CORBIS; 443 (t)©Gilbert Liz/CORBIS Sygma, (b)©Peter Turnley/CORBIS; 444 (t)©Owen Franken/CORBIS, (b)©Radu Sigheti/Reuters/CORBIS; 445 ©Marc Garanger/CORBIS; 446 ©Bettmann/CORBIS; 447 ©Shepard Sherbell/CORBIS Saba; 448 ©Jon Hicks/CORBIS; 449 ©Macduff Everton/CORBIS; 450 ©Owak/Kulla/CORBIS; 452 (t)©Gustavo Gilabert/CORBIS Saba, (b)©David Turnley/CORBIS

Acknowledgements for Primary Sources are found at the bottom of each Primary Source page.

The editor has made every effort to trace ownership of all copyrighted material and to secure the necessary permissions. Should there be a question regarding the use of any material, regret is hereby expressed for such error. Upon notification of any such oversight, proper acknowledgement will be made in future editions.

(t) top, (b) bottom, (m) middle, (l) left, (r) right